Gotthold Ephraim Lessing

NATHAN THE WISE, MINNA VON BARNHELM,

and Other Plays and Writings

Edited by Peter Demetz
Foreword by Hannah Arendt

CONTINUUM · NEW YORK

1995

The Continuum Publishing Company
370 Lexington Avenue, New York, NY 10017

The German Library
is published in cooperation with Deutsches Haus,
New York University.
This volume has been supported by a grant from
Doenne and Hellwig GmbH and Co. KG

Printed in the United States of America

Library of Congress Cataloging-in-Publication Data

Lessing, Gotthold Ephraim, 1729–1781.
    [Selections. English. 1991]
    Nathan the Wise, Minna von Barnhelm, and other plays and writings
/ Gotthold Ephraim Lessing ; edited by Peter Demetz ; foreword by
Hannah Arendt.
    p.   cm. — (The German library ; v. 12)
    Contents: Minna von Barnhelm / translated by Kenneth J. Northcott
— Emilia Galotti / translated by Anna Johanna Gode von Aesch — The
Jews / translated by Ingrid Walsøe-Engel — Nathan the Wise /
translated by Bayard Quincy Morgan — Ernst and Falk / translated by
William L. Zwiebel — Selections from Lessing's
philosophical/theological writings / translated by Henry Chadwick.
    ISBN 0-8264-0706-4 (cloth) — ISBN 0-8264-0707-2 (pbk.)
    1. Lessing, Gotthold Ephraim, 1729–1781—Translations, English.
I. Demetz, Peter, 1922–   . II. Title. III. Series.
PT2403.A1D4   1991
832'.6—dc20   91-19344
                                                        CIP

Acknowledgments will be found on page 336,
which constitutes an extension of the copyright page.

Gotthold Ephraim Lessing

NATHAN THE WISE,
MINNA VON BARNHELM,

and Other Plays and Writings

The German Library: Volume 12
Volkmar Sander, General Editor

Contents

Foreword

ON HUMANITY IN DARK TIMES:
Thoughts about Lessing

[. . .] Lessing experienced the world in anger and in laughter, and anger and laughter are by their nature biased. Therefore, he was unable or unwilling to judge a work of art "in itself," independently of its effect in the world, and therefore he could attack or defend in his polemics according to how the matter in question was being judged by the public and quite independently of the degree to which it was true or false. It was not only a form of gallantry when he said that he would "leave in peace those whom all are striking at"; it was also a concern, which had become instinctive with him, for the relative rightness of opinions which for good reasons get the worst of it. Thus even in the dispute over Christianity he did not take up a fixed position. Rather, as he once said with magnificent self-knowledge, he instinctively became dubious of Christianity "the more cogently some tried to prove it to me," and instinctively tried "to preserve it in [his] heart" the more "wantonly and triumphantly others sought to trample it underfoot." But this means that where everyone else was contending over the "truth" of Christianity, he was chiefly defending its position in the world, now anxious that it might again enforce its claim to dominance, now fearing that it might vanish utterly. Lessing was being remarkably farsighted when he saw that the enlightened theology of his time "under the pretext of making us rational Christians is making us extremely irrational philosophers." That insight sprang not only from partisanship in favor of reason. Lessing's primary concern in this whole debate was freedom, which was far more endangered by those who wanted "to compel faith by proofs" than by those who regarded faith as a gift of divine grace. But there was in addition his concern about the world, in which he felt both religion and philosophy should have their place, but separate places, so that behind the "partition . . . each can go its own way without hindering the other."

Criticism, in Lessing's sense, is always taking sides for the world's sake, understanding and judging everything in terms of its position in the world at any given time. Such a mentality can never give rise to a definite worldview which, once adopted, is immune to further experiences in the world because it has hitched itself firmly to one possible perspective. We very much need Lessing to teach us this state of mind, and what makes learning it so hard for us is not our distrust of the Enlightenment or of the eighteenth century's belief in humanity. It is not the eighteenth but the nineteenth century that stands between Lessing and us. The nineteenth century's obsession with history and commitment to ideology still looms so large in the political thinking of our times that we are inclined to regard entirely free thinking, which employs neither history nor coercive logic as crutches, as having no authority over us. To be sure, we are still aware that thinking calls not only for intelligence and profundity but above all for courage. But we are astonished that Lessing's partisanship for the world could go so far that he could even sacrifice to it the axiom of noncontradiction, the claim to self-consistency, which we assume is mandatory to all who write and speak. For he declared in all seriousness: "I am not duty-bound to resolve the difficulties I create. May my ideas always be somewhat disjunct, or even appear to contradict one another, if only they are ideas in which readers will find material that stirs them to think for themselves." He not only wanted no one to coerce him, but he also wanted to coerce no one, either by force or by proofs. He regarded the tyranny of those who attempt to dominate thinking by reasoning and sophistries, by compelling argumentation, as more dangerous to freedom than orthodoxy. Above all he never coerced himself, and instead of fixing his identity in history with a perfectly consistent system, he scattered into the world, as he himself knew, "nothing but *fermenta cognitionis.*"

Thus Lessing's famous *Selbstdenken*—independent thinking for oneself—is by no means an activity pertaining to a closed, integrated, organically grown, and cultivated individual who then as it were looks around to see where in the world the most favorable place for his development might be, in order to bring himself into harmony with the world by the detour of thought. For Lessing, thought does not arise out of the individual and is not the manifestation of a self. Rather, the individual—whom Lessing would say was created for action, not ratiocination—elects such thought because he discovers in thinking another mode of moving in the world in freedom. Of all the specific liberties which may come into our minds when we hear the word "freedom," freedom of movement is historically the oldest and also the

most elementary. Being able to depart for where we will is the pro-
totypal gesture of being free, as limitation of freedom of movement has
from time immemorial been the precondition for enslavement. Freedom of movement is also the indispensable condition for action, and it
is in action that men primarily experience freedom in the world. When
men are deprived of the public space—which is constituted by acting
together and then fills of its own accord with the events and stories that
develop into history—they retreat into their freedom of thought. That
is a very ancient experience, of course. And some such retreat seems to
have been forced upon Lessing. When we hear of such a retreat from
enslavement in the world to freedom of thought, we naturally remember the Stoic model, because it was historically the most effective.
But to be precise, Stoicism represents not so much a retreat from action
to thinking as an escape from the world into the self, which, it is
hoped, will be able to sustain itself in sovereign independence of the
outside world. There was nothing of the sort in Lessing's case. Lessing
retreated into thought, but not at all into his own self; and if for him a
secret link between action and thought did exist (I believe it did,
although I cannot prove it by quotations), the link consisted in the fact
that both action and thought occur in the form of movement and that,
therefore, freedom underlies both: freedom of movement.

Lessing probably never believed that acting can be replaced by thinking, or that freedom of thought can be a substitute for the freedom
inherent in action. He knew very well that he was living in what was
then the "most slavish country in Europe," even though he was allowed
to "offer the public as many idiocies against religion" as he pleased. For
it was impossible to raise "a voice for the rights of subjects . . . against
extortion and despotism," in other words, to act. The secret relationship of his "self-thinking" to action lay in his never binding his
thinking to results. In fact, he explicitly renounced the desire for
results, insofar as these might mean the final solution of problems
which his thought posed for itself; his thinking was not a search for
truth, since every truth that is the result of a thought process necessarily puts an end to the movement of thinking. The *fermenta cognitionis* which Lessing scattered into the world were not intended to
communicate conclusions, but to stimulate others to independent
thought, and this for no other purpose than to bring about a discourse
between thinkers. Lessing's thought is not the (Platonic) silent dialogue
between me and myself, but an anticipated dialogue with others, and
this is the reason that it is essentially polemical. But even if he had
succeeded in bringing about his discourse with other independent

thinkers and so escaping a solitude which, for him in particular, paralyzed all faculties, he could scarcely have been persuaded that this put everything to rights. For what was wrong, and what no dialogue and no independent thinking ever could right, was the world—namely, the thing that arises between people and in which everything that individuals carry with them innately can become visible and audible. In the two hundred years that separate us from Lessing's lifetime, much has changed in this respect, but little has changed for the better. The "pillars of the best-known truths" (to stay with his metaphor), which at that time were shaken, today lie shattered; we need neither criticism nor wise men to shake them any more. We need only look around to see that we are standing in the midst of a veritable rubble heap of such pillars.

Now in a certain sense this could be an advantage, promoting a new kind of thinking that needs no pillars and props, no standards and traditions to move freely without crutches over unfamiliar terrain. But with the world as it is, it is difficult to enjoy this advantage. For long ago it became apparent that the pillars of the truths have also been the pillars of the political order, and that the world (in contrast to the people who inhabit it and move freely about in it) needs such pillars in order to guarantee continuity and permanence, without which it cannot offer mortal men the relatively secure, relatively imperishable home that they need. To be sure, the very humanity of man loses its vitality to the extent that he abstains from thinking and puts his confidence into old verities or even new truths, throwing them down as if they were coins with which to balance all experiences. And yet, if this is true for man, it is not true for the world. The world becomes inhuman, inhospitable to human needs—which are the needs of mortals—when it is violently wrenched into a movement in which there is no longer any sort of permanence. That is why ever since the great failure of the French Revolution people have repeatedly reerected the old pillars which were then overthrown, only again and again to see them first quivering, then collapsing anew. The most frightful errors have replaced the "best-known truths," and the error of these doctrines constitutes no proof, no new pillar for the old truths. In the political realm restoration is never a substitute for a new foundation but will be at best an emergency measure that becomes inevitable when the act of foundation, which is called revolution, has failed. But it is likewise inevitable that in such a constellation, especially when it extends over such long spans of time, people's mistrust of the world and all aspects of the public realm should grow steadily. For the fragility of these repeatedly restored props of the public order is bound to become more apparent after every collapse, so that ultimately the public order is based on people's holding as self-evident precisely those "best-known truths" which secretly scarcely anyone still believes in.

2

History knows many periods of dark times in which the public realm has been obscured and the world become so dubious that people have ceased to ask any more of politics than that it show due consideration for their vital interests and personal liberty. Those who have lived in such times and been formed by them have probably always been inclined to despise the world and the public realm, to ignore them as far as possible, or even to overleap them and, as it were, reach behind them—as if the world were only a façade behind which people could conceal themselves—in order to arrive at mutual understandings with their fellow men without regard for the world that lies between them. In such times, if things turn out well, a special kind of humanity develops. In order properly to appreciate its possibilities we need only think of *Nathan the Wise,* whose true theme—"It suffices to be a man"—permeates the play. The appeal: "Be my friend," which runs like a leitmotif through the whole play, corresponds to that theme. We might equally well think of *The Magic Flute,* which likewise has as its theme such a humanity, which is more profound than we generally think when we consider only the eighteenth century's usual theories of a basic human nature underlying the multiplicity of nations, peoples, races, and religions into which the human race is divided. If such a human nature were to exist, it would be a natural phenomenon, and to call behavior in accordance with it "human" would assume that human and natural behavior are one and the same. In the eighteenth century the greatest and historically the most effective advocate of this kind of humanity was Rousseau, for whom the human nature common to all men was manifested not in reason but in compassion, in an innate repugnance, as he put it, to see a fellow human being suffering. With remarkable accord, Lessing also declared that the best person is the most compassionate. But Lessing was troubled by the egalitarian character of compassion—the fact that, as he stressed, we feel "something akin to compassion" for the evildoer also. This did not trouble Rousseau. In the spirit of the French Revolution, which leaned upon his ideas, he saw *fraternité* as the fulfillment of humanity. Lessing, on the other hand, considered friendship—which is as selective as compassion is egalitarian—to be the central phenomenon in which alone true humanity can prove itself.

Before we turn to Lessing's concept of friendship and its political relevance, we must dwell for a moment on fraternity as the eighteenth century understood it. Lessing, too, was well acquainted with it; he spoke of "philanthropic feelings," of a brotherly attachment to other human beings springs from hatred of the world in which men are treated "inhumanly." For our purposes, however, it is important that humanity manifests itself in such brotherhood most frequently in "dark times." This kind of humanity actually becomes inevitable when the times become so extremely dark for certain groups of people that it is no longer up to them, their insight or choice, to withdraw from the world. Humanity in the form of fraternity invariably appears historically among persecuted peoples and enslaved groups; and in eighteenth-century Europe it must have been quite natural to detect it among the Jews, who then were newcomers in literary circles. This kind of humanity is the great privilege of pariah peoples; it is the advantage that the pariahs of this world always and in all circumstances can have over others. The privilege is dearly bought; it is often accompanied by so radical a loss of the world, so fearful an atrophy of all the organs with which we respond to it—starting with the common sense with which we orient ourselves in a world common to ourselves and others and going on to the sense of beauty, or taste, with which we love the world—that in extreme cases, in which pariahdom has persisted for centuries, we can speak of real worldlessness. And worldlessness, alas, is always a form of barbarism.

In this as it were organically evolved humanity it is as if under the pressure of persecution the persecuted have moved so closely together that the interspace we have called world (and which of course existed between them before the persecution, keeping them at a distance from one another) has simply disappeared. This produces a warmth of human relationships which may strike those who have had some experience with such groups as an almost physical phenomenon. Of course I do not mean to imply that this warmth of persecuted peoples is not a great thing. In its full development it can breed a kindliness and sheer goodness of which human beings are otherwise scarcely capable. Frequently it is also the source of a vitality, a joy in the simple fact of being alive, rather suggesting that life comes fully into its own only among those who are, in worldly terms, the insulted and injured. But in saying this we must not forget that the charm and intensity of the atmosphere that develops is also due to the fact that the pariahs of this world enjoy the great privilege of being unburdened by care for the world. [. . .]

3

These and similar questions of the proper attitude in "dark times" are of course especially familiar to the generation and the group to which I belong. If concord with the world, which is part and parcel of receiving honors, has never been an easy matter in our times and in the circumstances of our world, it is even less so for us. Certainly honors were no part of our birthright, and it would not be surprising if we were no longer capable of the openness and trustfulness that are needed simply to accept gratefully what the world offers in good faith. Even those among us who by speaking and writing have ventured into public life have not done so out of any original pleasure in the public scene, and have hardly expected or aspired to receive the stamp of public approval. Even in public they tended to address only their friends or to speak to those unknown, scattered readers and listeners with whom everyone who speaks and writes at all cannot help feeling joined in some rather obscure brotherhood. I am afraid that in their efforts they felt very little responsibility toward the world; these efforts were, rather, guided by their hope of preserving some minimum of humanity in a world grown inhuman while at the same time as far as possible resisting the weird irreality of this worldlessness—each after his own fashion and some few by seeking to the limits of their ability to understand even inhumanity and the intellectual and political monstrosities of a time out of joint.

I so explicitly stress my membership in the group of Jews expelled from Germany at a relatively early age because I wish to anticipate certain misunderstandings which can arise only too easily when one speaks of humanity. In this connection I cannot gloss over the fact that for many years I considered the only adequate reply to the question, Who are you? to be: A Jew. That answer alone took into account the reality of persecution. As for the statement with which Nathan the Wise (in effect, though not in actual wording) countered the command: "Step closer, Jew"—the statement: I am a man—I would have considered as nothing but a grotesque and dangerous evasion of reality. [. . .]

Thus, in the case of a friendship between a German and a Jew under the conditions of the Third Reich it would scarcely have been a sign of humanness for the friends to have said: Are we not both human beings? It would have been mere evasion of reality and of the world common to both at that time; they would not have been resisting the world as it was. A law that prohibited the intercourse of Jews and Germans could be evaded but could not be defied by people who denied the reality of the distinction. In keeping with a humanness that had not lost the solid ground of reality, a humanness in the midst of the reality of persecution, they would have had to say to each other: A German and a Jew, and friends. But wherever such a friendship succeeded at that time (of course the situation is completely changed, nowadays) and was maintained in purity, that is to say without false guilt complexes on the one side and false complexes of superiority or inferiority on the other, a bit of humanness in a world become inhuman had been achieved.

4

The example of friendship, which I have adduced because it seems to me for a variety of reasons to be specially pertinent to the question of humanness, brings us back to Lessing again. As is well known, the ancients thought friends indispensable to human life, indeed that a life without friends was not really worth living. In holding this view they gave little consideration to the idea that we need the help of friends in misfortune; on the contrary, they rather thought that there can be no happiness or good fortune for anyone unless a friend shares in the joy of it. Of course there is something to the maxim that only in misfortune do we find out who our true friends are; but those whom we regard as our true friends without such proof are usually those to whom we unhesitatingly reveal happiness and whom we count on to share our rejoicing.

We are wont to see friendship solely as a phenomenon of intimacy, in which the friends open their hearts to each other unmolested by the world and its demands. Rousseau, not Lessing, is the best advocate of this view, which conforms so well to the basic attitude of the modern individual, who in his alienation from the world can truly reveal himself only in privacy and in the intimacy of face-to-face encounters. Thus it is hard for us to understand the political relevance of friendship. When, for example, we read in Aristotle that *philia*, friendship among citizens, is one of the fundamental requirements for the well-being of the City, we tend to think that he was speaking of no more than the absence of factions and civil war within it. But for the Greeks the essence of friendship consisted in discourse. They held that only the constant interchange of talk united citizens in a *polis*. In discourse the political importance of friendship, and the humanness peculiar to it, were made manifest. This converse (in contrast to the intimate talk in which individuals speak about themselves), permeated though it may be by pleasure in the friend's presence, is concerned with the common world, which remains "inhuman" in a very literal sense unless it is constantly talked about by human beings. For the world is not humane just because it is made by human beings, and it does not become humane just because the human voice sounds in it, but only when it has become the object of discourse. However much we are affected by the things of the world, however deeply they may stir and stimulate us, they become human for us only when we can discuss them with our fellows. Whatever cannot become the object of discourse—the truly sublime, the truly horrible or the uncanny—may find a human voice through which to sound into the world, but it is not exactly human. We humanize what is going on in the world and in ourselves only by speaking of it, and in the course of speaking of it we learn to be human.

The Greeks called this humanness which is achieved in the discourse of friendship *philanthropia,* "love of man," since it manifests itself in a readiness to share the world with other men. Its opposite, misanthropy, means simply that the misanthrope finds no one with whom he cares to share the world, that he regards nobody as worthy of rejoicing with him in the world and nature and the cosmos. Greek philanthropy underwent many a change in becoming Roman *humanitas.* The most important of these changes corresponded to the political fact that in Rome people of widely different ethnic origins and descent could acquire Roman citizenship and thus enter into the discourse among cultivated Romans, could discuss the world and life with them. And this political background distinguishes Roman *humanitas* from what moderns call humanity, by which they commonly mean a mere effect of education.

That humaneness should be sober and cool rather than sentimental; that humanity is exemplified not in fraternity but in friendship; that friendship is not intimately personal but makes political demands and preserves reference to the world—all this seems to us so exclusively characteristic of classical antiquity that it rather perplexes us when we find quite kindred features in *Nathan the Wise*—which, modern as it is, might with some justice be called the classical drama of friendship. What strikes us as so strange in the play is the "We must, must be friends," with which Nathan turns to the Templar, and in fact to everyone he meets; for this friendship is obviously so much more important to Lessing than the passion of love that he can brusquely cut the love story off short (the lovers, the Templar and Nathan's adopted daughter Recha [Rachel], turn out to be brother and sister) and transform it into a relationship in which friendship is required and love ruled out. The dramatic tension of the play lies solely in the conflict that arises between friendship and humanity with truth. That fact perhaps strikes modern men as even stranger, but once again it is curiously close to the principles and conflicts which concerned classical antiquity. In the end, after all, Nathan's wisdom consists solely in his readiness to sacrifice truth to friendship.

Lessing had highly unorthodox opinions about truth. He refused to accept any truths whatever, even those presumably handed down by Providence, and he never felt compelled by truth, be it imposed by others' or by his own reasoning processes. If he had been confronted with the Platonic alternative of *doxa* or *aletheia*, of opinion or truth, there is no question how he would have decided. He was glad that—to use his parable—the genuine ring, if it had ever existed, had been lost; he was glad for the sake of the infinite number of opinions that arise when men discuss the affairs of this world. If the genuine ring did exist, that would mean an end to discourse and thus to friendship and thus to humanness. On these same grounds he was content to belong to the race of "limited gods," as he occasionally called men; and he thought that human society was in no way harmed by those "who take more trouble to make clouds than to scatter them," while it incurred "much harm from those who wish to subject all men's ways of thinking to the yoke of their own." This has very little to do with tolerance in the ordinary sense (in fact Lessing himself was by no means an especially tolerant person), but it has a great deal to do with the gift of friendship, with openness to the world, and finally with genuine love of mankind.

The theme of "limited gods," of the limitations of the human understanding, limitations which speculative reason can point out and thereby transcend, subsequently became the great object of Kant's critiques. But whatever Kant's attitudes may have in common with Lessing's—and in fact they do have much in common—the two thinkers differed on one decisive point. Kant realized that there can be no absolute truth for man, at least not in the theoretical sense. He would certainly have been prepared to sacrifice truth to the possibility of human freedom; for if we possessed truth we could not be free. But he would scarcely have agreed with Lessing that the truth, if it did exist, could be unhesitatingly sacrificed to humanity, to the possibility of friendship and of discourse among men. Kant argued that an absolute exists, the duty of the categorical imperative which stands above men, is decisive in all human affairs, and cannot be infringed even for the sake of humanity in every sense of that word. Critics of the Kantian ethic have frequently denounced this thesis as altogether inhuman and unmerciful. Whatever the merits of their arguments, the inhumanity of Kant's moral philosophy is undeniable. And this is so because the categorical imperative is postulated as absolute and in its absoluteness introduces into the interhuman realm—which by its nature consists of relationships—something that runs counter to its fundamental relativity. The inhumanity which is bound up with the concept of one single truth emerges with particular clarity in Kant's work precisely because he attempted to found truth on practical reason; it is as though he who had so inexorably pointed out man's cognitive limits could not bear to think that in action, too, man cannot behave like a god.

Lessing, however, rejoiced in the very thing that has ever—or at least since Parmenides and Plato—distressed philosophers: that the truth, as soon as it is uttered, is immediately transformed into one opinion among many, is contested, reformulated, reduced to one subject of discourse among others. Lessing's greatness does not merely consist in a theoretical insight that there cannot be one single truth within the human world but in his gladness that it does not exist and that, therefore, the unending discourse among men will never cease so long as there are men at all. A single absolute truth, could there have been one, would have been the death of all those disputes in which this ancestor and master of all polemicism in the German language was so much at home and always took sides with the utmost clarity and definiteness. And this would have spelled the end of humanity.

It is difficult for us today to identify with the dramatic but untragic conflict of *Nathan the Wise* as Lessing intended it. That is partly because in regard to truth it has become a matter of course for us to behave tolerantly, although for reasons that have scarcely any connection with Lessing's reasons. Nowadays someone may still occasionally put the question at least in the style of Lessing's parable of the three rings—as, for example, in Kafka's magnificent pronouncement: "It is difficult to speak the truth, for although there is only one truth, it is alive and therefore has a live and changing face." But here, too, nothing is said of the political point of Lessing's antinomy—that is, the possible antagonism between truth and humanity. Nowadays, moreover, it is rare to meet people who believe they possess the truth; instead, we are constantly confronted by those who are sure that they are right. The distinction is plain; the question of truth was in Lessing's time still a question of philosophy and of religion, whereas our problem of being right arises within the framework of science and is always decided by a mode of thought oriented toward science. In saying this I shall ignore the question of whether this change in ways of thinking has proved to be for our good or ill. The simple fact is that even men who are utterly incapable of judging the specifically scientific aspects of an argument are as fascinated by scientific rightness as men of the eighteenth century were by the question of truth. And strangely enough, modern men are not deflected from their fascination by the attitude of scientists, who as long as they are really proceeding scientifically know quite well that their "truths" are never final but are continually undergoing radical revision by living research.

In spite of the difference between the notions of possessing the truth and being right, these two points of view have one thing in common: those who take one or the other are generally not prepared to sacrifice their view to humanity or friendship in case a conflict should arise. They actually believe that to do so would be to violate a higher duty, the duty of "objectivity"; so that even if they occasionally make such a sacrifice they do not feel they are acting out of conscience but are even ashamed of their humanity and often feel distinctly guilty about it. In terms of the age in which we live, and in terms of the many dogmatic opinions that dominate our thinking, we can translate Lessing's conflict into one closer to our experience, by showing its application to the twelve years and to the dominant ideology of the Third Reich. Let us for the moment set aside the fact that Nazi racial doctrine is in principle unprovable because it contradicts man's "nature." (By the way, it is worth remarking that these "scientific" theories were neither an invention of the Nazis nor even a specifically German invention.) But let us assume for the moment that the racial theories could have been convincingly proved. For it cannot be gainsaid that the practical political conclusions the Nazis drew from these theories were perfectly logical. Suppose that a race could indeed be shown, by indubitable scientific evidence, to be inferior; would that fact justify its extermination? But the answer to this question is still too easy, because we can invoke the "Thou shalt not kill" which in fact has become the fundamental commandment governing legal and moral thinking of the Occident ever since the victory of Christianity over antiquity. But in terms of a way of thinking governed by neither legal nor moral nor religious strictures—and Lessing's thought was as untrammeled, as "live and changing" as that—the question would have to be posed thus: *Would any such doctrine, however convincingly proved, be worth the sacrifice of so much as a single friendship between two men?*

Thus we have come back to my starting point, to the astonishing lack of "objectivity" in Lessing's polemicism, to his forever vigilant partiality, which has nothing whatsoever to do with subjectivity because it is always framed not in terms of the self but in terms of the relationship of men to their world, in terms of their positions and opinions. Lessing would not have found any difficulty in answering the question I have just posed. No insight into the nature of Islam or of Judaism or of Christianity could have kept him from entering into a friendship and the discourse of friendship with a convinced Mohammedan or a pious Jew or a believing Christian. Any doctrine that in principle barred the possibility of friendship between two human beings would have been rejected by his untrammeled and unerring conscience. He would instantly have taken the human side and given short shrift to the learned or unlearned discussion in either camp. That was Lessing's humanity.

This humanity emerged in a politically enslaved world whose foundations, moreover, were already shaken. Lessing, too, was already living in "dark times," and after his own fashion he was destroyed by their darkness. We have seen what a powerful need men have, in such times, to move closer to one another, to seek in the warmth of intimacy the substitute for that light and illumination which only the public realm can cast. But this means that they avoid disputes and try as far as possible to deal only with people with whom they cannot come into conflict. For a man of Lessing's disposition there was little room in such an age and in such a confined world; where people moved together in order to warm one another, they moved away from him. And yet he, who was polemical to the point of contentiousness, could no more endure loneliness than the excessive closeness of a brotherliness that obliterated all distinctions. He was never eager really to fall out with someone with whom he had entered into a dispute; he was concerned solely with humanizing the world by incessant and continual discourse about its affairs and the things in it. He wanted to be the friend of many men, but no man's brother.

He failed to achieve this friendship in the world with people in dispute and discourse, and indeed under the conditions then prevailing in German-speaking lands he could scarcely have succeeded. Sympathy for a man who "was worth more than all his talents" and whose greatness "lay in his individuality" (Friedrich Schlegel) could never really develop in Germany because such sympathy would have to arise out of politics in the deepest sense of the word. Because Lessing was a completely political person, he insisted that truth can exist only where it is humanized by discourse, only where each man says not what just happens to occur to him at the moment, but what he "deems truth."

But such speech is virtually impossible in solitude; it belongs to an area in which there are many voices and where the announcement of what each "deems truth" both links and separates men, establishing in fact those distances between men which together comprise the world. Every truth outside this area, no matter whether it brings men good or ill, is inhuman in the literal sense of the word; but not because it might rouse men against one another and separate them. Quite the contrary, it is because it might have the result that all men would suddenly unite in a single opinion, so that out of many opinions one would emerge, as though not men in their infinite plurality but man in the singular, one species and its exemplars, were to inhabit the earth. Should that happen, the world, which can form only in the interspaces between men in all their variety, would vanish altogether. For that reason the most profound thing that has been said about the relationship between truth and humanity is to be found in a sentence of Lessing's which seems to draw from all his works wisdom's last word. The sentence is:

JEDER SAGE, WAS IHM WAHRHEIT DÜNKT,
UND DIE WAHRHEIT SELBST SEI GOTT EMPFOHLEN!

(Let each man say what he deems truth,
and let truth itself be commended unto God!)

HANNAH ARENDT

Introduction

Gotthold Ephraim Lessing was the first German intellectual, in the modern sense of the word, yet to call him, as it is being done so often, a representative of the German Enlightenment obscures rather than reveals the contradictions of his life and work. He could be a poet, playwright, scholar, archaeologist, philosopher, or critic almost at will, and depending on the occasion, he published *rococo* poems, incisive book reviews, devastating analyses of bad translations, semiotic treatises about the arts of space and time, entertaining comedies, defenses of little known poets, theological polemics, and cryptic tragedies; yet he never wrote much of anything about his private life. Respect for tradition and desire for change were curiously mixed in his thought, and far from advocating immediate and sudden transformations, he believed in infinite patience and particularly in a slow unfolding of history in which individuals played their own part. He was famous and even feared for his abrasive way of arguing against people who defended ossified institutions, yet as unorthodox Christian, he never gave up his almost pietistic belief in the virtue of submitting to the divine, nor was he ever willing, as a critic, to abandon the authority of Aristotle, appropriately interpreted to be sure. He came too early to be able to make his living as a free-lance writer; and while he was always eager to be independent of the feudal institutions of the past and lived in nervous new cities such as bourgeois Berlin and Hamburg (instead of in the medieval towns of Augsburg or Nuremburg that were much revered by the later Romantics), he was never financially secure and was ultimately forced to be a court librarian constantly supervised by stern authorities. His life was a magnificent sketch of what future intellectuals would do.

Lessing (born on January 22, 1729) was the son of a Lutheran pastor at Kamenz in Saxony who came from a clan of respected magistrates, small-town mayors, and theologians. His father sent him, the third of twelve children, to St. Afra near Meissen, an elite school well known for its Spartan discipline and its rigorous curriculum, which included linguistic training in Hebrew, Greek, Latin, and French. Young Lessing never showed any signs of tiring as a student, and most of his teachers were as impressed by his quick intelligence as they were irritated by his airs of condescension. At any rate they did not object when he left the school before his classmates (after a learned parting speech on the mathematics of the barbarians) to begin the study of theology at the University of Leipzig (1746). He felt clumsy and boorish in the cosmopolitan city atmosphere, found himself interested in medicine, among other secular matters, and was attracted by the lively local theater, directed then by the famous star actress Caroline Neuber who at first allied herself with and later opposed J. C. Gottsched, professor of metaphysics and poetry at Leipzig University, the most influential critic of the thirties and forties. The young Lessing did a few translations for her and wrote a comedy in which he made fun of his own bookish inclinations. Unfortunately, many young actresses and actors soon departed for Vienna, and Lessing, the would-be-man-about-town, had guaranteed their local IOUs and found himself in legal trouble. He made a quick escape to Wittenberg, where he spent a few miserable months, penniless, lonely, in torn clothes, and sick, yet he was able to continue with his medical studies, which were concluded later with a dissertation on the Spanish physician-writer Huarte and an MA degree (1752).

In November 1748 Lessing arrived in Berlin, where he had long wanted to go, declared in a letter to his astonished parents that he planned to be the German Molière (he did not see why a good Christian could not write good comedies), and with the help of a distant young relative who was anathema at home, started to write for the *Berlinische Privilegierte Zeitung,* which later became the famous liberal *Vossische Zeitung.* He peddled translations and occasional pieces, tried his hand at publishing timely, if unperformable political plays and edited periodicals discussing the qualities of modern writing and the problems in contemporary theater. Berlin was the best choice he could have made. Frederick of Prussia, unsparing in his wars, was a brilliant French writer (his written German was always dubious) who had invited many French intellectuals, including Voltaire, to his court and the academy. French Huguenots, Czech Protestants, and a Jewish community of important merchants and gifted intellectuals were tolerated and often supported, if only for reasons of war production, and they contributed essentially to the rapidly awakening intellectual life of the city. In Berlin, as Lessing remembered, anything could be said against religion, but little, or virtually nothing, against the policies of the king.

Within the Berlin fifties, Lessing emerged as the brightest of the young critics and, together with his friend Moses Mendelssohn, scholar of the Jewish Bible and modern aesthetics, and the publisher Friedrich Nicolai, began to set the tone for a criticism committed to a rational analysis of past and present. These years in Berlin (1748–60) were immensely productive for Lessing, and, what he wrote there would shape German drama and the language of criticism for a long time to come. As a response to a bet with his friends, Lessing wrote *Miss Sara Sampson* (1755), the first German tragedy of private, not public, feelings, and he also published *Philotas* (1759) as his own examination of the king's war policies. Finally, he introduced, in German, Diderot's essays and plays (1760), which opened the way for a modern theater that concentrated on the serious problems of everyday people like you and me.

Lessing was a man of abrupt and willful decisions, and he surprised his Berlin friends when, one day, in November 1760 he simply disappeared from the city. It has never been adequately explained why he, a Saxon by birth, accepted employment with the victorious Prussian Army (Saxony's enemy) and then served for four years as secretary to General Bogislaw Friedrich von Tauentzien, commander in chief of the Prussian occupying forces in Breslau, even to the point of accompanying the general as the latter laid siege to another Silesian town still held by the enemy. Lessing himself said that he made himself rather unpopular by playfully taking the Prussian side when talking to Saxons and by defending the Saxon point of view among the Prussians, but preparing the general's official correspondence with the war ministry in Berlin or writing his decrees was quite another matter. These must have been lively, yet ultimately dissatisfying years (1760–65). He continued studying the aesthetics of the ancients, collected rare books, and gained and lost money at the elegant casinos, where he went regularly to try his luck. In 1765, he was back in Berlin, and after publishing his Laokoon (1766), a pioneering study in aesthetics and semiotics, he was again unemployed and quickly joined the new Hamburg National Theater when a group of art-loving citizens invited him to support their plans on the spot. It was not very clear what exactly he was to do. Some members of the consortium were rather shady characters who were involved with the actresses or even bankrupt, or both, and audiences soon tired of the serious fare. Within two years, the National Theater, established with great hopes, had to close, and so did a hapless little publishing house and printing press that Lessing had founded with a friend. Perhaps it was premature to expect the citizens rather than princes to subsidize a regular theater, but the attempt was an essential challenge to Lessing, who accompanied the performances with a running commentary that was published, in irregular intervals, as *Hamburg Dramaturgy* (often, as with his inclination, combining theatrical criticism with learned reevaluations of Aristotle's poetics). At the same time, in order to provide the actors with a contemporary play, he finished his *Minna von Barnhelm,* which, from the day of its premiere on September 30, 1767, has remained the most frequently performed comedy of the German repertory.

After the failures in Hamburg, the forty-year-old Lessing, alone and again without regular income, agreed (though with more than ambivalent feelings) to serve the duke of Braunschweig as the librarian of the magnificent manuscript and book collections in the small north German town of Wolfenbüttel (1769). It was, in the seventies, not a lively town of ducal splendor; the court had already moved elsewhere, and Lessing had to live in a cavernous castle, abandoned by light and laughter, as well as collaborate with invidious bureaucrats who sabotaged whatever he wanted to renew or change. Ultimately, he followed the example of the illustrious Leibniz, one of his predecessors in the directorship of the library, and rented himself rooms in nearby Braunschweig to be, at least occasionally, among more friendly people. There was a brief time of intimate happiness in Lessing's life when he wooed, in very civil letters, Eva Koenig, the widow of a Hamburg merchant and mother of four. Though an engagement was announced, Lessing hesitated to marry, and when he did (1776), they had only one blessed year together before she died after giving birth to his son, who "lived but twenty-four hours," as Lessing, tight-lipped and devastated, wrote to a close friend. In order to contribute to the celebrations of the duchess's birthday, he wrote the tragedy *Emilia Galotti* (1772), read by many critics then and now as an indictment of the feudal princes (Lessing did not attend the first performance, claiming a bad toothache). After joining the Freemasons, who could claim the duke as a member, Lessing expressed his quick disappointment with Freemasonry, unwilling to be truly egalitarian, in a series of *Conversations for the Freemasons.* He also published, although with reservations, the writings of a friend who was among the most radical critics of the Bible and thus found himself involved in bitter public disputes (in German instead of the scholars' Latin) on the essence of Christianity. Eager to explain his views from the pulpit of the theater, he wrote his play *Nathan the Wise* (1778/79) in which he, as wittily as George Bernard Shaw, probed the mutual relationship of the historical religions. Lessing died on February 15, 1781, and the announcement of his demise was signed by Malchen Koenig, Eva's sixteen-year-old daughter, whom the aging man had loved so dearly.

It is easy to recite the when and where of Lessing's life, yet it is much more difficult to grasp something of his elusive character. His letters to Moses Mendelssohn, his best friend (if there was one) and to his wife Eva do not lack wit and feeling, but unlike his romantic contemporary Rousseau, Lessing did not believe that showing off a wounded heart constituted an essential part of the writer's task. He could be personal in a friendly and ceremonial way, but when it came to real pain he was as terse as a Stoic philosopher. He was a devoted and lifelong reader, yet not entirely a library mole. The young and serious student of theology was charmed by a young actress; there were the long years of wooing Eva (mostly by correspondence); there was a mathematician's widow who wanted to make Lessing her very own; there was the remarkable Elise Reimarus, a trusted Hamburg friend and an intellectual in her own right, as well as sixteen-year-old Malchen about whom people talked a good deal in Wolfenbüttel. Many of the jokes and puns in his comedies show only all too clearly that he knew the alehouse, the gaming table, the city streets, and how the servants behaved downstairs. Most biographers would agree that Lessing was a man eager to make sudden decisions, to test, as would Dostoyevsky a century later, his luck at cards and other games of chance and fortune, and to take playful risks where others were more cautious. There is a good deal of Lessing in the comic figure of the French cardsharper and soldier of fortune in *Minna von Barnhelm*, as well as in Minna herself, who is not opposed to risking her money and perhaps, at the right moment, her reputation; and just as she does, Lessing himself put forth his ideas without hedging his bets. Lessing, the emblematic rational man of German intellectual history, was also a human being, vulnerable and eager to hazard ideas.

The Austrian playwright Franz Grillparzer, who was a splendid critic, once remarked that Lessing's admiration for Shakespeare, or at least for some of his major tragedies, did not prevent him, in his own plays, from showing himself as a disciple of Diderot. For centuries, European theatergoers had attended tragedies and comedies, but in the mid–eighteenth century, people had become more impatient with these inherited genres and the rules of decorum and language, which was either excessively noble or lowly comical, and Diderot was among the first outspoken critics who suggested that the time had come to show contemporary events and characters and the bittersweet fusion of tears and laughter as it often happened in experience. Lessing declared that Diderot was Aristotle's only true heir and began experimenting with a repertory of mixed possibilities. For the present anthology, I have selected his most enduring and challenging plays. *Minna von Barn-helm,* a Berlin comedy of manners with more feeling than is usually found in its British counterparts, suggests that after the Seven Years' War countries and people are still devastated. Two lovers, one from defeated Saxony, or rather Thuringia, the other a volunteer in the victorious Prussian army, have a difficult time picking up the pieces of their lives. Only when the young woman willfully plays out the fictional tragedy of her life, does she get her man, after she has cleansed him of his pride and his lack of compassion in strict accordance to Aristotle. *Emilia Galotti,* a tragedy in prose, has long resisted simple interpretations and, precisely because it is such a cryptic play, continues to demand that we unravel what is going on between daughter and father, not to mention the decadent prince. We must also ponder whether she commits suicide paradoxically by forcing her father to plunge his dagger into her pure (or even not so pure) heart. Lessing has been long revered as a resolute enemy of anti-Semitism, and I think that it might be useful to read closely together *The Jews,* a short piece written by the young Lessing, and *Nathan the Wise* from his later years. *The Jews* argues against facile judgments about entire groups of people, and the contemporary discussion that is reflected in the correspondence reprinted here demonstrates that young Lessing had touched a raw nerve in the educated. *Nathan the Wise,* a sophisticated comedy of ideas in the guise of a fairy tale, articulates the suspicion that perhaps, in the great religions of the Jews, the Muslims, and the Christians a fourth religion might be hidden, one that is essential to all of them. If I have taken the liberty of deleting a few scenes from the last acts, I have done so, following Friedrich Schiller's example, in order to do away with some of the theatrical claptrap and thus allow the conflict of ideas to emerge more clearly and without needless obstruction.

Lessing did not, by far, want to establish philosophical systems, and though many of his ideas about the theater were closely linked with Diderot, he is on his own, as far as matters political and theological are concerned. He was sensitive to contemporary events, yet also skeptical of quick change, and his later *Conversations for the Freemasons* (1778/80), actually a number of little playlets (somewhat shortened here), shows how disillusioned he was with this secret organization of the upper middle class and aristocratic elite. As a philosopher of religion, or more precisely as a thinking religious man, Lessing was as reluctant to support Protestant orthodoxy as he was unwilling to make common cause with the so-called neologists, who totally identified reason with revelation, and he distressed many of his enlightened Berlin friends by saying in his letters that though the waters of orthodoxy were impure he preferred them to the manure of the "neologians." On theological questions, he was a *Selbstdenker* (self-thinker) in the Kantian sense; in the *Proof of the Spirit and of Power* (1777), he suggested that it was impossible to legitimatize Christianity with the history of miracles instead of with the truth of reason; and in *The Education of the Human Race* (1780), he once again examined the demands of three historical religions (as he had done in *Nathan the Wise*) and suggested that God, that supreme pedagogue, had adjusted his progressing revelation to the intellectual development of humanity. In *The Testament of John* (1777) and in *The Religion of Christ* (1780), Lessing refused to identify the quiet intensity of his Christian feelings with the demands of Christian institutions and ultimately argued that we should help to prepare for a time when we shall make our ethical decisions by relying on the good as the supreme value in itself, instead of relying on other, transworldly justifications.

I am particularly thankful to Harcourt Brace Jovanovich Publishers (New York) for permission to reprint Hannah Arendt's "On Humanity in Dark Times: Thoughts on Lessing," originally published in *Men in Dark Times* (New York, 1968), 3–31 (with a few deletions, as indicated). Ms. Ingrid Walsøe-Engel (Yale University) and Mr. William L. Zwiebel (College of the Holy Cross, Worcester, Massachusetts) translated Lessing's *Die Juden,* and related correspondences, and *Ernst und Falk: Gespräche für Freimäurer,* respectively, for the present edition and thus essentially widened the range of Lessing's writings available to American readers. In the preparation of the manuscript I was, once more, loyally assisted by Melissa Vogelsang and I owe her a special debt of gratitude.

P. D.

MINNA VON BARNHELM

A Comedy in Five Acts
Written in 1767

CHARACTERS

MAJOR VON TELLHEIM
MINNA VON BARNHELM
COUNT OF BRUCHSAL, *her uncle*
FRANZISKA, *her maid*
JUST, *Tellheim's servant*
PAUL WERNER, *former sergeant major in Tellheim's battalion*
LANDLORD
LADY IN MOURNING
ORDERLY • SERVANTS
RICCAUT DE LA MARLINIÈRE
The scene alternates between two adjacent rooms of an inn.

Act I

Scene 1

JUST (*seated in a corner, sleeping and talking in his sleep*): Bugger of a landlord . . . you . . . us? . . . On guard! *(He goes through the motions of drawing his sword and in doing so wakes himself up.)* Bah! I can't even close my eyes without getting into a fight with him. I wish he'd been on the receiving end of half the blows I've dealt him. . . . *(Yawns)* But it's light out, I've got to find the master. As far as I'm concerned, he'll not set foot in this damn house again. I wonder where he spent the night.

Scene 2

Just and Landlord.

LANDLORD: Good morning, Herr Just, good morning. You're up early, or should I say you're still up so late?

JUST: You can say what you damn well like.

LANDLORD: I wasn't saying anything but "Good morning," and surely, Herr Just, you ought to say "Thank you" to that.

JUST: Thanks.

LANDLORD: Everyone feels a bit touchy when they don't get their proper rest. But never mind. So the major didn't come in last night, and you waited up for him?

JUST: You're clever, you are.

LANDLORD: Just guessing, Herr Just, just guessing.

JUST (*turning and about to leave*): Your servant, sir!

LANDLORD: Oh no, Herr Just, no!

JUST: All right then, I'm not your servant.

LANDLORD: Herr Just, I do hope that you're not still angry about yesterday. You shouldn't let the sun go down on your wrath, you know.

JUST: Well, I do and I shall let it go down on it till doomsday.

LANDLORD: Now, I ask you, is that Christian?

JUST: It's just as Christian as throwing an honest man out of the house because he can't pay his rent on the dot.

LANDLORD: Well, now, who could be so godless as to do a thing like that?

JUST: A Christian landlord. . . . To think the master, a man like that, an officer of his stamp!

LANDLORD: And I'm the one who's supposed to have thrown him out of the house into the street? I'm afraid I have too much respect for officers to do that, and in any case too much sympathy with one who's just been discharged. I was obliged to ask him to move into another room, that's all—because of an emergency. Think no more about it, Herr Just. *(Shouts offstage.)* Hey there! I'll make it up to you in another way. *(Enter servant.)* Bring us a glass. Herr Just would like a drop of something special.

JUST: Don't bother. Anything you offered me would turn to gall in my mouth. By God . . . No I mustn't blaspheme, I'm still sober.

LANDLORD *(to servant who enters carrying a bottle of liqueur and a glass):* Give it to me. All right, you can go! Now, Herr Just, here's a drop of something special; strong, but gentle, and it'll do you good. *(Fills the glass and offers it to Just.)* Just the thing for a stomach that's been up all night.

JUST: Well, I shouldn't really . . . but why should I sacrifice my good health to his bad manners? *(Takes the glass and drinks.)*

LANDLORD: Your health, Herr Just.

JUST *(giving him back the glass):* Not bad, but it doesn't make you any less of a scoundrel.

LANDLORD: Now, what about another quick one? You can't balance properly on one leg.

JUST *(having drunk the second glass):* Well, I must admit it's good, very good . . . homemade, of course?

LANDLORD: Not likely, real Danziger Goldwasser!

JUST: Now look here, Landlord, if something like this could make me play the hypocrite, I would; but I can't, and so I tell you straight to your face—you're a scoundrel.

LANDLORD: That's the first time in my life that anyone ever called me that. Another one, Herr Just, all good things come in threes.

JUST: All right *(Drinks.)* Hm. Good, *very* good, but so is the truth. . . . Truth's a good thing too. . . . Landlord, you're a scoundrel.

LANDLORD: Now, I ask you, if I was a scoundrel, would I be standing here listening to you call me one?

JUST: Yes, you would. Scoundrels seldom have any guts.

LANDLORD: Won't you have another one, Herr Just? A four-stranded rope holds better, you know.

JUST: No, enough is enough. Besides, what's the use? If I drank the bottle down to the last drop, I wouldn't change my mind. Ugh, such a good drop of Danziger and such rotten manners. Throwing out a man like the master, who's lived here day and night and spent many a pretty penny here; throwing him out just because he wasn't spending quite as much—and behind his back into the bargain.

LANDLORD: But I needed the room. It was an emergency, and I knew the major would gladly have left it of his own free will if only we could have waited until he got back. Was I to turn a stranger away? I ask you. Was I to shove the trade down another landlord's throat? And besides, I don't think they could have found another place to stay. All the places are full up at the moment. You shouldn't have wanted a lovely young lady like that to have to stay out in the street. No, Herr Just, your master's too much of a gentleman to allow that. Besides, what does he stand to lose? Didn't I move him into another room?

JUST: Yes, right behind the pigeon loft . . . with a nice view between the chimneys of the houses next door. . . .

LANDLORD: Well, the view was all right until they started building. The rest of the room's nice enough—and it's got wallpaper.

JUST: You mean it had.

LANDLORD: It still has on one side. And you've got your little room next door, Herr Just . . . what's wrong with your room? There's a fireplace . . . well, perhaps it does smoke a bit in the winter. . . .

JUST: But it looks all right in the summer. . . . You're not trying to needle us, are you?

LANDLORD: Now, now, Herr Just, Herr Just. . . .

JUST: Don't you get Herr Just excited, or else. . . .

LANDLORD: Me? Get you excited? . . . No, that's the Danziger.

JUST: An officer like my master. Or perhaps you reckon that a discharged officer isn't an officer and couldn't break your neck. I wonder why you landlords were always such a help in the war. Every officer was an honest chap then. Does a bit of peace make you so cocksure?

LANDLORD: Now what are you getting angry about, Herr Just?

JUST: I want to get angry. . . .

Scene 3

Tellheim, Landlord, and Just.

TELLHEIM (*entering*): Just!

JUST *(thinking it is the landlord who is talking to him):* Just? Oh, so we're on those terms now, are we?

TELLHEIM: Just!

JUST: I thought I was Herr Just to you.

LANDLORD *(becoming aware of Tellheim's presence):* Sh! Sh! Herr Just, Herr Just. . . . Look behind you . . . your master.

TELLHEIM: Just, I believe you're quarreling. What did I tell you?

LANDLORD: Quarrel, Your Grace? Would I, Your Grace's most humble servant, take it upon myself to quarrel with one who has the honor to be in Your Grace's service?

JUST: I'd like to give that humbug what for.

LANDLORD: It's true that Herr Just was speaking out on behalf of his master . . . perhaps a little heatedly, but he was right to do so. I think all the more of him for it; in fact I admire him for it.

JUST: It's a wonder I don't knock his teeth down his throat.

LANDLORD: It's really a shame, getting upset over nothing. I'm as sure as can be that Your Grace would not bring any disgrace on me for what I have done . . . because it was necessary, because I had to.

TELLHEIM: Enough, sir. I owe you money. You moved me out of my room in my absence. You must be paid. I have to find somewhere else to stay. It's perfectly understandable.

LANDLORD: Somewhere else? You're moving out, sir? Oh, what a wretch I am! No, never! I'd sooner have the lady moved out. The major can . . . well . . . if you don't want to give her your room . . . the room's yours. She'll have to go. I can't help it. I'll see to it at once, Your Grace.

TELLHEIM: My friend, please do not do two stupid things instead of one. The lady must, of course, retain possession of my room.

LANDLORD: And to think that Your Grace thought I mistrusted you, thought I was worried about my money! As if I didn't know that Your Grace could pay whenever he wanted to! That sealed purse with the five hundred talers in it which Your Grace left in the desk. . . . Don't worry, it's in good hands.

TELLHEIM: I hope so—like the rest of my things. Just will take charge of them when he pays the bill.

LANDLORD: Honestly, Your Grace, I was quite scared when I found that purse. I always thought you were an orderly and careful man, who wouldn't allow himself to run out of money. But, well, if I'd really thought that there was money in the desk. . . .

TELLHEIM: You would have been a little more polite with me.

LANDLORD: But Your Grace . . .

TELLHEIM: Come, Just, this gentleman is apparently not going to permit me to tell you what to do, while we are in his house.

LANDLORD: I'm going, Your Grace! My whole establishment is at your service.

Scene 4

Tellheim and Just.

JUST (*stamping his foot and spitting on the ground*): Pah!

TELLHEIM: What's the matter?

JUST: I'm fairly choking with rage!

TELLHEIM: That's about the same as having a plethora.

JUST: And you, sir, I just don't know you any more. Let me die before your very eyes if you aren't the guardian angel of this cunning, this merciless, dog. In spite of the gallows, in spite of the sword and the wheel, I'd have strangled him with my own hands and torn him to pieces with my own teeth.

TELLHEIM: Animal!

JUST: I'd rather be an animal than be like that.

TELLHEIM: What do you want?

JUST: All I want is for you to understand how they're insulting you.

TELLHEIM: And then?

JUST: I want you to have your revenge on him. But no! No, this fellow's not worth your bothering with.

TELLHEIM: Would you rather I told you to avenge me? That was my first thought. I hadn't intended him to see me again, and he was to receive his payment from you. I know that you can toss away a handful of money with a pretty disdainful gesture.

JUST: Ha! Ha! That would have been a good way of paying him off.

TELLHEIM: But one which I'm afraid we shall have to put off for the time being. I haven't a penny of ready money, and I don't know how to get any.

JUST: No ready money? What about that little purse with the five hundred talers which the landlord found in your writing desk?

TELLHEIM: That is money which was given to me to keep.

JUST: Not the five hundred talers which your old sergeant major, Paul Werner, brought you four or five weeks ago?

TELLHEIM: The very same. They belong to Paul Werner; why not?

JUST: You mean to say you haven't used them yet? You can do what you like with them, sir; I'll take responsibility.

TELLHEIM: Really?

JUST: I told Werner how long the paymaster general was taking to put your demands to rights. He heard . . .

TELLHEIM: That I would certainly be reduced to beggary, if I weren't already. I'm very grateful to you, Just. And this piece of news permitted Werner to share his bit of poverty with me. I'm glad to have got to the bottom of it. Now listen to me, Just; give me your bill as well; our partnership is at an end.

JUST: Eh? What?

TELLHEIM: Quiet! Someone is coming.

Scene 5

A lady in mourning, Tellheim, and Just.

LADY: I beg your pardon, sir.

TELLHEIM: Who are you looking for, madam?

LADY: Simply the worthy man with whom I have the honor to be speaking. You do not recognize me any longer. I am the widow of your former captain.

TELLHEIM: For heaven's sake, madam, but you are changed.

LADY: I have just risen from my sickbed to which I had retired because of my sorrow at my husband's death. I am sorry to have to bother you so early, Major Tellheim. I am going to the country where a good-natured, though not exactly fortunate, friend has offered me a haven.

TELLHEIM *(to Just):* Go, leave us alone.

Scene 6

Lady in mourning and Tellheim.

TELLHEIM: Speak freely, madam. You have no need to be ashamed of your misfortune in my presence. Can I be of service to you in any way?

LADY: Major . . .

TELLHEIM: I sympathize with you, madam. How can I be of service to you? You know that your husband was my friend—I repeat, my friend; and this is a title with which I have always been very sparing.

LADY: Who knows better than I how well he deserved your friendship and how well you deserved his? You would have been his last thought, your name the last word to escape his lips, had the ties of nature not reserved that right for his unfortunate son and for his unfortunate wife . . .

TELLHEIM: Enough. Madam! I would gladly weep with you, but today

I have no tears. Spare me. You come upon me at a moment when I might easily be led to rail against Providence. O, my honest Marloff! Quickly, madam, what is your command? If I am in a position to help you . . . if I am . . .

LADY: I may not leave without fulfilling his last wish. He remembered just before his end that he was dying in your debt and made me swear to discharge this debt with the first money that I should receive. I sold his equipment, and I have come to redeem his note.

TELLHEIM: I beg your pardon, madam, it is for this that you have come?

LADY: For this. Please let me pay you the money.

TELLHEIM: Madame, I beg you. Marloff owed me money? That can scarcely be so. Let me see. *(Takes out his notebook and looks at it.)* I see nothing here.

LADY: You must have mislaid his note, and in any case, the note has nothing to do with it. Permit me . . .

TELLHEIM: No, madam, I am not in the habit of mislaying things of that sort. If I do not have it, then that is evidence that I never had it, or that it was canceled and returned to him.

LADY: Major Tellheim!

TELLHEIM: Most certainly, madam. Marloff owed me nothing. In fact I cannot even recall that he was ever in my debt. On the contrary, madam, I regard myself as having been left in his debt. I have never been able to pay off my debts to a man who for six years shared my happiness and my misfortune, my honor and my danger. I shall not forget that he has left a son. He shall be my son as soon as I can be his father. The confusion in which I find myself at the moment . . .

LADY: Generous man! But please do not think too lowly of me. Take the money, Major Tellheim; in this way I shall at least be put at ease.

TELLHEIM: What do you need to set you at ease, beyond my assurance that this money does not belong to me? Or do you want me to steal from my friend's infant and fatherless child? Steal, madam, that's what it would be in the truest meaning of the word. The money belongs to him, and you should invest it for him.

LADY: I understand you; please forgive me if I have not yet learned to accept favors. But how did you know that a mother will do more for her son than for her own life? I am going now . . . .

TELLHEIM: Go, madam, go. Farewell. I shall not ask you to send me news of yourself, for such news might come at a time when I could make no use of it. But I forgot one thing, madam. Marloff still had money owing him from our former regiment. His demands are just as valid as my own. If mine are met, then his will be too. My word on it.

LADY: Sir. . . . No, I would rather say nothing. . . . To grant future favors is, in God's eyes, to have granted them already. I give you my thanks and my tears. *(Exit.)*

Scene 7

Tellheim.

TELLHEIM: Poor woman! I must not forget to destroy that note. *(Takes some papers from his wallet and tears them up.)* Who can guarantee that my own need might not one day make me put them to use?

Scene 8

Just and Tellheim.

TELLHEIM: Are you there?

JUST *(wiping his eyes):* Yes.

TELLHEIM: You have been crying?

JUST: I have been writing out my bill in the kitchen, and the kitchen is full of smoke. Here it is.

TELLHEIM: Give it to me.

JUST: Have a bit of mercy on me, sir. I know people don't have much on you, but . . .

TELLHEIM: What do you want?

JUST: Well, I'd expected to die before getting the sack from you.

TELLHEIM: I have no further use for you. I have now to learn how to look after myself without servants. *(Opens the bill and reads.)* "The major owes me: three and a half months pay at six talers per month—twenty-one talers. From the first of the month I have paid out the following sums for him: one taler, seven groschen, nine pfennigs. Sum total, twenty-two talers, seven groschen, nine pfennigs." Just, I think I should pay you for the whole of the current month.

JUST: Look at the other side first, would you, major?

TELLHEIM: There's more? *(Reads.)* "I owe the major! Advanced on my account to the surgeon, twenty-five talers. For board and lodging during my convalescence, thirty-nine talers. Advanced to my father, whose house was burned and plundered, not to mention the two horses which he gave him, fifty talers. Sum total, one hundred and fourteen talers. Deduct the twenty-two talers, seven groschen, nine pfennigs brought forward: I remain in the major's debt to the tune of ninety-one talers, sixteen groschen, three pfennigs." Just, you're mad!!

JUST: I'm ready to believe that I've cost you a great deal more than that, but it would have been a waste of ink writing any more down. I can't pay you; and if you want to take my uniform away from me, which I also haven't paid for, then I'd rather you'd let me kick the bucket in some field hospital.

TELLHEIM: What do you take me for? You don't owe me anything, and I'll give you a recommendation to one of my friends who will look after you better than I can.

JUST: I don't owe you anything, yet you still want to throw me out.

TELLHEIM: Because I don't want to owe you anything.

JUST: Oh, just because of that? As sure as I know that I'm in your debt, I'm just as sure you don't owe me a penny, and just as sure that you shan't throw me out. You can do what you like, major, I'm going to stay with you, I've got to stay with you.

TELLHEIM: And your obstinacy, your defiance, your wild and impetuous conduct against everyone who you think has no right to interfere with you, your malicious spite, your desire for revenge . . .

JUST: You can paint me as black as you like, I won't think any worse of myself than of my dog. One evening last winter, in the twilight, I was walking along the canal and heard something whining. I climbed down, reached toward the voice, thinking that I was rescuing a child, and pulled a poodle out of the water. Well, that's all right too, I thought. The poodle followed me. Now I don't particularly like poodles. I chased him away, but it was no use. I beat him, but it was no use. I refused to let him into my room at night; he stayed in front of the door all night. If he got too close to me, I gave him a kick; he yelped, looked at me, and wagged his tail. I've never given him a thing to eat, but I'm the only one he obeys and the only one who can touch him. He runs along in front of me and does his tricks for me without being asked. He's an ugly poodle, but a very good dog. If he goes on like this, I'll have to stop disliking him.

TELLHEIM *(aside):* Exactly as I am to him! No, there *are* no completely inhuman people . . . Just, we'll stay together.

JUST: Certainly! . . . And you wanted to get on without a servant? You forget about your wounds and that you're only got the use of one arm. You can't get dressed by yourself. You can't do without me, and . . . not wishing to praise myself . . . and I am a servant, who . . . if worst comes to worst . . . can beg and steal for his master.

Tellheim: Just, we are not staying together.
JUST: All right!

Scene 9

Servant, Tellheim, and Just.

SERVANT: Hey!
JUST: What is it?
SERVANT: Can you show me the officer who was living in this room until yesterday? *(pointing to the side from which he has just come.)*
JUST: Yes, I can. What've you got for him?
SERVANT: What we've always got when we haven't got anything. A greeting. It's come to my mistress's ears as how she turned him out of his room. My mistress knows what's what, and so I'm to beg his pardon.
JUST: All right, beg his pardon, there he is.
SERVANT: What is he? What do you call him?
TELLHEIM: My friend, I have already heard your commission. It is an unnecessary piece of courtesy on the part of your mistress, which I recognize for what it is worth. Please give her my respects. . . . What is your mistress's name?
SERVANT: What's her name? Oh, she's called "madam."
TELLHEIM: And her family name?
SERVANT: I've never heard that, and it's not my business to ask. I arrange things so that . . . well, I change masters about every six weeks. As far as I'm concerned, to hell with their names!
JUST: Bravo, mate!
SERVANT: I only started with the mistress a few days ago, in Dresden. I think she's looking for her fiancé here.
TELLHEIM: Enough, my friend. I wanted to know your mistress's name, not her secrets. Go!
SERVANT: Brother, I don't think he'd be much of a master for me!

Scene 10

Tellheim and Just.

TELLHEIM: Just, I want you to arrange to get out of this place. I find myself more sensitive to the courtesy of this strange woman than I am to the ill manners of the landlord. Here, take this ring; it's the one valuable thing I have left and the one which I never thought I'd have to put to this use. Pawn it. Raise four hundred talers on it. The innkeeper's bill can't be more than thirty talers. Pay the landlord and then move my things. Where to? . . . Wherever you like. The cheaper the inn the better. You can meet me in the café next door. I am leaving now; see that you do it properly.

JUST: Don't you worry about that, Major.

TELLHEIM (*returning*): And most important of all, don't forget my pistols, which were hanging behind the bed.

JUST: I won't forget anything. Hm, so the master had this valuable ring, and carried it in his pocket and not on his finger. So, landlord, we're not as poor as we seem to be. I know what! I'll pawn it with the landlord. A pretty little ring. He'll be angry, I know, because we're not going to spend all the money in his place. A pretty little ring, I'll . . .

Scene 11

Paul Werner and Just.

JUST: Well, if it isn't Werner! Hello, Werner. Welcome to the big city.

WERNER: Damned village! I can't get used to it again. Cheer up, children, cheer up! I am bringing some more money. Where's the major?

JUST: He must have passed you. He just went downstairs.

WERNER: I came up the backstairs. How is he? I would have been here last week, but . . .

JUST: What held you up?

WERNER: Just . . . Just, have you heard of Prince Heraclius?

JUST: Heraclius? Not that I know of.

WERNER: Haven't you heard about the great hero in the East?

JUST: Well, I know about three wise men from the East, who run about with a star around New Year's time.

WERNER: Man, I think you must read the paper about as little as you read the Bible. You don't know Prince Heraclius. You don't know about the great man who has conquered Persia and is now going to finish off the Turks. Thank God there's somewhere left in the world where there's a war on! I kept hoping it would break out here again. But they're still sitting round licking their wounds. No, once a soldier, always a soldier. But listen. (*looking round shyly to make sure no one is listening.*) In confidence, Just, I'm going to Persia to fight a campaign or two against the Turks under the leadership of His Royal Highness, Prince Heraclius.

JUST: You?

WERNER: Me! As sure as I'm standing here. Our ancestors used to fight the Turks, and we would too if only we were honest men and good Christians. I know a campaign against the Turks isn't nearly such fun as one against the French. But then the rewards should be greater in this life and the next. Did you know that all Turks' swords are encrusted with diamonds?

JUST: I wouldn't budge a foot to have my head split open by a sword like that. You surely aren't crazy enough to want to leave your farm?

WERNER: I'm taking it with me. Didn't you know? My farm has been sold . . .

JUST: Sold?

WERNER: Sh! . . . Here are the four hundred I got yesterday. They're for the major.

JUST: And what is he supposed to do with them?

WERNER: What d'you think he's supposed to do with them? Eat 'em up, gamble 'em away, drink 'em up . . . well . . . I don't know; he can do what he likes with them. The man's got to have some money, and it's bad enough for him having all this trouble to get his own. I know what I'd do if I was in your place. I'd think, "To hell with the lot of them! I'll go with Paul Werner to Persia." Hell! Prince Heraclius must have heard of Major Tellheim, too, even if he doesn't know his old sergeant major, Paul Werner. That business at Katzenberg . . .

JUST: Shall I tell you about it?

WERNER: *You* tell *me?* . . . I can tell that a good battle plan is something you don't appreciate. I'm not going to throw my pearls before swine. Take the four hundred talers and give them to the major. Tell him to keep them for me. I've got to go to the market now. I've brought forty bushels of rye with me, and he can have that too.

JUST: Werner, I know you mean well, but we don't want your money. Keep your talers, and you can have the other five hundred back as soon as you like; we've not touched them.

WERNER: Really? The major's still got some money, has he?

JUST: No, he hasn't.

WERNER: Well, has he borrowed some then?

JUST: No.

WERNER: What are you living on then?

JUST: Credit, and when we can't get any more credit and they throw us out, we shall pawn what we've still got left and clear out. Listen, Paul, we've got to get even with this landlord here.

WERNER: If he's done something to the major, I'm with you.

JUST: What about waiting for him when he comes out of the to-bacconist's this evening and giving him a going over?

WERNER: This evening? Wait for him? Two against one? No, that's not right.

JUST: Suppose we burn his house about his ears?

WERNER: Burn it down? You know, it's easy to tell you were with the baggage train and not in the infantry . . . . Pah!

JUST: Supposing we seduced his daughter? Though it's true she's ugly.

WERNER: She'll stay ugly for a long time. Anyway, you don't need my help for that. But what's the matter, what's up?

JUST: Come on and I'll tell you something that'll surprise you.

WERNER: There's the devil to pay round here.

JUST: Come on!

WERNER: So much the better! To Persia! To Persia!

Act II

Scene 1

The lady's boudoir

Minna von Barnhelm and Franziska, her maid.

MINNA *(in her negligée and looking at her watch):* Franziska, we got up very early, we are going to be bored.

FRANZISKA: Well, I don't know who can get any sleep in these big cities, what with the coaches, night watchmen, drums, cats, corporals . . . no end of rattling, shouting, swearing, meowing, just as if the night were made for anything but peace. Would you like a cup of tea, madam?

MINNA: No, I don't feel like tea.

FRANZISKA: I'll get them to make some of our chocolate.

MINNA: Yes do, for yourself.

FRANZISKA: Just for myself? I'd just as soon talk to myself as drink alone. . . . Well, it's going to be a long day. . . . Out of sheer boredom we shall have to make our toilet and then choose the dress in which we are going to make our first assault.

MINNA: Why do you talk about assaults? You know that I have only come here to demand a surrender.

FRANZISKA: And that officer we turned out, the one we sent our apologies to—he doesn't seem to have the best of manners, otherwise he would at least have asked for the honor of being allowed to pay his respects to us.

MINNA: Not all officers are Tellheims. To tell you the truth, I only sent him my apologies so that I could have the chance to ask him about Tellheim. . . . Franziska, my heart tells me that our journey will be successful and that I shall find him.

FRANZISKA: Your heart, madam? I shouldn't put too much trust in your heart. The heart likes to tell us what we want to hear. If our mouths were as ready to say what our hearts wanted them to, we'd have got into the fashion of wearing locks on our mouths long ago.

MINNA: Ha! Ha! You and your locks and mouths! That's a fashion I'd approve of.

FRANZISKA: It's better to keep even the prettiest teeth hidden than to have your heart leaping out over them every few minutes.

MINNA: Really, are you so reserved?

FRANZISKA: No, madam, but I wish I was. People talk very seldom about the virtues they have, but all the more frequently about the ones they don't have.

MINNA: You know, Franziska, that's a very good observation you've made.

FRANZISKA: That I made? Do you really *make* something that just occurs to you?

MINNA: And do you know why I think it's such a good observation? Because it has a lot to do with my Tellheim.

FRANZISKA: Do you ever come across anything that doesn't have some connection with him?

MINNA: Friends and enemies alike say that he is the bravest man in the world. But did anyone ever hear him talk about bravery? He has the most honest heart in the world, but did anyone ever hear him talk about honesty or nobility?

FRANZISKA: What virtues does he talk about then?

MINNA: He doesn't talk about any, because he lacks none of them.

FRANZISKA: That's just what I wanted to hear.

MINNA: Wait a minute, Franziska, I do remember one thing. He often talks about economy. You know, in strictest confidence, Franziska, I think he's a bit of a spendthrift.

FRANZISKA: There's one other thing, madam. I've often heard him talk about his constancy and his faithfulness to you. Supposing he was a bit of a flirt?

MINNA: You beast! . . . But you are not serious, are you, Franziska?

FRANZISKA: How long is it since he wrote to you?

MINNA: He has only written once since the armistice.

FRANZISKA: Another complaint against peace. Wonderful! Peace is supposed to make good all the evil caused by the war, but it also seems to destroy whatever good the war brought about. Peace ought not to be so obstinate, and anyway, how long have we been at peace? Time really drags when there's so little news. There's not much point in having the mails working again—nobody ever writes, because nobody has anything to write about.

MINNA: "Peace has come," he wrote to me, "and I am approaching the fulfillment of my wishes." But that he should have only written to me once . . .

FRANZISKA: So that we have to hasten to help him to the fulfillment of his wishes. If we come across him, we'll make him pay. . . . But supposing he had in the meantime fulfilled his wishes, and we were to find out here . . .

MINNA *(fearful and quickly)*: That he was dead?

FRANZISKA: Dead to you, madam, in the arms of another.

MINNA: Oh! You torture me. Just you wait, Franziska, he'll pay you out for that! But go on talking or we shall fall asleep. His regiment was disbanded after the armistice. Who knows what confusion he may have got into with his records and accounts. Who knows whether he may not have been posted to another regiment in some distant province? Who knows what the circumstances are? . . . There's a knock.

FRANZISKA: Come in!

Scene 2

Landlord, Minna, and Franziska.

LANDLORD *(his head thrust forward)*: May I come in, gracious ladies?

FRANZISKA: Oh! The landlord. Please come in.

LANDLORD *(a pen behind his ear, a sheet of paper and writing utensils in his hand)*: I come, madam, to wish you a most humble good morning . . . *(to Franziska)* and you too, my dear.

FRANZISKA: What a polite man!

MINNA: We thank you.

FRANZISKA: And wish you a good morning, too.

LANDLORD: May I take the liberty of asking how Your Graces rested on your first night under my miserable roof?

FRANZISKA: Well, the roof isn't all that bad, but the beds could have been better.

LANDLORD: What! Don't tell me that you didn't sleep! Perhaps you were overtired from the journey.

MINNA: Perhaps.

LANDLORD: Of course, of course. For otherwise, otherwise. . . . In the meantime, if there is anything which is not completely as it should be for Your Graces' comfort, Your Graces have only to tell me.

FRANZISKA: Very well, Sir, very well, and incidentally, we are not stupid and an inn is the last place where you should be stupid. We'll tell you how we should like things arranged.

LANDLORD: And now there's another thing . . . *(He takes the pen from behind his ear.)*

FRANZISKA: Well?

LANDLORD: I am sure that Your Graces are familiar with the regulations which, in their wisdom, our police have made.

MINNA: I'm afraid I am completely unfamiliar with them, sir.

LANDLORD: We landlords are directed not to put up any stranger, no matter what his social class or his sex, for more than twenty-four hours without handing in a report to the proper authority as to his name, his home address, character, the business which brings him here, the proposed duration of his visit, etc., etc.

MINNA: Very well.

LANDLORD: Would Your Graces object, therefore . . . *(He goes to the table and prepares to start writing.)*

MINNA: Gladly, my name is . . .

LANDLORD: One moment, if you please. *(writing)* Date: 22d August, *anni currentis,* arrived here at the King of Spain. . . . Now, your name, madam?

MINNA: Fräulein von Barnhelm.

LANDLORD *(writing):* "Von Barnhelm" . . . and you come from where, madam?

MINNA: From my estates in Saxony.

LANDLORD *(writes):* "Estates in Saxony" . . . Saxony! Ha! Ha! Saxony, madam, Saxony?

FRANZISKA: Well, and why not? I take it it isn't a sin around here to come from Saxony?

LANDLORD: A sin? Oh, heaven forbid! That would be a brand-new sin! So you come from Saxony? Saxony, dear old Saxony. Well, if I'm right, Saxony isn't exactly what you would call small, and it has several . . . what should I say . . . districts, provinces . . . our police are very precise, madam.

MINNA: I understand; from my estates in Thuringia.

LANDLORD: From Thuringia. Well now, that's better, madam, that's much more precise . . . *(Writes and then reads aloud.)* "Fräulein von Barnhelm coming from her estates in Thuringia together with a lady-in-waiting and two servants."

FRANZISKA: A lady-in-waiting, is that me?

LANDLORD: That's right, my dear.

FRANZISKA: Now, sir, I think you'd better change that to lady's *maid*. I understand that the police here are very precise; there might be a misunderstanding, which could cause me trouble when my banns are read. For I really am still a maid, and my name is Franziska, surname Willing; my father used to be a miller on one of the lady's estates. The village was called Klein-Rammsdorf. My brother owns the mill now. I went to court when I was still very young and was brought up with madam, here. We are the same age, twenty-one next Candlemas. Madam and I learned exactly the same things. It is very important that the police should know exactly who I am.

LANDLORD: Very well, my child, I'll make a note of it in case anyone should enquire. But now, madam, what is your business here?

MINNA: My business?

LANDLORD: Is Your Grace perhaps seeking something from His Majesty the king?

MINNA: Oh, no!

LANDLORD: Or from the High Court of Justice?

MINNA: No, not that either.

LANDLORD: Or? . . .

MINNA: No, no. I'm just here to look after my own affairs.

LANDLORD: Very well, madam, but where are they?

MINNA: They are . . . Franziska, do you know, I think we're being cross-examined.

FRANZISKA: Sir, surely the police would never insist on knowing a young lady's secrets?

LANDLORD: Oh certainly, my dear, the police want to know everything, absolutely everything, and especially secrets.

FRANZISKA: What shall we do, madam? Listen, sir . . . but it must stay between us and the police.

MINNA *(aside):* Whatever is the idiot going to tell him now?

FRANZISKA: We've come to steal an officer from the king.

LANDLORD: What's that, my dear?

FRANZISKA: Or to let ourselves be stolen by an officer.

MINNA: Franziska, are you mad? Sir, this saucy girl is pulling your leg.

LANDLORD: Well, I hope not. I mean, as far as my humble person is concerned, she can joke with me as much as she likes, but when it comes to our police authorities . . .

MINNA: Do you know what, sir? I really don't know what to do about all this. I should have thought that you might have left all this form-filling business until my uncle arrives. I told you yesterday why he couldn't come with me right away. He had an accident with his coach a couple of miles from here and was determined that the accident shouldn't cause me another night's delay, so I came on ahead. At the very most he'll only be a day later than I.

LANDLORD: All right then, madam, we'll wait for him.

MINNA: He will be able to answer your questions better than I. He knows who he has to tell things to, how much to tell, and what he can keep quiet about.

LANDLORD: So much the better. It's true, you can't ask a young woman *(He looks meaningfully at Franziska.)* to treat a serious matter seriously among serious people.

MINNA: And the rooms for my uncle, are they ready?

LANDLORD: Absolutely, madam, absolutely, except for one . . .

FRANZISKA: From which you have had to turn out another honest man?

LANDLORD: It seems, madam, that the lady's maids who come from Saxony are a very sympathetic lot.

MINNA: That's right, sir. What you did was not right. It would have been better for you not to have taken us in at all.

LANDLORD: What do you mean, madam, what do you mean?

MINNA: I hear that the officer who was turned out on our behalf . . .

LANDLORD: Was only a discharged officer, madam.

MINNA: Even so!

LANDLORD: Who's on his last legs.

MINNA: So much the worse. He seems to be a very deserving man . . .

LANDLORD: But I tell you, he is discharged.

MINNA: But the king cannot possibly know every deserving man in his service.

LANDLORD: Oh, yes he does, he knows them, all of them.

MINNA: But he can't reward them all.

LANDLORD: They'd all be rewarded if they'd lived properly. But as long as the war was on, these gentlemen lived as if it was going to last forever, as if the idea of "mine" and "yours" had been abandoned for good. And so now all the inns are full of them, and a landlord has to be pretty careful of them. I've managed to get on pretty well with this one. If he didn't actually have any money left, he had the equivalent. And he could easily have stayed on for another two or three months. Still, it's all for the best. By the way, madam, do you know anything about jewels?

MINNA: Not especially.

LANDLORD: I'm sure Your Grace does. I must show you a ring, a valuable ring. You know, you have a very beautiful one on your own finger, and I must say that I'm surprised, because the more I look at it the more it looks like the one I have myself. Look, look! *(He takes the ring out of its case.)* Look at that fire, the center diamond alone weighs more than five carats!

MINNA *(looking at the ring)*: Where am I? What do I see? This ring . . .

LANDLORD: At a fair estimate it is worth 1,500 talers.

MINNA: Franziska, have a look! . . .

LANDLORD: I didn't hesitate for a moment to offer him four hundred for it.

MINNA: Don't you recognize it, Franziska?

FRANZISKA: It's the very same! Sir, where did you get this ring?

LANDLORD: Surely you're not claiming it, my dear?

FRANZISKA: Not claim it? Madam's name is engraved on the inside of it. Show him, madam.

MINNA: This is it! This is it! How did you come by this ring, landlord?

LANDLORD: Me? In the most honorable fashion in the world. Madam, you surely don't want to cause me disgrace and misfortune? How should I know where the ring actually came from? I do know that during the war a lot of things changed hands very often, with or without the knowledge of the rightful owner. War's war, after all. More than one thing has come over the border from Saxony. Give it back to me, madam, please give it back!

MINNA: First tell us who you got it from.

LANDLORD: From a man who I should never have thought such a thing of. From a man, otherwise a very good man . . .

MINNA: From the best man under the sun, if you got it from its rightful owner. Hurry, bring this man to me! He must be the man himself, or at least must know where he is.

LANDLORD: Who, who, madam?

FRANZISKA: Are you deaf? Our major.

LANDLORD: Major, that's right, he is a major, the man who had this room before you, and it's him I got it from.

MINNA: Major von Tellheim?

LANDLORD: Von Tellheim, yes! Do you know him?

MINNA: Do I know him! He was here? Tellheim here? Living in this room? And it was he who pawned the ring with you? How did he get into such an embarrassing situation? Where is he? Does he owe you money? Franziska, bring me the strongbox. Open it! *(Franziska places the box on the table and opens it.)* How much does he owe you? Who else does he owe money to? Bring all his creditors to me here. Here's cash, paper money. Everything belongs to him!

LANDLORD: What's all this?

MINNA: Where is he, where is he?

LANDLORD: He was still here an hour ago.

MINNA: You horrible man, how could you be so unkind to him, so harsh, so cruel?

LANDLORD: Your Grace will forgive me?

MINNA: Hurry, bring him here to me.

LANDLORD: His servant may still be here. Would Your Grace wish me to look for him?

MINNA: Would I? Hurry, run! If you do me this service, I'll overlook your bad treatment of him.

FRANZISKA: Hurry, sir, hurry, hurry, hurry! *(Pushes him out.)*

Scene 3

Minna and Franziska

MINNA: I've got him back, Franziska! You see, now I've got him back! I don't know where I am, for sheer joy. Rejoice with me, dear Franziska. But why should you? But you must, you must rejoice with me. Come, Franziska, I'll give you gifts so that you will rejoice with me. Say something, Franziska, what shall I give you? What would you like best of all the things I have here? Take whatever you like, but rejoice with me. I can see you won't take anything. Wait a minute! *(She looks in the strongbox.)* There you are, dear Franziska *(She gives her money.)*, buy yourself something you'd like. Ask me for more if that's not enough. But rejoice with me! Oh, it's so sad to have to rejoice alone! Come, take it! . . .

FRANZISKA: I'd be stealing it from you, madam; you're drunk with happiness, drunk.

MINNA: Now, Franziska, I may be a little tipsy, but take it . . . *(She forces her to take the money, pressing it into her hand.)* And don't thank me! Wait a minute, it's a good thing I thought of it. *(She puts her hand into the strongbox again and takes out some more money.)* And this, dear Franziska, set this aside for the first poor wounded soldier who speaks to us.

Scene 4

Landlord, Minna, and Franziska.

MINNA: Well, is he coming?
LANDLORD: What a miserable, rude fellow he is!
MINNA: Who?
LANDLORD: His servant. He refuses to go and fetch him.
FRANZISKA: Bring the wretch in here. I know all of the major's servants. Which of them was it?
MINNA: Bring him here, quickly. When he sees us, he'll go. *(Exit landlord.)*

Scene 5

Minna and Franziska.

MINNA: I can hardly wait. But Franziska, why are you still so cold? Don't you want to rejoice with me?
FRANZISKA: I would like to, from the bottom of my heart, if only . . .
MINNA: If only?
FRANZISKA: We have found the man again, but how have we found him? From all that we hear, things are not going very well with him. He must be unhappy, and that makes me feel sad.
MINNA: Makes you feel sad? Let me hug you for those words, my dearest friend! I will never forget what you said. I am merely in love, but you are really good.

Scene 6

Landlord, Just, Minna, and Franziska.

LANDLORD: I managed to bring him, but it wasn't easy.
FRANZISKA: A stranger, I don't know him.
MINNA: My friend, you are in the service of Major von Tellheim?
JUST: Yes.

MINNA: Where is your master?

JUST: Not here.

MINNA: But you know where to find him?

JUST: Yes.

MINNA: Will you bring him here quickly?

JUST: No.

MINNA: You would be doing me a favor.

JUST: Ha!

MINNA: And your master a service.

JUST: Maybe, maybe not.

MINNA: What makes you think that?

JUST: Aren't you the strangers that sent their regards to him this morning?

MINNA: Yes.

JUST: I'm right then.

MINNA: Does your master know my name?

JUST: No, but he dislikes overpolite ladies as much as he dislikes overrude landlords.

LANDLORD: Are you referring to me?

JUST: Yes.

LANDLORD: You don't need to take it out on madam, here. Bring your master here quickly.

MINNA *(to Franziska)*: Give him a little something.

FRANZISKA *(trying to press money into Just's hand)*: We're not asking you to do this service for nothing.

JUST: And I'm not asking you for money without doing you a service.

FRANZISKA: Fair exchange.

JUST: I can't do it. My master has told me to move his things out. That's what I'm doing, and I'd be grateful if you didn't hold me up any longer. When I'm finished, I'll tell him that he can come here. He's next door in the cafe, and when he can't find anything better to do there, he'll probably come up here. *(Starts to leave.)*

FRANZISKA: Wait a moment. . . . Madam is the major's . . . sister.

MINNA: Yes, yes, his sister.

JUST: I know better than that. The major hasn't got any sisters. Twice in six months, he sent me to his family in the Kurland. Of course, there are all kinds of sisters.

FRANZISKA: You scoundrel!

JUST: Don't you have to be a scoundrel if you're going to get people to let you go? *(Exit.)*

FRANZISKA: Devil!

LANDLORD: Well, I told you. Let him go. I know now where his master is. I'll fetch him myself at once. But, madam, I ask you most humbly to make excuses to the major, for my having had the misfortune to have to turn away, against my will, a man of his worth.

MINNA: Go quickly, landlord. I will see that everything is all right. *(Exit landlord.)* Franziska, run after him, quickly, he must not mention my name. *(Exit Franziska.)*

Scene 7

Minna and, afterwards, Franziska.

MINNA: I have him again! . . . Am I alone? I don't want to be alone for nothing. *(She folds her hands.)* I am not alone! *(looking up)* One single, thankful thought directed to heaven is the most perfect prayer. I have found him, I have found him! *(She flings her arms wide.)* I am happy, what can be more pleasing to God's eyes than a joyful creature. *(Enter Franziska.)* Back again, Franziska? . . . You feel sorry for him. I don't feel sorry for him. I am not sorry for him. Unhappiness is good, too. Perhaps heaven took everything away from him just so that I could give him everything back in the shape of myself.

FRANZISKA: He may be here any moment, and you are still in your negligée, madam. Why don't you get dressed quickly?

MINNA: Go, please. From now on he will see me like this more often than he will see me in full toilette.

FRANZISKA: You certainly know what suits you best, madam.

MINNA: Right again.

FRANZISKA: A beautiful woman is most beautiful without makeup.

MINNA: Do we have to be beautiful? I suppose it's necessary for us to think that we are beautiful. As long as he thinks I'm beautiful . . . Franziska, if all young girls feel as I do at this moment, we are . . . Strange feelings! Tender and proud, virtuous yet vain, voluptuous, and pious . . . You can't understand me, I don't think that I understand myself. Joy makes you dizzy, giddy.

FRANZISKA: Please, pull yourself together, madam, I hear someone coming.

MINNA: Pull myself together? Shall I receive him without showing him my feelings?

Scene 8

Tellheim, Landlord, Minna, and Franziska.

TELLHEIM *(seeing Minna and at once rushing up to her):* Minna!

MINNA *(going toward him):* Tellheim!

TELLHEIM *(stopping suddenly and turning back):* Forgive me, madam
. . . but to find Fräulein von Barnhelm here . . .

MINNA: Surely it can't be entirely unexpected? *(As she moves nearer to
him, he withdraws further.)* Am I to forgive you because I am still
your Minna? Heaven forgive you that I am still Fräulein von Barnhelm!

TELLHEIM: Madam . . . *(He looks at the landlord and shrugs his
shoulders.)*

MINNA *(growing aware of the landlord waves to Franziska):* My good
man . . .

TELLHEIM: If we are not both mistaken . . .

FRANZISKA: Sir, who's this you've brought us? Come along, quickly,
let's go and find the right one.

LANDLORD: Isn't he the right one? He must be!

FRANZISKA: Oh no, he mustn't. Hurry up, I haven't said good morning
to your daughter yet.

LANDLORD *(without budging):* Oh, a great honor, I'm sure . . .

FRANZISKA *(taking hold of him):* Come, we have to look at the menu,
Let's see what we're going to have . . .

LANDLORD: The first thing you're going to have . . .

FRANZISKA: Quiet, quiet, if madam knows beforehand what she's
going to have for lunch, it spoils her appetite. Come, you must tell
me on my own what we are going to have. *(Forces him to go.)*

Scene 9

Tellheim and Minna.

MINNA: Are we still making a mistake?

TELLHEIM: I wish to heaven we were! But there is only one Minna, and
you are she.

MINNA: What a lot of fuss! Why shouldn't the whole world hear what
we have to say to one another.

TELLHEIM: You here? What are you doing here, madam?

MINNA: I have done what I wanted to. *(Runs to him with open arms.)* I
have found everything that I was looking for.

TELLHEIM *(backing away):* You were looking for a happy man, worthy of your love, and you find . . . a wretched one.

MINNA: So you love me no longer; you love someone else.

TELLHEIM: A man who could love someone else could never have loved you.

MINNA: You remove but one sting from my heart. If I have lost your love, what difference does it make whether it is indifference or another woman's charms which have taken you from me. You no longer love me, and yet you do not love another. Unhappy man, if you have no one to love!

TELLHEIM: True, madam. He who is unhappy must not love anyone or anything at all. He deserves his misfortune if he does not know how to gain this victory over himself, if he can permit himself to stand by and allow those whom he loves to participate in his misfortune. Ever since reason and necessity have bidden me to forget Minna von Barnhelm, what an effort I have made! I had just begun to hope that this effort would not forever be in vain . . . and you appear, madam.

MINNA: Do I understand you correctly? One moment, sir, let us see where we are before we say anything more. Would you answer me just one question?

TELLHEIM: As many as you like, madam.

MINNA: Will you answer me without quibbling or evading the issue? With nothing but a simple yes or no?

TELLHEIM: I will if I can.

MINNA: You can. Good! Forget for the moment the effort which you made to forget me. . . . Do you still love me, Tellheim?

TELLHEIM: Madam, this question . . .

MINNA: You promised to answer only yes or no.

TELLHEIM: But I did add, "If I can."

MINNA: You can. You must know what is happening in your own heart. Do you still love me, Tellheim, yes or no?

TELLHEIM: If my heart . . .

MINNA: Yes or no?

TELLHEIM: Well, yes.

MINNA: Yes?

TELLHEIM: Yes, yes, except . . .

MINNA: Patience! . . . You still love me, that is enough for me. . . . What kind of tone am I using? A hostile, melancholic, infectious one. I shall use my own again. Now, my beloved, unhappy one. You still love me and you still have your Minna, why are you unhappy?

Let me tell you what a vain and foolish creature your Minna was . . .
still is. She allowed herself, allows herself, to dream that she was your
whole happiness. Quickly, show her the cause of your unhappiness
and let her see how much of it she can counterbalance. Well?

TELLHEIM: Madam, I am not in the habit of complaining.

MINNA: Very well. I certainly cannot imagine a quality, after
boastfulness, which would please me less in a soldier than complaining. But there is a certain cold, disinterested way in which we can
speak about misfortune and bravery.

TELLHEIM: Which is still boasting and complaining nevertheless.

MINNA: Argue, argue, argue! In that case you should never have called
yourself unhappy. Either you should keep quiet about the whole
business or else bring it all out into the open. So reason and necessity
bid you forget me? I am a great admirer of reason, and I have a great
deal of respect for necessity; but tell me, at least, how reasonable this
reason is, how necessary this necessity.

TELLHEIM: Very well, then, madam, listen. You call me Tellheim, and
that is indeed my name. But you imagine at the same time that I am
the same Tellheim you knew in your native country, a man in the
bloom of youth, full of prospects, full of ambition, a man completely
in control of his body and his soul, to whom every frontier of honor
and happiness was open, who was worthy of your hand and your
heart, and even if he was not worthy of you yourself, hoped daily to
grow more worthy. I am as far from being this Tellheim as I am from
being my own father. Both belong to the past. I am Tellheim, the
discharged soldier, with his honor wounded, Tellheim the cripple
and the beggar. You promised yourself to the other Tellheim; do you
wish to keep your word to this one?

MINNA: That sounds very tragic . . . but, sir, until I find the other one
again—for after all, I am really rather fond of Tellheims—this one
will do for the moment. Give me your hand, dear beggar. *(Takes his
hand.)*

TELLHEIM *(putting his other hand in front of his face and turning away
from her):* This is too much! . . . Where am I? Let me go, madam!
Your goodness tortures me! Let me go!

MINNA: What has come over you? Where do you want to go?

TELLHEIM: Away from you!

MINNA: Away from me? *(Draws his hand to her breast.)* Dreamer!

TELLHEIM: My dear, desperation will throw me at your feet.

MINNA: Away from me?

TELLHEIM: Yes, away from you, never, never to see you again, or at least I am so firmly resolved, so absolutely resolved to do nothing contemptible—nor to allow you to do anything thoughtless. Let me go, Minna! *(Breaks away, exit.)*

MINNA *(calling after him):* Minna let you go? Tellheim! Tellheim!

Act III

Scene 1

The parlor

JUST *(a letter in his hand):* Have I got to come back into this damned house again? A note from my master to the young lady who says she's his sister. I hope there's nothing brewing there. Otherwise there'll be no end of carrying notes backward and forward. I'll be glad to get rid of this note, but I don't want to have to go up to the room. The women ask such a lot of questions, and I don't like answering them. Wait a minute, the door's opening. How lucky! It's the lady's maid.

Scene 2

Franziska and Just.

FRANZISKA *(calling back through the door through which she has just come).* Don't worry, I'll take care. *(She catches sight of Just.)* Look out, here's something got in my way already; but there's nothing I can do with this brute.

JUST: Your servant . . .

FRANZISKA: I wouldn't want a servant like that.

JUST: Oh well, it's only a matter of speaking. I was just bringing a note from my master to your mistress, the young lady . . . his sister . . . wasn't that it? Sister?

FRANZISKA: Give it to me! *(Snatches the note from his hand.)*

JUST: "Will you be good enough," my master says, "to give it to her? And afterwards would you be good enough," my master says . . . I don't want you to think that *I* am asking for anything.

FRANZISKA: Well?

JUST: My master knows what's what. He knows that the way to a young lady is through her maid . . . at least, I imagine so. Would the young maid be so good, my master says, and let him know whether he might have the pleasure of speaking to the young maid for a quarter of an hour.

FRANZISKA: Do you mean me?

JUST: You'll excuse me if I'm giving you a title which you no longer have any right to. . . . Yes, you . . . . Just a quarter of an hour, but alone, absolutely alone, tête-à-tête. He has something very important to tell you.

FRANZISKA: Well, I've got a few things to tell him. He can come if he wants to. I'll wait for him.

JUST: But when can he come? When is most convenient? This evening?

FRANZISKA: What do you mean? Your master can come when he wants to, and now be off with you.

JUST: With pleasure. *(Starts to leave.)*

FRANZISKA: Wait a minute, there's just one more thing. Where are the major's other servants?

JUST: The other ones? They're . . . here, there, and everywhere.

FRANZISKA: Where's William?

JUST: The valet? The major sent him off on a trip.

FRANZISKA: Oh? and Philip, where is he?

JUST: The gamekeeper? The major left him in good hands.

FRANZISKA: Doubtless because there's no hunting at the moment. But what about Martin?

JUST: The coachman? He went out for a ride.

FRANZISKA: And Fritz?

JUST: The footman? He's been given a promotion.

FRANZISKA: Where were you, then, when the major was with us in Thuringia in his winter quarters? You weren't with him at that time.

JUST: Oh yes, I was a groom, but I was in the hospital at the time.

FRANZISKA: A groom? But what are you now?

JUST: A bit of everything—valet, gamekeeper, footman, and groom.

FRANZISKA: Well I declare! Letting so many good people go and keeping the worst one of all. I'd like to know what your master sees in you.

JUST: Perhaps he thinks I'm an honest man.

FRANZISKA: People who are just honest don't amount to much. William was a different sort of chap . . . and your master's let him go off on a trip?

JUST: Yes, he's let him . . . he can't stop him.

FRANZISKA: What do you mean?

JUST: William'll cut a good figure on his travels; he took the master's whole wardrobe with him.

FRANZISKA: What? Do you mean he made off with it?

JUST: Well, you couldn't exactly say that, but after we left Nuremberg, he didn't bother to follow us with it.

FRANZISKA: What a rogue!

JUST: He was quite a chap—could cut your hair, shave you, chat with you . . . and charm you . . . couldn't he?

FRANZISKA: But still! I wouldn't have let the gamekeeper go if I'd been the major. Even if he couldn't use him as a gamekeeper, he was a hardworking sort of a chap. . . . Who's looking after him now?

JUST: The commandant of Spandau.

FRANZISKA: The fort? There surely isn't much hunting on the ramparts, is there?

JUST: Well, Philip isn't actually hunting there, either.

FRANZISKA: What's he doing then?

JUST: He's pushing a wheelbarrow.

FRANZISKA: Pushing a wheelbarrow?

JUST: Only for three years. He hatched a little plot among the soldiers in my master's company and wanted to take six deserters through the lines.

FRANZISKA: I can't believe it! The devil!

JUST: Oh! He's a hardworking chap all right; he knows all the highways and byways for fifty miles round, and he can shoot, too.

FRANZISKA: It's lucky the major still has his good old coachman.

JUST: Has he still got him?

FRANZISKA: I thought you said that Martin was out somewhere, so I suppose he'll be back?

JUST: Do you think so?

FRANZISKA: Where's he gone to?

JUST: It's about ten weeks since he rode off with the master's one and only horse.

FRANZISKA: And the rogue hasn't come back yet?

JUST: Of course he may have taken a drop more to drink than his horse. . . . He was a proper coachman, he was! He'd driven in Vienna for ten years. The master won't get another like him. Why, when the horses were at full gallop, he only had to say, "Whoa," and they stood stock-still. And what's more, he was a trained horse-doctor.

FRANZISKA: After all that, I feel a bit worried about the footman's promotion.

JUST: No, no, that worked out all right. He's a drummer in a garrison regiment.

FRANZISKA: I thought he'd be all right.

JUST: Fritz got in with a bad lot, never came home at night, ran up debts everywhere in the master's name, and got into a thousand dirty bits of business. In short, the major saw that he really wanted to rise in the world *(He pantomimes hanging),* so he helped him along the way.

FRANZISKA: Wretch!

JUST: But he's a perfect footman. Give him a fifty-pace start, and my master couldn't overtake him with the fastest horse. But I wouldn't mind betting that Fritz could give the gallows a thousand-pace start and he'd still catch up with it. They were all close friends of yours, were they? William, Philip, Martin, and Fritz? Well, Just, the last of 'em, bids you good day.

Scene 3

Franziska and, afterwards, the landlord.

FRANZISKA *(looking earnestly after him):* I deserved that. Thank you, Just. I set too low a price on honesty. I won't forget the lesson you've taught me. Oh, what an unlucky man! *(Turns and is about to go into Minna's room when the landlord enters.)*

LANDLORD: Wait a minute, my dear.

FRANZISKA: I don't have time at the moment.

LANDLORD: Just one little moment. . . . Still no more news of the major? Surely he hasn't left?

FRANZISKA: What else?

LANDLORD: Didn't your mistress tell you? When I left you down in the kitchen, my dear, I happened to come back into this room.

FRANZISKA: You just happened to, so that you could do a bit of eavesdropping.

LANDLORD: My dear child, how could you think such a thing of me? There's nothing worse than an inquisitive landlord. I hadn't been here long when the door of madam's room suddenly burst open. The major rushed out, the young lady following him, both in such a hurry and looking like . . . you can't describe it. She grabbed hold of him, he tore himself away, she grabbed him again. "Tellheim!" "Madam, let me go!" "Where are you going?" He dragged her to the head of the stairs like this, and I was afraid they were going to fall down, but he slipped out of her clutches. The young lady stood there wringing her hands. Then she suddenly turned round, ran to the window, from the window back to the stairs; from the stairs she turned to pacing up and down in this room. I was standing there, and she passed me three times without seeing me. Then she seemed to see me but—and God save us!—I think the young lady thought I was you, my dear. "Franziska," she cried, looking at me. "Am I happy now?" I looked straight up at the ceiling. And again, "Am I happy now?" Honestly, I didn't know what to do till she ran to her door. Then she turned to me again and said, "Come along, Franziska," and went in.

FRANZISKA: You must have dreamt it.

LANDLORD: Dreamt it? No, my child, you don't dream as clearly as that. Yes, I'd give a lot . . . not that I'm nosy mind . . . but I'd give a lot to have the key to that.

FRANZISKA: The key? To our door? That's on the inside, sir. We took it in last night; we're scared.

LANDLORD: I don't mean a key like that. What I mean, my dear, is a key, like an explanation, of everything I saw.

FRANZISKA: Ah, yes! . . . Adieu, sir. Are we going to eat soon?

LANDLORD: Don't forget, my dear, what I really wanted to say.

FRANZISKA: Well? But make it quick!

LANDLORD: The young lady still has my ring; I call it mine . . .

FRANZISKA: It's in good hands, I can assure you.

LANDLORD: I'm not worried about that. I just wanted to remind you. You see, I don't even want it back again. I can easily guess how she knew the ring and why it looked so like her own. She's the best one to look after it. I don't want it any more, and I'll charge the young lady's account with the five hundred talers I lent on it. That's all right, my dear, isn't it?

Scene 4

Paul Werner, Landlord, and Franziska.

WERNER: There he is!

FRANZISKA: Five hundred talers? I thought it was only four hundred.

LANDLORD: That's right, four hundred and fifty, only four hundred and fifty, all right my dear, that's what I'll do.

FRANZISKA: All right, we'll see.

WERNER (*coming up behind her and then clapping her on the shoulder*): Little lady, little lady!

FRANZISKA (*alarmed*): Hey!

WERNER: Don't be frightened, little lady. You're pretty and a stranger here, and pretty strangers have to be warned. Little lady, beware of this man. *(Points at landlord.)*

LANDLORD: What an unexpected pleasure! Herr Paul Werner! Welcome to my house, welcome. Still the same old jolly, comical, honest Paul Werner. . . . You beware of me, my dear. Ha! Ha! Ha!

WERNER: Keep out of his way.

LANDLORD: Out of my way? Am I a danger? Ha! Ha! Ha! It gets better and better, doesn't it, my dear? He knows how to joke. Me, a danger? Me? Now twenty years ago there might have been something in it. Yes, my dear, then I was a danger, but now . . .

WERNER: There's no fool like an old fool.

LANDLORD: That's the trouble. When we get old, we're not a danger any longer. You'll be in the same boat, one day, Herr Werner!

WERNER: I've never heard anything like it! Young lady, you know that I wasn't talking about that sort of danger. One devil was cast out, and seven others have taken its place.

LANDLORD: Listen to him, just listen to him! See how he's managed to bring the subject round again! One joke after another, and always something new. Oh he's a splendid man, is our Paul Werner! *(whispering to Franziska)* And a wealthy man, too, and a bachelor. He has a farm about three miles away. He made a little pile in the war . . . and was a sergeant major in the major's regiment. Oh, yes, he's a real friend, one who would die for him.

WERNER: Yes, and you're a friend of my major's . . . one he ought to have killed.

LANDLORD: What! No, Herr Werner, that's not a nice joke at all. Me not a friend of the major's? . . . No, that's a joke I can't understand.

WERNER: Just told me a few nice things about you.

LANDLORD: Just? I thought I recognized the voice of Just in this. Just is an evil-speaking, mean fellow. Now here's a nice young thing who can tell you whether I'm a friend of the major's or not, whether I haven't done him a few services. And why shouldn't I be a friend of the major's? Isn't he a worthy man? It's true he had the misfortune to be discharged, but what does that matter? The king can't know all the worthy men under his command, and if he did know them, he can't reward all of them.

WERNER: Lucky for you that you said that! But Just . . . there's certainly nothing special about Just, but he isn't a liar. And if what he told me was true . . .

LANDLORD: I don't want to hear anything about Just. As I said, this pretty child here can speak.—*(whispering)* You know, my dear, the ring.—Tell Herr Werner. That way he'll get to know me better. And so that it won't appear as if you're just talking to please me, I'll leave you. But you'll have to repeat it to me, Herr Werner, repeat it and tell me whether Just isn't a filthy slanderer.

Scene 5

Paul Werner and Franziska.

WERNER: Well, little lady, so you know my major?

FRANZISKA: Major von Tellheim? Certainly I know him; he's a good man.

WERNER: Isn't he a good man? Are you perhaps a friend of his?

FRANZISKA: From the bottom of my heart.

WERNER: Really? You know, little lady, when you say that, you seem twice as pretty to me. But what are these services that the landlord says he did for the major?

FRANZISKA: I'm sure I don't know, unless he's trying to take credit for something which happened by chance because of his rotten behavior.

WERNER: So it was true, what Just told me? *(turning to the side where the Landlord has exited)* Lucky for you that you left! He really turned him out of his room! Imagine playing a trick like that on a man like that, simply because the idiot thought the major didn't have any money left! The major, no money!

FRANZISKA: What, you mean the major does have money?

WERNER: Piles of it! He doesn't know how much he's got. He doesn't know who owes him what. I owe him money myself, and I'm bringing him a bit here. Look, little lady, here in this purse *(taking a purse from his pocket)* are five hundred talers. And in this little roll *(He takes the roll from his other pocket.)*, three hundred. All his money.

FRANZISKA: Really? Then why does the major have to pawn things? He pawned a ring . . .

WERNER: Pawned! Don't you believe it! Perhaps he just wanted to get rid of the rubbish.

FRANZISKA: But it's not rubbish! It's a valuable ring which he received from a very dear person.

WERNER: That's it then. From a very dear person. A thing like that often reminds you of something you'd rather not be reminded of. So you get rid of it.

FRANZISKA: What?

WERNER: Some funny things happen to a soldier when he's in winter quarters. There's nothing to do, so out of boredom and to amuse himself, he strikes up acquaintances which he intends only for the winter, but which the kind hearts with whom he forms them assume are for life; and the next thing you know, someone's popped a ring on his finger. He doesn't know how it got there. And as often as not, he'd gladly cut off his finger to get rid of the ring.

FRANZISKA: Oh! And do you think that happened to the major?

WERNER: I'm sure of it. Especially in Saxony. If he'd had ten fingers on each hand, all twenty of them would have had rings on them.

FRANZISKA *(aside)*. This sounds odd. We'll have to look into it. Herr Werner . . .

WERNER: Little lady, if it's all the same to you, I'd rather you called me sergeant major.

FRANZISKA: All right, sergeant major, but I've got a note here from the major to my mistress. I'll just take it in quickly, and I'll be back at once. Will you be good enough to wait? I'd like to stay and chat with you a bit longer.

WERNER: Do you like having a chat, little lady? It's all right with me. Go on. I like a chat, too. I'll wait for you.

FRANZISKA: Yes, please wait! *(Exit.)*

Scene 6

Werner.

WERNER: That's not a bad little lady; but I should never have promised to wait, because the most important thing is to find the major. So, he doesn't want my money and would rather pawn things. That's typical, but I've thought of a dodge. When I was in town two weeks ago, I visited Marloff's widow. The poor woman was ill and was lamenting the fact that her dead husband owed the major four hundred talers, and she didn't know how she was going to pay him. I was going to see her again today and tell her that when I get the money for my farm, I could lend her five hundred talers. I wanted some of the money to be safe in case things don't work out in Persia. But she'd left, and I'm certain she hasn't been able to pay the major. Yes, that's what I'll do, and the sooner the better. The little lady mustn't mind, but I can't wait for her at the moment. *(Exits deep in thought and almost collides with Tellheim who enters at that moment.)*

Scene 7

Tellheim and Werner.

TELLHEIM: Lost in thought, Werner?

WERNER: Ah, there you are. I was just coming to call on you in your new quarters, Major.

TELLHEIM: So that you could bombard my ears with curses against the landlord of my old ones? Please spare me that.

WERNER: I would probably have done that as well. But what I really wanted to do was to thank you for looking after the five hundred talers for me. Just gave them back to me. I must admit that I would have been grateful if you could have kept them for me a bit longer. But you've moved to new quarters which neither of us knows anything about. Who knows what it's like there. They might be stolen from you, and then you'd have to replace them. There'd be no help for it. And I can't give you that responsibility.

TELLHEIM *(smiling):* How long have you been that careful, Werner?

WERNER: It's something you learn. You can't be too careful with your money these days. And there was another thing, Major, from Frau Marloff. I just came from her. Her husband owed you four hundred talers; here are three hundred as a payment. She'll send you the rest next week. It could be that I'm the cause of her not sending the whole sum, because she owed me a taler and eighty groschen, and as she thought I'd come to dun her for it, she paid me out of the money she'd set aside for you. It's easier for you to wait a few days for your money than it is for me to do without my few groschen. There you are. *(Hands him the roll of money.)*

TELLHEIM: Werner!

WERNER: What are you staring at me like that for? Take it, sir!

TELLHEIM: Werner!

WERNER: What's the matter, what's upset you?

TELLHEIM *(bitterly, striking himself on the forehead and stamping his foot)):* That . . . that the whole four hundred talers aren't there.

WERNER: But, Major, didn't you understand what I said?

TELLHEIM: It's just because I did understand you! Why is it that today it is the finest people who torment me the most?

WERNER: What did you say?

TELLHEIM: You're only half the trouble . . . Leave me, Werner! *(He pushes aside the hand in which Werner holds the money.)*

WERNER: As soon as I've got rid of this.

TELLHEIM: Werner, supposing I was to tell you that Frau Marloff had been here early this morning?

WERNER: Well?

TELLHEIM: That she doesn't owe me anything?

WERNER: Really?

TELLHEIM: That she paid everything down to the last penny? What would you say to that?

WERNER *(pausing for a moment)*: I'd say that I'd lied and that lying is a foul game, because you can get caught.

TELLHEIM: And would you feel ashamed of yourself?

WERNER: But what about the person who forced me into lying, what about him? Shouldn't he be ashamed of himself? Now look, Major, if I didn't come straight out and tell you that I don't like the way you're carrying on, I'd be lying again, and I don't want to lie any more.

TELLHEIM: Don't be angry, Werner! I recognize your goodness of heart and your affection for me, but I don't need your money.

WERNER: You don't need it, and you'd rather sell things and pawn things and have people talking about you?

TELLHEIM: I don't care if people know that I have nothing left. No one should wish to appear more wealthy than he is.

WERNER: But why should he appear poorer? As long as our friends have means, we have means ourselves.

TELLHEIM: It would not be proper for me to be in your debt.

WERNER: Wouldn't be proper? Don't you remember that day when the sun and the enemy were warming things up for us and your groom had got lost with the canteens and you came to me and said, "Werner, have you got anything to drink?" and I handed you my water bottle and you took it and drank? Was that proper? God bless my soul! If a drink of stagnant water at that time wasn't worth more than all this rubbish! *(taking out the purse and offering that to Tellheim)* Please take it, Major! Imagine it's water. God made money for everybody, too.

TELLHEIM: You're torturing me. You heard me; I do not want to be in your debt.

WERNER: First it wasn't proper, and now you don't want to be. Well that's something different again. *(somewhat angrily)* You don't want to be in my debt, but supposing you were already in my debt, Major? Or don't you owe anything to the man who warded off the blow that would have split your head in two, or who another time chopped off the arm which was going to shoot you through the heart? How can you get further into his debt? Or is my neck worth less than my purse? If that's your way of thinking, then God bless my soul, it's a pretty poor way.

TELLHEIM: Who are you talking to like this, Werner? We are alone, and now I can say it. If a third party were to hear, it would sound like a lot of humbug. I'll gladly admit that I have you to thank for saving my life on a couple of occasions. But my friend, wouldn't I, if the opportunity had arisen, have done exactly the same for you?

WERNER: If the opportunity had arisen? No one has any doubts about that. Haven't I seen you risk your life for the commonest of soldiers when he was in a jam?

TELLHEIM: Very well!

WERNER: But . . .

TELLHEIM: Why can't you understand me? I say, it is not proper for me to be in your debt; I do not wish to be in your debt. At least not under the circumstances in which I find myself at the moment.

WERNER: Ah ha! You want to wait till things get better. You want to borrow money from me another time, when you don't need it, when you've got money and I haven't.

TELLHEIM: No one should borrow if they don't know how they're going to pay the money back.

WERNER: But a man like you can't always be in need.

TELLHEIM: You know the world. The last person to borrow money from is someone who needs it himself.

WERNER: Oh! That's me, is it? What do I need it for? If you need a sergeant major, then you pay him.

TELLHEIM: You need it so that you can become more than a mere sergeant major. So that you can make your way in a career in which even the worthiest man cannot succeed if he has no money.

WERNER: Be more than a sergeant major? I wouldn't dream of it. I'm a good sergeant major; I might become a bad captain and certainly a worse general. I've seen plenty of that.

TELLHEIM: Please don't make me think anything which is not worthy of you, Werner. I was not exactly pleased to hear what Just told me. You've sold your farm and want to go off on your travels again. I would rather not have to think that it's not the career that you enjoy, but the wild dissolute life which, regrettably, goes with it. A man should be a soldier in order to fight for his country or for a cause, not to serve here today and there tomorrow. That's no better than being a butcher's boy.

WERNER: Well, you're right major. I follow you. You know better what is right and proper. I'll stay with you. . . . But major, please take my money for the time being. Sooner or later your whole business will be settled. You'll get piles of money. Then you can pay me back with interest. I'm only doing it for the interest.

TELLHEIM: Be quiet!

WERNER: God bless my soul! I'm only doing it for the interest. Sometimes when I think, "What's going to happen to you in your old age, when you're hacked to bits, when you're penniless, when you have to go begging?"; then I conclude, "No, you won't have to go begging; you'll go to Major Tellheim; he'll share his last penny with you; he'll look after you on your deathbed; he'll see that you die as an honest man."

TELLHEIM *(taking Werner's hand):* And, my friend, don't you still think so?

WERNER: No, I don't think so any more. If someone won't accept something from me when he needs it and I have it, he won't give me anything when he has it and I need it. . . . That's all! *(Starts to exit.)*

TELLHEIM: Don't drive me out of my mind! Where are you going? *(Holds him back.)* Suppose I were to assure you, on my honor, that I still have some money, that I will tell you when I haven't got any more, and that you will be the first and only person from whom I will borrow any? Will that satisfy you?

WERNER: It'll have to. . . . Give me your hand on it, Major!

TELLHEIM: There, Paul! . . . Now, that's enough. I came here to talk to a certain young lady.

Scene 8

Franziska, coming out of Minna's room, Tellheim, and Werner.

FRANZISKA *(coming out):* Are you still there, Sergeant Major? *(She sees Tellheim.)* And you're there too, Major? I will be with you in an instant. *(Goes quickly back into the room.)*

Scene 9

Tellheim and Paul Werner.

TELLHEIM: That was her! . . . But it sounds as if you know her, eh, Werner?

WERNER: Yes, I know the little lady.

TELLHEIM: And yet if I remember correctly, when I was in winter quarters in Thuringia, you were not with me?

WERNER: No, I was seeing about some pieces of equipment in Leipzig.

TELLHEIM: Then how do you come to know her?

WERNER: Our acquaintanceship is still in its infancy. It dates from today. But a young acquaintanceship is a warm one.

TELLHEIM: Then have you also met her mistress?

WERNER: Is her mistress a young lady? She told me that you knew her mistress.

TELLHEIM: Didn't you hear? From Thuringia.

WERNER: Is the lady young?

TELLHEIM: Yes.

WERNER: Beautiful?

TELLHEIM: Very beautiful.

WERNER: Rich?

TELLHEIM: Very rich.

WERNER: Is the young lady as friendly with you as the girl? That would be splendid.

TELLHEIM: What do you mean?

Scene 10

Franziska, coming out of the room again with a letter in her hand, Tellheim, and Paul Werner.

FRANZISKA: Major . . .

TELLHEIM: My dear Franziska, I haven't had the chance to bid you welcome yet.

FRANZISKA: I'm sure you've already done so in your thoughts. I know that you like me. And I like you, too. But it is not fair to frighten people whom you like.

WERNER *(aside):* Ha! Now I understand! That's right.

TELLHEIM: What is my fate, Franziska? Have you given her the letter?

FRANZISKA: Yes, and this one is for you. *(Hands him the letter.)*

TELLHEIM: An answer?

FRANZISKA: No, your own letter back.

TELLHEIM: What? Would she not read it?

FRANZISKA: She wanted to, but . . . we can't read writing very well.

TELLHEIM: You're teasing me.

FRANZISKA: And we think that letter writing is not for those who can communicate by word of mouth whenever they like to.

TELLHEIM: What an excuse! She must read it. It contains the justification . . . all the reasons and grounds . . .

FRANZISKA: Madam would like to hear them from your own lips and not read about them.

TELLHEIM: To hear them from my own lips? So that her every word, her every expression will confuse me? So that I shall be able to see in her every glance how great my loss is?

FRANZISKA: She shows no mercy! . . . Take it! *(Gives him the letter.)* She will expect you at three. She wants to drive out and look at the town. You are to go with her.

TELLHEIM: Go with her?

FRANZISKA: And what will you give me if I let you go alone? I am going to stay at home.

TELLHEIM: Alone?

FRANZISKA: In a nice closed carriage.

TELLHEIM: Impossible!

FRANZISKA: Yes, yes. In a carriage you will have to face the music. You can't escape from us in a carriage. That's why we've arranged it like that. In short, Major, you will come at three sharp. Well? You wanted to speak to me alone as well. What have you got to say to me? . . . But we are not alone. *(She catches sight of Werner.)*

TELLHEIM: Oh yes, Franziska, we would be alone, but as your mistress has not read the letter, I have nothing to say to you.

FRANZISKA: Oh? So we would be alone? You have no secrets from the sergeant major?

TELLHEIM: No, none.

FRANZISKA: And yet it seems to me that there are some you should have.

TELLHEIM: What do you mean?

WERNER: Why should he, little lady?

FRANZISKA: Especially secrets of a certain sort . . . all twenty, Sergeant Major? *(holding up both hands with the fingers spread apart)*

WERNER: Sh, Sh, little lady!

TELLHEIM: What's that?

FRANZISKA: "And the next thing you know someone's popped a ring on your finger before you know where you are," eh, Sergeant Major?

TELLHEIM: What are you two talking about?

WERNER: Little lady, little lady, surely you understand a joke?

TELLHEIM: Werner, surely you haven't forgotten what I have told you so many times? There is a certain point beyond which you should not joke with women.

WERNER: God bless my soul, I may have forgotten. . . . Little lady, please . . .

FRANZISKA: Well, if it was a joke, I'll forgive you this time.

TELLHEIM: If I really have to come, Franziska, please see that your mistress reads the letter before I arrive. That will save me some of the pain of having to think things and say things again, which I would so gladly forget. There, give it to her. *(He gives the letter back to her, and in so doing becomes aware that it has been opened.)* Do my eyes deceive me, Franziska, or has this letter been opened?

FRANZISKA: Perhaps it has. *(Looks at it.)* That's right, it has been opened. I wonder who did that. But we really haven't read it, Major, really. We don't want to read it, because the writer is coming in person. But please come and . . . do you know what, Major? Don't come as you are now, in boots, with your hair scarcely combed. Of course we excuse you; you hadn't expected us. Come in shoes, and have your hair combed. This way you look much too virtuous, much too Prussian!

TELLHEIM: Thank you, Franziska.

FRANZISKA: You look as if you'd camped out last night.

TELLHEIM: You may not be so far wrong.

FRANZISKA: We are going to get ready right away too, and then eat. We would be happy to invite you to join us, but we fear that your presence might hinder our eating; and we are not so much in love that our appetites have been spoiled.

TELLHEIM: I'm going. Franziska, please prepare her a little so that I shall not grow despicable in her eyes or my own. Come, Werner, you shall eat with me.

WERNER: Here in the inn? I shouldn't enjoy a bite.

TELLHEIM: No, in my room.

WERNER: I'll follow you at once, but first I want a word with the little lady.

TELLHEIM: I should be delighted. *(Exit.)*

Scene 11

Paul Werner and Franziska.

FRANZISKA: Well, Sergeant Major? . . .

WERNER: Little lady, when I come back again, shall I get dressed up too?

FRANZISKA: Come as you please, Sergeant Major, my eyes won't hold anything against you. But my ears will have to be all the more on their guard. . . . Twenty fingers, and all full of rings! Eh, Sergeant Major?

WERNER: No, little lady, that was just what I wanted to tell you. That cock-and-bull story just slipped out. There's nothing in it. I think one ring is enough for anybody. And I've heard the major say hundreds and hundreds of times that he's a rotten kind of soldier that would lead a girl on. And that's what I think too, little lady. Rely on it! Now I must go after him. Good-bye, little lady!

Scene 12

Minna and Franziska.

MINNA: Has the major gone again? Franziska, I think I am now calm enough for him to have stayed.

FRANZISKA: And I can make you a bit more calm.

MINNA: So much the better. His letter, oh, his letter! Every line told me what an honorable, noble man he is. Every refusal to accept me spoke of his love for me. I suppose he noticed that we'd read the letter. It doesn't matter as long as he comes. He is coming, isn't he? Perhaps a little too much pride in his behavior, Franziska. Not wanting to owe his good fortune to his beloved is pride, unforgivable pride. If I found too much pride in him, Franziska . . .

FRANZISKA: You'd give him up?

MINNA: So you're feeling sorry for him again already? No, my dear, you don't give up a man because of one flaw; but I have thought of a trick to give him some of his own medicine.

FRANZISKA: Oh, you must really be very calm, madam, if you're thinking of playing tricks again.

MINNA: I am; but come, you have a part to play in this as well.

Act IV

Scene 1

Minna's boudoir

Minna, richly but tastefully dressed and Franziska. They are just getting up from the table, which is being cleared by a servant.

FRANZISKA: You surely can't have had enough to eat, madam?

MINNA: Don't you think so, Franziska? Perhaps I wasn't hungry when I sat down at the table.

FRANZISKA: We had agreed not to mention him during the meal; perhaps we ought to have undertaken not to think of him as well.

MINNA: You're right. I was thinking of nothing but him.

FRANZISKA: I noticed that. I started to talk about a hundred different things, and each time you answered me absurdly. *(A second servant enters with coffee.)* Dear, melancholy coffee.

MINNA: Caprices? I have none. I am just thinking about the lesson I'm going to give him. Do you understand what to do, Franziska?

FRANZISKA: Oh yes, but it would be better if he saved us the trouble.

MINNA: You'll see that I know him through and through. The man who refuses me when he thinks I am wealthy will fight the whole world for me when he learns that I am poor and forlorn.

FRANZISKA *(very earnestly):* And a thing like that must tickle even the most sensitive egotism.

MINNA: Don't moralize. You used to catch me out in vanity, now it's egotism. Now just leave me alone, dear Franziska. You ought to be able to wrap your sergeant major round your little finger, too.

FRANZISKA: My sergeant major?

MINNA: Yes, even if you deny it, it's still true. I haven't seen him yet, but from all that you've said about him, I'd prophesy that you are going to marry him.

Scene 2

Riccaut de la Marlinière, Minna, and Franziska.

RICCAUT *(offstage): Est-il permis, monsieur le Major?*

FRANZISKA: What is that? Is it coming to us? *(Moves toward the door.)*

RICCAUT: *Parbleu!* I 'ave made ze mistake . . . *Mais non* . . . I 'ave not made ze mistake . . . *C'est sa chambre.*

FRANZISKA: Madam, this man obviously thinks that Major von Tellheim is still here.

RICCAUT: Zat eez right. *Le Major de Tellheim; juste, ma belle enfant, c'est lui que je cherche. Où est-il?*

FRANZISKA: He doesn't live here any longer.

RICCAUT: *Comment?* Before twenty-four hour 'e is 'ere. And eez not staying any longer? Ver 'e stay?

MINNA *(coming up to him):* Sir . . .

RICCAUT: *Ah, madame . . . mademoiselle . . .* Your Grace, forgive . . .

MINNA: Sir, your mistake is a pardonable one, and your surprise quite natural. The major was kind enough to give up his room to me, as a stranger who did not know where she could find accommodation.

RICCAUT: *Ah, voilà de ses politesses! C'est un très galant homme que ce major.*

MINNA: I am ashamed to say that I do not know where he has gone in the meantime.

RICCAUT: Your Grace not know? *C'est dommage; j'en suis fâché.*

MINNA: I should have made enquiries. I am quite sure that his friends will go on looking for him here.

RICCAUT: I am very much of 'is friend, Your Grace.

MINNA: Franziska, do you know perhaps?

FRANZISKA: No, madam.

RICCAUT: I am needing to speak wis 'im. I come to bring 'im a *nouvelle* which will make 'im very 'appy.

MINNA: That makes me even more sorry; but I hope to speak to him myself, perhaps soon. If it is not important from whose mouth he hears this news, then I am happy to offer my services, sir.

RICCAUT: I understand. *Mademoiselle parle français? Mais sans doute; telle que je la vois! La demande etait bien impolie; Vous me pardonnerez, mademoiselle.*

MINNA: Sir . . .

RICCAUT: No? You are not speaking French?

MINNA: Sir, in France I would try to speak it. But why should I do so here? I can tell that you understand me, and I also understand you. You may speak however you like.

RICCAUT: Good, good! I can myself explain in German too. *Saches donc, mademoiselle* . . . I must tell Your Grace that I come from eating wis ze minister . . . minister of . . . minister of . . . 'ow eez calling 'imself ze minister . . . in ze long street . . . on ze big square?

MINNA: I am a complete stranger here.

RICCAUT: Well, ze minister of ze War Department. I dine zere at midday . . . I dine *à l'ordinaire* wis'im . . . and zen we start to talk about Major Tellheim; *et le ministre m'a dit en confidence, car son Excellence est de mes amis, et il n'y a point de mystères entre nous* . . . 'Is Excellency, vat I vish to say, 'as told me in confidence, zat ze case of our major eez on ze point of ending. And ending good. 'E 'as made a report to ze king, and ze king 'as resolved *tout à fait en faveur du major*. "Monsieur," *m'a dit son Excellence,* "*vous comprenez bien, que tout dépend de la manière, dont on fait envisager les choses au Roi, et vous me connaissez. Celà fait un très joli garçon que ce Tellheim, et ne sais-je pas que vous l'aimez? Les amis de mes amis sont aussi les miens. Il coûte un peu cher au Roi ce Tellheim, mais est-ce que l'on sert les rois pour rien? Il faut s'entr'aider en ce monde; et quand il s'agit de pertes, que ce soit le roi, qui en fasse, et non pas un honnête-homme de nous autres. Voilà le principe, dont je ne me dépars jamais."* Vot say Your Grace? Is 'e not a good man? *Ah! que son Excellence a le coeur bien placé!* 'E assured me *au reste,* zat if ze major 'as not already received *une lettre de la main*—a letter from ze royal 'and—zat 'e must *infailliblement* receive one today.

MINNA: Indeed, sir, this news will be most welcome to Major von Tellheim. I only wish that I might tell him the name of the friend who is taking such an interest in his good fortune.

RICCAUT: Your Grace vish my name? *Vous voyez en moi. . . .* Your Grace see in me *le Chevalier Riccaut de la Marlinière, Seigneur de Prêt-au-vol, de la Branche de Prensd'or.* Your Grace is very surprised zat I come from such a great family, *qui est véritablement du sang royal. . . . Il faut le dire; je suis sans doute le cadet le plus aventureux, que la maison a jamais eu . . .* I am serving since I am eleven years old. An *affaire d'honneur* forced me to run avay. Zen I served 'Is 'Oliness, ze Pope, ze Republic of San Marino, ze crown of Poland, and in 'Olland, till at last I come 'ere. *Ah, mademoiselle, que je voudrais n'avoir jamais vu ce pays-là.* If only I could 'ave stayed in 'Olland, zen I would be now a colonel. But 'ere I remain a *capitaine,* and now a discharged *capitaine.*

MINNA: That's a great misfortune.

RICCAUT: *Oui, mademoiselle, me voilà reformé, et par la mis sur le pavé!*

MINNA: I am very sorry.

RICCAUT: *Vous êtes bien bonne, mademoiselle,* but as ze proverb goes, each misfortune brings 'is brother wis 'im; *qu'un malheur ne vient jamais seul;* zat is what 'appens to me. What can an *honnête-homme* of my *extraction* do for resources but to gamble? Always I 'ave played wis fortune, as long as I did not need fortune. But now I need 'er, *mademoiselle, je joue avec un guignon, qui surpasse toute croyance.* In ze last fifteen days, not a day 'as passed when I was not broken. Yesterday I was broken sree times. *Je sais bien, qu'il y avait quelque chose de plus que le jeu. Car parmi mes pontes se trouvaient certaines dames . . .* I say no more. You must be gallant to ze ladies. Zey invited me today, to give me *revanche; mais . . . vous m'entendez mademoiselle . . .* first you must earn ze living, before you can gamble.

MINNA: Sir, I will not hope . . .

RICCAUT: *Vous êtes bien bonne, mademoiselle . . .*

MINNA *(taking Franziska aside):* Franziska, I really am sorry for this man. Do you think he would be offended if I offered him something?

FRANZISKA: He doesn't look as though he would.

MINNA: Good! . . . Sir, I hear . . . that you gamble, that you keep the bank, doubtless at places where there is something to be won. I must confess to you that I too . . . like to gamble . . .

RICCAUT: *Tant mieux, mademoiselle, tant mieux! Tous les gens d'esprit aiment le jeu à la fureur.*

MINNA: And to confess to you that I like to win and to entrust my money to one who . . . knows how to gamble. Would you have any interest, sir, in taking me into partnership? To grant me a share of your bank?

RICCAUT: *Comment, mademoiselle, vous voulez être de moitié avec moi? De tout mon coeur.*

MINNA: To begin with, just a bagatelle . . . *(She goes and takes money from her strongbox.)*

RICCAUT: *Ah, mademoiselle, que vous êtes charmante!*

MINNA: Here is something I won a short time ago, fifty talers. . . . I must say that I am ashamed it is not more . . .

RICCAUT: *Donnez toujours, mademoiselle, donnez. (Takes the money.)*

MINNA: Of course, I have no doubt that your gaming house is a very respected one . . .

RICCAUT: Oh, very respected. Fifty talers? Your Grace shall 'ave a sird interest, *pour le tiers*—per'aps a little more. But wis a beautiful lady we do not take zings too precisely. I congratulate me to 'ave come into *liaison* with Your Grace, *et de ce moment je recommence à bien augurer de ma fortune.*

MINNA: But, unfortunately, I shall not be able to be present when you are playing, sir.

RICCAUT: Why does Your Grace need to be present? We gamblers are honest people among one anozer . . .

MINNA: If we are lucky, sir, then I shall expect you to return my portion, but if we have bad fortune . . .

RICCAUT: Zen I come and get some new recruits, eh, Your Grace?

MINNA: The recruits may run out if it goes on too long. So guard your money well, sir.

RICCAUT: What does Your Grace take me for? A simpleton, a block'ead?

MINNA: Forgive me, sir

RICCAUT: *Je suis des bons, mademoiselle. Savez vous ce que celà veut dire?* I 'ave experience . . .

MINNA: But nevertheless, sir . . .

RICCAUT: *Je sais monter un coup . . .*

MINNA *(astonished):* But should you?

RICCAUT: *Je file une carte avec une adresse . . .*

MINNA: Never!

RICCAUT: *Je fais sauter la coupe avec une dextérité . . .*

MINNA: But sir, you surely wouldn't?

RICCAUT: Why not, Your Grace, why not? *Donnez moi un pigeonneau à plumer, et . . .*

MINNA: Play false? Cheat?

RICCAUT: *Comment, mademoiselle? Vous appelez cela* "cheat"? *Corriger la fortune, l'enchaîner sous ses doigts, être sûr de son fait,* is zat what ze Germans call "cheat"? "Cheat"! Oh, what a poor language German is, what a crude language!

MINNA: No, sir, if that is the way you think . . .

RICCAUT: *Laissez-moi faire, mademoiselle,* and do not worry. Why should you worry 'ow I play? Zat's enough, either Your Grace will see me tomorrow wis five hundred talers, or you never see me again . . . *Votre très humble, mademoiselle, votre très humble . . . (Hurries out.)*

MINNA *(looking after him with astonishment and displeasure):* I hope it will be the latter, sir, I hope it will be the latter!

Scene 3

Minna and Franziska.

FRANZISKA *(bitterly):* I'm dumbfounded! Oh, beautiful, beautiful!

MINNA: All right, jeer at me, I deserve it. *(She pauses and then continues more calmly.)* Don't jeer at me, Franziska, I don't deserve it.

FRANZISKA: Marvellous, you've really done a kind act, you put a rogue back on his feet!

MINNA: I thought I was helping out an unfortunate.

FRANZISKA: And the funny thing is, the rogue thinks you're another of his sort . . . I must go after him and get the money back from him. *(Starts to leave.)*

MINNA: Franziska, don't let the coffee get completely cold. Pour me a cup.

FRANZISKA: He must give it back to you. You've changed your mind; you don't want to go into partnership with him. Fifty talers! You heard him say, madam, that he was a beggar. *(Minna meanwhile pours out her own coffee.)* Whoever would give that much money to a beggar? And at the same time try to spare him the indignity of having had to beg for it? The generous man who pretends, out of his generosity, not to recognize a beggar is in his turn not recognized by the beggar. How would you like it, madam, if he looks on your gift as . . . I don't know what . . . (*Minna gives her a cup of coffee.*) Are you trying to get me even more worked up? I don't want anything to drink. (*Minna removes the cup. Franziska imitates Riccaut.*) "Parbleu, Your Grace, one 'as no recognition 'ere for eez service." Of course not, when they let rogues like that go running round loose without hanging them.

MINNA (*cold and meditative, while drinking*): My dear girl, you have such sympathy for good people, but when are you going to learn to put up with the bad ones? After all, they are people too . . . and often not nearly such bad people as they seem to be. You simply have to find their good side. I imagine that this Frenchman is nothing worse than vain. It's sheer vanity which makes him pretend to be a cheat. He doesn't want to feel obliged to me; he doesn't want to have to thank me. Perhaps he'll go and pay off some of his small debts and live on what's left, as long as it holds out, quietly and frugally, without a thought about gambling. If that's the case, then let him fetch his recruits whenever he wants to. (*Hands her the cup.*) Here, put it away. But tell me, shouldn't Tellheim be here by now?

FRANZISKA: No, madam, I can't do either. I can't find a bad side to a good person or a good side to a bad one.

MINNA: But he is really coming?

FRANZISKA: He'd do better to stay away! Just because you see a little pride in him, the best of men, you want to play such a cruel trick on him?

MINNA: Are you back on that subject again? Say no more; that's the way I want it to be. Don't spoil the game for me. If you don't do exactly as I told you and say exactly what I told you to say, I'll leave you alone with him, and then. . . . That must be him now.

Scene 4

Paul Werner, rather stiffly, Minna, and Franziska.

FRANZISKA: No, it's just his dear sergeant major.

MINNA: *Dear* sergeant major? What's all this about *dear*?

FRANZISKA: Madam, please don't confuse him. Your servant, Sergeant Major, what have you brought for us?

WERNER (*ignoring Franziska and going directly to Minna*): Major von

Tellheim asks me, Sergeant Major Paul Werner, to pay his most humble respects to Fräulein von Barnhelm and to tell her that he will be here immediately.

MINNA: Where is he then?

WERNER: Your Grace will pardon him; we left our quarters before the stroke of three, but the paymaster general stopped us on the way, and since once you start talking to people like that you never stop, he gave me the nod to come and report the occurrence to you.

MINNA: That's all right, Sergeant Major. I hope, though, that the paymaster general had something pleasant to say to the major.

WERNER: Officers like that very seldom do . . . Has Your Grace any further orders? *(Starts to leave.)*

FRANZISKA: Where are you off to, Sergeant Major? I thought we were going to have a little chat?

WERNER *(softly and seriously):* Not here, little lady, it's not respectful and it would be insubordinate. . . . Madam . . .

MINNA: Thank you for your trouble, Sergeant Major. It has been a great pleasure for me to meet you. Franziska has told me a lot of good things about you. *(Werner exits with a stiff bow.)*

Scence 5

Minna and Franziska.

MINNA: Is that your sergeant major, Franziska?

FRANZISKA: Since you mock me, I don't have time to take you up on that "your" . . . Yes, madam, that is my sergeant major. I'm sure that you find him a little stiff and wooden. He even seemed that way to me just now. But I noticed that in front of Your Grace he felt as if he was on parade. And when soldiers are on parade . . . they certainly do look more like marionettes than men. But you ought to see and hear him when he's on his own.

MINNA: Yes, I certainly ought.

FRANZISKA: He must still be outside, may I go and talk to him for a while?

MINNA: You know how reluctant I am to deny you this pleasure, but you must stay here, Franziska. You must be present while I am talking to the major. Oh, and something else occurs to me. Take my ring and look after it, and give me the major's. *(She takes her ring off her finger.)*

FRANZISKA: Why?

MINNA *(while Franziska is getting the other ring):* I really don't know myself, but I have a feeling that I might have a use for it. . . . There's a knock. . . . Give it to me quickly! *(She puts it on.)* It's him!

Scene 6

Tellheim, in the same uniform, but otherwise dressed as Franziska prescribed, Minna, and Franziska.

TELLHEIM: Madam, you will excuse my being late . . .

MINNA: Oh, Major, we don't want to be quite that military with one another. You are here, and looking forward to a pleasure is a pleasure in itself! . . . Well? *(She looks smilingly into his face.)* Dear Tellheim, don't you think that we were being rather childish earlier?

TELLHEIM: Yes, madam, it is childish to go on struggling when you should resign yourself.

MINNA: I thought we might go for a drive, Major . . . take a look at the city . . . and then go to meet my uncle.

TELLHEIM: What?

MINNA: You see, we still have not had a chance to talk to each other about the most important matters. Yes, he arrives today. It is mere chance that I arrived a day ahead of him.

TELLHEIM: The Count of Bruchsal, has he returned?

MINNA: The disturbances caused by the war drove him to Italy, but peace has brought him back home again. . . . Don't worry, Tellheim, even if we thought previously that the greatest obstacle to our union would come from his side . . .

TELLHEIM: Our union?

MINNA: He is your friend. He has heard too many good things from too many people about you not to be. He is dying to meet the man who has been chosen by his only heir. He is coming as uncle, as guardian, as father, to give me to you.

TELLHEIM: Madam, why didn't you read my letter? Why didn't you wish to read it?

MINNA: Your letter? Oh, yes, I remember, you did send me one. What happened to that letter, Franziska? Did we or didn't we read it? What did you write to me, dear Tellheim?

TELLHEIM: Nothing but what honor bids me.

MINNA: Which was that you should not leave an honorable girl, who loves you, in the lurch. Certainly honor would bid you write that. I certainly should have read the letter. But what I have not read, I can hear.

TELLHEIM: Yes, you shall hear it . . .

MINNA: No, I don't even need to hear it. It is obvious. Could you be capable of so mean a trick as not to want me now? Don't you know that all my life I would be in disgrace? My fellow countrymen would point their fingers at me. "That's her," they would say. "That's Fräulein von Barnhelm, who thought that just because she was rich, she could get the brave Tellheim—as if brave men are to be bought!" That's what they would say, for my fellow countrymen are all jealous of me. They can't deny that I am wealthy, but they don't want to know that in addition I am really quite a good girl and worthy of a man. Isn't that right, Tellheim?

TELLHEIM: Yes, yes, madam, I know your compatriots. I'm sure they would envy you as an officer who has been discharged, whose honor has been besmirched, and who is a cripple and a beggar into the bargain.

MINNA: And are you supposed to be all those things? I heard something of the sort, if I am not mistaken, this morning. This seems to be a mixture of good and bad. Let's look at each point more closely. You are discharged? So I have heard, but I thought that your regiment had simply been absorbed into another. Why didn't they keep a man of your merit?

TELLHEIM: What had to happen has happened. The authorities have convinced themselves that a soldier does very little out of love for them, not much more from a sense of duty, but everything from the standpoint of his own reputation. Why then should they feel that they owe him anything? Peace has made several people like me dispensable to them, and in the final analysis no one is indispensable.

MINNA: You talk like a man who finds that, for his part, the authorities are very easily dispensable. And certainly this was never more true than at this moment. I am grateful to the authorities that they have renounced their claim to a man whom I would very unwillingly have shared with them. . . . I am your commander, Tellheim, you don't need any other master. I could scarcely have dreamt that I would have the good fortune to find you discharged. . . . But you are not simply discharged; you are more. Now let's see, what else is there? You are a cripple, you said. Well *(She looks him up and down)*, for a cripple you seem to be pretty straight and in one piece, you seem pretty strong and well. Tellheim, if you're going begging on the strength of the loss of your limbs, I predict that you'll get very little except from good-hearted girls like myself.

TELLHEIM: At the moment you sound mischievous rather than good-hearted, my dear Minna.

MINNA: And all I hear in your rebuff, is "dear Minna."—I don't want to poke fun anymore, because I'm aware that you are a partial cripple. A shot did take away some of the use of your right arm. But, taken all in all, it's not so bad. . . . I shall be in less danger from your beatings.

TELLHEIM: Madam!

MINNA: What you want to say is that you have even less to fear from mine.

TELLHEIM: You wish to laugh, madam. I am only sorry that I cannot laugh with you.

MINNA: Why not? What do you have against laughter? Can one not be serious even when laughing? Dear major, laughter keeps us more reasonable than melancholy. The proof is here at hand. Your beloved, though laughing, judges your situation far more accurately than you do yourself. You say that your honor is besmirched because you have been discharged; you say that you are a cripple because you were shot in the arm. Is that right? Isn't this an exaggeration? And isn't it my view that all exaggerations are comic? I'll bet that if we look into this beggar nonsense, it will prove to have as little basis as the rest. You've probably lost your equipment two or three times; some of your funds may have disappeared from this or that bank; you probably have no hope of being repaid for this or that advance that you made while you were in the service—but are you a beggar because of this? Even if you had nothing left but what my uncle is bringing you . . .

TELLHEIM: Your uncle is bringing me nothing.

MINNA: Nothing but the ten thousand talers which you so generously advanced to our government.

TELLHEIM: If only you had read my letter, madam!

MINNA: Oh, very well, I did read it. But I am completely puzzled about what you said on this point. No one is going to try to make a crime out of what was a noble act. . . . Please explain it to me.

TELLHEIM: You will remember, madam, that I had orders to collect the levy in all the districts of your region with the utmost severity, and in cash. I wished to spare myself this severity, and so I advanced the sum which was lacking.

MINNA: Yes, I remember. I loved you for this even though I had not yet met you.

TELLHEIM: Your government gave me its promissory note, and I wanted to include this among the debts which had to be settled when the armistice was signed. The note was acknowledged as valid, but my right to it was disputed. People sneered when I assured them that I had advanced the money in cash. They declared that it was a bribe from your government because I had so quickly agreed to the lowest possible sum for the levy. Thus the note was taken from me, and if it is paid, it will certainly not be paid to me. It is for this reason, madam, that I regard my honor as having been besmirched. Not for my discharge, which I should have asked for in any case had I not received it—Are you serious, madam? Why aren't you laughing? Ha! Ha! Ha! I'm laughing.

MINNA: Oh, stop this laughter Tellheim! I beg you! It is the terrible laughter of the misanthrope. No, you are not the man to regret a good act merely because it had bad effects. No, these evil effects cannot persist. The truth must come to light. My uncle's evidence, the evidence of our legislature . . .

TELLHEIM: Your uncle! Your legislature! Ha, ha, ha!

MINNA: Your laughter is killing me, Tellheim! If you believe in virtue and providence, Tellheim, then don't laugh. I've never heard curses more dreadful than your laughter. And even at the worst, supposing you are misunderstood here, you would not be misunderstood in Thuringia. No, we cannot, we shall not misunderstand you, Tellheim. And if our legislature has the least concept of honor, then I know what they must do. But I'm foolish: why should that be necessary? Imagine, Tellheim, that you had lost the ten thousand talers in one wild evening. The king was your unlucky card, but the queen will be all the more favorable. Providence, believe me, always indemnifies the man who is honorable, and very often ahead of time. The deed, which first was to cost you ten thousand talers, was the very thing that won me for you. Without this deed I should never have been eager to meet you. You know that I came uninvited to the first party at which I thought I should find you. I only came because of you. I came with the firm intention of loving you—I loved you already—with the firm intention of possessing you, even if I had found you as black and ugly as the Moor of Venice. You aren't as black and ugly, nor would you be so jealous. But Tellheim, Tellheim, you do have a lot in common with him. Oh, these wild inflexible men who can fix their obstinate eyes on nothing but the ghost of their honor and who steel themselves against any other feeling! . . . Look at me, Tellheim! (*Tellheim, meanwhile, has been staring fixedly in front of himself.*) What are you thinking about ? Can't you hear me?

TELLHEIM *(absent-mindedly):* Oh yes! But tell me, madam, how did the Moor enter Venetian service? Why did he sell his strength and his blood to a foreign country?

MINNA *(shocked):* Where are you, Tellheim? . . . Now it is time to leave. Come! *(She takes his arm.)* Franziska, have them send the carriage round.

TELLHEIM *(breaking free from Minna and following Franziska):* No, Franziska, I fear that I cannot have the honor of accompanying Fräulein von Barnhelm. Madam, I pray you, leave me today to my commonsense, and excuse me. You are doing your best to make me lose it. I shall resist as much as I can . . . but since I still have some sense left, listen, madam, to the firm resolve which I have made and from which nothing in the world shall shake me. If there is not still a lucky throw left for me in the game, if the tables are not completely turned, if . . .

MINNA: I'm afraid I have to interrupt you, Major. . . . We should have told him straightaway, Franziska. You never remind me of anything. . . . Our conversation would have been quite different if I had begun it with the good news which the Chevalier de la Marlinière just brought you.

TELLHEIM: The Chevalier de la Marlinière? Who is that?

FRANZISKA: He seems to be quite a good man, except . . .

MANNA: Silence, Franziska! He is also a discharged officer who comes from service in Holland . . .

TELLHEIM: Oh, Lieutenant Riccaut!

MINNA: He assured me that he was your friend.

TELLHEIM: And I can assure you that I am not his.

MINNA: And that one of the ministers, I forget which, had told him that your affair was close to a favorable conclusion. Apparently a letter from the king is on its way to you.

TELLHEIM: How on earth could Riccaut have been meeting with a minister? It's true that something should have been decided, because the paymaster general just now told me that the king had dismissed all the charges from the written parole which I gave not to leave here until everything was settled. But that must be all there is to it. They're simply going to let him go. But they are mistaken; I shall not go. I would rather die in penury before the very eyes of my defamers . . .

MINNA: Obstinate man!

TELLHEIM: I need no grace; I seek justice. My honor . . .

MINNA: The honor of a man like you . . .

TELLHEIM *(with heat):* No, madam, you may be a good judge of everything else, but not of this. Honor is not the voice of conscience, not the testimony of those who are less noble. . . .

MINNA: No, no, I know! Honor is . . . honor . . .

TELLHEIM: One moment, madam, you have not permitted me to say all that I had to. . . . I wanted to say that if I am to be unscrupulously denied that which is mine, if I do not find complete satisfaction for my honor, then, madam, I cannot be yours. For in the eyes of the world, I am not worthy to be. Fräulein von Barnhelm deserves a man of irreproachable character. A love which allows its object to be the man who is not ashamed to depend upon a girl for his happiness, whose blind tenderness . . .

MINNA: Are you serious, Major? *(turning her back upon him)* Franziska. . . .

TELLHEIM: Don't be angry, Madam.

MINNA *(aside to Franziska):* Now is the moment! What do you advise, Franziska?

FRANZISKA: I advise nothing, but he is certainly making it hard for you.

TELLHEIM *(advancing to interrupt them):* You are angry, madam . . .

MINNA *(Scornfully):* Me? Not in the least.

TELLHEIM: If I loved you less, madam . . .

MINNA *(in the same tone):* That would be my misfortune. . . . And Major, believe me, I do not wish to be your misfortune. We must remain unselfish in our love. It's just as well that I was not more openhearted. Perhaps your sympathy would have granted me what your heart denies *(slowly taking the ring from her finger).*

TELLHEIM: What do you mean by that, madam?

MINNA: No, neither of us should make the other either more or less happy. That is the meaning of true love. I believe you, Tellheim, and you have too much honor not to recognize true love.

TELLHEIM: Are you laughing at me, madam?

MINNA: Here, take back the ring with which you pledged your love to me. *(Gives him the ring.)* There, now we'll pretend we never knew each other.

TELLHEIM: What are you saying?

MINNA: Why are you surprised? Take it, sir. . . . You surely weren't playing coy?

TELLHEIM *(taking the ring from her hand):* Oh, God, can Minna talk like this?

MINNA: You cannot be mine in one case; I cannot be yours in any. Your misfortune is only apparent; mine is certain. *(Starts to exit.)*

TELLHEIM: Where are you going, my dearest Minna?

MINNA: Sir, you insult me now with this familiarity.

TELLHEIM: What is the matter, madam? Where are you going?

MINNA: Let me go. Let me hide my tears from you . . . traitor! *(Exits.)*

Scene 7

Tellheim and Franziska.

TELLHEIM: Her tears? And I am supposed to let her go. *(Starts to follow Minna.)*

FRANZISKA *(restraining him):* Major, you surely wouldn't follow her into her bedroom?

TELLHEIM: Her misfortune, did she not speak of her misfortune?

FRANZISKA: Certainly. Her misfortune to lose you after . . .

TELLHEIM: After? After what? There's something else. What is it, Franziska? Speak, tell me . . .

FRANZISKA: After she . . . I wanted to say . . . had sacrificed so much for you.

TELLHEIM: Sacrificed? For me?

FRANZISKA: Listen, I will be quite brief. It is just as well, Major, that you got rid of her in this manner. . . . Why shouldn't I tell you? It can't remain secret much longer. . . . We fled! . . . The Count of Bruchsal has disinherited my mistress because she would not accept a man of his choice. She has lost everything and renounced everything. What are we to do? We decided to search for the one who . . .

TELLHEIM: Enough! Come, I must throw myself at her feet.

FRANZISKA: What are you thinking about? You ought to thank your lucky stars . . .

TELLHEIM: Wretch! Whom do you take me for? No, dear Franziska, such advice did not come from your heart. Forgive me!

FRANZISKA: Don't delay me any longer. I must go and see what she is doing. How easily something might have happened to her! . . . Leave us. Come back later if you wish to. *(Exits to Minna.)*

Scene 8

Tellheim.

TELLHEIM: But Franziska! . . . I will await you here. . . . No, this is more urgent! . . . If she sees how serious I am, she cannot refuse me her forgiveness. . . . Now I do have need of you, honest Werner. . . . No, Minna, I am not a traitor! *(Exit in haste.)*

Act V

Scene 1

The parlor.

Tellheim from one side, Werner from the other.

TELLHEIM: Werner, I've been looking everywhere for you. Where have you been?

WERNER: And I've been looking for you, Major. I bring you some good news.

TELLHEIM: It's not your news I need at the moment; I need your money. Hurry, Werner, give me as much as you have, and then go and see if you can borrow as much as possible!

WERNER: Major? . . . Bless my soul, didn't I say he'd only borrow from me when he had something to lend himself?

TELLHEIM: Surely you're not looking for excuses?

WERNER: So that I shall have nothing to reproach him with, he takes it with one hand and gives it back with the other.

TELLHEIM: Don't delay, Werner! I certainly intend to repay, but when and how, God only knows!

WERNER: Then you don't know that the court treasury has received orders to pay you your money. I just heard from . . .

TELLHEIM: What are you talking about? Who are you letting fool you? Surely you must know that if it were true, I would be the first to hear about it? Quickly, Werner, money, money!

WERNER: By God! With pleasure! Here is some. The five hundred talers and the three hundred. *(Hands him both.)*

TELLHEIM: The five hundred talers! Go and get Just, Werner, He's to redeem at once the ring which he pawned this morning. But where are you going to get more, Werner? I need a lot more.

WERNER: Let me worry about that. The man who bought my farm lives in town. We were not due to close for two weeks, but the money is there, and for a half-percent discount.

TELLHEIM: Very well, Werner. Don't you see that you are my only source of refuge? . . . I must confide in you completely. . . . The young lady here . . . you saw her . . . is unhappy.

WERNER: That's bad.

TELLHEIM: But tomorrow she will be my wife.

WERNER: That's good.

TELLHEIM: And the day after tomorrow I shall leave with her. I have permission to leave, and I wish to leave. I would rather leave everything here in the lurch. Who knows where else I may find good fortune? If you like, Werner, come with me. We'll enlist again.

WERNER: Really? . . . But someplace where there's a war on, Major?

TELLHEIM: Where else? But go, my dear Werner, we'll talk about this later.

WERNER: A major after my own heart! The day after tomorrow? Why not, rather, tomorrow? . . . I'll get everything in order. . . . Major, there's a wonderful war in Persia! What do you think of that?

TELLHEIM: We'll think about it. Go now, Werner!

WERNER: Hurrah, hurrah! Long live Prince Heraclius! *(Exit.)*

Scene 2

Tellheim.

TELLHEIM: What has happened to me? My soul is newly inspired. My own misfortune cast me down, made me angry, shortsighted, shy, indolent. Her misfortune raises me up again. I look around again as a free man and feel the strength and the will to undertake everything for her. . . . Why am I waiting? *(Is about to go to Minna's room when Franziska comes out.)*

Scene 3

Franziska and Tellheim.

FRANZISKA: So, it's you? I thought I heard your voice. What do you want, Major?

TELLHEIM: What do I want? . . . What is your mistress doing? Come!

FRANZISKA: She's just going out.

TELLHEIM: Alone? Without me? Where is she going?

FRANZISKA: Have you forgotten, Major?

TELLHEIM: Have you no sense, Franziska? I upset her and she was offended. I shall ask her forgiveness and she will forgive me.

FRANZISKA: What? After you took back the ring?

TELLHEIM: I did that without knowing what I was doing. . . . I have just remembered the ring. . . . Where did I put it? *(Looks for it.)* Here it is.

FRANZISKA: Is that it? *(Tellheim replaces the ring.)* *(aside)* If only he would look at it a little more closely.

TELLHEIM: She forced it on me with such bitterness . . . but I have forgotten this bitterness already. When you are under stress, you don't always weigh your words very carefully. But she won't refuse for a moment to take back the ring. And don't I still have hers?

FRANZISKA: She's expecting to get that back. . . . Where is it, Major? Show it to me.

TELLHEIM *(Somewhat abashed):* I . . . I forgot to bring it with me . . . Just . . . Just is going to bring it to me at once.

FRANZISKA: I suppose one is very much like the other. Let me have a look at this one; I love looking at things like that.

TELLHEIM: Another time, Franziska. Come . . .

FRANZISKA *(aside):* He simply won't see his mistake.

TELLHEIM: What did you say? Mistake?

FRANZISKA: I meant to say that it is a mistake if you still think my mistress is still a good match. Her own estate is a very modest one, and her guardians could reduce it to nothing by a few self-seeking calculations. She expected to inherit everything from her uncle, but this cruel uncle . . .

TELLHEIM: Don't talk of him. Am I not man enough to recompense her for everything?

FRANZISKA: Did you hear? She's ringing for me; I must go in.

TELLHEIM: I'm going with you.

FRANZISKA: Oh for heaven's sake, no! She expressly forbade me to talk to you. At least wait and come after I have gone in.

Scene 4

Tellheim.

TELLHEIM *(calling after her):* Announce me to her! Speak for me, Franziska! I'll come after you immediately! . . . What shall I say to her? When you speak from the heart, there is no need of preparation. The one thing that might need careful handling is her reticence, her hesitation to throw herself into my arms because of her misfortune, her eagerness to pretend to a good fortune which she lost on my account. To excuse herself for this lack of trust in my honor, in her own value, to excuse herself . . . I have already excused it. . . . Ah, but here she comes.

Scene 5

Minna, Franziska, and Tellheim.

MINNA *(coming out as though unaware of the major's presence):* The carriage is waiting, isn't it Franziska? . . . My fan, please.

TELLHEIM *(going up to her):* Where are you going, madam?

MINNA *(with affected coldness):* Out, Major. I can guess the reason for your coming back here—to give me my ring back as well. . . . Very well, Major, please have the goodness to hand it to Franziska. Franziska, take the ring from the major! I'm afraid I have no time to lose. *(About to go.)*

TELLHEIM *(walking in front of her):* Madam! What's this I hear, madam? I am not worthy of such love?

MINNA: Well, Franziska, so you told the major . . .

FRANZISKA: Everything.

TELLHEIM: Please don't be angry with me, madam. I am no traitor. You have lost much on my account in the eyes of the world, but not in my own. In my eyes you have gained incalculably by this loss. It was all too new. You feared that you might make an unfavorable impression upon me. At first you wanted to conceal it from me. I don't complain about this lack of trust. I know that it came from your desire to keep me, and this desire is a source of pride to me. You found that I too had suffered misfortune, and you didn't want to pile misfortune upon misfortune. You couldn't imagine how much more your misfortune meant to me than my own.

MINNA: That's all well and good, Major, but it has happened once and for all. I have released you from your obligation by taking back this ring.

TELLHEIM: I have agreed to nothing . . . indeed, I regard myself as under a greater obligation than before. You are mine, Minna, for ever mine! *(He takes out the ring.)* Here, take for a second time this pledge of my faithfulness.

MINNA: Me? Take this ring back? This ring?

TELLHEIM: Yes, dearest Minna, yes!

MINNA: What do you take me for? This ring?

TELLHEIM: The first time you took this ring from my hand, our circumstances were equal and we both enjoyed good fortune. They are no longer fortunate, but they are at least equal again. Equality is always the strongest bond of love. Allow, me, my dearest Minna. . . . *(Seizes her hand to place the ring on it.)*

MINNA: What, by force, Major? No, there is no power in the world which would make me take this ring back. Do you think I have a need for rings? You see, don't you, that I have one here which is not in the least inferior to yours?

FRANZISKA: He still doesn't see it!

TELLHEIM *(letting Minna's hand drop):* What does this mean? I see

Fräulein von Barnhelm, but it is not her that I hear. You are playing coy, madam. . . . Forgive my imitating you and using this expression.

MINNA *(in her true tone):* Did this word insult you, Major?

TELLHEIM: It hurt me.

MINNA *(touched):* It was not meant to, Tellheim . . . Forgive me, Tellheim.

TELLHEIM: Thank God! This warmth of tone tells me that you are coming to yourself, madam, that you love me, Minna.

FRANZISKA *(bursting out):* The joke almost went too far.

MINNA *(imperiously):* Please do not interfere, Franziska!

FRANZISKA *(aside and taken aback):* Still not enough?

MINNA: Yes, sir. It would be feminine vanity to remain cold and disdainful. Away with all that! You deserve to find in me someone just as truthful as you are yourself. . . . I still love you, Tellheim, I still love you, but nevertheless . . .

TELLHEIM: No more, dearest Minna, no more! *(Seizes her hand again to put the ring on it.)*

MINNA *(withdrawing her hand):* But nevertheless . . . it is for this very reason that I can never again allow this to happen . . . never again! . . . What are you thinking about, Major! I thought you had enough to think about with your own misfortune. . . . You must remain here, you must extort the most complete satisfaction. In my haste I can think of no other word but extort . . . even if the most extreme misfortune were to consume you under the very eyes of your slanderers.

TELLHEIM: That was my first thought; that's what I said when I didn't know what I was saying and thinking. Vexation and stifled rage had clouded my whole soul. Love itself in the fullest splendor of good fortune could not dispel the gloom. But Love sent her daughter, Pity, who being more familiar with the blackness of pain, dispelled the clouds and opened my whole soul once again to impressions of tenderness. I felt the urge for self-preservation because I had something to preserve which was more valuable than myself and which had to be preserved by me. Please do not be insulted by this word "pity," Madam. You can hear it without humiliation because it comes from the innocent cause of our misfortune. I am the cause. It is on my account, Minna, that you are losing friends and relatives, possessions and fatherland. And it is through me and in me that you must find all these again, or I shall have the ruin of the most lovable of your sex on my conscience. Please don't make me even think about a future in which I would have to hate myself. . . . No, nothing shall keep me here any longer. From this moment on I shall show nothing but scorn for the injustice which has been meted out to me here. Is this country the whole world? Is this the only place where the sun rises? Where may I not go? Who will refuse me service even if I have to seek it under the farthest sky? Follow me with confidence, dearest Minna. We shall lack for nothing. I have a friend who will gladly help me . . .

Scene 6

An orderly, Tellheim, Minna, and Franziska.

FRANZISKA *(catching sight of the orderly):* Sh, Major!

TELLHEIM *(to the orderly):* Who are you looking for?

ORDERLY: I am looking for Major von Tellheim. . . . Ah! So it's you. Sir, this royal letter *(He takes the letter out of his wallet.)* I am to hand you.

TELLHEIM: For me?

ORDERLY: According to the address.

MINNA: Franziska, do you hear? The chevalier was speaking the truth after all!

ORDERLY *(as Tellheim takes the letter):* I must beg your pardon, sir. You would have received it yesterday, but it was impossible to find you. It was only today on parade that I learned your address from Lieutenant Riccaut.

FRANZISKA: Madam, did you hear? . . . This is the chevalier's minister. . . . " 'Ow is calling 'imself ze minister on ze big square?"

TELLHEIM: I am most grateful to you for your trouble.

ORDERLY: It is my pleasure, Major.

Scene 7

Tellheim, Minna, and Franziska.

TELLHEIM: Madam, what do I have here? What are the contents of this letter?

MINNA: I have no right to extend my curiosity so far.

TELLHEIM: What, do you still think of your fate as separate from mine? . . . But why am I waiting to open it? It can scarcely make me more unhappy than I am now. No, dearest Minna, it cannot make us more unhappy . . . but perhaps it can make us happier! Permit me, madam. *(Opens the dispatch and reads it. The landlord enters.)*

Scene 8

Landlord, Tellheim, Minna, and Franziska.

LANDLORD *(to Franziska):* Psst, my dear, a word!

FRANZISKA *(going up to him):* Sir? I'm afraid we don't know ourselves what's in the letter.

LANDLORD: Who wants to know about the letter? I've come about the ring. Your mistress must return it to me at once. Just is here and wants to redeem it.

MINNA *(who has also come up to the landlord):* Tell Just that the ring has already been redeemed; and tell him by whom—by me.

LANDLORD: But . . .

MINNA: I take full responsibility. You may go! *(Exit landlord.)*

Scene 9

Tellheim, Minna, and Franziska.

FRANZISKA: And now, madam, it's time to stop teasing the major.

MINNA: Stop your pleading! Don't you know that the knot will untie itself at any moment?

TELLHEIM *(after reading the letter with the most lively show of emotion):* Ah, here, too, he has revealed his true self. . . . Oh, madam, what justice! . . . what grace! . . . This is more than I had expected . . . more than I deserve. . . . My fortune, my honor, everything is restored. Surely, I am still dreaming! *(looking once more at the letter as though to reassure himself)* No, it is not an illusion called forth by my own wishes. . . . Read it for yourself, madam, read it for yourself!

MINNA: I would not be so presumptuous, Major.

TELLHEIM: Presumptuous? The letter is to me, to your Tellheim, Minna. It contains . . . something that your uncle cannot take away from you. You must read it; please read it!

MINNA: If, in so doing, I do you a favor, Major. . . . *(She takes the letter and reads it.)*

"My dear Major Tellheim:

We hereby inform you that the matter which had given us concern for your honor has been explained to your advantage. Our brother was informed of it in greater detail, and his evidence has shown you to be innocent. The treasury has orders to restore to you the letters of credit which were called into question and to repay the advances which you made. We have also commanded that all claims which the paymaster had against you be dismissed. Please inform us if your state of health permits you to take up service again. We would not readily wish to lose a man of your courage and temper.

Your most affectionate Majesty, etc."

TELLHEIM: What do you say to that?

MINNA *(folding up the letter and returning it to him):* I? Nothing.

TELLHEIM: Nothing?

MINNA: Well, yes: that your king is a great man and probably also a good man. . . . But that is no concern of mine. He is not my king.

TELLHEIM: And do you have nothing else to say? Nothing about us?

MINNA: You are going back into his service. The major will become a lieutenant colonel, perhaps a full colonel. I give you my heartiest congratulations.

TELLHEIM: Do you not know me better than that? No, since fortune is restoring so much to me—more than enough to satisfy the wishes of any reasonable man—it will depend entirely upon Minna whether or not I belong to anyone else but her. May my whole life to devoted to your service! It is dangerous to serve the mighty, and such service offers no recompense for the humiliation and the duress which it brings. Minna is not one of those vain women who only love their men for their title and rank. She will love me for myself, and for her sake I shall renounce the rest of the world. I became a soldier because of a certain partisanship. I do not know, myself, the political principles for which I fought. And it was a whim of mine that soldiering is good for every man of honor for a time at least, so that he may become familiar with everything that men call danger and so learn boldness and determination. Only the most extreme necessity could have compelled me to make a vocation out of this experiment, to make a profession out of this temporary occupation. But now that I am no longer under any sort of pressure, now my total ambition is to be a peaceful and contented human being. With you, dearest Minna, that is what I shall surely become. That is what, in your company, I shall constantly remain. . . . May the most holy bond of matrimony join us tomorrow, and then we will search throughout the whole wide world for the most peaceful, pleasing, and delightful corner, which has all that is needed for a true paradise except a loving couple. There we will live; there shall all of our days. . . . What is the matter, Minna? *(Minna moves uneasily back and forth, trying to conceal her emotion.)*

MINNA *(pulling herself together):* You are cruel, Tellheim, to describe so attractively a happiness which you know I must reject. My loss . . .

TELLHEIM: Your loss? What do you mean by your loss? Anything which Minna could lose would not be Minna's. You are the sweetest, loveliest, most enchanting creature under the sun, full of goodness and generosity, full of innocence and happiness . . . mixed now and then with a little wantonness, perhaps, and now and again a touch of obstinacy. . . . But so much the better! So much the better! Otherwise, Minna would be an angel whom I should have to worship with awe, whom I could not love. *(Takes her hand to kiss it.)*

MINNA *(taking her hand back)*: No, sir! . . . What is this change which has suddenly come over you? Is this flattering, tempestuous lover the cold Tellheim? Could only the return of his fortune kindle these fires in him? I trust that you will permit me in these sudden fits of heat and cold to preserve a little judgment for both of us. When he himself was in a position to turn things over in his mind, he said that it was an unworthy love which did not hesitate to subject is object to scorn. . . . That is so, but I too am seeking a love which is as pure and noble as his. . . . And now that honor summons him, now that a great king seeks his favor, am I to allow him to give himself up to dreams of love with me? And have the famous warrior degenerate into a dallying swain? . . . No, sir, follow the summons of your own better fate.

TELLHEIM: Very well, then, if you find the big world more attractive, Minna . . . good, then let us remain in the big world! . . . How insignificant, how poor this big world is! You know it only from its tinsel side. But in truth, Minna, you will. . . . Never mind! Until that time, all right! There will be no lack of admirers for your perfection and no lack of people jealous of my good fortune.

MINNA: No, Tellheim, that's not what I meant. I'm directing you back into the big world, back to the path of your honor, but I don't wish to follow you. . . . In that world, Tellheim needs a wife who is beyond reproach. A girl from Saxony who has thrown herself into his arms. . . .

TELLHEIM *(starting up and looking wildly around him)*: Who dares to talk like that? . . . Minna, I tremble when I think that anyone but you should have said this. My rage against him would have known no bounds.

MINNA: You see, that's what I fear. You would not suffer the smallest piece of ridicule about me, but day in and day out you would have to put up with the most bitter mockery. In short, Tellheim, listen to the decision which I have made and from which nothing in the world will shake me.

TELLHEIM: Before you finish, madam . . . I beg you, Minna . . . think for a moment that you are passing a verdict of life or death on me.

MINNA: Without a further thought . . . as surely as I gave you back the ring with which you once pledged me your faith, and as surely as you took this same ring back, so surely shall the unfortunate Barnhelm never become the wife of the more fortunate Tellehim.

TELLHEIM: And this is your sentence, madam?

MINNA: Equality is the only firm bond of love. The fortunate Barnhelm wished to live only for the fortunate Tellheim. Even the unhappy Minna might have let herself be persuaded to increase or decrease the misfortune of her friend. . . . He must have noticed, before this letter came to make us unequal once more, how my refusal was only feigned.

TELLHEIM: Is that true, madam? . . . I thank you, Minna, that you have not passed the final sentence. . . . Is it only the unfortunate Tellheim that you want? He can be had. *(coldly.)* I have the feeling that it is not right for me to accept this long-overdue vindication; that it might be better if I did not seek the return of that which has so shamefully been taken from my honor. . . . Yes, I will pretend not to have received the letter. That shall be my answer! *(about to tear the letter up)*

MINNA *(taking his hand):* What are you going to do, Tellheim?

TELLHEIM: Possess you.

MINNA: Wait!

TELLHEIM: Madam, I swear to you that I shall tear it up unless you change your mind. Then we shall see what further objections you have.

MINNA: What, in this tone? . . . Have I to grow despicable in my own eyes? Never! Only a worthless creature would not be shamed to owe her whole good fortune to the blind tenderness of a man.

TELLHEIM: False, absolutely false!

MINNA: Surely you don't dare deny your own words when they come from my lips?

TELLHEIM: Sophistry! Will the weaker sex be dishonored by everything which is unsuited to the stronger? May a man permit himself what a woman does? Which sex was determined by nature to be the support of the other?

MINNA: Calm yourself, Tellheim! I shall not be completely without protection . . . even if I have to reject the honor of yours. My needs will still be attended to. I have called upon our ambassador. He wishes to talk to me today. I hope that he will take me under his protection. But the time is getting on. Permit me, Major.

TELLHEIM: I will accompany you, madam.

MINNA: No, sir, leave me.

TELLHEIM: Your shadow shall leave you before I do. Come, madam, we will go where you want, to whom you want. Everywhere, a hundred times a day and in your presence, I shall tell friends and strangers alike of the bond which holds you to me, and of the cruel obstinacy which makes you want to break these bonds.

Scene 10

Just, Tellheim, Minna, and Franziska.

JUST *(rushing in):* Major! Major!

TELLHEIM: Yes?

JUST: Come quickly, quickly!

TELLHEIM: Why? Come here! Tell me, what is it?

JUST: Listen. . . . *(Whispers to Tellheim.)*

MINNA *(aside to Franziska):* Do you notice anything, Franziska?

FRANZISKA: Oh, you are a merciless creature! I have been on tender-hooks.

TELLHEIM *(to Just):* What did you say? . . . It's impossible! . . . You? *(looking wildly at Minna)* Say it out loud, say it to her face. . . . Listen, madam!

JUST: The landlord says that Fräulein von Barnhelm has redeemed the ring which I pawned. She recognized it as her own and refused to give it back.

TELLHEIM: Is this true, madam? No, it can't be true!

MINNA *(smiling):* And why can't it be true, Tellheim?

TELLHEIM *(passionately):* All right, it is true! A terrible light suddenly dawns upon me. . . . Now I recognize you, false, faithless one!

MINNA *(frightened):* Who? Who is faithless?

TELLHEIM: You, whom I can no longer name by name.

MINNA: Tellheim!

TELLHEIM: Forget my name! You came here to break with me, that much is clear . . . and chance played into your hands! It restored the ring to you, and by your own trickery you made me take my own ring back.

MINNA: Tellheim, what ghosts are you conjuring up? Pull yourself together and listen to me.

FRANZISKA *(to herself):* Now she'll get it!

Scene 11

Werner, with a purse, Tellheim, Minna, Franziska, and Just.

WERNER: Here I am back already, Major!

TELLHEIM *(without looking at him):* Who sent for you?

WERNER: Here's money, five thousand talers.

TELLHEIM: I don't want it!

WERNER: Tomorrow, sir, you can have the same amount again if you want it.

TELLHEIM: Keep your money!

WERNER: It's your money, sir. I don't think you know who you're talking to.

TELLHEIM: Take it away, I say!

WERNER: What's the matter? I'm Paul Werner.

TELLHEIM: All goodness is sheer hypocrisy, all kindness mere deceit.

WERNER: Is that true of me?

TELLHEIM: Just as you like!

WERNER: I only carried out orders.

TELLHEIM: Then carry out this one as well, and be off!

WERNER: Sir! *(angry)* I am a man . . .

TELLHEIM: That's something to be proud of!

WERNER: Who has something of a temper . . .

TELLHEIM: Good! Temper is the best thing we have.

WERNER: Please, sir . . .

TELLHEIM: How often do I have to tell you? I don't need your money!

WERNER *(angry):* All right, then, let him have it who wants it! *(He throws the purse down and goes to one side.)*

MINNA: Oh, Franziska, my dear, I should have followed your advice. I've carried the joke too far. . . . But he only needs to listen to me. . . . *(Going up to him.)*

FRANZISKA: Sergeant major!! *(She has moved up to him without answering Minna.)*

WERNER *(angry):* Go away!

FRANZISKA: Ugh! What sort of men are these?

MINNA: Tellheim! Tellheim! *(Tellheim is biting his fingers in rage and has turned away from Minna, refusing to listen to her.)* I went too far! . . . Listen to me! . . . You are deceiving yourself . . . a sheer misunderstanding . . . Tellheim! . . . Won't you listen to your Minna? . . . Can you nurse such a suspicion? . . . I wanted to break with you? . . . And that's the reason I came here? . . . Tellheim!

Scene 12

Two servants (they enter from opposite sides and run across the room), Werner, Tellheim, Minna, Franziska, and Just.

FIRST SERVANT: Madam, His Excellency, the count!

SECOND SERVANT: He is coming, madam!

FRANZISKA *(runs to the widow):* It's him, it's him!

MINNA: Is it him? . . . Hurry, Tellheim, hurry!

TELLHEIM *(suddenly coming to himself):* Who, who's coming? Your uncle, madam? This cruel uncle? All right, let him come, let him! Have no fear! He shall not harm you with so much as a glance. He has me to reckon with. . . . It's true that you don't deserve it of me. . . .

MINNA: Oh, hurry, Tellheim! Put your arms around me and forget everything. . . .

TELLHEIM: If only I thought you might regret your treatment of me!

MINNA: No, I cannot regret having caught a glimpse of your whole heart! . . . What a wonderful man you are! Put your arms around your Minna, your happy Minna, and happy most of all on your account. *(She falls into his arms.)* And now, let's go to meet him. . . .

TELLHEIM: Meet whom?

MINNA: The best of your unknown friends.

TELLHEIM: What?

MINNA: The count, my uncle, my father, your father. . . . My flight, his anger, my disinheritance . . . don't you know that it was all made up? How gullible you are, my dear!

TELLHEIM: Made up? But the ring? The ring?

MINNA: Where is the ring I gave back to you?

TELLHEIM: You'll take it back? . . . How happy you make me! . . . Here, Minna! *(Takes it out.)*

MINNA: Look at it first. . . . Oh, there's none so blind as those who won't see! . . . Which ring is it? The one I had from you or the one you had from me?—Isn't it the very one I didn't wish to leave in the landlord's hands?

TELLHEIM. My God, what is this? What are you saying?

MINNA: Shall I take it back now? Shall I? . . . Give it to me, give it to me! *(She takes it from his hand and places it on his finger.)* Now, is everything all right?

TELLHEIM: Where am I? . . . *(Kisses her hand.)* Oh, you wicked angel! To torture me like that! . . .

MINNA: This was just a proof, my dear husband, that you can never play a trick on me without my playing one on you immediately after. Don't you think that you tortured me as well?

TELLHEIM: You actress! I should have known you better than that.

FRANZISKA: No, really, I don't think I could be an actress. I was trembling and shuddering and had to hold my hand to my mouth to keep it shut.

MINNA: My role didn't come easily to me either. But come!

TELLHEIM: I still can't get over it. . . . How well I feel, yet how frightened! It's like waking from a nightmare.

MINNA: We're delaying. I hear him.

Scene 13

Count of Bruchsal, accompanied by landlord, Minna, Franziska, Tellheim, Just, Werner, and servants.

COUNT: You arrived safely, then?

MINNA *(going towards him):* Ah, Father! . . .

COUNT: Yes, here I am, my dearest Minna. *(He puts his arms round her.)* But what's this, girl? *(seeing Tellheim)* You've only been here twenty-four hours, and you've already made some acquaintances and are beginning to entertain?

MINNA: Can you guess who it is?

COUNT: Surely not your Tellheim?

MINNA: Who else but him? . . . Come, Tellheim! *(She takes him to the Count.)*

COUNT: Sir, we have never made each other's acquaintance, and yet I thought I recognized you as soon as I saw you. I hoped it might be you. Come, embrace me. . . . You enjoy my deepest respect. I ask your friendship. . . . My niece, my daughter, loves you.

MINNA: Do you know that, father? . . . And is my love blind?

COUNT: No, Minna, your love is not blind, but your beloved . . . is mute.

TELLHEIM *(going into his arms):* Please let me pull myself together, Father.

COUNT: Very well, My Son. I hear that, even if your mouth cannot speak, your heart can. As a rule I do not care for officers who wear this color *(Points to Tellheim's uniform)*, but you are an honest man, Tellheim, and an honest a man can wear what he likes; people will still like him.

MINNA: If only you knew everything!

COUNT: But why shouldn't I learn everything? . . . Where are my rooms, landlord?

LANDLORD: If Your Excellency would do me the honor of stepping this way.

COUNT: Come, Minna! Come, sir! *(Exit with landlord and servants.)*

MINNA: Come, Tellheim!

TELLHEIM: I'll follow you in a minute, madam. Just one more word with this man here. *(Turns to Werner.)*

MINNA: And make it a good one. I think you owe it to him. Right, Franziska?

Scene 14

Tellheim, Werner, Just, and Franziska.

TELLHEIM *(pointing to the purse which Werner has just thrown away)*: Here, Just, pick up that purse and take it home. Go on! *(Just picks it up and exits.)*

WERNER *(who has been standing angrily in the corner and not participating in any of the foregoing)*: Well?

TELLHEIM *(going up to him confidentially)*: Werner, when can I have the other five thousand talers?

WERNER *(regaining his good temper at once)*: Tomorrow, sir, tomorrow.

TELLHEIM: I no longer need to become your debtor, but I will become your banker. You good-natured people all need a guardian. You're a sort of spendthrift. . . . I'm afraid I made you angry a while ago, Werner.

WERNER: God bless my soul, you did! I shouldn't have been such a fool. Now I see it all. I really deserved a hundred strokes, and you can give them to me, as long as you aren't angry any more, sir.

TELLHEIM: Angry? *(shaking his hand)* Read in my eyes everything I cannot put into words . . . I'd like to see the man who has a finer girl and a better friend than I have! . . . Isn't that right, Franziska? *(Exits.)*

Scene 15

Franziska and Werner.

FRANZISKA *(aside):* Yes, he is a good man. I'll never meet another like him. I have to admit it. *(Shyly and modestly coming up to Werner)* Sergeant Major . . .

WERNER *(Wiping his eyes):* Well?

FRANZISKA: Sergeant Major . . .

WERNER: What do you want, little lady?

FRANZISKA: Look at me, Sergeant Major.

WERNER: I can't yet; I don't know what I've got in my eye.

FRANZISKA: Just look at me!

WERNER: I'm afraid I looked at you a bit you too much already, little lady. . . . All right, now I'm looking at you. What's the matter?

FRANZISKA: Sergeant Major, don't you need a Mrs. Sergeant Major?

WERNER: Are you serious, little lady?

FRANZISKA: Absolutely!

WERNER: Would you like to go to Persia with me?

FRANZISKA: Wherever you like!

WERNER: Really? Hey, Major, don't boast! I've got a girl who's at least as good as yours and a friend who's just as honest! . . . Give me your hand, little lady. . . . Done! . . . In ten years you'll either be a general's wife or a widow.

Curtain

Translated by Kenneth J. Northcott

EMILIA GALOTTI

A Tragedy in Five Acts
Written in 1772

CHARACTERS

EMILIA GALOTTI
ODOARDO *and* CLAUDIA GALOTTI, *parents of Emilia*
HETTORE GONZAGA, *Prince of Guastalla*
MARINELLI, *chamberlain to the Prince*
CAMILLO ROTA, *one of the Prince's councilors*
CONTI, *painter*
COUNT APPIANI
COUNTESS ORSINA
ANGELO *and several* SERVANTS

Act I

The prince's study

Scene 1

The Prince, a valet.

THE PRINCE *(seated at a desk and glancing through some of the letters and papers with which it is covered):* Complaints, nothing but complaints! Petitions, nothing but petitions!—Oh, these wretched chores. And yet there are those who think of us with envy!—Indeed, if we could help them all—all those who ask—that would be grounds for envy.—Emilia? *(as he opens another petition and looks for the signature)* An Emilia?—But an Emilia Bruneschi—not Galotti. Not Emilia Galotti!—What does she want, this Emilia Bruneschi? *(He reads.)* She asks for much, very much.—But her name is Emilia. Granted! *(He signs and rings, whereupon a valet enters.)* I suppose none of the councilors has appeared in the antechamber?

THE VALET: No.

THE PRINCE: I began this day too early—It is such a beautiful morning. I shall go for a drive. The Marquis Marinelli shall accompany me. Have him called. *(Exit valet.)*—I cannot go on working anyway.—I was so calm, I fancy, so calm—suddenly this poor Bruneschi woman must come along and call herself Emilia;—gone is my calm and everything!—

THE VALET *(enters again):* The Marquis has been called. And here is a letter from the Countess Orsina.

THE PRINCE: Orsina? Put it there.

THE VALET: Her footman is waiting.

THE PRINCE: I will send the answer if one is needed.—Where is she? In the city? or at her villa?

THE VALET: She came to the city yesterday.

THE PRINCE: So much the worse—better, I mean. All the less reason for the footman to wait. *(Exit valet)* My dear Countess! *(bitterly, as he picks up the letter)* As good as read! *(and throws it down again)*— Well, yes; I thought I loved her! All the things one believes! And maybe I did love her really. But—I did!

THE VALET *(who enters once again):* The painter Conti requests the privilege—

THE PRINCE: Conti? Very well; show him in.—This will divert my thoughts.—*(Stands up.)*

Scene 2

Conti, the Prince.

THE PRINCE: Good morning, Conti. How have you been? What has your art been doing?

CONTI: Looking for bread, my Prince.

THE PRINCE: It should not do that, and it shall not,—at least not in my small domain.—But of course, the artist must be willing to work.

CONTI: Work? That is his delight. But being forced to work too much can cost him the name of artist.

THE PRINCE: I do not mean many things, I mean great things: a little, but with high resolve.—You do not come empty-handed, do you, Conti?

CONTI: I bring the portrait which you ordered, my lord. And bring another, which you did not order; but because it deserves to be seen—

THE PRINCE: The first is?—I can hardly remember—

CONTI: The Countess Orsina.

THE PRINCE: True!—Though that was ordered quite some time ago.

CONTI: Our fair ladies cannot be painted every day. In the past three months the Countess has agreed to sit just once.

THE PRINCE: Where are the pieces?

CONTI: In the antechamber; I will get them.

Scene 3

THE PRINCE: Her picture!—So be it!—Her picture in any case is not herself.—And maybe I shall find in the picture again what I no longer see in the person.—Though, I do not want to find it again.—This bothersome painter! I should not be surprised if she bribed him.—And what if she did! If another picture, painted in other colors on another background,—will let her take her place once more in my heart: why, I really think I would not mind. When I loved her I was always so lighthearted, so gay, so free from care.—Now I am the opposite of all that.—But no; no, no! More at my ease or less at my ease; I am better this way.

Scene 4

The Prince, Conti with the pictures, one of which still turned around; he leans against a chair.

CONTI *(as he arranges the other):* I must ask you, my Prince, to take into consideration the limitations of our art. A large part of Beauty's attraction lies entirely outside its boundaries.—Please step over here!—

THE PRINCE *(after a moment's scrutiny):* Excellent, Conti;—simply excellent!—I refer to your art, your brush;—but flattering, Conti; infinitely flattering!

CONTI: The subject did not seem to share that opinion. And in truth, it is no more flattering than art must be flattering. Art must paint the picture as Plastic Nature—if there is such a thing—imagined it: without the falling off which recalcitrant matter makes unavoidable; without the decay with which time attacks it.

THE PRINCE: The artist who thinks doubles his worth.—But the subject, you say, nevertheless considered—

CONTI: Forgive me, Prince. The subject is a person who commands my respect. I did not mean to imply anything disparaging.

THE PRINCE: Imply as much as you wish!—But what did the subject say?

CONTI: I am satisfied, said the Countess, as long as I am not uglier than that.

THE PRINCE: Not uglier?—Ah, how like her!

CONTI: And she said it with a look—of which this portrait, to be sure, does not show a trace, not the slightest trace.

THE PRINCE: That is what I meant; that is precisely where I see the infinite flattery.—Ah! I know it, that proud, scornful look. It would distort the face of one of the Graces!—I do not deny that a pretty mouth twisted just a trifle mockingly is often only the prettier. But, mark my word, just a trifle: the twisting must not become a grimace, as it does with our Countess. And there must be eyes to keep the wanton mockery in check,—eyes, such as the good Countess certainly has not at all. Not even in this picture.

CONTI: My lord, I am distressed beyond words—

THE PRINCE: And what for? All that art can make of those great, protruding, icy, staring Medusa-eyes of the Countess, all that—Conti—you have made of them in honest endeavor.—Honest, I say?—Less of that honest endeavor would have been more honest.

For, judge for yourself, Conti, is the character of the person to be inferred from this picture? It should be, you will agree. Pride you have transformed into dignity, scorn into smiles, a tendency toward gloomy reverie into gentle melancholy.

CONTI *(somewhat angered):* Ah, my Prince,—we painters count on having the finished picture find the lover as warm as he was when he ordered it. We paint with the eyes of love, and eyes of love alone should judge us.

THE PRINCE: Come now, Conti;—why did you not bring it one month sooner?—Put it away.—What is the other piece?

CONTI *(getting it and holding it, still turned away, in his hand):* Also a portrait of a lady.

THE PRINCE: Then I would almost—rather not see it at all. For it would never answer the ideal I have here *(pointing to his head)*, or rather here *(pointing to his heart)*.—I should like to admire your art, Conti, in other genres.

CONTI: A more admirable art than mine does exist, but surely not a more admirable subject than this.

THE PRINCE: Then, Conti, I wager it is the artist's own mistress.—*(as the painter turns the picture toward him)* What do I see? Your work, Conti? Or the work of my imagination?—Emilia Galotti!

CONTI: What, my prince? You know this angel?

THE PRINCE *(as he tries to control himself, but without taking his eyes from the picture):* More or less—just enough to recognize her again.—It was several weeks ago that I met her with her mother at a soiree.—Since then I have seen her only in holy places,—where staring at people is not so very proper.—And then I know her father, too. He is no friend of mine. He was the one who most strongly opposed my claims to Sabionetta.—An old soldier, proud and rough, otherwise upright and good!—

CONTI: The father! But here we have his daughter.—

THE PRINCE: By God! as if stolen from a mirror!—*(his eyes still riveted on the picture)* Ah, well you know, my dear Conti, that one praises the artist most when, in looking at his work, one forgets to praise him.

CONTI: And yet, this piece still leaves me greatly dissatisfied with myself.—Although, on the other hand, I am also greatly satisfied with this dissatisfaction with myself.—Ah! would that we were able to paint directly with our eyes! On that long path from the eye through the arm to the brush, how much is lost!—But, as I say, the fact that I know what was lost and how it was lost and why it had to be lost: of that I am as proud as I am of all that I did not allow to be lost. Prouder even. For in that knowledge, more than in this product of my art, I recognize that I am a truly great artist, although my hand is not always equally great.—Or do you believe, Prince, that Raphael would not have been the greatest artistic genius even if he had had the misfortune to be born without hands? You don't believe that, prince, or do you?

THE PRINCE *(looking away, for only a moment, from the picture):* What did you say, Conti? What do you want to know?

CONTI: Oh nothing, nothing!—Just prattle! Your soul was in your eyes, I see. I love such souls and such eyes.

THE PRINCE *(with forced detachment):* So then, Conti, you do count Emilia Galotti among the distinguished beauties of our city?

CONTI: What? Among? ". . . among the most distinguished"? ". . . the most distinguished of our city"?—You are mocking me, my Prince. Or you have seen, all this while, just as little as you have heard.

THE PRINCE: Dear Conti,—*(his eyes directed once more toward the picture)* how can such as we trust our eyes? In the fullest sense, only a painter knows how to judge beauty.

CONTI: And men's reactions should wait for the word from a painter?—Into a monastery with him who wants to learn from us what is beautiful! But one thing I must tell you as a painter, my Prince: one of the greatest delights in my life is the fact that Emilia Galotti sat for me. This head, this face, this brow, these eyes, this nose, this mouth, this chin, this throat, this bosom, this stature, this entire figure have been ever since my one concern in the study of feminine beauty.—The first canvas, the one for which she sat, went to her absent father. But this copy—

THE PRINCE *(turning quickly toward him):* Yes, Conti? It has not been promised to someone else?

CONTI: It is for you, Prince, if it meets with your approval.

THE PRINCE: Approval!—*(smiling)* This, your one concern in the study of feminine beauty, Conti, what better thing could I do than to make it mine also?—That portrait over there you may take with you again,—to order a frame.

CONTI: Good!

THE PRINCE: As beautiful, as richly ornamented as the carver can possibly make it. It is to be placed in the gallery.—But this one stays here. A study is not treated with such ceremony; nor is it hung; it should be near at hand.—I thank you, Conti; I thank you very much.—And once again: art shall not go looking for bread in my domain,—not until I myself have none.—Send word to my treasurer, Conti, and let him pay you for both portraits against your receipt. Whatever you want, Conti. As much as you want.

CONTI: Can it be, Prince, that you want to reward something other than art in this way? I am almost afraid it is.

THE PRINCE: Ah, the jealous artist! Of course not!—Remember, Conti, as much as you want. *(Exit Conti.)*

Scene 5

THE PRINCE: As much as he wants!—*(toward the picture)* At any price, I have gotten you too cheaply.—Ah! beautiful work of art, is it true that I own you?—Now to own you too, more beautiful masterpiece of nature!—As much as you want, good mother! Whatever you want, surly old man! Just ask! Just ask, the two of you!—Happiest would I be, could I buy you, enchantress, from yourself!—This glance, so full of charm and modesty! This mouth! and when it opens to speak! when it smiles! This mouth!—I hear someone coming.—I am still too jealous of you. *(as he turns the picture to the wall)* It must be Marinelli. If only I had not sent for him! What a morning I could have!

Scene 6

Marinelli, the Prince.

MARINELLI: My lord, forgive me.—I had not expected so early a summons.

THE PRINCE: I wanted to go for a drive. The morning was so beautiful.—But now the morning seems almost over, and I no longer feel like it.—*(after a short pause)* What is new, Marinelli?

MARINELLI: Nothing of importance, that I know of.—The Countess Orsina arrived in town yesterday.

THE PRINCE: And here already is her good morning, *(pointing to her letter)* or whatever else it may be! I am not at all curious about it.— You have spoken to her?

MARINELLI: Am I not unfortunately her confidant?—But if ever again I become one to a lady who decides to love you in all sincerity, then, Prince—

THE PRINCE: Swear to nothing, Marinelli!

MARINELLI: Yes? Is it true, Prince? Could it be?—Ah! Then perhaps the Countess is not so mistaken after all.

THE PRINCE: On the contrary, quite mistaken!—My approaching marriage with the Princess of Massa requires that I break off all that sort of thing for the present.

MARINELLI: If it were only that, then Orsina would of course have to be as resigned to her fate as the prince is to his.

THE PRINCE: Which is undeniably more cruel than hers. My heart is to be sacrificed to a miserable interest of state. Hers she only needs to take back, but she need not give it away against her will.

MARINELLI: Take it back? Why take it back? asks the Countess: if it is nothing more than a wife, who is brought to the Prince not by love but by politics? Beside such a wife, the mistress still sees her place. She does not fear being sacrificed to such a wife, but rather—

THE PRINCE: To a new love.—And what if she were? Do you mean to say that that would be a crime, Marinelli?

MARINELLI: I?—Ah! Please do not confuse me, my Prince, with the foolish lady whose case I plead,—plead out of pity. For yesterday, I must admit, she moved me most singularly. She did not want to speak of her relationship with you at all. She wanted to appear entirely calm and cool. But in the midst of the most casual conversation, one expression, one comment after the other slipped from her lips, betraying her tortured heart. In the gayest way she said the most melancholy things, and then again the most foolish nonsense with the saddest face. She has taken refuge in books and I fear they will give her the final blow.

THE PRINCE: Just as they gave her poor limited mind its first shock too.—But, my dear Marinelli, you are not trying to use the very thing that separated me from her, to get me to return?—If love makes her go mad, then sooner or later she would have gone mad even without love—And now enough of her.—Let us talk about something else!— Is nothing at all happening in the city?

MARINELLI: As good as nothing.—The fact that the marriage of Count Appiani is to take place today,—is not much more than nothing.

THE PRINCE: Of Count Appiani? and to whom, may I ask?—I have yet to hear that he is betrothed.

MARINELLI: The matter has been kept a great secret. I may add, there was not much to be made of it anyway.—You will laugh, my Prince. But that is how it is with these sensitive souls! Love always plays the worst tricks on them. A girl without fortune and without station has known how to ensnare him,—with a trace of good looks and a grand display of virtue and feeling and wit and so on.

THE PRINCE: The man who can abandon himself thus freely and

completely to the impression which innocence and beauty makes on him,—I should think he is more to be envied than to be laughed at.—And what is the name of this happy girl?—For after all, Appiani is—I know full well that you, Marinelli, do not like him, just as little as he likes you—yet after all, he is a very worthy young man, a handsome man, a rich man, a man of honor. It would have pleased me greatly had I been able to secure his services. I must give it further consideration.

MARINELLI: If it is not too late.—For, as I have heard, he does not plan to seek his fortune at court at all.—He intends to take his fair sovereign to his valleys in the Piedmont,—to hunt chamois in the Alps and to train marmots.—What more can he do? Here, of course, because of the misalliance which he is about to contract it is all over for him. From now on the circle of the best families is closed to him—

THE PRINCE: You and your best families!—where ceremony, restraint, boredom, and not infrequently paltriness reign supreme.—But now tell me the name of the girl for whom he makes his great sacrifice.

MARINELLI: It is a certain Emilia Galotti.

THE PRINCE: What, Marinelli? A certain—

MARINELLI: Emilia Galotti.

THE PRINCE: Emilia Galotti?—Never!

MARINELLI: Assuredly, my lord.

THE PRINCE: No, I say; that is not, that can not be true.—You are mistaken about the name.—The Galotti family is large.—It can be a Galotti; but not Emilia Galotti; not Emilia!

MARINELLI: Emilia—Emilia Galotti!

THE PRINCE: Then there is another one who has both those names.—In any case, you said, a certain Emilia Galotti—a certain one. Only a fool could speak of the real one in such a way.—

MARINELLI: You are beside yourself, my lord.—Do you know this Emilia Galotti?

THE PRINCE: I ask the questions, Marinelli, not my servants.—Emilia Galotti? The daughter of Colonel Galotti, of Sabionetta?

MARINELLI: The same.

THE PRINCE: Who lives here in Guastalla with her mother?

MARINELLI: The same.

THE PRINCE: Not far from the Church of All-Saints?

MARINELLI: The same.

THE PRINCE: In short—*(as he reaches for the portrait and puts it into Marinelli's hand)* Here!—This one? This Emilia Galotti?—Utter your accursed "the same" once more and drive the blade into my heart.

MARINELLI: The same!

THE PRINCE: Devil!—This one?—This Emilia Galotti, is to become this day—

MARINELLI: The Countess Appiani!—*(The Prince snatches the picture out of Marinelli's hand and throws it aside.)* The marriage is to take place quietly at the father's country estate near Sabionetta. Mother and daughter, the count, and perhaps a few friends will set out from here about noon.

THE PRINCE *(in desperation, throws himself into a chair):* Then I am lost!—Then I do not want to live!

MARINELLI: What is coming over you, my lord?

THE PRINCE *(springing up again and rushing toward him):* Traitor!— what is coming over me? I will tell you what; I love her, I worship her. Now you know! As though you had not known all along, all of you who would rather that I bear forever the shameful chains of the wild Orsina!—But that you, Marinelli, you who so often assured me of your most heartfelt friendship—oh, a prince has no friend! can have no friend!—that you, so faithlessly, so maliciously, could conceal from me, until this moment, the danger that was threatening my love: if ever I forgive you that—may no sin of mine be forgiven me!

MARINELLI: I can scarcely find words, Prince,—even if you were to let me—to show you my astonishment.—You love Emilia Galotti?— Well then, vow against vow: if I knew about this love, had as much as the slightest inkling of it, may neither saint nor angel lend me his ear.—And I would swear exactly the same of Orsina. Her suspicions are off on a completely different track.

THE PRINCE: Then forgive me, Marinelli,—*(throwing himself into his arms)* and have pity on me.

MARINELLI: Now then, Prince! Look at what your reserve has brought you!—"Princes have no friend! can have no friend!"—And the reason, if this is so!—Because they do not want one.—Today they honor us with their trust, share with us their most secret wishes, open the innermost recesses of their minds to us, and tomorrow we are again as much strangers to them as if they had never exchanged a single word with us.

THE PRINCE: Ah, Marinelli, how could I confide in you a thing I scarcely dared admit to myself?

MARINELLI: And which you have, no doubt, admitted even less to her who is the cause of your torment?

THE PRINCE: To her?—All my endeavors to speak with her a second time have been in vain.—

MARINELLI: And the first time—

THE PRINCE: I spoke with her—Oh, I am going mad! And you want me to explain at length?—You see me carried away by the flood: Why do you keep asking how it happened? Save me, if you can, and ask later.

MARINELLI: Save? Is there much to save?—What you neglected to confess, my lord, to Emilia Galotti, you will now confess to the Countess Appiani. Goods that one cannot have first hand, one buys secondhand:—and not infrequently all the cheaper for being secondhand.

THE PRINCE: Seriously, Marinelli, seriously, or—

MARINELLI: Though of course, all the worse, too—

THE PRINCE: Don't be impertinent!

MARINELLI: Moreover, the Count plans to leave the country with his catch.—Well, so we must think of something else.

THE PRINCE: And of what?—Dearest, most excellent Marinelli, think for me. What would you do, if you were in my place?

MARINELLI: First of all, consider a small matter a small matter—and tell myself that I do not propose to be what I am—the master—for nothing.

THE PRINCE: Do not flatter me with a power for which I see no use here.—Today you say? today already?

MARINELLI: Not till today—it still is to happen. And it is only things that have already happened that cannot be remedied.—*(after a moment's thought)* Will you allow me free rein, Prince? Will you agree to anything I do?

THE PRINCE: Anything, Marinelli, anything that can avert this blow.

MARINELLI: Then let us lose no time.—But do not stay in town. You must drive immediately to your villa, to Dosalo. The road to Sabionetta passes by there. If I do not succeed in getting the Count out of the way immediately, then I think—But, no; I am very sure he will fall into this trap. You are planning to send an envoy to Massa concerning your marriage, Prince, are you not? Let the Count be the envoy, on condition that he leave this very day.—Do I make myself clear?

THE PRINCE: Excellent!—Bring him out to me. Go, hurry. And I shall jump into my carriage at once. *(Exit Marinelli.)*

Scene 7

THE PRINCE: At once! At once!—Where is it?—*(looking at the portrait)* On the floor? That is mad. *(Picking it up)* But I cannot look at you now. For a while I do not want to look at you.—Why should I drive the arrow yet more deeply into the wound? *(setting it aside)*—I have yearned and sighed long enough,—longer than I ought, but I did nothing! and through this tactful inactivity, by a hair's breadth, all could have been lost!—And if all is lost even now? If Marinelli accomplishes nothing? Why should I rely on him all the way? It occurs to me,—at this hour, *(looking at the clock)* at this precise hour every morning, the devout girl goes to hear Mass in the Dominician Church.—What if I were to try to speak to her there?—But today, the day of her marriage—today she will be thinking of other things than the Mass.—And yet, who knows?—It is worth trying.— *(He rings, and as he hastily gathers together several of the papers on the desk, the valet enters.)* The carriage!—Has no councilor arrived yet?

THE VALET: Camillo Rota.

THE PRINCE: He is to come in. *(Exit valet.)* But he must not try to detain me. Not this time!—I will gladly wait on his scruples that much longer some other time.—But there was a petition from an Emilia Bruneschi.—*(searching for it)* This is it.—My dear Bruneschi, since she who pleads for you—

Scene 8

Camillo Rota, papers in hand. The Prince.

THE PRINCE: Come in Rota, come.—Here is what I have opened this morning. Not much to make one feel better.—You will see for yourself what decisions need to be made.—Take all this with you.

CAMILLO ROTA: Very good, my lord.

THE PRINCE: And here is a petition from a certain Emilia Galot . . . Bruneschi I mean.—I have already signed my consent.—And yet—it is no small matter—Let the official answer wait,—or not wait; as you wish.

CAMILLO ROTA: Not as I wish, my lord.

THE PRINCE: Is there anything more? Something to sign?

CAMILLO ROTA: A death sentence is to be signed.

THE PRINCE: With pleasure!—Just give it to me! Quickly.

CAMILLO ROTA (*startled and staring at the Prince in amazement*): A death sentence—I said.

THE PRINCE: I heard you.—The matter might be settled already. I am in a hurry.

CAMILLO ROTA (*looking through his papers*): I do not seem to have brought it along after all!—Forgive me, my lord. It can wait until tomorrow.

THE PRINCE: That too!—Now take your things: I must leave.—Tomorrow, Rota, we will go on! (*Exit.*)

CAMILLO ROTA (*shaking his head as he gathers up the papers and leaves*): With pleasure?—A death sentence, with pleasure?—I would not have wanted to let him sign it in such a moment, even if it had been for the murderer of my only son.—With pleasure! with pleasure!—It cuts me through and through, this horrible "With pleasure"!

Act II

Scene 1

A hall in the Galotti residence

Claudia Galotti, Pirro.

CLAUDIA (*entering, to Pirro, who enters from the opposite side*): Who came galloping into the court just now?

PIRRO: Our master, my lady.

CLAUDIA: My husband? Is that possible?

PIRRO: He follows me directly.

CLAUDIA: So unexpected?—(*hurrying toward him*) Ah! my dearest!—

Scene 2

Odoardo Galotti, Claudia Galotti, Pirro.

ODOARDO: Good morning, my dear!—This *is* a surprise, is it not?

CLAUDIA: And of the nicest sort!—Provided it is meant as a surprise.

ODOARDO: Nothing more! Do not worry.—The joy of this day awakened me so early; it was such a lovely morning; the trip is so short; I imagined you so busy here—How easily they may forget something! I suddenly thought.—In short: I come and see and leave again at once.—Where is Emilia? Undoubtedly busy making herself beautiful?—

CLAUDIA: Not herself, her soul!—She went to Mass.—"I must pray today, more than on any other day, for mercy from above," she said and left everything and took her veil and hurried—

ODOARDO: All alone?

CLAUDIA: Those few steps—

ODOARDO: One is enough to turn into a false step!—

CLAUDIA: Do not be angry, my dearest, and come in, to rest yourself for a moment and if you wish, to take some refreshment.

ODOARDO: As you please, Claudia.—But she should not have gone alone.—

CLAUDIA: And Pirro, you remain here in the anteroom to turn away all visitors for the rest of the day.

Scene 3

Pirro and shortly thereafter Angelo.

PIRRO: Those visitors, who come only out of curiosity anyway.—All the questions they have asked me this past hour!—But who is that coming there now?

ANGELO *(still partially offstage in a short coat, which he holds up to cover his face, his hat pulled down over his forehead):* Pirro!—Pirro!

PIRRO: Someone I know?—*(as Angelo comes into full view and throws open his coat)* Heavens! Angelo?—You?

ANGELO: As you see.—I walked around the house long enough, waiting for a chance to speak to you.—Just a word or two.—

PIRRO: And you dare show your face in broad daylight again?—After your last murder you were declared an outlaw; there is a price on your head—

ANGELO: Which surely you will not want to earn?—

PIRRO: What do you want? I beg you, do not get me into trouble.

ANGELO: With this perhaps? *(showing him a bag of money)*—Take it! It is yours!

PIRRO: Mine?

ANGELO: Have you forgotten? That German, your former master,—

PIRRO: Be quiet!

ANGELO: Whom you led into our trap on the way to Pisa—

PIRRO: If someone heard us!

ANGELO: Had the goodness to leave us a valuable ring, too.—Don't you remember?—It was too valuable, that ring, for us to exchange for money just then without arousing suspicion. I finally managed to get it done. I received one hundred pistoles for it: and this is your share. Take it!

PIRRO: I don't want any of it,—keep it all.

ANGELO: For all I care!—If it makes no difference to you how much you sell your head for—*(as if he were pocketing the bag again)*

PIRRO: All right then, give it to me! *(Takes it.)*—And now what? That you should look me up just for that—

ANGELO: Does not seem very likely to you?—Scoundrel! What do you think of us?—That we would deprive a man of his rightful due? That may be the fashion among so-called honest people, not among us.— Fare thee well!—*(He acts as if he were about to leave, then turns again.)* But one little question I want to ask anyway.—That was old man Galotti galloping all alone into town, wasn't it? What does he want?

PIRRO: He wants nothing; he simply felt like taking a ride. Tonight his daughter and Count Appiani are to be married on the estate from where he just came. He can't stand waiting for the moment—

ANGELO: And will soon ride away again?

PIRRO: So soon, that he will see you here, if you wait much longer.— But you cannot have any plot against him! Be careful. He is a man—

ANGELO: Don't I know him? Didn't I serve under him?—Anyway, there is not enough to be gotten out of him.—When do the young people follow?

PIRRO: Toward noon.

ANGELO: With a large group?

PIRRO: Just one carriage: the mother, the daughter, and the count. A few friends are coming from Sabionetta as witnesses.

ANGELO: And servants?

PIRRO: Only two besides me—I am to ride ahead on horseback.

ANGELO: Good.—One more thing: whose carriage is it? Is it yours? or the Count's?

PIRRO: The Count's.

ANGELO: Not good! Then there is a courier besides the able-bodied coachman. Still!—

PIRRO: I don't understand this. What do you want?—The bit of jewelry the bride might have, will hardly be worth the trouble—

ANGELO: Then the bride herself will make it worthwhile!

PIRRO: And in this crime too I am to be your accomplice?

ANGELO: You are to ride ahead. Ride on then, ride on! and pay no attention to anything else!

PIRRO: Never!

ANGELO: What? I almost think you want to play at having a conscience.—Listen, fellow! I think you know me.—If you blab! Or if every single thing is not exactly as you have described it!—

PIRRO: But Angelo, for Heaven's sake!—

ANGELO: Do what you cannot help doing! *(Exit.)*

PIRRO: Ha! let the Devil get you by one hair and you are his forever! Wretched me!

Scene 4

Odoardo and Claudia Galotti, Pirro.

ODOARDO: She is taking too long—

CLAUDIA: Just one minute more, Odoardo! It would grieve her to have missed seeing you.

ODOARDO: I must still go for a word with the Count. I can hardly wait for the moment when I may call that worthy young man my son. Everything about him delights me. And above all the decision to live his own life in the valleys of his ancestral estates.

CLAUDIA: It breaks my heart to think of it.—We shall lose her so completely, our only, beloved daughter.

ODOARDO: How do you mean, lose her? To know her in the arms of love? Do not confuse your joy in her with her own happiness.—You might renew my old suspicion:—that it was more the excitement and diversion of the world, more the nearness to the court than the necessity of giving our daughter a proper education, that made you stay here in the city with her—away from a husband and father who loves you both so deeply.

CLAUDIA: How unfair, Odoardo! But let me say just one thing today for this city, for this nearness to the court which are so odious to your strict sense of virtue.—Here, only here could love bring together what was meant to be together. Only here could the Count find Emilia, and here he did find her.

ODOARDO: I will grant that. But, dear Claudia, were you right, just because the outcome is right?—I am glad that it turned out this way, with this city education! Let us not claim we were wise, when in fact we were only lucky! I am glad that it all turned out this way!—Now they have found each other; now let them go where a life of virtue and peace awaits them.—What should the Count do here? Bow and flatter and grovel and try to outdo the Marinellis only in order to attain in the end the kind of success he does not need? Only to be considered in the end worthy of an honor which for him would be no honor?—Pirro!

PIRRO: Here I am.

ODOARDO: Go and take my horse to the Count's house. I will follow and remount there. *(Exit Pirro.)*—Why should the Count be servant here, when there he can be master?—Then too, you have not considered that through our daughter he has ruined his chances with the Prince entirely. The prince hates me—

CLAUDIA: Perhaps less than you fear.

ODOARDO: Fear! I should fear such a thing!

CLAUDIA: Have I told you yet that the Prince has seen our daughter?

ODOARDO: The Prince? And where was that?

CLAUDIA: During the last soiree given by the Chancellor Grimaldi, which he honored with his presence. He acted so graciously toward her—

ODOARDO: So graciously?

CLAUDIA: He talked with her for such a long time—

ODOARDO: Talked with her?

CLAUDIA: Seemed so entranced with her gaiety and wit—

ODOARDO: So entranced?—

CLAUDIA: Has spoken of her beauty with such high praise—

ODOARDO: High praise? And you tell me all this in a tone of delight? Oh Claudia! Claudia! Vain, foolish mother!

CLAUDIA: Why?

ODOARDO: All right, all right! That too has turned out well.—Ha! If I imagine—That is just the spot where I could be hurt most mortally!—A libertine who admires, covets.—Claudia! Claudia! the mere thought puts me into a rage.—You should have told me of this immediately.—And yet, I do not want to say anything unpleasant to you today. And I would *(as she grasps his hand)*, if I stayed longer.— So let me be! let me be!—God be with you, Claudia!—And have a safe trip following me!

Scene 5

CLAUDIA GALOTTI: What a man!—O the harshness of virtue!—if indeed it deserves that name.—To it everything seems suspicious, everything guilty!—Or, if that is called knowing people:—who would want to know them?—But what is keeping Emilia?—He is her father's enemy: it follows—it follows that if he has an eye for his daughter, it can only be to shame him?—

Scene 6

Emilia, Claudia Galotti.

EMILIA *(rushes in, frightened and distraught)*: Thank heaven! Thank heaven! Now I am safe. Or did he perhaps follow me? *(as she throws back her veil and sees her mother)* Did he, my mother? did he?—No, heaven be thanked!

CLAUDIA: What is it, my daughter? what is it?

EMILIA: Nothing, nothing—

CLAUDIA: And still you look so wildly about you? And tremble all over?

EMILIA: What did I have to hear! And where, where did I have to hear it!

CLAUDIA: I thought you were in church—

EMILIA: Even there. What does church and altar mean to vice?—Oh, Mother! *(throwing herself into her arms)*

CLAUDIA: Speak, my daughter!—Resolve my fears.—What dreadful thing could have befallen you there, in a sacred place?

EMILIA: Never should my devotion have been more intense, more ardent than today; never has it been less what it ought to be.

CLAUDIA: We are human beings, Emilia. The gift of prayer is not always within our power. For Heaven the desire to pray is the same as prayer.

EMILIA: And the desire to sin is the same as sinning.

CLAUDIA: That my Emilia did not desire!

EMILIA: No, my mother, God's grace did not let me sink so low. But oh, that another's vice can make us guilty with him against our will!

CLAUDIA: Pull yourself together: —Collect your thoughts, as best you can.—Tell me at once what happened to you.

EMILIA: I had just—farther from the altar than usual, for I arrived late—gone down on my knees. I had just begun to lift up my heart to God, when something took a place behind me. So close behind me!—I could move neither forward nor aside,—much as I wanted to, for fear that I was letting another's prayers disturb me in mine.— Prayers! that was the worst that I feared.—But it was not long before I heard, close to my ear,—the name,—do not be angry with me, my mother—the name of your daughter!—my name!—Oh, would that claps of thunder had kept me from hearing more!—It spoke of beauty, of love—It complained that this day which was to bring me happiness—if indeed it did—would forever decide the speaker's unhappiness.—It implored me—All this I had to hear. But I did not turn around; I wanted to act as though I did not hear it—What else could I do?—Beg my guardian angel to strike me deaf, were it, were it forever!—That I begged; that was all I could pray.—Finally it was time to rise again. The Mass was over. I trembled at the thought of turning around. I trembled at the thought of seeing the one who had allowed himself such desecration. And when I turned around, when I saw who it was—

CLAUDIA: Who, my daughter?

EMILIA: Guess, my mother, guess.—I thought I would sink into the earth.—He himself.

CLAUDIA: Who himself?

EMILIA: The prince.

CLAUDIA: The prince!—O, blessed be the impatience of your father, who was just here and would not wait for you!

EMILIA: My father here!—and would not wait for me?

CLAUDIA: If in your distraught state you had let him hear this, too!

EMILIA: Speak, my mother?—What could he have found wrong in what I did?

CLAUDIA: No more than in what I did. And yet, yet—Ah, you do not know your father! In his wrath it would have seemed to him that I had caused what I could neither prevent nor foresee.—But go on, my daughter, go on! When you recognized the prince—I hope you were sufficiently in control of yourself to show him in one look all the scorn that he deserves.

EMILIA: That I was not, my mother! After that first look with which I recognized him, I did not have the courage to cast another in his direction. I fled—

CLAUDIA: And the prince followed you—

EMILIA: Which I did not know until in the outer hall I felt myself grasped by the hand. And by him! My sense of shame made me stay still; breaking from his grasp would have attracted the attention of the passersby. That was all I could think of—or all I can now remember having thought. He spoke; and I answered him. But what he spoke, what I answered him, if I ever remember it, then of course, then I will tell you, my mother. Now I know nothing about what happened. My senses had left me.—In vain do I try to remember how I came away from him and out of the hall. When I reached the street, I finally regained my senses; and heard him come after me; and heard him enter the house with me, climb the stairs with me—

CLAUDIA: Fear has its own peculiar sense, my daughter!—I shall never forget the expression on your face when you came rushing in.—No, he could not have dared follow you so far.—Oh God! Oh God! if your father knew this!—How wild he already was when he merely heard that the prince had met you recently and had not seemed displeased!—However, calm yourself, my daughter! Take what has happened to you as a dream. Indeed, it will have fewer consequences than even a dream. Today you will escape his pursuit, once and for all.

EMILIA: But you agree, my mother, do you not? The count must know this. I must tell him.

CLAUDIA: Not for anything in the world! Why? What for? Do you want to perturb him for a thing that is less than nothing? And even if he is not perturbed by it now: let me assure you, my child, a poison which does not work immediately is not for that reason a less dangerous poison. A thing that makes no impression on the lover, can still make one on the husband. It might even flatter the lover to get the better of so important a rival. But once he has gotten the better of him: ah! my child,—then very often the lover turns into a very different creature. May your lucky star spare you that lesson.

EMILIA: You know, my mother, how eager I am to submit to your better judgment in everything.—But if he were to hear from someone else that the prince spoke to me today? Would not my silence, sooner or later, increase his concern?—I should think, it would be better not to keep anything from him that I have on my mind.

CLAUDIA: Weakness! lovers' weakness!—No, by no means, no, my daughter! Tell him nothing. Let him suspect nothing!

EMILIA: Then so be it! I have no will to oppose yours.—Aah! *(drawing a deep breath)* Now I feel much easier.—What a foolish, timid thing I am!—Is that not true, my mother?—I might well have behaved differently and still have just as little compromised myself.

CLAUDIA: I did not want to tell you that, my daughter, until your own common sense told you. And I knew it would tell you, as soon as you had come to yourself again.—The prince is a man of the world. You are too little accustomed to the trifling language of the world. In it a mere courtesy assumes the appearance of true emotion, a flattery that of a protestation, a whim appears as a desire, a desire as a decision. A nothing sounds in this language like everything, and everything in it is as much as nothing.

EMILIA: O mother!—I must indeed feel quite foolish having had such fears!—Now he will certainly hear nothing about it, my good Appiani! He might well think me more vain than virtuous.—Ah! there he comes himself! It is his step.

Scene 7

Count Appiani, Emilia and Claudia Galotti.

APPIANI *(enters deep in thought, with downcast eyes and advances without seeing Emilia until she rushes toward him)*: Ah, my dearest!—I did not expect you to be here in the anteroom.

EMILIA: I would like you to be cheerful, my Count, even when you do not suspect my presence.—So solemn? so serious?—Does not this day seem worthy of a more joyful emotion?

APPIANI: It is of greater worth than my entire life. But promising so much bliss for me,—perhaps it is this very bliss that makes me so serious, makes me, as you call it, my lady, so solemn.—*(noticing her mother)* Ha! you too are here, madam!—whom soon I shall revere by a more tender name!

CLAUDIA: Which will be my greatest pride!—How fortunate you are, my Emilia!—Why did not your father want to share our delight?

APPIANI: I have just torn myself from his arms,—or rather he from mine.—What a man, my Emilia, your father! A paragon of all manly virtues! In his presence my soul is raised to such lofty thoughts! Never is my resolve to be ever noble, ever virtuous, more alive than when I see him,—when I think of him. And how, except by realizing this resolve, can I make myself worthy of the honor of being yours and thus being called his son, my Emilia?

EMILIA: And he did not want to wait for me!

APPIANI: I think it was because for so short a visit his Emilia would have moved him too greatly, would have overwhelmed him too completely in his innermost being.

CLAUDIA: He expected to find you busy with your bridal dress, and heard—

APPIANI: What I then heard from him with the most tender admiration.—That is right, my Emilia! In you I will have a God-fearing wife and one who is not proud of her piety.

CLAUDIA: But, my children, while doing one thing neglect not the other!—Now it is high time; go now, Emilia!

APPIANI: To do what, madam?

CLAUDIA: You do not want to lead her to the altar, Count, like that, as she is now?

APPIANI: It is true, I only notice it now.—Who can look at you, Emilia, and pay attention to your dress?—And why not like that, as she is now?

EMILIA: No, my dear Count, not like this, not quite. But not much more splendid either, not much.—One little moment and I am ready!—Nothing, nothing at all from the set of jewels, the most recent gift of your extravagant generosity! Nothing, nothing at all that would only go with such jewelry!—I could resent it, this jewelry, if it were not from you.—For I have dreamed of it three times—

CLAUDIA: You did? You had not told me.

EMILIA: As if I were wearing it, and as if suddenly every stone in it turned into a pearl.—But pearls, my mother, pearls mean tears.

CLAUDIA: Child! The meaning is more of a dream than the dream itself.—Have you not always liked pearls better than stones?—

EMILIA: True, mother, quite true—

APPIANI *(pensive and sad):* Pearls mean tears!—mean tears!

EMILIA: What? That strikes you? You?

APPIANI: Yes, it is true; I should be ashamed of myself.—But once the imagination is keyed to unhappy visions—

EMILIA: But why should it be?—Now, what would you imagine I have decided?—What was I wearing, how did I look, the first time you felt attracted to me?—Do you remember?

APPIANI: Do I remember? In my thoughts, I see you just so, and just so I see you even when I do not see you so.

EMILIA: Well then, a dress of that same color, of that same cut; wide and loose—

APPIANI: Excellent!

EMILIA: And my hair—

APPIANI: In its own russet brilliance; in curls, as nature formed them—

EMILIA: Let us not forget the rose in it! Right! Right!—A little patience, and I will stand before you just so!

Scene 8

Count Appiani, Claudia Galotti.

APPIANI *(glancing after her with a downcast expression):* Pearls mean tears!—A little patience?—Yes, if only time were outside of us!—If a minute by the hand of the clock were not able to expand in us into years!—

CLAUDIA: Emilia's observation, Count, was as quick as it was correct. You are more serious today than usual. One last step away from the goal of your longing,—could it be that you regret, Count, that it was the goal of your longing?

APPIANI: Oh, my mother, can you suspect this of your son?—Yet it is true that I am unusually sad and gloomy today.—But consider, madam:—being one last step away from the goal or not having started out yet, is actually the same thing.—Since yesterday and the day before yesterday, all that I see, all that I hear, all that I dream has argued this truth. This *one* thought attaches itself to every other thought that I am made to have and that I want to have.—What is that? I do not understand it.—

CLAUDIA: You perturb me, Count—

APPIANI: One thing leads thus to another!—I am angry—angry at my friends and angry at myself—

CLAUDIA: Why?

APPIANI: My friends insist as a matter of course that I inform the prince of my marriage, before it takes place. They admit that I do not owe it to him, but respect toward him forbids every other course. And I was weak enough to give them this promise. I was just planning to drive to the palace.

CLAUDIA *(startled):* To the prince's palace?

Scene 9

Pirro, followed immediately by Marinelli, Count Appiani, Claudia Galotti.

PIRRO: Madam, the Marquis Marinelli is at the door asking for the count.

APPIANI: For me?

PIRRO: Here he is already. *(Opens the door for him and leaves.)*

MARINELLI: I beg your pardon, madam.—Count, I stopped at your house and was told that I could find you here. I have an urgent message for you—madam, I beg your pardon once more; we will be through in a few moments.

CLAUDIA: Which I do not want to delay. *(Curtsies and leaves.)*

Scene 10

Marinelli, Appiani.

APPIANI: Well, sir?

MARINELLI: I come from His Highness the Prince.

APPIANI: What is his command?

MARINELLI: I am proud to be the bearer of so distinguished a privilege.—And if Count Appiani will not stubbornly refuse to recognize in me one of his most devoted friends—

APPIANI: Without further preliminaries, if you please.

MARINELLI: Very well!—The Prince must immediately send an envoy to the Duke of Massa in matters concerning his marriage to the Princess, the Duke's daughter. He was long undecided about whom he should appoint. At long last, Count, his choice fell upon you.

APPIANI: Upon me?

MARINELLI: And that—if friendship may be boastful—not without a word from me.—

APPIANI: In truth, you make it hard for me to find words to thank you.—I had long since stopped expecting that the prince might ever deign to use my services.—

MARINELLI: I am certain that he merely lacked a worthy occasion. And if this too should not be deemed worthy of a man such as the Count: then I admit that my friendship was too hasty.

APPIANI: Every third word is friendship!—With whom am I speaking? I would never have dreamed of the friendship of the Marquis Marinelli.—

MARINELLI: I recognize my error, Count,—my unforgivable error, of wanting to be your friend without your permission.—In the face of all this, what does it matter? The offer of the prince, the honor bestowed upon you remain what they are, and I am sure you will accept them most eagerly.

APPIANI *(after a few moments' reflection):* I do.

MARINELLI: Well then, come.

APPIANI: Where to?

MARINELLI: To Dosalo, to the Prince.—Everything is ready; you are to leave before this day is over.

APPIANI: What did you say?—This day?

MARINELLI: Better this very hour than the one following. The matter is of the utmost urgency.

APPIANI: Really?—Then I am sorry that I must decline the honor the Prince had intended for me.

MARINELLI: What?

APPIANI: I cannot leave today;—not tomorrow;—nor even the day after tomorrow.—

MARINELLI: You are jesting, Count.

APPIANI: With you?

MARINELLI: Incomparable, indeed! If the jest involves the prince, it is only the funnier.—You cannot leave today?

APPIANI: No, sir, no.—And I hope that the Prince himself will find my excuse valid.

MARINELLI: I am anxious to hear it.

APPIANI: Oh, a small matter!—You see, this very day I am to take a wife.

MARINELLI: Well? And so?

APPIANI: And so?—and so?—Your question is dreadfully naive.

MARINELLI: There have been instances, Count, to show that marriages can be postponed.—I do not think, of course, that the bride's or the groom's interests are always served that way. The matter may have its unpleasant sides. And yet, I should think, a command from the master—

APPIANI: A command from the master? the master? A master whom we ourselves choose is not exactly our master—I admit that you owe the Prince unqualified obedience. But not I.—I came to his court of my own free will. I wanted the honor of serving him but not of becoming his slave. I am the vassal of a greater master—

MARINELLI: Greater or smaller: master is master.

APPIANI: That I should argue this with you!—Enough, tell the Prince what you have heard:—that I am sorry to be unable to accept his trust; because this very day I am to contract an alliance upon which all my happiness depends.

MARINELLI: Would you not, at the same time, inform him to whom?

APPIANI: To Emilia Galotti.

MARINELLI: The daughter of this house?

APPIANI: Of this house.

MARINELLI: Hm! hm!

APPIANI: You wish to say something?

MARINELLI: I should think, in that case it would be still easier to postpone the ceremony till after you return.

APPIANI: The ceremony? Just the ceremony?

MARINELLI: The good parents will not be so particular.

APPIANI: The good parents?

MARINELLI: And Emilia will no doubt remain true to you.

APPIANI: No doubt true?-You with your "no doubt"—are no doubt a complete jackass!

MARINELLI: You say that to me, Count?

APPIANI: Why not?

MARINELLI: Heaven and Hell!—You shall answer for this.

APPIANI: Bah! This jackass is a spiteful one; but—

MARINELLI: Death and damnation!—I demand satisfaction, Count.

APPIANI: Obviously.

MARINELLI: And would take it right now;—except that I do not want to ruin this day for the loving groom.

APPIANI: Kindhearted creature! But don't, don't! *(grasping his hand)* It is true, I don't feel like being sent to Massa today; but I do have time to spare for a walk with you.—Come with me, come!

MARINELLI *(who frees himself and leaves):* Just wait, Count, just wait!

Scene 11

Appiani, Claudia Galotti.

APPIANI: Go, you vile creature!—Ha! that did me good. It made my blood boil. I feel different and better.

CLAUDIA *(in haste and with grave concern)*: Great God! Count—I heard sharp words between you.—Your face is flushed. What happened?

APPIANI: Nothing, madam, nothing at all. The Chamberlain Marinelli has done me a great service. He has spared me the trip to the prince.

CLAUDIA: Really?

APPIANI: Now we can leave that much earlier. I go now to tell my men to hurry and shall be back at once. Meanwhile Emilia will be ready, too.

CLAUDIA: Can I be completely reassured, Count?

APPIANI: Completely reassured, madam. *(She goes inside and he leaves.)*

Act III

Scene 1

An anteroom in the Prince's villa

The Prince, Marinelli.

MARINELLI: All for nothing; he turned down the proffered honor with the utmost disdain.

THE PRINCE: And so everything remains as before? So it will happen? So this very day Emilia will become his?

MARINELLI: It would seem so.

THE PRINCE: I had hoped for so much from your idea!—Who knows how stupidly you went about it.—If a fool happens to have a good idea, then a clever man must carry it out. I should have remembered that.

MARINELLI: What a nice reward!

THE PRINCE: Reward for what?

MARINELLI: For being ready to risk my life in this business.—When I saw that neither serious talk nor banter could move the Count to place honor above love, I tried to rouse his wrath. I said things to him which made him forget himself. He hurled insults at me and I demanded satisfaction—and demanded it then and there.—I thought of it this way: either he me, or I him. I him: then our path is clear. Or he me: well, even so; then he must flee and the Prince wins at least time.

THE PRINCE: You would have done that, Marinelli?

MARINELLI: Ha! one should realize beforehand, when one is so foolishly prepared to sacrifice oneself for the great—one should realize beforehand how grateful they will be—

THE PRINCE: And the Count?—He has the reputation of being one who, in such matters, does not wait to be told a second time.

MARINELLI: As the case may be, no doubt.—Who can blame him?—He said he had more important things to attend to today than blowing his brains out with me. And so he called me for eight days after his marriage.

THE PRINCE: To Emilia Galotti! The very thought drives me wild!—On that note you let things go and departed—and now you come and boast that you risked your life for me, sacrificed yourself for me—

MARINELLI: But what more, my lord, would you have had me do?

THE PRINCE: What more?—As if he had done something!

MARINELLI: Let me hear then, my lord, what you have done for yourself.—You were fortunate enough to speak once more with her in church. What did you arrange with her?

THE PRINCE (*scornfully*): Curiosity more than enough!—which I am just needed to satisfy.—Oh, everything went as I wished.—You need not trouble yourself any more, my all too obliging friend!—She met my wishes more than half-way. I could have taken her with me right away. (*coldly and in a commanding tone*) Now you know what you want to know—and can go!

MARINELLI: And can go!—Yes, of course, of course; that is the end of the song! and would be, even supposing that I still wanted to try the impossible.—The impossible, I say?—It would not be so impossible, but daring!—If we had the bride in our power, I would guarantee that nothing would come of the marriage.

THE PRINCE: Aye! Just hear how much that man would guarantee! Now I need but give him a detachment of my guard and he would lie in ambush at the roadside and attack, fifty strong, a carriage and drag out a girl, whom he would triumphantly bring to me.

MARINELLI: It has happened before that a girl was abducted by force, without its appearing like a forced abduction.

THE PRINCE: If you knew how to do that, you would not spend so much time talking about it.

MARINELLI: But one should not have to account for the results.—There might be accidents—

THE PRINCE: And of course I am in the habit of holding people to account for things they cannot help!

MARINELLI: Well then, my lord—*(a shot is heard in the distance.)* Ha! what was that?—Did I hear right?—Did you not hear a shot also, my lord?—And there another!

THE PRINCE: What is that? what is happening?

MARINELLI: What do you suppose?—What if I were more a man of action than you think?

THE PRINCE: Of action?—Out with it, speak—

MARINELLI: In short: what I was talking about is happening.

THE PRINCE: Can it be?

MARINELLI: But do not forget, Prince, the assurances you gave me just now.—I have your word again—

THE PRINCE: But the arrangements are—

MARINELLI: As best as could be!—The execution of the plan is in the hands of people whom I can trust. The road goes hard by the enclosure of the animal park. There, one party will have attacked the carriage, as it were, to plunder it. And another party, in which I put one of my servants, will have rushed out of the park to the aid, as it were, of the attacked. In the ensuing scuffle, which both parties pretend to enter, my servant is to seize Emilia, as if wanting to save her, and bring her through the park to the villa.—That is the plan.— What do you say now, Prince?

THE PRINCE: You surprise me in a most singular manner.—A feeling of apprehension wells up in me—*(Marinelli steps to the window.)* What are you looking for?

MARINELLI: It must be over there!—Right!—and a masked man already comes galloping from around the enclosure;—undoubtedly to report to me the results.—Leave me for a moment, my lord.

THE PRINCE: Ah, Marinelli—

MARINELLI: Well? You mean, do you not, that now I have done too much, as before I did too little?

THE PRINCE: It is not that. But still, I cannot imagine—

MARINELLI: Imagine?—Better see it then as an accomplished fact!— Now leave quickly.—The masked man must not see you. *(Exit the Prince.)*

Scene 2

Marinelli and shortly thereafter Angelo.

MARINELLI *(who steps once more to the window):* Over there the carriage is slowly returning to the city.—That slowly? And at every door a servant?—Those are signs I do not like: that the plan was only half successful;—that they are gently taking away a wounded man—and not a dead one.—The masked man dismounts.—It is Angelo himself. Reckless fool!—Well, after all, here he knows his way around.—He is signaling to me. He must be sure of himself.—Ha, my dear Count, you who did not want to go to Massa and now must go much farther!—Who taught you so much about jackasses? *(going toward the door)* They are spiteful indeed.—Well, Angelo?

ANGELO *(who has removed his mask):* Just watch, Chamberlain! They will bring her right away.

MARINELLI: And how did it go otherwise?

ANGELO: Quite well, I think.

MARINELLI: How is the Count?

ANGELO: So, so! If you please.—But he must have had wind of what was coming. For he was not completely unprepared.

MARINELLI: Tell me quickly what you have to tell!—Is he dead?

ANGELO: I feel sorry for the good man.

MARINELLI: Well then, take this for your soft heart! *(Gives him a purse with gold.)*

ANGELO: To top it all, my brave old Nicolo, he too was made to pay for it.

MARINELLI: So? Casualties on both sides?

ANGELO: I could cry over the loss of that honest boy! Although his death makes this *(weighing the purse in his hand)* better for me by one-fourth. For I am his heir, since I avenged him. That is a law with us: as good a one, I think, as was ever made for faith and friendship. This Nicolo, Chamberlain—

MARINELLI: You and your Nicolo!—But what about the Count, the Count—?

ANGELO: Dash it! The Count got him squarely. And for that I got the Count!—He fell; and if he got back into the coach alive, I guarantee he will not get out of it alive.

MARINELLI: As long as that is certain, Angelo.

ANGELO: I will gladly lose your patronage, if it is not certain!—Is there anything else I can do for you? You know, I have the longest way to go: we still want to get across the border today.

MARINELLI: Then go!

ANGELO: If something else comes up, Chamberlain,—you know where I can be reached. What someone else dares do, will not be magic for me either. And I am cheaper than anyone else. *(Exit.)*

MARINELLI: Well, that is all right!—And yet, not altogether all right.— For shame, Angelo! to be so niggardly! After all, he would have been worth a second shot.—And how much he may have to suffer now, the poor Count!—For shame, Angelo! I call that doing one's handiwork cruelly—and bungling it.—But of that the Prince need not be told for a while. First let him realize how well this death suits him.—This death!—What would I not give for the certainty of it!—

Scene 3

The Prince, Marinelli.

THE PRINCE: There she is, coming up the esplanade. She is hurrying on ahead of the servant. Fear, it seems, has set wings to her feet. She does not seem to suspect anything. She thinks she is saving herself from bandits, and no more.—But how long can that last?

MARINELLI: At least we have her now.

THE PRINCE: And won't her mother come for her? Won't the Count follow her? What will we have gained then? How can I keep her from them?

MARINELLI: I must admit that I have no answers to all that as yet. But we shall see. Be patient, my lord. The first step had to be taken first—

THE PRINCE: What for? If we have to retrace it later!

MARINELLI: Maybe we shall not have to.—There are a thousand and one things for us to build on.—And are you not forgetting the point that is the most important of all?

THE PRINCE: How can I forget what apparently I have not even thought of?—The most important point? what is that?

MARINELLI: The art of pleasing, of persuading,—which a Prince, who loves, never lacks.

THE PRINCE: Never lacks? Except when he needs it most.—I have already made an all too miserable attempt at this art today. With every possible kind of flattery and vow I yet could not get a single word out of her. Mute and trembling, with downcast eyes she stood there, like a criminal hearing her death sentence. Her fear was contagious; I trembled with her and finally begged her forgiveness. I scarcely dare speak to her again.—At her entrance, at least, I dare not be present. You, Marinelli, must receive her. I shall listen nearby to see how matters go, and shall come when I have recovered my composure.

Scene 4

Marinelli and shortly thereafter his servant, Battista, with Emilia.

MARINELLI: If only she did not herself see him fall.—But I suppose she did not, since she hurried away so quickly—There she comes. I prefer not to be the first thing she lays eyes on here. (*He withdraws into a corner of the room.*)

EMILIA (*out of breath*): Oh!—Oh!—I thank you, my friend; I thank you.—But Lord, oh Lord! where am I?—And completely alone? Where is my mother? Where did the Count go?—They are coming too, aren't they? right after me?

BATTISTA: I think so.

EMILIA: You think so? You do not know? You did not see them?— Wasn't there shooting right behind us?—

BATTISTA: Shooting?—What a terrible thing to say!—

EMILIA: I am certain of it! And it hit the Count or my mother.—

BATTISTA: I will go out after them right away.

EMILIA: Not without me.—I want to go with you; I must go with you: come, my friend!

MARINELLI (*joining them suddenly as though he had just entered*): Ah, my lady! What misfortune, or rather what good fortune,—what fortunate misfortune brings us the honor—

EMILIA (*startled*): What? You here, sir?—Then I must be on your estate?—Forgive me, Chamberlain. We were attacked by bandits not far from here. Some good people came to our rescue;—and this honest man lifted me from the carriage and brought me here.—But I am terrified, seeing myself saved alone. My mother is still in danger. And behind us there was shooting. Perhaps she is dead;—and I live?—You will excuse me. I must go; I must go back,—where I should have stayed to begin with.

MARINELLI: Calm yourself, my lady. All is well; they will be with you shortly, your loved ones, for whom you feel such tender fears.—In the meantime, Battista, go, hurry: perhaps they do not know where the young lady is. Perhaps they are looking for her in one of the buildings in the park. Bring them here immediately. (*Exit Battista.*)

EMILIA: Are you certain? Are they all safe? did nothing happen to

them?—Ah, what a day of horrors this day has been for me!—But I
should not stay here; I should hurry out to meet them—

MARINELLI: Why, my lady! As it is, you are breathless and exhausted.
You should recover instead and, if you please, move to another room
where there is more comfort.—I wager the Prince himself is already
with your beloved venerable mother and is bringing her to you.

EMILIA: Who did you say?

MARINELLI: Our most gracious Prince himself.

EMILIA *(in utmost confusion)*: The Prince?

MARINELLI: As soon as he heard the news he hastened to your aid.—
He is highly incensed that such a crime could be perpetrated so close
by, under his very eyes as it were. He has ordered the pursuit of those
daring criminals, and their punishment, if they are caught, will be
commensurate with the deed.

EMILIA: The Prince!—Where am I then?

MARINELLI: At Dosalo, the Prince's villa.

EMILIA: What a coincidence!—And you think he himself might come
in here presently?—But certainly in the company of my mother?

MARINELLI: Here he is now.

Scene 5

The Prince, Emilia, Marinelli.

THE PRINCE: Where is she? where?—We are looking for you everywhere, my dear young lady.—But you are well, are you not?—Then
all is well! The Count, your mother—

EMILIA: Ah, my lord! where are they? Where is my mother?

THE PRINCE: Not far; just a few steps away.

EMILIA: God, in what state will I find perhaps the one or the other!
Find most certainly!—For you are hiding from me, my lord—I see it,
you are hiding from me—

THE PRINCE: But of course not, my dear young lady.—Give me your
arm and come with me without fear.

EMILIA *(uncertain)*: But—if nothing has happened to them—if my
premonitions deceive me:—why are they not here? Why did they not
come with you, my lord?

THE PRINCE: All the more reason to hurry, my lady, to see all these
visions of horror vanish at once.

EMILIA: What shall I do? *(wringing her hands)*

THE PRINCE: What, my lady? Could you be doubting me?

EMILIA *(falling down before him):* At your feet, my lord—

THE PRINCE *(raising her):* I am most terribly mortified.—Yes, Emilia, I deserve this silent reproach.—My behavior this morning is not to be justified,—to be forgiven at the very most. Excuse my weakness. I should not have harried you with a confession of which I can expect no advantage. And it was but right that you punished me by the speechless dismay with which you listened, or rather did not listen.— And even if I could declare this fortuitous meeting, which gives me once more, before all my hope vanishes forever,—which gives me once more the joy of seeing you, of speaking to you—even if I could declare this fortuitous meeting to be an omen of fortune's favor and the most miraculous delay in my final doom, to be allowed to beg once more to be heard: still I must—do not tremble, my lady—put myself entirely at the mercy of the decision I shall read in your eyes. No word, no sigh is to insult you.—Only, do not wrong me with your mistrust. Only, do not doubt for a single moment the most boundless power you have over me. Only, may you never think that you are in need of further protection against me.—And now come, my lady,—come to where delights await you which you will find more to your liking. *(He leads her away, not without resistance on her part.)* Follow us, Marinelli.—

MARINELLI: Follow us,—that probably means: follow us not!—And why should I follow them anyway? Let him see for himself how far he succeeds with her with no one else about.—All I have to do is—to prevent their being disturbed. At least not by the Count, I have reason to hope. But by the mother; by the mother! I should be very much surprised if she withdrew so quietly and left her daughter to her fate.—Well, Battista? what is it?

Scene 6

Battista, Marinelli.

BATTISTA *(in great haste):* The mother, Chamberlain—

MARINELLI: Just as I thought!—Where is she?

BATTISTA: If you do not forestall her, she will be here in a moment.—I was not trying to look for her at all, as you bade me pretend to do, when I heard her cries from afar. She knows where her daughter is and—Heaven forbid—everything else about our scheme. Not a human being in this lonely region but has joined the crowd around her, and everybody wants to be the one to show her the way. I do not know whether she has been told yet that the Prince is here, that you are here.—What are you going to do?

MARINELLI: Let me see!—*(He thinks.)* Deny her entrance when she knows that her daughter is here?—That won't do.—Of course, she will rub her eyes when she sees the wolf with her little lamb.—Rub her eyes? That would be just fine. But Heaven have mercy on our ears!—What of it? the best of lungs get tired, even a woman's.—They all stop screaming when they are exhausted. Then too, let us not forget, the mother is precisely the one we ought to have on our side.—If I know mothers:—to be a sort of mother-in-law of a Prince, flatters most of them.—Let her come, Battista, let her come!

CLAUDIA GALOTTI *(within):* Emilia! Emilia! My child, where are you?

MARINELLI: Go, Battista, and try at least to get rid of her prying companions.

Scene 7

Claudia Galotti, Battista, Marinelli.

CLAUDIA *(stepping in at the door, as Battista tries to leave):* Ha! he is the one who lifted her out of the carriage! He led her away! I recognize you. Where is she? Speak, you wretch!

BATTISTA: Is that how you thank me?

CLAUDIA: Oh, if you deserve to be thanked *(in a mild tone)*—then forgive me, good man!—Where is she?—Do not keep me from her any longer. Where is she?

BATTISTA: Ah, madam, she could not be better cared for were she in Paradise.—My master here will lead you to her. *(to several people, trying to follow)* Get back, there! You!

Scene 8

Claudia Galotti, Marinelli.

CLAUDIA: Your master?—*(Sees Marinelli and shrinks back.)*—Oh!—That—your master?—You here, sir? And my daughter here, too? And you, you are to lead me to her?

MARINELLI: With great pleasure, madam.

CLAUDIA: Wait!—I just remember—it was you—was it not?—who came to my home this morning to see the Count? with whom I left him alone? with whom he argued?

MARINELLI: Argued?—Not, as I took it: an insignificant exchange of words in matters concerning the realm.

CLAUDIA: And Marinelli is your name?

MARINELLI: Marquis Marinelli.

CLAUDIA: Then it fits.—Listen to me, Marquis.—Marinelli was—the name Marinelli was the last word spoken by the dying Count.

MARINELLI: The dying Count? Count Appiani?—You hear, madam, what strikes me most in your strange speech.—The dying Count? Whatever else you are trying to say, I do not understand.

CLAUDIA (*bitterly and slowly*): The name Marinelli was the last word spoken by the dying Count!—Do you understand now?—At first I did not understand it either, although it was said in a tone—in a tone!—I hear him still! Where were my senses, that they did not grasp the meaning of this tone that very moment?

MARINELLI: Well, madam?—I have always been the Count's friend, his closest friend. So, if he spoke my name in dying—

CLAUDIA: In that tone?—I cannot imitate it; I cannot describe it: but it expressed everything! everything!—What? I am to believe they were bandits who attacked us?—they were murderers, hired murderers!— And Marinelli, Marinelli was the the last word spoken by the dying Count! In such a tone!

MARINELLI: In what tone?—Is it right to establish an accusation against a righteous man on the basis of a tone, heard in a moment of horror?

CLAUDIA: Oh, if only I could bring it to court, this tone!—But, woe is me! With all this I am forgetting my daughter.—Where is she?— What? dead too?—Could my daughter help it, that Appiani was your enemy?

MARINELLI: I forgive the frightened mother.—Come, madam,—your daughter is here in one of these rooms: and has already, I hope, fully recovered from her fright. The Prince himself is helping her with his most tender attention—

CLAUDIA: Who?—Who himself?

MARINELLI: The Prince.

CLAUDIA: The Prince? Are you really saying the Prince?—Our Prince?

MARINELLI: What other Prince could it be?

CLAUDIA: Well then!—Hapless mother that I am!—and her father! her father!—He will curse the day she was born. He will curse me.

MARINELLI: For Heaven's sake, madam! What are you imagining now?

CLAUDIA: It is clear!—Is it not?—Today in the House of God! before the eyes of the All-Immaculate! Nearest to the Eternal!—there the infamous scheme was started; there it began! (*to Marinelli*) Ha, murderer! cowardly, miserable murderer! Not brave enough to murder with his own hand, but base enough to murder for the satisfaction of someone else's lust! to have murder done!—Scum of all murderers!—No honest murderers would tolerate you among them!—You! You!—And why should I not spit all my gall, all my venom into your face with one single word?—You! You, procurer!

MARINELLI: You rave, good woman.—But at least control your wild shouting and remember where you are.

CLAUDIA: Where I am? Remember where I am?—What cares the lioness, whose young have been stolen, in whose forest she roars?

EMILIA *(within):* Ah, my mother! I hear my mother!

CLAUDIA: Her voice? It is she? She heard me; she heard me. And I was not to shout?—Where are you, my child? I am coming, I am coming! *(She dashes into the room with Marinelli after her.)*

Act IV

Scene 1

The scene as before

The Prince, Marinelli.

THE PRINCE *(coming from the room where he had been with Emilia):* Come, Marinelli! I must catch my breath—and must have some enlightenment from you.

MARINELLI: Oh, a mother's wrath! Ha! ha! ha!

THE PRINCE: You laugh?

MARINELLI: If you had seen, Prince, how insane the mother behaved here, here in this room—you must have heard her scream!—and how calm she suddenly became the moment she saw you—Ha! ha!—I knew it all along: no mother will scratch out a Prince's eyes if he finds her daughter beautiful.

THE PRINCE: You are a poor observer!—The daughter fell fainting into her mother's arms. It was because of this, that the mother forgot her wrath, not because of me. She was sparing her daughter, and not me, by not saying more loudly, by not saying more clearly,—what I myself would rather not have heard, not have understood.

MARINELLI: What, my lord?

THE PRINCE: Why the pretense?—Out with it. Is it true? or is it not true?

MARINELLI: And if it were?

THE PRINCE: And if it were?—Then it is?—He is dead? dead?— *(threateningly)* Marinelli! Marinelli!

MARINELLI: Well?

THE PRINCE: Oh God! all-righteous God! I am innocent of this bloody deed.—Had you told me beforehand that it would cost the Count his life—No, no! and had it cost me mine!—

MARINELLI: If I had told you beforehand?—As if his death had been in my plan! I instructed that fellow Angelo most solemnly to prevent harm being done to anyone. And it would have come off with no violence too, if the Count had not done violence first. Right off, he shot one man down.

THE PRINCE: You mean, he should have been able to understand a jest!

MARINELLI: That Angelo thereupon became furious and avenged the death of his friend—

THE PRINCE: Of course, that is quite natural!

MARINELLI: I reprimanded him enough for it.

THE PRINCE: Reprimanded? How friendly!—Warn him not to let himself be seen in my territories. My reprimand might not be so friendly.

MARINELLI: Very well!—I and Angelo, design and chance: it is all one.—To be sure, it was agreed beforehand, to be sure, it was promised beforehand, that I should not be held to account for any accident that might occur—

THE PRINCE: That *might* occur, you say? or that was meant to occur?

MARINELLI: Still better!—And yet, my lord, before you tell me in plain and simple language, what you take me to be—just one observation! The death of the Count is anything but unimportant to me. I had challenged him; he owed me satisfaction; he went out of this world without giving it to me, and my honor remains blemished. Granting even that under any other circumstances I would deserve the suspicion which you hold against me: but under these too?—*(with affected passion)* Whoever can think that of me!—

THE PRINCE *(giving in)*: All right, all right—

MARINELLI: That he were still alive! Oh, that he were still alive! I would give anything, anything in the world just for that—*(bitterly)* even the goodwill of my Prince,—this priceless, never to be trifled with goodwill—even that I would give for it!

THE PRINCE: I understand.—All right, then. His death was an accident, just an accident. You swear to it, and I, I believe it.—But who else? The mother too? Emilia too?—The world too?

MARINELLI *(coldly)*: Hardly.

THE PRINCE: And if it is not believed, what is it that will be believed?—You are shrugging your shoulders?—Your Angelo will be considered the tool and I the author of the crime.—

MARINELLI *(even more coldly):* In all probability!

THE PRINCE: I! I myself!—Or else, from this moment on I must renounce all interest in Emilia—

MARINELLI *(with great indifference):* As you would have had to do as well—if the Count were still alive.—

THE PRINCE *(heatedly, but gaining control of himself immediately):* Marinelli!—But no, I will not let you drive me to distraction.—Be it so—and so it is! This is all you want to say anyway, isn't it: the death of the Count is a bit of good fortune for me—the greatest bit of good fortune that could benefit my love. And as such,—what matter how it happened!—One Count more or less in the world! Is this how you want me to think?—Very well, then! I too am not afraid of a little crime. But, my dear friend, it must be a quiet little crime, a helpful little crime. And ours, you see, is precisely neither quiet nor helpful. It did clear the way, but it blocked it at the same time. Everybody would put the blame on us and tell us so to our faces,—and yet, unfortunately we did not even commit it!—That, I submit, is what has come of your wise, wonderful preparations.

MARINELLI: If that is how you want to see it—

THE PRINCE: How else, then?—I want you to answer me!

MARINELLI: More things are charged to my account than belong there.

THE PRINCE: You still have not answered me.

MARINELLI: As you wish! What could there be about my preparations that would cause open suspicion against the Prince in this accident?—It is because of the master stroke which he himself was pleased to mingle with my preparations?

THE PRINCE: I?

MARINELLI: May the Prince permit me to tell him that the step he took in the church this morning,—with no matter how much decorum he may have taken it,—as unavoidable as it may have been for him—that this step nevertheless did not belong to the dance.

THE PRINCE: But what harm did it do?

MARINELLI: It did not spoil the whole dance, to be sure, but for the present at least the rhythm.

THE PRINCE: Hm! Do I understand you correctly?

MARINELLI: Well then, briefly and simply. When I took over the matter—it is true, is it not?—Emilia knew nothing as yet of the Prince's love? Emilia's mother even less. What now if I based my plan on this circumstance? What if the Prince, meanwhile, undermined the foundation on which my scheme was built?—

THE PRINCE *(slapping his forehead):* Confound it!

MARINELLI: What if he himself betrayed what his real designs were?

THE PRINCE: Curse the thought!

MARINELLI: But suppose that he did not himself betray it.—Indeed! I would like to know from which of my preparations mother or daughter could gather the slightest suspicion against him?

THE PRINCE: Oh, that you must be right!

MARINELLI: That, I admit, is very wrong of me—you will forgive me, my lord.—

Scene 2

Battista, the Prince, Marinelli.

BATTISTA *(in great haste):* The Countess has just arrived.

THE PRINCE: The Countess? What Countess?

BATTISTA: Orsina.

THE PRINCE: Orsina?—Marinelli!—Orsina?—Marinelli!

MARINELLI: I am no less surprised than you.

THE PRINCE: Go, hurry, Battista: she is not to get out of her carriage. I am not here. For her, I am not here. She is to turn back immediately. Go, hurry!—*(Exit Battista.)* What does that foolish woman want? Such brazenness! How does she know that we are here? Is she coming to spy on us perhaps? Has she perhaps heard something already?—Ah, Marinelli! Say something, answer me!—Is he pretending to feel hurt, the man who claims he is my friend? And hurt because we exchanged a few miserable harsh words? Should I beg his pardon?

MARINELLI: Ah, my Prince, as soon as you are yourself again, I am again yours with my whole heart!—The arrival of Orsina is a puzzle to me, as it is to you. But she will hardly let herself be turned away. What do you wish to do?

THE PRINCE: Certainly not speak with her; I must leave—

MARINELLI: Very well! but quickly. I will receive her—

THE PRINCE: But only to tell her to leave.—You are not to get involved with her beyond that. We have other things to do—

MARINELLI: I beg your pardon, Prince! These other things are done. Take courage! What is still lacking, will certainly come of itself.— But do I not hear her already?—Hurry, Prince!—There *(pointing to a cabinet, which the Prince enters)*, if you wish, you will be able to hear us.—I am afraid, I am afraid, she did not take this step under the most propitious stars.

Scene 3

Countess Orsina, Marinelli.

ORSINA *(at first without seeing Marinelli):* What is this?—No one comes to greet me except some impudent fellow who would rather have refused me entrance?—I am at Dosalo, am I not? The Dosalo, where a whole army of fawning lackeys used to rush out to bid me welcome? where love and delight used to await me?—This is the place: but, but!—Look, there is Marinelli!—It's good the Prince took you along.—No, not good! What I have to settle with him, I have to settle with him alone.—Where is he?

MARINELLI: The Prince, my dear Countess?

ORSINA: Who else?

MARINELLI: You expect him to be here then? know him to be here?— He at least does not expect the Countess Orsina here.

ORSINA: No? Then he did not receive my letter this morning?

MARINELLI: Your letter? Oh yes, of course; I remember he mentioned a letter from you.

ORSINA: Well? did I not ask him in this letter to meet me here at Dosalo today?—It is true he did not deign to answer me in writing. But I heard that he actually left for Dosalo an hour later. I thought that was enough of an answer, and I came.

MARINELLI: A strange coincidence!

ORSINA: Coincidence?—But I tell you, it was agreed. As good as agreed. On my part, the letter, on his, the action.—How he stands there, the good Marquis! How he stares! Is that little brain of his surprised? and at what?

MARINELLI: Yesterday it seemed so remote that you would ever set eyes on the Prince again.

ORSINA: Better counsel often comes by night.—Where is he?—I wager, he is in that room where I heard that shrieking and screaming.—I wanted to go in, but that scoundrel of a servant stepped in my way.

MARINELLI: My dearest Countess—

ORSINA: It was a woman shrieking. What do you wager, Marinelli?— Oh, tell me, tell me—if I am, as you say, your dearest Countess—This court rabble be damned! So many words, so many lies!—Well, what does it matter whether you tell me beforehand or not? I shall see for myself. *(about to leave)*

MARINELLI *(holding her back):* Where to?

ORSINA: Where I should have been all this time.—Do you think it is proper that I dally in idle chatter with you here in the anteroom, while the Prince waits for me within?

MARINELLI: You are mistaken, Countess. The Prince does not wait for you. The Prince cannot speak with you here—does not wish to speak with you.

ORSINA: And nevertheless is here? and nevertheless is here in answer to my letter?

MARINELLI: Not in answer to your letter—

ORSINA: Which he did receive though, you said—

MARINELLI: Did receive, but did not read.

ORSINA *(vehemently):* Did not read?—*(less vehemently)* Did not read?—*(sadly and wiping a tear from her eye)* Did not even read?

MARINELLI: Because he was distracted, believe me.—Not because he meant to show his contempt—

ORSINA *(proudly):* Contempt?—Who is thinking of that?—To whom do you say that?—You are an impudent comforter, Marinelli!—Contempt! Contempt! And for me! Contempt for me!—*(more gently, almost sadly)* I know he no longer loves me. That is clear. And in place of love something else has come into his heart. That is quite natural. But why should it be contempt? It might be just indifference. Is it not so, Marinelli?

MARINELLI: Of course, of course.

ORSINA *(scornfully):* Of course?—Oh, the wise man who can be made to say whatever one wishes!—Indifference! Indifference in place of love?—That means, nothing in place of something. Now learn this, you parroting little courtier, learn this from a woman: indifference is an empty word, a mere sound, that corresponds to nothing, nothing whatever. The soul is indifferent only to that of which it does not think, only to a thing which for it is no thing.—And being only indifferent to a thing that is no thing,—that is as much as not indifferent at all.—Is that too deep for you?

MARINELLI *(to himself):* O heavens! how true, what I feared.

ORSINA: What are you mumbling there?

MARINELLI: Pure admiration!—And who does not know, Countess, that you are a philosopher?

ORSINA: That is true, isn't it?—Yes, yes, I am.—But have I shown it now, that I am?—Shame on me, if I have shown it, and if I have frequently shown it! Is it surprising then, that the Prince holds me in contempt? How can a man love a thing that wants to think in spite of him? A woman who thinks is as loathsome as a man who powders his nose. She should laugh, only laugh in order to keep him ever in good spirits, the stern lord and master of Creation.—Well, what do you want me to laugh about now, Marinelli?—Of course! About the coincidence! that I should write to the Prince, asking him to come to Dosalo; that the Prince does not read my letter, and that he comes to Dosalo anyway. Ha! ha! ha! Certainly a strange coincidence! Very funny, very amusing!—And you are not laughing with me, Marinelli?—The stern lord and master of Creation may join in laughing—may he not?—even though we poor creatures may not join in thinking?—*(seriously and commandingly)* Then laugh!

MARINELLI: Right away, Countess, right away!

ORSINA: You log! And with that the moment is past. No, no, please, do not laugh.—For you see, Marinelli, *(thoughtfully, almost movingly)* what makes me laugh so heartily has also its serious—very serious side. As everything in the world!—Coincidence? Should it be a coincidence for the Prince not to think of speaking to me here and then being forced to speak to me here anyway? A coincidence?—Believe me, Marinelli: the word *coincidence* is blasphemy. Nothing under the sun is coincidence;—least of all something of which the purpose is so absolutely clear.—Almighty, all-loving Providence, forgive me for following this foolish sinner in calling something a coincidence that is so obviously your doing, perchance your doing even by an immediate act.—*(passionately to Marinelli)* Don't you dare mislead me again into such wickedness.

MARINELLI *(to himself)*: This goes too far!—But, my dear Countess—

ORSINA: Be careful with your "buts"! The "buts" must be paid for with thought:—and my head! my head! *(putting her hand to her forehead)*—See to it, Marinelli, see to it that I speak with him soon, the Prince; else I may not be able to at all.—You see we are meant to speak with each other; we must speak with each other—

Scene 4

The Prince, Orsina, Marinelli.

THE PRINCE *(to himself, stepping out of the cabinet)*: I must come to his rescue.

ORSINA *(seeing him, but not certain whether or not she should go toward him)*: Ha! there he is.

THE PRINCE *(goes straight across the room, past her, toward the other rooms, without interrupting his speech)*: Ah, look! our lovely

Countess.—How sorry I am, Madam, that I can take so little advantage today of the honor of your visit! I am occupied. I am not alone.—Some other time, my dear Countess! Some other time.—Do not stay here any longer now. No, not any longer!—And you, Marinelli, I shall be waiting for you.—

Scene 5

Orsina, Marinelli.

MARINELLI: Have you heard now from his own lips, my dear Countess, what you would not believe coming from me?

ORSINA *(as in a daze):* Have I? have I really?

MARINELLI: Really.

ORSINA *(with emotion):* "I am occupied. I am not alone." Is that all the excuse that I am worth? Whom does one turn away with that? Every tiresome fool, every beggar. For me not a single lie anymore? Not a single little lie for me anymore?—Occupied? with what? Not alone? and who might be with him?—Come, Marinelli; have pity, dear Marinelli! Tell me a little lie of your own. What can a lie cost you?—What does he have to do? Who is with him?—Tell me; tell me whatever happens to come to your tongue first,—and I will go.

MARINELLI *(to himself):* On that condition I could even tell her a bit of the truth.

ORSINA: Well? Quickly, Marinelli, and I will go.—In any case he said, the Prince did: "Some other time, my dear Countess!" Did he not say so?—So that he may keep his word, so that he may have no excuse not to keep his word: quickly, Marinelli, your lie, and I go.

MARINELLI: The Prince, my dear Countess, is in truth not alone. There are people with him who make it impossible for him to spare a single moment; people who have just escaped from a great danger. Count Appiani—

ORSINA: Is with him?—I am sorry that I must catch you up on this lie. Quick, a new one.—For Count Appiani, in case you have not heard, has just been shot and killed by bandits. The carriage with his corpse passed me just outside the city.—Or is he not? Did I merely dream it?

MARINELLI: Unfortunately, you did not merely dream it!—But the others, who were with the Count, were fortunate enough to escape to safety in this villa: to be exact, the bride and the mother of the bride, with whom he was on his way to Sabionetta for the wedding ceremony.

ORSINA: Then it is they? They are with the Prince? the bride? and the mother of the bride?—Is the bride pretty?

MARINELLI: The Prince feels very deeply with her in her misfortune.

ORSINA: I should hope so, even if she were ugly. For her fate is dreadful.—Poor, dear girl, just when he was to become yours forever, he is torn from you forever!—But who is she, this bride? Do I perhaps know her?—I have been away from the city for so long that I know nothing at all.

MARINELLI: It is Emilia Galotti.

ORSINA: Who?—Emilia Galotti? Emilia Galotti?—Marinelli! Help me, lest I take this lie for the truth!

MARINELLI: Why?

ORSINA: Emilia Galotti?

MARINELLI: Whom you can hardly know—

ORSINA: But I do! I do! Even though only as of today.—Seriously, Marinelli? Emilia Galotti?—Emilia Galotti is the unfortunate bride, whom the Prince is comforting?

MARINELLI *(to himself)*: Can it be that I have told her too much already?

ORSINA: And Count Appiani was the bridegroom of this bride? the Appiani who was just shot?

MARINELLI: That is correct.

ORSINA: Bravo! oh, bravo! bravo! *(clapping her hands)*

MARINELLI: What is this?

ORSINA: I could kiss the devil who misled him into this!

MARINELLI: Whom? Misled? Into what?

ORSINA: Yes, I could kiss him, kiss him—Even if you yourself were this devil, Marinelli.

MARINELLI: Countess!

ORSINA: Come here! Look at me! directly! Straight in the eye!

MARINELLI: Well?

ORSINA: Don't you know what I am thinking?

MARINELLI: How can I know?

ORSINA: Have you no part in it?

MARINELLI: In what?

ORSINA: Swear to it!—No, do not swear. You might commit yet another sin. But then, go ahead and swear. What is one sin more or less to one already damned?—Have you no part in it?

MARINELLI: You frighten me, Countess.

ORSINA: Really?—Come now, Marinelli, does your kind heart suspect nothing?

MARINELLI: What? Suspect what?

ORSINA: Well,—in that case I shall confide something to you,—something that should make every hair on your head stand on end.—But here, so near the door, someone might hear us. Come over here.— And! *(putting her finger to her lips)* Listen! Just between you and me! just between you and me! *(and bringing her mouth close to his ear as if wanting to whisper something to him, which instead, she loudly screams at him)* The Prince is a murderer!

MARINELLI: Countess,—Countess—have you gone completely mad?

ORSINA: Mad? Ha! ha! ha! *(laughing at the top of her voice)* I have seldom or never been more satisfied with the soundness of my powers of reason than at this very moment.—Believe me, Marinelli;—but it must remain a secret—*(lowering her voice)* the Prince is a murderer!—The murderer of Count Appiani!—Not bandits, the Prince's henchmen, the Prince himself did kill him!

MARINELLI: How can so loathesome a thought come from your lips, come to your mind?

ORSINA: How?—Quite naturally.—This Emilia Galotti, who is here with him,—whose bridegroom had to take such a headlong departure from this world,—this Emilia Galotti is the very person with whom the Prince spoke at great length this morning in the outer hall of the Dominican Church. I know it; my informants saw it. They heard what he said to her, too.—Well, my dear sir? Have I gone mad? I am putting together, it seems to me, just about all the pieces that belong in this puzzle.—Or does this also fit merely as a matter of chance? Is this also coincidence in your book? Ah, Marinelli, then you understand as little about the wickedness of men as you do about Providence.

MARINELLI: Countess, you would be talking away your life—

ORSINA: If I said more?—All the better, all the better!—Tomorrow I will proclaim it in the marketplace.—And whoever contradicts me— whoever contradicts me, he was the murderer's accomplice. Farewell. *(As she is about to leave, she meets Odoardo Galotti who enters in great haste.)*

Scene 6

Odoardo Galotti, the Countess, Marinelli.

ODOARDO GALOTTI: I beg your pardon, madam—

ORSINA: I have here no power of pardon. For I have here no right of resentment.—This is the man you want to address. *(pointing to Marinelli)*

MARINELLI *(seeing him, to himself):* This caps it all! the old man!—

ODOARDO: You will forgive a father, sir, who is extremely perturbed,—for entering thus unannounced.

ORSINA: Father? *(turns around again)* Of Emilia, no doubt.—Ha, welcome!

ODOARDO: A servant came galloping back to meet me on the road and inform me that my family were in danger somewhere in this vicinity. As I hurry to this place I hear that Count Appiani was wounded; that he is returning to the city; that my wife and daughter found refuge in this villa.—Where are they, sir, where are they?

MARINELLI: Rest assured, Colonel. Your wife and your daughter suffered no harm, except the shock. They are both well. The Prince is with them. I will go immediately and announce you.

ODOARDO: Why announce? Why first announce?

MARINELLI: For good reasons—because—because of the Prince. You know, Colonel, how things stand between you and the Prince. Your terms with him are not the friendliest. As gracious as he may be toward your wife and daughter:—they are ladies—will that help make your unexpected visit opportune to him?

ODOARDO: You are right, sir, you are right.

MARINELLI: But, Countess,—may I first have the honor of escorting you to your carriage?

ORSINA: Never mind, never mind.

MARINELLI *(grasping her hand, not unceremoniously)* Allow me to observe my duty.—

ORSINA: Do not hurry me!—I relieve you of that duty, sir! How the like of you always manage to make a duty of polite formalities, just for the sake of handling what ought to be your real duty as a matter of secondary concern.—To announce this worthy man, the sooner the better, that is your duty.

MARINELLI: Have you forgotten what the Prince himself commanded you to do?

ORSINA: He may come and command once again. I intend to wait for him.

MARINELLI *(quietly to the Colonel, whom he draws aside):* My dear sir, I must leave you here with a lady, who—whom—with whose mind—you understand me. I tell you this so that you will know what to make of her words—which are frequently extremely odd. It would be best, if you did not let yourself be drawn into conversation with her.

ODOARDO: Certainly.—But hurry, sir.

Scene 7

Countess Orsina, Odoardo Galotti.

ORSINA *(after several moments of silence, during which she watches the Colonel with an expression of pity, just as he watches her with one of curiosity):* I wonder what he said to you just now, you poor unfortunate man!—

ODOARDO *(partly to himself, partly to her):* Poor?

ORSINA: In any case, it was not the truth;—least of all, one of the truths that are in store for you.

ODOARDO: That are in store for me?—Do I not know enough already?—Madam!—But go ahead and speak, go ahead and speak.

ORSINA: You know nothing.

ODOARDO: Nothing?

ORSINA: Good and loving father!—What would I give to have you as my father too!—Forgive me! the wretched are so eager to cling together.—I would faithfully share with you pain and fury.

ODOARDO: Pain and fury? Madam!—But I forget—Go ahead and speak.

ORSINA: If she is your only daughter—your only child!—Though, an only child or not. A hapless child is always the one and only.

ODOARDO: Hapless? Madam!—What do I want with her?—And still, by God, no madwoman speaks like that!

ORSINA: Madwoman? So that is what he told you about me?—Well, well, it may well be that it is one of his lesser lies.—I sense something of the sort!—And believe me, believe me, sir: whoever does not lose his mind over certain things, does not have a mind to lose.—

ODOARDO: What should I think?

ORSINA: That you should most certainly not despise me!—For you, too, have a mind, dear sir, you too.—I see it by your resolute, venerable countenance. You too have a mind;—yet, it costs me but one word,—and you lose it.

ODOARDO: Madam!—Madam!—I shall have lost it even before you say the word, if you do not say it soon.—Say it! say it!—Or it is not true,—it is not true that you belong to that kindly species of the insane, a species so deserving of our sympathy and respect—you are a cruel, foolish woman. You have not now, what you never had at all.

ORSINA: Then mark me well!—What do you know, you who claim to know enough already? That Appiani was wounded? Only wounded?—Appiani is dead!

ODOARDO: Dead? dead?—Ha, woman, that is against our agreement.

You wanted to make me lose my mind, and you break my heart.

ORSINA: That only in passing!—But, to proceed.—The bridegroom is dead: the bride—your daughter—worse than dead.

ODOARDO: Worse? worse than dead?—But at the same time also dead?—For I know of only one thing worse—

ORSINA: Not at the same time also dead. No, good father, no!—She lives, she lives. Her life is just beginning.—A life of rapture! the most beautiful, the merriest life of idle leisure—while it lasts.

ODOARDO: The word, madam, the one word that is to make me lose my mind! Out with it!—Do not pour your drop of poison into a bucket.—The one word! Quickly.

ORSINA: Well now; spell it out for yourself!—In the morning the Prince spoke with your daughter during Mass, in the afternoon he has her at his pleasure—pleasure resort.

ODOARDO: Spoke with her during Mass? The Prince with my daughter?

ORSINA: With such intimacy! with such ardor!—It was no small matter they had to agree upon. And well and good if it was by agreement; well and good if your daughter took refuge here of her own free will! You see: then at least it was no forced abduction, but merely a little—a little assassination.

ODOARDO: Slander! damnable slander! I know my daughter. If it be assassination, then it is abduction also.—*(he glances wildly about, stamping and fuming)* Well, Claudia? Well, you loving mother?—what joy we have had! Hurrah for the gracious Prince! Hurrah for this very special honor!

ORSINA: Is it taking effect, old man? is it taking effect?

ODOARDO: Here I am now, standing before the thief's den—*(opening wide his coat and seeing himself without weapons)* I am surprised that in my haste I did not leave my hands behind as well!—*(feeling all his pockets, as if looking for something)* Nothing! nothing at all! nowhere!

ORSINA: Ha, I see!—I can help you out!—I brought one along. *(drawing out a dagger)* There, take it! take it quickly, before someone sees us!—I might have something else for you too,—poison. But poison is only for us women, not for men.—Take this! *(forcing the dagger into his hand)* Take it!

ODOARDO: Thank you, thank you.—Dear child, whoever says once more that you are mad will have to deal with me.

ORSINA: Put it away! quickly!—I shall be denied the opportunity to use it. But you will not be without it, without this opportunity: and you will seize it, the first, the best,—if you are a man.—I, I am only a woman; but that is how I came here! firmly resolved!—I and you, old man, we can tell each other everything. For we are both wronged; wronged by the very same seducer.—Oh, if you knew,—if you knew how supremely, how unspeakably, how unbelievably I have been wronged by him, and still am:—you might, you would forget your own wrongs over mine.—Do you know me? I am Orsina, the betrayed, forsaken Orsina.—Although perhaps forsaken only because of your daughter.—Yet, what fault is it of your daughter's?—Soon she too will be forsaken.—And then another!—And again another!—And again another!—Ha! *(as though in raptures)* what a heavenly dream! If some day we all,—we, the entire forsaken multitude—we all, transformed into Bacchantes, into Furies, if we all had him at our mercy, tore him to pieces, limb from limb, mangled him, wallowed in his entrails,—to find his heart, the heart that the traitor promised each of us and gave to none! Ha! that would turn out to be a dance! that would!

Scene 8

Claudia Galotti, Odoardo Galotti, Countess Orsina.

CLAUDIA *(who upon entering looks around and, seeing her husband, immediately rushes toward him)*: I knew it!—Ah, our protector, our savior! Are you here, Odoardo? Are you here?—Their whispering, the expression in their faces told me so.—What should I tell you, if as yet you know nothing?—What should I tell you if already you know everything?—But we are innocent. I am innocent. Your daughter is innocent. Innocent, in everything innocent!

ODOARDO *(who upon seeing his wife has tried to compose himself)*: Yes, yes. Now calm yourself, calm yourself—and answer me. *(to Orsina)* Not, madam, that I still doubt your word—Is the Count dead?

CLAUDIA: Dead.

ODOARDO: Is it true that the Prince spoke with Emilia this morning during Mass?

CLAUDIA: True. But if you knew what a fright it gave her, in what confusion she came home—

ORSINA: Well, did I lie?

ODOARDO *(laughing bitterly)*: You better hadn't—much better.

ORSINA: Am I mad?

ODOARDO *(pacing wildly to and fro)*: Oh—nor am I as yet.

CLAUDIA: You bade me be calm, and I am calm.—Dearest husband, may I too—implore you—

ODOARDO: What do you want? Am I not calm? Could anyone be more calm than I am?—*(mastering himself)* Does Emilia know that Appiani is dead?

CLAUDIA: She could not know. But I fear that she suspects it, since he does not come.—

ODOARDO: And she is wailing and whimpering—

CLAUDIA: No longer.—That is past: that is how she is; you know her. She is the most timid and the most resolute of her sex. Never in control of her first impressions, but finding her way through anything after only a moment's thought, prepared for anything. She keeps the Prince at such a distance, she speaks with him in such a tone—See to it, Odoardo, just see to it that we get away from here.

ODOARDO: I have come on horseback.—What can we do?—But madam, you are returning to the city, are you not?

ORSINA: I am, indeed.

ODOARDO: Would you have the kindness to take my wife with you?

ORSINA: Why not? With pleasure.

ODOARDO: Claudia,—*(introducing the Countess to her)* the Countess Orsina, a woman of great understanding, my friend, my benefactress.—You must go with her and send the carriage out for us as soon as you get there. Emilia may not return to Guastalla. She is to go with me.

CLAUDIA: But—if only—I do not like to be separated from the child.

ODOARDO: Won't her father be near her? He will be admitted, sooner or later. No objections!—Come, madam, *(quietly to Orsina)* You will hear from me.—Come, Claudia. *(He leads her off.)*

Act V

Scene I

The scene as before

Marinelli, the Prince.

MARINELLI: Here, my Lord, you can see him from this window. He is pacing up and down the arcade.—He is just turning in; he is coming.—No, he is going back again—He cannot quite make up his mind as yet. But he is certainly a great deal calmer—or seems so. For us it amounts to the same thing!—Of course! No matter what notions the two women may have put into his head, will he dare speak up?—According to what Battista overheard, his wife is to order the carriage out as soon as she can. For he came on horseback.—Wait and see, when he finally appears before you, he will most humbly thank Your Highness for the gracious protection which his family found here after this unfortunate occurrence; will commend himself and his daughter to your continued goodwill; will quietly take her to the city and await in deepest submission whatever further interest it may please Your Highness to take in his unfortunate beloved daughter.

THE PRINCE: But what if he is not that tame? I doubt, I doubt very much that he will be. I know him too well.—If now he merely manages to stifle his suspicions and to swallow his anger, and, instead of taking Emilia to the city, takes her with him? keeps her by his side? or even sends her off to a convent outside my territory? What then?

MARINELLI: Love that worries looks far ahead. Indeed!—But I suppose he won't—

THE PRINCE: But what if he does! What then? Of what avail then will it be to us that the hapless Count lost his life in this affair?

MARINELLI: Why dwell on this sad but secondary sight? Onward! says the conqueror, be it friend or foe who falls to his right, to his left.—And even if! Even if the old grudger wanted to do what you are so afraid of, Prince:—*(thinking)* I have it! That will work!—He certainly won't get beyond wanting to do it. Certainly not!—But we must not let him out of our sight!—*(steps to the window again)* He almost caught us off our guard! He is coming.—Let us avoid him for the moment and let me tell you first, my Prince, what we must do in case the thing we fear should come to pass.

THE PRINCE *(threateningly)*: But, Marinelli!—

MARINELLI: The most innocent thing in the world!

Scene 2

ODOARDO GALOTTI: No one here yet?—Good, I am to cool off still further. So much the better.—There is nothing more despicable than an adolescent hothead with gray hair! How often have I not told myself. And still, I have let myself be carried away again, and by whom? By a jealous woman, by a woman out of her wits with jealousy.—What has insulted virtue to do with the revenge of vice? It is only the first of these that I must save.—As for your cause—my son! my son!—I have never known how to cry;—and do not want to learn it at this late hour—One quite different will make your cause his. For me it must be enough if your murderer never tastes the fruit of his crime! May this torture him more than the crime itself! And if surfeit and loathing soon drive him from lust to lust, may the memory that this one lust remained unindulged gall his enjoyment of them all! In his every dream may the bleeding bridegroom lead the bride to his bedside; and if, even so, he stretches out his lustful arms toward her, let him hear of a sudden the scornful laughter of Hell, and awake!

Scene 3

Marinelli, Odoardo Galotti.

MARINELLI: Where have you been, sir? where have you been?

ODOARDO: Was my daughter here?

MARINELLI: Not she, but the Prince.

ODOARDO: He will forgive me.—I accompanied the Countess.

MARINELLI: Well?

ODOARDO: The good lady!

MARINELLI: And your wife?

ODOARDO: Is with the Countess,—so that she may order the carriage for us at once. May the Prince permit me to stay here with my daughter until then.

MARINELLI: Why so much trouble? Would not the Prince have considered it a pleasure to escort himself both mother and daughter to the city?

ODOARDO: My daughter at least would have had to refuse this honor.

MARINELLI: Why?

ODOARDO: She is not to return to Guastalla.

MARINELLI: No? and why not?

ODOARDO: The Count is dead.

MARINELLI: All the more reason—

ODOARDO: For her to return with me.

MARINELLI: With you?

ODOARDO: With me. I have already told you, the Count is dead—in case you do not know it yet—What is there now for her to do in Guastalla?—She shall go with me.

MARINELLI: Where the daughter stays in future is of course exclusively for her father to decide. But for the time being—

ODOARDO: What, for the time being?

MARINELLI: You will have to allow, Colonel, that she be brought to Guastalla.

ODOARDO: My daughter? brought to Guastalla? and why?

MARINELLI: Why? Consider for a moment—

ODOARDO (*heatedly*): Consider! consider! I consider that there is nothing to consider here.—She shall, she must go with me.

MARINELLI: Oh, sir,—why should we grow heated over this? Perhaps I am mistaken, perhaps what I think necessary is not necessary.—The Prince will know best. Let the Prince decide.—I shall go and fetch him.

Scene 4

ODOARDO GALOTTI: What?—Never!—Tell me where she should go?—Keep her from me?—Who wants to do that? Who has the right to do that?—The one who can do anything here he pleases? Let it be, let it be; then I shall show him how much, *I* can do, even though I should not! Shortsighted tyrant! I shall prove myself a match for you. He who heeds no law is as powerful as he who has no law. Don't you know that? Come on! come on!—But look! There we have it again: my wrath running off again with my reason.—What do I want? Let it first come to pass at least, the thing I am raging over. What nonsense cannot such a flunky talk! And why did I not just let him talk! Why did I not listen at least to his excuse for wanting to send her back to Guastalla!—Then I could prepare myself for an answer now.—Though, what excuse is there to which the answer might fail me? But if it does fail me; if—Somebody is coming. Calm yourself, old fellow, calm yourself!

Scene 5

The Prince, Marinelli, Odoardo Galotti

THE PRINCE: Ah, my dear, honest Galotti,—this is what must happen if I am to see you here. For anything less you would not do it. But I don't mean to chide you!

ODOARDO: My lord, I deem it ill-mannered in all cases for a man to force himself upon his sovereign. Those whom he knows he will have summoned when he has need of them. Even now I beg forgiveness—

THE PRINCE: How I would wish this proud modesty for many another!—But now to the business at hand. You must be anxious to see your daughter. She is again distraught because of the sudden departure of her loving mother.—And why this departure? I was only waiting for dear Emilia to recover completely to accompany both ladies triumphantly to the city. You have reduced this triumph for me by one half but I shall not let it be taken away from me entirely.

ODOARDO: Too gracious!—Permit me, Prince, to spare my hapless child all the diverse grief that friend and foe, pity and ill will hold in readiness for her at Guastalla.

THE PRINCE: It would be a crime to deprive her of the sweet grief which friends and their pity will cause her. But let me, my dear Galotti, see to it that grief through foe and ill will do not reach her.

ODOARDO: Prince, fatherly love does not like to share its grief.—I think I know what alone is proper for my daughter under the present circumstances—Departure from this world,—a convent,—as soon as possible.

THE PRINCE: A convent?

ODOARDO: Until then, let her weep under the eyes of her father.

THE PRINCE: Such beauty is to fade away in a convent?—Can a single unfulfilled hope make us so unreconciled to this world?—And yet, of course: one ought not contradict a father. Take your daughter, Galotti, wherever you please.

ODOARDO *(to Marinelli)*: Well, sir?

MARINELLI: If you insist on my talking!—

ODOARDO: Oh certainly not, certainly not.

THE PRINCE: What is this between you two?

ODOARDO: Nothing, my lord, nothing.—We are just wondering which of us was wrong about you.

THE PRINCE: Why?—You tell me, Marinelli.

MARINELLI: It grieves me greatly to interfere with the magnanimity of my Prince. And yet, when friendship demands that above all else he be called upon in his role as judge—

THE PRINCE: Which friendship?—

MARINELLI: You know, my lord, how dearly I loved the Count Appiani, how closely our two hearts seemed entwined—

ODOARDO: You know that, Prince? Then in truth you alone know it.

MARINELLI: Appointed by him to avenge him—

ODOARDO: You?

MARINELLI: Just ask your wife. Marinelli, the name Marinelli was the last word on the lips of the dying Count, and in a tone of voice! in a tone!—May it never cease ringing in my ears, this dreadful tone, if I do not do everything in my power to have his murderers found and punished!

THE PRINCE: You may count on my full support.

ODOARDO: And my most fervent good wishes!—Good, good!—But what else?

THE PRINCE: That is what I ask too, Marinelli.

MARINELLI: There is the suspicion that it may not have been bandits who attacked the Count.

ODOARDO *(scornfully):* No? not really?

MARINELLI: That a rival had him put out of the way.

ODOARDO *(bitterly):* Ah! A rival?

MARINELLI: Just that.

ODOARDO: Well then,—God damn him, that conspiring assassin!

MARINELLI: A rival, and a favored rival—

ODOARDO: What? favored?—What are you saying?

MARINELLI: Nothing but what the rumors are spreading.

ODOARDO: Favored? favored by my daughter?

MARINELLI:Certainly not that. That cannot be. There I disagree, more vehemently even than you.—But nevertheless, my lord,—for even the soundest judgment before proof weighs nothing in the scales of justice:—and so it seems there is no way to avoid that the hapless girl be questioned in the matter.

THE PRINCE: Yes, of course; indeed.

MARINELLI: And where else can that be done except in Guastalla? where else?

THE PRINCE: There you are right, Marinelli; there you are right.—Well now, that changes the situation, my dear Galotti. Does it not? You can see for yourself—

ODOARDO: Oh yes, I see—I see what I see.—God! God!

THE PRINCE: What is it? What is wrong now?

ODOARDO: That I did not foresee, what I now see. That vexes me, nothing more.—Well then; she will return to Guastalla. I shall return her to her mother: and until she has been cleared by the most severe inquiry, I myself shall not leave Guastalla either. For who knows,—*(with a bitter laugh)* who knows if justice may not find it necessary to question me too.

MARINELLI: Quite possibly! In such cases justice would rather do too much than too little.—For that reason I even fear—

THE PRINCE: What? what do you fear?

MARINELLI: That for the present mother and daughter cannot be permitted to speak with each other.

ODOARDO: Not speak with each other?

MARINELLI: That it will be necessary to separate mother and daughter.

ODOARDO: To separate mother and daughter?

MARINELLI: Mother and daughter and father. The established form of legal inquiry absolutely demands this precaution. And I am sorry, my lord, to find myself obliged to make the express recommendation that at least Emilia be brought into special custody.

ODOARDO: Special custody?—Prince! Prince!—But yes; of course, of course!—Certainly: into special custody! Not so, Prince? not so?— Oh, what a wonderful thing is justice! Magnificent! *(reaches quickly for the pocket in which he has the dagger)*

THE PRINCE *(moves toward him, flatteringly)*: Calm yourself, my dear Galotti.—

ODOARDO *(aside, withdrawing his hand again, empty)*: His guardian angel made him speak those words!

THE PRINCE: You are mistaken; you do not understand him. The word *custody* makes you think perhaps of prison and dungeon.

ODOARDO: Let me think that and I shall be calm!

THE PRINCE: Not a word about prison, Marinelli! In this case the harshness of the laws may be reconciled quite easily with the high regard we have for blameless virtue. If Emilia must be brought into special custody, then I know—the most appropriate. The home of my Chancellor.—I want no argument from you, Marinelli!—I myself shall bring her there. And there, too, I shall put her in the care of a most worthy lady. She will be responsible to me for Emilia's well-being.—You go too far, Marinelli, really too far, if you demand more.—You of course know my Chancellor Grimaldi and his wife, do you not, Galotti?

ODOARDO: How could I fail to? I know even the charming daughters of this noble couple. Who does not know them?—*(to Marinelli)* No, sir, do not permit this. If Emilia must be put in custody, then it must be in the deepest dungeon. You must demand this, I beg you.—What a fool I am, with my pleading! What an old fool!—So she spoke true, the kind Sybil: who does not lose his mind over certain things, has no mind to lose!

THE PRINCE: I do not understand you.—My dear Galotti, what more can I do?—Let us keep it that way, I beg you.—Yes, at the home of my Chancellor! She is to go there, I shall bring her there myself; and if she is not treated there with the utmost respect, then my word is worth nothing. But have no fear.—That settles it!—As for yourself, Galotti, you may do as you please. You may follow us to Guastalla; you may return to Sabionetta, as you wish. It would be ridiculous to dictate to you.—And now, good-bye, my dear Galotti!—Come, Marinelli, it is getting late.

ODOARDO *(who has been standing in deep thought):* What? then I am not even to speak with her, my daughter? Not even here?—After all, I accept everything; I think everything is perfect. The home of a Chancellor is of course a sanctuary of virtue. Oh, my lord, please bring my daughter there, nowhere else but there.—But I would like to speak with her first. The death of the Count is not yet known to her. She will not understand why she is being separated from her parents. To let her know as best I can about this death, to ease her mind about this separation:—I must speak to her, my lord, I must speak to her.

THE PRINCE: Then come along—

ODOARDO: Oh, a daughter can certainly come to her father.—Here, with the two of us alone, I shall be done with her in a moment. Just send her to me, my lord.

THE PRINCE: That too!—Oh Galotti, if only you were willing to be my friend, my guide, my father! *(Exit the Prince and Marinelli.)*

Scene 6

ODOARDO GALOTTI *(looking after him, after a pause):* Why not?— With pleasure.—Ha! ha! ha!—*(Glances wildly about.)* Who is laughing?—Oh God, I think it was I myself.—So let it be! Merry, merry! The play is drawing to a close. One way or another!—But— *(pause)* what if she is hand in glove with him? What if she is not worthy of what I plan to do for her?—*(pause)* Do for her? And what do I plan to do for her?—Have I the heart to tell myself?—Here I am, thinking a thing! A thing that can only be thought!—Monstrous! Begone, begone! I cannot wait for her. No!—*(heavenward)* He who plunged her, in her innocence, into this abyss, let him draw her out again. What need has he of my hand to help him? Begone! *(He starts to leave and sees Emilia coming.)* Too late! Ah! he wants my hand, he wants it!

Scene 7

Emilia, Odoardo.

EMILIA: What? You are here, my father?—And you alone?—And my mother? not here?—And the Count? not here?—And you, so distraught, my father?

ODOARDO: And you so calm, my daughter?

EMILIA: Why not, my father?—Either nothing is lost, or all. Calmness by will or necessity, does it not amount to the same thing?

ODOARDO: But, what do you think is the case here?

EMILIA: That all is lost;—and that calmness must come by necessity, my father.

ODOARDO: And you are calm because necessity bids you—Who are you? A young girl? and my daughter? Then man and father should feel ashamed before you?—But tell me: what do you mean by "all is lost"?—that the Count is dead?

EMILIA: And why he is dead! Why! Ha, so it is true, my father? So it is true, the entire dreadful story which I read in the weeping and frantic eyes of my mother?—Where is my mother? Where has she gone, my father?

ODOARDO: On ahead;—provided we follow.

EMILIA: The sooner, the better. For if the Count is dead, if he is dead for that reason—for that reason! why do we stay here? Let us flee, my father!

ODOARDO: Flee?—What is the need of that?—You are, you remain in the hands of your captor.

EMILIA: I remain in his hands?

ODOARDO: And alone, without your mother, without me.

EMILIA: I alone in his hands?—Never, my father.—Or you are not my father.—I alone in his hands?—Good, then leave me, leave me.—I should like to see who keeps me,—who compels me,—who it is that can compel a human being.

ODOARDO: I thought you were calm, my child.

EMILIA: And I am. But what do you call being calm? Folding one's hands? Suffering what one ought not to suffer? Bearing what one ought not to bear?

ODOARDO: Ha! if that is how you think!—Let me embrace you, my daughter!—I have always said: nature meant to make woman her masterpiece. But she selected the wrong clay, she selected it too fragile. Apart from that, everything in you is better than in us.—Ha, if that is your calm, then I have found mine again through it! Let me embrace you, my daughter!—Imagine: under the pretext of a legal inquiry,—ah, what a devilish farce—he has decided to tear you from our arms and take you to the Grimaldi women.

EMILIA: Has decided to tear me? decided to take me?—pretends to tear me, pretends to take me: pretends to! pretends to!—As if we, as if we had no will, my father!

ODOARDO: Indeed, I grew so furious, that I reached for this dagger *(pulling it out)*, to stab one of them,—both of them!—through the heart.

EMILIA: For Heaven's sake, my father, no!—This life is all these wicked men possess.—To me, my father, give this dagger to me.

ODOARDO: Child, it is not a hairpin.

EMILIA: Then the hairpin must serve as a dagger.—It is all the same.

ODOARDO: What? It would have come to that? But no, no! Think, my child.—You too have only one life to lose.

EMILIA: And only one innocence!

ODOARDO: That stands above the power of brute force.—

EMILIA: But not above all seduction.—Brute force! Brute force! Who cannot defy brute force? What we call brute force is nothing: seduction is the only true force.—I have blood pulsing in my veins, my father, blood that is as youthful, as warm as anyone's. And my senses are senses too. I vouch for nothing. I will be responsible for nothing. I know the house of the Grimaldi. It is a house of pleasures. Only one hour there, under the eyes of my mother;—and there arose within me such diverse passions as weeks of the strict discipline of religion could scarcely calm.—Of religion? And of what religion?—To escape a fate not worse than that, thousands have leaped into torrential waters and are saints!—Give me, my father, give me this dagger.

ODOARDO: If you knew this dagger, if you knew it!—

EMILIA: Even if I do not know it!—An unknown friend is still a friend.—Give it to me, my father; give it to me.

ODOARDO: And if I give it to you now—Here! *(Gives it to her.)*

EMILIA: And here! *(About to stab herself, her father grabs it out of her hand.)*

ODOARDO: See, how hasty!—No, this is not for your hand.

EMILIA: It is true, with a hairpin I must—*(She reaches up quickly to find one in her hair and touches the rose.)* Are you still here?—Away with you! you do not belong in the hair of such a one as—my father wants me to become.

ODOARDO: Oh, my daughter!—

EMILIA: Oh, my father, if I can read your thoughts!—But no; you do not want that either. Why else would you hesitate?—*(bitterly, as she tears the rose apart)* Long ago there was a father who, to save his daughter from disgrace, took the first steel that came to hand and plunged it into her heart—and brought her thus to life a second time. But all such deeds are of long ago! There are no such fathers any more!

ODOARDO: Yes there are, my daughter, there are! *(stabbing her)* God, what have I done! *(She is about to fall and he catches her in his arms.)*

EMILIA: Broken a rose, ere the storm scattered its petals.—Let me kiss it, this, my father's hand.

Scene 8

The Prince, Marinelli, Emilia, Odoardo.

THE PRINCE *(as he enters)*: What is this?—Is Emilia not well?

ODOARDO: Very well, very well!

THE PRINCE *(coming closer)*: What do I see—Horror!

MARINELLI: Woe unto me!

THE PRINCE: Cruel father, what have you done?

ODOARDO: Broken a rose, ere the storm scattered its petals.—Was it not so, my daughter?

EMILIA: Not you, my father—I myself—I myself—

ODOARDO: Not you, my daughter;—not you!—Do not depart from this world with a lie. Not you, my daughter! Your father, your hapless father!

EMILIA: Ah—my father—*(She dies and he lays her gently on the floor.)*

ODOARDO: Farewell!—Well now, Prince! Does she still please you? Does she still arouse your passion? Still, in this blood, that cries out against you for revenge? *(after a pause)* But you are waiting for the result of all this? Maybe you are waiting for me to turn the dagger on myself, to end my doing as an insipid tragedy?—You are mistaken. Here! *(throwing the dagger at his feet)* Here it is, the bloody witness to my crime! I go now to give myself up at the prison. I go and await you as my judge.—And then beyond—I shall await you before Him, who is the Judge of us all!

THE PRINCE *(after a prolonged silence, during which he regards the body with horror and despair, to Marinelli)*: Here! pick it up.— Well? you hesitate?—Wretch!—*(tearing the dagger from his hand)* No, your blood and this blood may not be mixed.—Go, and show yourself nevermore!—Go! I say.—God! God!—Is it not enough, for the misery of the many, that princes are human: must it also be that devils disguise themselves as their friends?

Translated by Anna Johanna Gode von Aesch

THE JEWS

A Comedy in One Act
Written in 1749

and related correspondence

CHARACTERS

MICHEL STICH
MARTIN KRUMM
A TRAVELER
CHRISTOPH, *his servant*
THE BARON
A YOUNG LADY, *his daughter*
LISETTE

Scene 1

Michel Stich. Martin Krumm.

MARTIN KRUMM: You're an idiot, Michel Stich!

MICHEL STICH: You're an idiot, Martin Krumm!

MARTIN KRUMM: We may as well admit that we were both incredibly stupid. Killing one more wouldn't have made any difference!

MICHEL STICH: But how could we have gone about it more cleverly? Weren't we well disguised? wasn't the coachman on our side? was it our fault that Lady Luck thwarted our plans? If I've said it once, I've said it a hundred times: rotten luck! you can't even be a good criminal without it!

MARTIN KRUMM: Yes, you know, when I really think about it, it didn't even help us to avoid the noose for a few more days.

MICHEL STITCH: Oh, shut up about the noose! If all thieves were hanged, the gallows would have to stand a lot closer together. You only ever see one every two miles; and where there is one, it's usually empty. I think that the judges, just to be polite, will simply let them fade out of use. What are they good for, anyway? For nothing, except that, at the most, one of our kind, whenever he goes by, gives them a wink.

MARTIN KRUMM: Oh! I don't even do that! My father and my grandfather died on them, should I ask for something better? I'm not ashamed of my parents.

MICHEL STITCH: But those honest people will be ashamed of you. You haven't done enough by a long shot for people to begin to think of you as their right and proper son.

MARTIN KRUMM: Oh! so you think then that because of that our master should get off easy? And I certainly want to revenge myself too on that wretched stranger, who tore such a tasty morsel out of our mouths. He's really going to have to drop us his watch—Ha! See, there he comes now. Quick! Get out of here! I'll prove I'm a master at this!

MICHEL STITCH: But we have to go halves! halves!

Scene 2

Martin Krumm. The Traveler.

MARTIN KRUMM: I'll play dumb.—Your humble servant, sir. They call me Martin Krumm, and here, on this estate, I'd be the highly esteemed steward.

TRAVELER: And well I believe you, my friend. But have you seen my servant?

MARTIN KRUMM: At your service, sir, no. But I have had the honor of hearing many good things about your most excellent person. And so I rejoice in having the honor of enjoying the honor of your acquaintance. They say that yesterday evening, on his journey, you snatched our master from a very dangerous situation. And as I can do no other than rejoice in the good fortune of my master, I rejoice—

TRAVELER: I think I know what you want; you want to thank me for helping your master—

MARTIN KRUMM: Yes, quite right! just that!

TRAVELER: You're an honest man—

MARTIN KRUMM: That I am! And honesty is the best policy, I always say!

TRAVELER: It is no small pleasure for me that, because of such a small kindness, I have made so many upstanding people so obliged to me. Your gratitude is an unnecessary reward for what I did. The common love of mankind obliged me to it. It was my duty, and I would needs be content, if it had been seen for nothing other than that. You are all too kind, dear people, to thank me for that which, without doubt, you would have done for me just as eagerly, had I found myself in similar danger. Can I be of any further service to you, my friend?

MARTIN KRUMM: Oh, I don't want to burden you with service, sir. I have my servant, who has to wait on me whenever it's necessary. But—what I'd really like to know is, what really happened? Where was it? Were there many criminals? Did they actually want to kill our master, or did they just want to relieve him of his money? One would certainly have been better than the other.

TRAVELER: I'll briefly tell you the whole course of things. It was probably just an hour from here where the robbers attacked your master on a deserted road. I was traveling just that same road, and his frightened cries for help prompted me to ride upon them in all haste along with my servant.

MARTIN KRUMM: Oh my! my!

TRAVELER: I found him in an open carriage—

MARTIN KRUMM: Oh my! my!

TRAVELER: Two disguised fellows—

MARTIN KRUMM: Disguised? Oh my! my!

TRAVELER: Yes! They had already set upon him.

MARTIN KRUMM: Oh my! my!

TRAVELER: Whether they wanted to kill him, or just tie him up, to plunder him all the more thoroughly, I don't know.

MARTIN KRUMM: Oh my! my! Oh, they surely wanted to kill him, the godless people!

TRAVELER: That's just what I don't want to say for fear of accusing them of too much.

MARTIN KRUMM: Yes, yes, believe me, they wanted to kill him. I know, I know for a fact—

TRAVELER: How could you know that? But, so be it. As soon as the robbers saw me, they left their prey and ran head over heels into the nearby shrubbery. I got off a shot at one of them. But it was already too dark, and he was already too far away, so that I cannot be at all sure that I hit him.

MARTIN KRUMM: No, you didn't hit him;—

TRAVELER: How do you know that?

MARTIN KRUMM: I just mean, because it was already dark: and I hear that nobody can aim well in the dark.

TRAVELER: I cannot describe to you, how grateful your master was to me. A hundred times he called me his savior, and pressed me to return to his estate with him. I only wish that my circumstances permitted me to remain longer in the company of this pleasant man; as it is, however, I must set out again today—And for just that very reason, I'm looking for my servant.

MARTIN KRUMM: Oh, don't stay on my account! But pardon just one more thing—Yes! what was it that I wanted to ask? The robbers,— tell me now,—what did they really look like? Were they on foot? They had disguised themselves, but as what?

TRAVELER: Your master absolutely insists that they were Jews. It's true they had beards, but their speech was the normal speech of a peasant from these parts. If they were disguised, as I most certainly believe, then the twilight really did come in handy for them. For I simply can't understand how Jews would be able to make the streets unsafe when so few of them are tolerated in this country.

MARTIN KRUMM: Yes, yes, I'm positive that they were Jews too. Perhaps you aren't really well enough acquainted with that godless trash yet. As many as there are of them, without exception, are swindlers, thieves, and highwaymen. And that's why it's a people which the Good Lord has cursed. It's a good thing I'm not the king. I wouldn't leave one of them, not a single one of them, alive. Oh! may God protect all upstanding Christians from these people. If the Good Lord didn't hate them himself, then why, in that terrible catastrophe a while back in Breslau, why did twice as many of them die as Christians? Our Reverend Preacher pointed that out very wisely in his last sermon. Why, it's as if they'd been listening and wanted to get revenge on our good master right away because of it. Oh! dear sir, if you want happiness and prosperity in the world watch out for Jews worse than for the plague!

TRAVELER: Would to God that that were only the voice of the common horde.

MARTIN KRUMM: Sir, for example: I was at the fair once—yes! when I think of the fair, straightaway I'd like to poison all the damn Jews all at once, if only I could. In the crowd they palmed this one's handkerchief, another's snuffbox and a third's watch, and I don't know what else! They're quick, unbelievably quick when it comes to stealing. A lot nimbler than our schoolmaster ever is on the organ. For example, sir: first of all they press up against you, just like I'm doing to you now—

TRAVELER: Just a bit more polite there, my friend!—

MARTIN KRUMM: Oh! Just let me show you. When they're standing like this—you see—then as quick as lightning they've got their hands on your pocket watch *(Instead of reaching for the pocket watch, he takes the snuffbox from his coat pocket.)* But then they can do all this with such skill, that you'd swear, their hands were going here when they're going there! If they are talking about the snuffbox, then they're surely aiming for your watch, and if they're talking about your watch, then what they really want to steal is your snuffbox. *(He's about to reach neatly for the watch, but is caught.)*

TRAVELER: Not so fast! Not so fast! What's your hand doing here?

MARTIN KRUMM: There, now, you can see, sir, what kind of a clumsy criminal I'd be. If a Jew had made a move like that, it would have been all over with the watch, that's for sure—But, I can see that I'm bothering you, so I'll take the liberty of commending myself to you, and for the good deeds you have rendered us, I'll remain forever Martin Krumm, your most obedient servant, most revered sir, the highly esteemed steward of this most noble nobleman's estate.

TRAVELER: Just go! Go!

MARTIN KRUMM: Just remember what I told you about the Jews. They're nothing but a godless thieving people!

Scene 3

The Traveler.

TRAVELER: Maybe this fellow, however stupid he is or pretends to be, is a more mischievous rogue than any Jew ever was! When a Jew practices deception, then, seven out of nine times, a Christian probably forced him into it. I doubt if many Christians can boast of having dealt honestly with a Jew: and they are surprised if he tries to repay them in kind? If trust and honesty are to reign between the two peoples, then both must contribute an equal share. But what's going to happen if for one of them it's an article of faith and practically a good deed to persecute the other? But—

Scene 4

The Traveler. Christoph.

TRAVELER: It's too bad that I always have to search for you for an hour whenever I want you.

CHRISTOPH: Surely you jest, sir. You'll certainly agree that I can only be in one place at a time, won't you? So is it my fault that you don't show up at that place? You can always find me right where I am, you know.

TRAVELER: Really? and you're already staggering? Now I understand why you're so insightful. Do you have to get drunk so early in the morning?

CHRISTOPH: You're talking about being drunk and I've hardly begun drinking! Except for a few good bottles of local wine, and a few glasses of brandy, and a bread roll, absolutely nothing has crossed my lips, as true as I'm standing here! I'm still completely sober.

TRAVELER: Oh! I can tell that just by looking at you! So I'm telling you as a friend, you should double your serving!

CHRISTOPH: Excellent advice! I will not neglect, as is my duty, to regard it as an order. I'll be off and you'll see just how obedient I can be!

TRAVELER: Don't be stupid! Instead of that, go and saddle the horses and pack up! I want to leave this morning.

CHRISTOPH: If you were only joking when you advised me to double the size of my breakfast, how can I begin to imagine that you are speaking in earnest now? You seem to want to have fun at my expense today! Does the young lady put you in such a good mood? Oh, she's the sweetest child.—Just a little bit older, if only she were just a little bit older. Isn't that right, sir? If a young lady has not reached a certain maturity,—

TRAVELER: Go and carry out my orders!

CHRISTOPH: You're getting serious. Nevertheless, I'll wait until you tell me for the third time. It's too important a point! You could have been too rash. And I have always been in the habit of allowing my master time to think things over. Give it some thought,—departing so early from a place where we're practically waited on hand and foot. We only just got here yesterday. We really deserve so much from this gentleman for what we've done, and for all that, we've hardly enjoyed as much as a supper and a breakfast here.

TRAVELER: Your rudeness is unbearable. Once one has decided to be a servant, one should get used to making less fuss.

CHRISTOPH: Good, sir! You're beginning to moralize, that is: you're getting angry. Calm down! I'm on my way!

TRAVELER: You really must not be used to thinking about things much. What we did for this gentleman can no longer be called a good deed as soon as we seem to expect the slightest gratitude for it. I should not even have allowed myself to be pressed into coming here. The pleasure of having—with no end in mind—come to the aid of a stranger, is great enough in itself. And he himself would have wished more blessings our way as we left, than he now gives us in exaggerated thanks. Whomever one obliges to extensive gratitude with attendant expenses, he bestows a service in return that may well be more bitter to him than our good deed was to us. Most people are far too corrupt to experience the presence of a benefactor as anything but highly inconvenient. It seems to humble their pride;—

CHRISTOPH: Your philosophy, sir, leaves you out of breath. Good! You'll see, that I am just as magnanimous as you. I'm going; in a quarter of an hour, you should be able to ride off.

Scene 5

The Traveler. The Lady.

TRAVELER: The more I try to keep aloof from this fellow, the more he forces himself on me.

LADY: Why are you leaving us, sir? Why are you all alone here? In the few hours that you have been with us, has our company become so repugnant to you? That would cause me great regret. I try to please all the world; and you, more than anyone else, I'd hate to displease.

TRAVELER: Excuse me, miss. I was just ordering my servant to make everything ready for our departure.

LADY: What are you talking about? your departure? But when did you arrive? It would be one thing if, a year from now, a melancholy hour were to give you such a notion. But what is this? you can't even bear to endure one whole day? That is too awful. I'll tell you, I'll get angry if you even so much as think about it again.

TRAVELER: You couldn't threaten me with anything more upsetting.

LADY: No? seriously? You would be upset if I were angry with you?

TRAVELER: Who could be indifferent to the wrath of a charming lady?

LADY: Your words sound almost as if you were making fun of me: but I will take them seriously; let's suppose I did make a mistake. So, good sir—I am moderately charming, as I have been told, and I'll tell you once again, I will be terribly, terribly angry if between now and the New Year, you give your leaving one more thought.

TRAVELER: How lovingly you've set the date. In the middle of winter, that's when you'd show me the door, in the most uncomfortable weather—

LADY: Oh dear! Who said that? I'm only saying that that's when, just for the sake of propriety, you can give a thought to leaving. We won't allow you to leave because of it; we'll ask you to—

TRAVELER: Also for the sake of propriety perhaps?

LADY: Oh dear! Who would think that such an honest face could be so mocking.—Oh! here comes Papa. I must be off! Don't tell him I was with you. As it is he reproaches me often enough for enjoying the company of men.

Scene 6

The Baron. The Traveler

BARON: Wasn't that my daughter with you? What on earth is the wild child running for?

TRAVELER: It is an inestimable good fortune to have such a pleasant and cheerful daughter. She's enchanting in her conversation, in which reigns the most charming innocence, the most unstudied wit.

BARON: You judge her too kindly. She has seldom been among her peers and possesses the art of pleasing, which one can hardly learn in the country, and which can often have a greater effect than beauty itself, in but very small measure. Everything about her is still just the way nature created it.

TRAVELER: And that is all the more charming, the less one encounters it in the cities. Everything there is dissembled, forced, and artificial. Yes, it's even got to the point where the words *stupidity, rudeness,* and *nature* are thought to mean exactly the same thing.

BARON: What could please me more than seeing how exactly our thoughts and opinions correspond! Oh, if only I'd had a friend like you long ago!

TRAVELER: You being unfair to your other friends.

BARON: To my other friends, you say? I am fifty years old. Acquaintances I've had, but never a single friend. And never has friendship seemed so attractive to me as in the few hours that I've been striving to win yours. How can I be worthy of it?

TRAVELER: My friendship has so little meaning, that the simple desire for it is of sufficient merit to receive it. Your request is worth far more than what you're asking for.

BARON: Oh, sir, the friendship of a benefactor—

TRAVELER: If I may,—is no friendship! If you think of me under this false aspect, then I cannot be your friend. Let's assume, for one moment, that I were your benefactor, would I not have to be afraid that your friendship were nothing more than an effective gratitude?

BARON: Shouldn't one be able to combine the two?

TRAVELER: With great difficulty! The latter considers a noble spirit to be a duty; the former demands only voluntary movements of the soul.

BARON: But how can I—Your overly sensitive discernments in these matters leave me completely confused.—

TRAVELER: Just don't value me more highly than I deserve. At the most, I am a person who did his duty with pleasure. Duty, in and of itself, is worth no gratitude. That I did it with pleasure, however, for that, I am sufficiently rewarded by your friendship.

BARON: This magnanimity confuses me even more.—But perhaps I am too bold—I have not yet dared to ask your name, you station in society. Perhaps I am offering my friendship to someone who—who would despise—

TRAVELER: Forgive me, sir! You—You are making yourself—You have far too high an opinion of me.

BARON *(aside):* Should I really ask him then? He could be offended by my curiosity.

TRAVELER *(aside):* If he asks me, what will I answer him?

BARON *(aside):* I won't ask him then; he could think it an impertinence.

TRAVELLER *(aside):* Should I tell him the truth?

BARON *(aside):* So I'll chose the safest path. First I'll have his servant questioned.

TRAVELER *(aside):* If only I could be spared this confusion!—

BARON: Why so thoughtful?

TRAVELER: I was just about to ask you the same question, sir—

BARON: I know—one forgets oneself now and again. Let's talk about something else—You know, it really was Jews who attacked me. Just now my steward told me that he came upon three of the them on the highway a few days ago. The way he described them to me, they looked more like criminals than honest people. And why should I even have any doubts about it? A people that is so bent on profit asks little whether it makes it justly or unjustly, by cunning or by force. They seem to be made for trade, or, to call a spade a spade, for swindling. Polite, free, enterprising, discreet, these are characteristics that would make them laudable, if they didn't use them all too often for our misfortune.—*(He stops a moment)*—Jews have already caused me no end of harm and aggravation. When I was still in the military, I let myself be talked into cosigning a note for an acquaintance, and the Jew on whom it was drawn not only drove me to the point where I had to pay him, but where I had to pay him twice—Oh! they are the most evil, the most despicable people—What do you say? You seem quite depressed.

TRAVELER: What should I say? I must say, that I have heard this complaint very often—

BARON: And isn't it true that their facial features have something about them that sets us against them right away? It's almost as if you can see the spitefulness, unscrupulousness, selfishness, deceit, and perjury clearly in their eyes—But why are you turning away from me?

TRAVELER: As I hear, sir, you are such a great expert in physiognomy, and I'm worried lest mine—

BARON: Oh! You insult me! How could you even suspect such a thing? Without being an expert in physiognomy I must tell you that I have never seen such an upright, magnanimous, and pleasant expression as yours.

TRAVELER: To tell you the truth: I am not partial to general judgments about whole peoples—You won't take this liberty of mine the wrong way.—I would like to believe that among all nations there were good and evil souls. And among the Jews—

Scene 7

The Young Lady. The Traveler. The Baron.

LADY: Oh! Papa!—

BARON: Well, well! You're fine wild one! You ran away from me before: what was the meaning of that?

LADY: I didn't run way from you, Papa; but only from your reprimands.

BARON: The difference is very subtle. But what was it then that had earned my reprimand?

LADY: Oh, surely you know. After all, you saw it. I was with the gentleman—

BARON: So?—

LADY: And the gentleman is a man, and you've ordered me not to have all that much to do with men.—

BARON: You should have noticed that this gentleman is an exception. I would only wish that he could tolerate you—I would view it with great pleasure if you were constantly in his company.

LADY: Oh!—I'm sure it was the first and the last time. His servant was already packing—And that's just what I wanted to tell you.

BARON: What? who? his servant?

TRAVELER: Yes, sir, I ordered him to. My duties, and my fear of being a burden to you—

BARON: What in the name of Heaven am I to think of that? Am I to be denied the good fortune of being able to show you even better that you have bound a grateful heart to you? Oh! I beg you, add yet a second to your good deed which will be as valuable to me as was saving my life; stay awhile with me—at least a few days; I would needs reproach myself for all eternity if I were to allow a man like you to depart from me—unknown, unhonored, unrewarded—if it be in my power to do otherwise. I have invited some of my relations today, to share my pleasure with them, and to afford them the good fortune of making the acquaintance of my guardian angel.

TRAVELER: Sir, I simply must—

LADY: Stay here, sir, stay here! I'll run and tell your servant to unpack again. But there he is now.

Scene 8

Christoph, in boots and spurs, with two valises under his arms. The others.

CHRISTOPH. Well! Everything is ready, sir. Let's be off! Shorten your farewells a little. What's the use of all that talking if we can't stay here?

BARON: Whatever is preventing you from staying here?

CHRISTOPH: Certain considerations, Baron, sir, which have the subbornness of my master as their cause and his magnanimity as their pretext.

TRAVELER: My servant is often rather stupid: forgive him. I see that your requests really are more than just compliments. I surrender, so that I might not, from fear of being rude, be guilty of rudeness.

BARON: Oh! What thanks I owe you!

TRAVELER: You can go and unpack again! We won't leave until tomorrow.

LADY: Well! can't you hear? What are you standing there for? Go and unpack again.

CHRISTOPH: By rights I should be angry. I almost feel as though my wrath were about to erupt, but because nothing worse has come of this than that we are to stay here and be wined and dined and well taken care of—so be it! Usually I don't like people making unnecessary work for me,—don't you know?

TRAVELER: Be quiet! You are too impudent.

CHRISTOPH: Only because I tell the truth.

LADY: Oh! this is splendid that you're staying with us. Now I like you twice as well. Come, I'll show you our garden; you'll like it.

TRAVELER: If you like it, miss, that's as good as certain.

LADY: Come on now;—it's almost dinnertime. Papa, we have your permission, don't we?

BARON: I'll even accompany you myself.

LADY: No, no, we can't expect that of you! You must have things to do.

BARON: I have nothing more important to do now than to please my guest.

LADY: He won't hold it against you—isn't that right, sir? *(softly to him)* Do say no! I would so like to go alone with you.

TRAVELER: I will regret having so easily allowed myself to be convinced to stay here, as soon as I see that I am causing you the slightest inconvenience. So I beg you—

BARON: Oh why pay any attention to the child's talk?

LADY: Child?—Papa!—Don't embarrass me like that!—The gentleman will think I'm just a baby!—Don't worry about it! I'm old enough to go for a walk with you. Come!—But just look, your servant is still standing there with the valises under his arms.

CHRISTOPH: I would have thought that was only of concern to the one who was sweating over them!

TRAVELER: Be quiet! They do you more honor here than you deserve—

Scene 9

Lisette. The former.

BARON *(sees Lisette coming):* Sir, I'll follow you in just a moment, if you would like to accompany my daughter into the garden.

LADY: Oh! Stay as long as you want. We won't be at a loss to pass the time. Come! *(The Lady and the Traveler depart.)*

BARON: Lisette, I have something to say to you!—

LISETTE: Oh, what?

BARON *(softly to her):* I still don't know who our guest is. And for certain reasons, I don't want to ask him, either. Couldn't you talk to his servant and—

LISETTE: I know what you want. My own curiosity is driving me to that very thing—and that's why I came here.—

BARON: Do your best then,—and bring me the news. You will earn my gratitude.

LISETTE: Go on now.

CHRISTOPH: You won't take it amiss sir, that we like it here with you. But I beg you, don't put yourself out on my account; I'm satisfied with everything you have here.

BARON: Lisette, I give him into your care. Let him want for nothing. *(off)*

CHRISTOPH: So, mademoiselle, I commend myself to your good care, which will let me want for nothing. *(about to leave)*

Scene 10

Lisette. Christoph.

LISETTE *(stops him):* No, sir, I can't find it in my heart to let you be so discourteous. Am I not enough of a lady to be worth a short conversation?

CHRISTOPH: Jesus! You're very particular about these things, mamselle. Whether you're enough or too much of a lady I can't say. Judging by your talkative mouth, I could almost assert the latter. But be that as it may; you'll grant me my leave now;—As you can see, I have my hands and arms full.—As soon as I'm hungry or thirsty, I'll be at your door.

LISETTE: That's just what our master of the harness does too!

CHRISTOPH: Hang it! He must be a clever fellow: he does it like me.

LISETTE: If you want to meet him, he's on a chain at the back of the house.

CHRISTOPH: Damn! I do believe you mean the dog. I see that you must have thought I meant physical hunger and thirst. But that's not what I meant—I meant the hunger and thirst of love. That, mademoiselle, that! Are you satisfied with my explanation now?

LISETTE: More than with what it was you explained!

CHRISTOPH: Oh my! Just between us:—Are you saying then that it would not be unwelcome to you if I were to offer you my love?

LISETTE: Perhaps! Do you want to offer it to me? in all seriousness?

CHRISTOPH: Perhaps!

LISETTE: For shame! What kind of an answer is that? perhaps?

CHRISTOPH: And yet it wasn't one whit different from yours!

LISETTE: Yes, but in my mouth it meant something entirely different! "Perhaps" is a lady's greatest insurance. For no matter how bad our game, we must never let anybody see our cards.

CHRISTOPH: Well, if that's the way it is!—I thought we were going to get down to businss.—*(He hurls both valises to the ground.)* I don't know why I'm making myself sweat like this! It's like this!—I love you, mamselle.

LISETTE: That's what I call saying a lot with very little. Let's analyze this more closely—

CHRISTOPH: No, let's just drop it entirely. But—just so we can divulge our thoughts to each other in peace;—Would you care to have a seat?—Standing makes me tired.—No need for ceremony! *(He forces her to sit on the valise)*—I love you, mamselle.—

LISETTE: But,—This seat's awfully hard—you know, I think there are books in here—

CHRISTOPH: And very romantic and clever ones at that;—and still you find them hard to sit on? It's my master's traveling library. It consists of comedies to make you cry, and tragedies to make you laugh, of romantic epics, profound drinking songs, and whatever other new things like that he has. But let's change seats! You sit on mine!—No need for ceremony!—mine is the softest.

LISETTE: Forgive me—I would not be so rude—

CHRISTOPH: No need for ceremony,—No fuss now!—You don't want to? Then I'll carry you.—

LISETTE: Well, if you're ordering me to—*(She stands up and is about to sit on the other one.)*

CHRISTOPH: Ordering? God forbid!—No! ordering, that's going too far.—If you're going to take it like that, then you'd better stay where you are! *(He sits down on his valise again.)*

LISETTE *(aside):* The ruffian! But I'll just have to put up with it—

CHRISTOPH: Where were we then?—Yes,—talking about love—So, I love you, mamselle. *Je vous aime,* I'd say, if you were a French marquise.

LISETTE: Jesus! You're not French are you?

CHRISTOPH: No, I must confess my disgrace: I'm only a German. But I have had the good fortune of keeping company with various Frenchmen, and that's how I kind of learned just what makes for an upright fellow! I think you can tell just by looking at me.

LISETTE: So you and your master come from France, perhaps?

CHRISTOPH: Oh no!—

LISETTE: Well then where do you come from then?

CHRISTOPH: Where we come from is a few miles past France.

LISETTE: You don't mean from Italy?

CHRISTOPH: Not far from there.

LISETTE: From England then?

CHRISTOPH: Almost; England is a province of it. We live over fifty miles from here. But—my God!—my horses,—the poor creatures are still saddled. Excuse me, mamselles!—Hurry up! Stand up! *(He puts the valises under his arm again).*—Despite my fervent love, I have to go and do what must be done. We still have the whole day, and more importantly, the whole night in front of us. We'll still come together on this. I'll know how to find you.

Scene 11

Martin Krumm. Lisette.

LISETTE: I won't be able to learn very much from him! Either he's too stupid or too shrewd, and both make you inscrutable.

MARTIN KRUMM: Well, Miss Lisette? So that's the man that's supposed to replace me in your affections?

LISETTE: He didn't have to.

MARTIN KRUMM: Didn't have to? And here I thought I was firmly ensconced in your heart.

LISETTE: That's just it, Steward, you *thought* so. People of your sort have the right to think tasteless thoughts. That's why I'm not upset that you thought it, but just that you told me. I'd like to know what business my heart is of yours? With what favors, with what presents have you won a right to it? It's not the done thing anymore to give one's heart away just any old time. And do you think that I'm really so hard up with mine? I'll surely find an honest man for it before I cast it to the swine.

MARTIN KRUMM: Jesus! That's made me all stuffed up! I'll have to take a pinch of tobacco now. Perhaps it'll go away again if I sneeze. *(He pulls out the stolen box, plays with it in his hands, and finally takes a pinch in an absurdly arrogant manner.)*

LISETTE *(eyeing him furtively from the side):* Damn! where did this fellow get that box from?

MARTIN KRUMM: Would you care for a pinch?

LISETTE: Oh, your most humble servant, Mr. Steward, sir! *(She takes a pinch.)*

MARTIN KRUMM: What a difference a silver box makes!—Could an earwig be more pliant?

LISETTE: Is it a silver box?

MARTIN KRUMM: If it weren't silver, it wouldn't be Martin Krumm's.

LISETTE: Aren't I allowed to have a look at it?

MARTIN KRUMM: Yes, but only if I don't let go of it.

LISETTE: The design is superb.

MARTIN KRUMM: Yes, it weighs almost three ounces.

LISETTE: Just for the design, I'd like to have a box like that.

MARTIN KRUMM: When I have it melted down, the design will be all yours.

LISETTE: You're too kind! Of course, it must be a present.

MARTIN KRUMM: Yes—it didn't cost me a penny!

LISETTE: You know, a present like that could really dazzle a lady! You'll be able to get anything you want with that, Steward. At least, *I* would hardly be able to defend myself if someone were to come at me with a silver box. With a box like that, a lover would have an easy time of it with me.

MARTIN KRUMM: I see, I see!—

LISETTE: Seeing as it didn't cost you anything, Steward, I'd advise you to make a good friend for yourself with it—

MARTIN KRUMM: I see, I see!—

LISETTE *(in a flattering voice):* Wouldn't you like to give it to me then?—

MARTIN KRUMM: Oh, forgive me!—It's not the done thing anymore to give away silver boxes just any old time. And do you think, Miss Lisette, that I'm so hard up with mine? I'm sure I'll be able to find an honest man for it, before I cast it to the swine.

LISETTE: Has anyone ever seen such stupid rudeness!—Thinking a snuffbox is as precious as a heart?

MARTIN KRUMM: Well, a heart of stone and a snuffbox of silver—

LISETTE: Perhaps it would cease to be of stone if—But all my words are in vain—You are not worthy of my love—What a good-hearted fool I am!—*(almost in tears)* and I almost believed that the steward was one of those honest people who mean what they say—

MARTIN KRUMM: And what a good-hearted fool I am, to believe that a woman means what she says. There, my little Lisette, don't cry!—*(He gives her the box.)* But now I really am worthy of your love, aren't I? Just to begin with, I won't ask for anything more than to give your hand a little kiss!—*(He kisses her.)* Oh, how wonderful that tastes!—

Scene 12

The Lady. Lisette. Martin Krumm.

LADY *(she comes creeping up and pushes his head onto Lisette's hand)*: Hey, Steward—kiss my hand too!

LISETTE: What the—

MARTIN KRUMM: Gladly, milady—*(about to kiss her hand)*

LADY *(slaps his face)*: You lout! Can't you understand a joke?

MARTIN KRUMM: The devil takes jokes like that!

LISETTE: Ha! ha! ha! *(Laughs at him.)* Oh, I' sorry for you, my dear Steward—Ha! ha! ha!

MARTIN KRUMM: Oh?? and you're laughing too? Is that the thanks I get? Well that's fine, just fine! *(off)*

LISETTE: Ha! ha! ha!

Scene 13

Lisette. The Lady.

LADY: I wouldn't have believed it if I hadn't seen it with my own eyes. You let yourself be kissed? And by the Steward at that?

LISETTE: I'm sure I don't know what right you have to spy on me? I thought you'd gone for a walk in the garden with the foreigner.

LADY: Yes, and I'd still be with him if Papa hadn't come along! But as it was I couldn't say one witty thing to him. Papa is much too serious.

LISETTE: Oh? What do you call witty? What do you have to say to him that your Papa couldn't hear.

LADY: Thousands of things!—But you'll make me angry if you ask me any more. All right, I like the foreign gentleman. I can certainly admit that, can't I?

LISETTE: But you'd probably have a terrible fight with your Papa if he were to bring you a bridegroom like that one day, wouldn't you? And in all seriousness, who knows what he will do? It's just a pity that your aren't a few years older: otherwise it could happen very soon.

LADY: Oh, if it's only a matter of age, Papa can just make me a few years older. I certainly won't contradict him.

LISETTE: No, I know something even better. I'll give you a few of my years, then we'll both get something out of it. Then I won't be too old and you won't be too young.

LADY: Yes, that's true! That will work!

LISETTE: Here comes the foreigner's servant; I have to speak with him. It's all in your best interest—Leave me alone with him.—Go on!

LADY: Don't forget about the years though—Do you hear, Lisette?

Scene 14

Lisette. Christoph.

LISETTE: Sir, surely you must be hungry or thirsty to be back again already, eh?

CHRISTOPH: Yes, of course!—But don't forget how I explained that hunger and thirst. To tell you the truth, my dear young lady, I had already cast my eye on you as soon as I got off my horse yesterday. But because I would only be staying here a few hours, I didn't think it would be worth the trouble to introduce myself to you. What would we have been able to do in such a short time? We would have had to have begun our story at the end. And it's not completely certain yet that we can still pull this off.

LISETTE: That's true! but at least now we can go about it properly. You can make me your proposal; I can give you my answer. I can tell you my doubts, you can refute them. We can think carefully about every step we take and neither of us will be able to sell the other a pig in a poke. If only you had made me your offer of love first thing yesterday; it's true, I would have accepted it. But just think how much I would have been risking had I not even had time to inquire about your station, wealth, country, service, and other such things?

CHRISTOPH: Jesus! Would that really have been so necessary? So much fuss? You really couldn't make more if we were getting married?—

LISETTE: Oh, if I only thought of it as a plain old wedding it would be absurd to be so conscientious. But with a love affair it is quite something else indeed! In that case the silliest trifle becomes an important point! So don't think you'll get the slightest kindness from me if you don't satisfy my curiosity in every detail.

CHRISTOPH: Oh? How far does this curiosity of yours extend?

LISETTE: Because you can best judge a servant by his master, I want to know first and foremost—

CHRISTOPH: Who my master is? Ha! ha! that's funny. You're asking me something I'd like to ask you, if I thought you knew more than I.

LISETTE: And you think you can get away with that trite excuse? In short, I must know who your master is, or our whole friendship is over.

CHRISTOPH: I've only known my master for four weeks. That's how long ago he took me into his service in Hamburg. From that point on I attended him, but I never bothered to inquire about his station or his name. This much is certain—he must be rich; for he let neither himself nor me suffer any want on the journey. What more do I need to worry about?

LISETTE: What can I expect from your love when you won't even trust such a trifle to my discretion. I would never ever treat you like that. For example, here I have a beautiful silver snuffbox—

CHRISTOPH: Yes? And?

LISETTE: You'd only have to ask me just a little and I'd tell you whom I got it from—

CHRISTOPH: Oh! Well, that's really not very important to me! I'd rather know who's supposed to get it from you.

LISETTE: On that point I really haven't decided anything yet. But if you shouldn't get it then you have nobody else to blame but yourself. I certainly wouldn't let your honesty go unrewarded.

CHRISTOPH: Or rather my talkativeness. But, as true as I'm an honest fellow, if I am being closemouthed this time, then it's from necessity. Because I know nothing that I could blab about. Damn it! I'd be happy to pour out my secrets if I only had some.

LISETTE: Adieu! I won't assail your virtue any longer. I only hope it helps you get a silver box and a sweetheart soon, just as it's deprived you of both now. *(about to go)*

CHRISTOPH: Where are you going? Be patient! *(aside)* I'm going to have to lie. For surely I shouldn't let a present like that slip through my fingers? What will it hurt anyway?

LISETTE: Well, do you want to be more specific? But,—I can see that it's too much for you. No, no, I don't want to know anything.

CHRISTOPH: Yes, yes. You shall know everything!—*(aside)* If only I really knew how to lie well. Just listen! My master is—is a nobleman. He comes—together we come from—from—Holland. Because of certain unpleasantnesses—a trifle—because of a murder—he had to—flee.

LISETTE: What? Because of a murder?

CHRISTOPH: Yes,—but because of an honorable murder—flee because of a duel—And right now—he's on the run.

LISETTE: And you, my friend?

CHRISTOPH: I'm on the run with him too. The victim had us—I mean the friends of the victim are pursuing us; and because of this pursuit—Now you can easily guess the rest—What the devil is one to do? Think about it yourself; a saucy young fop insults us. My master knocks him down. That's what had to happen. If someone insults me, I do the same thing,—or—or I box his ears. An honest fellow can't put up with anything.

LISETTE: That's good! I like people like that! Because I'm a bit intolerant too. But look, your master's coming. You wouldn't think to look at him that he could be so angry, so cruel.

CHRISTOPH: Come on! let's get out of his way. He might be able to tell that I've betrayed him just by looking at me.

LISETTE: I'm satisfied with—

CHRISTOPH: But the silver box—

LISETTE: Come on. *(aside)* First I want to see what I'll get from my master for the secret I've discovered: if all my trouble was worth it, then he shall have it.

Scene 15

The Traveler.

TRAVELER: I miss my box. It's a trifle; still the loss is painful to me. Could the Steward have?—But no, I could have lost it—I could have pulled it out carelessly.—I mustn't insult anyone with my suspicions. Nevertheless—He pressed himself up against me;—he reached for my watch:—I caught him; could he have also reached for my box without my having caught him?

Scene 16

Martin Krumm. The Traveler.

MARTIN KRUMM *(when he becomes aware of the traveler, he starts to turn around again):* Oh dear!

TRAVELER: Well, well, come closer, my friend! *(aside)* He's as shy as if he knew my thoughts!—Well? come closer!

MARTIN KRUMM *(defiantly):* Oh! I don't have time. I already know you want to chat with me. I have more important things to do. I don't want to hear about your exploits ten times. Tell them to someone who doesn't know about them yet.

TRAVELER: What's this I'm hearing? Before, the Steward was ingenuous and polite. Now he's impudent and rude. Which is your real mask then?

MARTIN KRUMM: Oh! Where the devil do you get off calling my face a mask? I don't want to fight with you,—otherwise—*(He's about to leave.)*

TRAVELER: His impudent behavior confirms my suspicion.—No, no, be patient! There's something important I have to ask you—

MARTIN KRUMM: And I won't give you an answer, no matter how important it is. So just spare yourself the question.

TRAVELER: I'll risk it—But, how sorry I would be if I were to do him wrong—My friend, have you seen my box? It's missing.—

MARTIN KRUMM: What sort of a question is that? Is it my fault that someone stole it from you? What do you think I am? the fence? or the thief?

TRAVELER: Who said anything about stealing? You're practically giving yourself away—

MARTIN KRUMM: I'm giving myself away? So you think I have it? Do you know what it means when you accuse an honest fellow of something like that? Do you know?

TRAVELER: Why are you shouting like that? I haven't accused you of anything yet. You're your own accuser. And for all that, I don't know if I would be so wrong. Who was it that I caught before when he was trying to reach for my watch?

MARTIN KRUMM: Oh, you're a man who can't understand a joke. Listen!—*(aside)* If only he didn't see Lisette with it—surely the girl won't be a fool and show off with it—

TRAVELER: Oh, I understand your joke so well that I think you want to joke around with my box too. But if you take the joke too far, then it finally gets serious. I'm sorry about your good name. Even suppose I were convinced what you really didn't mean any harm, would others also—

MARTIN KRUMM: Oh,—others!—others! Others would long since be sick of being accused of something like this. But, if you think that I have it: pat me down,—search me—

TRAVELER: That's not my job. And moreover, people don't carry everything with them in their pockets.

MARTIN KRUMM: All right! so you can see that I'm an honest fellow, I'll turn my pockets inside out myself! Pay attention! *(aside)* It would be really bad luck if it were to fall out!

TRAVELER: Oh, don't go to any bother!

MARTIN KRUMM: No, no: you'll see, you'll see. *(He turns one pocket inside out.)* Is that a box? There are bread crumbs in there: goodness me! *(He turns the second inside out.)* There's nothing in there either! Oh,—yes, there is! a little piece of a calendar.—I keep it for the verses over the months. You're really queer!—All right, let's get on with it. Pay attention: I'll turn the third one inside out. *(When he turns it inside out, two big beards fall out.)* Jesus! what did I drop there? *(He tries to pick them up quickly, but the traveler is quicker and grabs one of them.)*

TRAVELER: What's this supposed to be?

MARTIN KRUMM *(aside):* Oh, damn it! I thought I'd gotten rid of that stuff a long time ago.

TRAVELER: Why, that's a beard. *(He holds it up to his chin.)* Don't I look like a Jew now?—

MARTIN KRUMM: Oh, give it here! give it here! Who knows that you're thinking this time? I sometimes frighten my little boy with it. That's what it's for.

TRAVELER: You'll be so kind as to let me have it. I want to do some frightening with it too.

MARTIN KRUMM. Oh! Don't try and take me on! I have to have it back! *(He tries to rip it out of his hand.)*

TRAVELER. Go, or—

MARTIN KRUMM *(aside):* Jesus! Now I'll have to find a way out of this somehow.—It's all right; it's all right! I see that you came here to be my undoing. But, devil take me, I am an honest fellow, and I'd like to see the man that can spread foul gossip about me. Just you take note of that. No matter what happens, I can swear that I didn't use the beard for anything bad.—*(off)*

Scene 17

The Traveler.

TRAVELER: The man himself makes me suspect something very prejudicial to him.—Couldn't he have been one of the disguised robbers?—But I would rather be cautious in my suspicion.

Scene 18

The Baron. The Traveler.

TRAVELER: Would you believe that yesterday when I got into that fight with those Jewish highwaymen I pulled out one of their beards? *(He shows him the beard.)*

BARON: What do you make of that, sir?—But why did you leave me so suddenly in the garden?

TRAVELER: Forgive my discourtesy. I meant to come right back to you. I only went to look for my box which I must have lost somewhere around here.

BARON: That wounds me to the quick. That you should suffer a loss while here with me?

TRAVELER: It would be no great loss—But just have a look at this handsome beard!

BARON: You've already showed it to me. Why?

TRAVELER: I'll explain myself to you more clearly. I think—but no, I'll keep my suspicions to myself.—

BARON: Your suspicions? Explain yourself?

TRAVELER: No; I've been too rash. I could be mistaken—

BARON: You're making me nervous.

TRAVELER: What do you think of our steward?

BARON: No, no; we're not going to steer the conversation to something else—I beg you by the good deed you have done me, tell me what you believe, what you suspect, what you could be mistaken about!

TRAVELER: Only your answer to my question can impel me to tell you.

BARON: What I think of my steward? I think him an honest and upstanding man.

TRAVELER: Then forget that I wanted to say anything.

BARON: A beard,—suspicions,—the steward,—how am I to put all these things together? Do my requests have no effect on you? You could be mistaken? Let's assume you were mistaken; what risk would you be running with a friend?

TRAVELER: Your entreaties are too much for me. I'll tell you then, that the steward carelessly dropped this beard; that he had another one, which he hastily put back in his pocket; that his words betrayed a person who believes that people will think him as evil as his deeds; that I also caught him in a none too honest, at least, none too clever move.

BARON: It's as if my eyes had suddenly been opened. I fear,—You are not mistaken. And you had doubts about telling me something like this? I'll go this instant and make every effort to get to the truth! Could it be that I have my murderer in my own house?

TRAVELER: But don't be angry with me, if, fortunately, you should find my suspicions to be false. You forced them out of me, otherwise I would most certainly have kept silent about them.

BARON: Whether I find them to be true or false, I will always be grateful to you for them.

Scene 19

The Traveler, and afterwards, Christoph.

TRAVELER: If only he doesn't deal too hastily with him. For no matter how great the suspicion is, the man could still be innocent. I am quite ill at ease. Indeed, it is no small matter to make a master so suspicious of his subordinates. Even if he finds them to be innocent, still he loses his trust in them forever.—Now, on second thoughts, I'm sure I should have kept silent.—Won't people think that my suspicion had selfishness and revenge as its cause? What if they learn that I blame him for my loss?—I'd give anything if I could still prevent the investigation—

CHRISTOPH *(approaches laughing):* Ha! ha! ha! Do you know who you are, sir?

TRAVELER: Do you know that you're a fool? What are you asking?

CHRISTOPH: Good, if you don't know, I'll tell you. You are a nobleman. You come from Holland. You had some trouble and a duel there. You had the good fortune of skewering a young know-it-all. The friends of the victim are pursuing you vigorously. You are on the run! And I have the honor of attending you on the run.

TRAVELER: Are you dreaming or are you mad?

CHRISTOPH: Neither. Then for a madman, my speech is too clever, and for a dreamer, too crazy.

TRAVELER: Who told you this absurd tale?

CHRISTOPH: Oh? So you think someone would have had to make it up for me? But don't you think it extremely well devised? In the short time I had to lie, I'm sure I couldn't have come up with anything better. At least now you are safe from further curiosity.

TRAVELER: But what am I to make of all this?

CHRISTOPH: Nothing more than you want to; leave the rest to me. Listen to how it happened. They asked me for your name, station, country, duties; I didn't keep them waiting for an answer, I said everything I knew; that is, I said I knew nothing. You won't have any difficulty believing that this news was very inadequate, and that they had little cause to be satisfied with it. So they kept on pressing me for more; but in vain! I said nothing, because I had nothing to say. But finally, a present they offered me made me say more than I knew; that is: I lied.

TRAVELER: Wretch! I see I'm in fine hands with you.

CHRISTOPH: Surely my lies can't have been the truth just by coincidence?

TRAVELER: Insolent liar! You've gotten me in such a muddle, out of which—

CHRISTOPH: Out of which you can immediately extricate yourself as soon as you make that lovely little name, which you were so kind as to call me just now, better known.

TRAVELER: But won't I be forced to reveal myself then?

CHRISTOPH: All the better! Then I'll finally have a chance to make your acquaintance too. But judge for yourself whether, in all good conscience, I could have had a bad conscience about these lies. *(He pulls the box out.)* Look at this box! Could I have earned it more easily?

TRAVELER: Show it to me!—*(He takes it in his hand.)* What's this I see?

CHRISTOPH: Ha! ha! ha! I thought you'd be amazed! You would have lied up a storm yourself if you could have earned a box like this.

TRAVELER: So you're the one who stole it from me?

CHRISTOPH: What? What was that?

TRAVELER: Your disloyalty does not vex me as much as the all too rash suspicion I have brought upon an honest man because of it. And you're shamelessly brazen enough to try to convince me that it was a—although obtained almost as despicably—present? Go! Get out of my sight and don't come back!

CHRISTOPH: Are you dreaming, or—out of respect I won't mention the other. Jealousy couldn't possibly be the cause of such excesses. The box is supposed to be yours? I'm supposed to have stolen it from you, *salva venia.* If that were the case, I'd have to be a stupid idiot to flaunt it in front of you of all people! Good—here comes Lisette! Come quickly! Help me bring my master to his senses again.

Scene 20

Lisette. The Traveler. Christoph.

LISETTE: Oh sir, what a commotion you're causing here. What ever did our steward do to you? You made the master absolutely furious with him. They're talking about beards, and boxes, and plundering; the steward is crying and cursing and saying that he's innocent, and that you're lying. The master can't be calmed down, he's even sent for the warden and the bailiff, to have him locked up. What's the meaning of all that?

CHRISTOPH: Oh, that's not all yet, just listen, just listen to what he has in mind for me—

TRAVELER: Yes, indeed, my dear Lisette, I have been too rash. The steward is innocent. It was my godless servant who plunged me into this trouble. He's the one who stole my box from me—and I suspected the steward of doing it; and the beard really could have been a children's game, as he said. I'll go and give him satisfaction, I'll confess my mistake; whatever he demands, I'll—

CHRISTOPH: No, no, stay! First you must give me satisfaction. To hell with it, Lisette, speak up, say how things really are. I wish you were swinging from the gallows with your wretched box. Am I supposed to let myself be called a thief because of it? Didn't you give it to me?

LISETTE: Yes, of course! And you should keep it too.

TRAVELER: So it's true then? But the box belongs to me!

LISETTE: To you? I didn't know that!

TRAVELER: And so Lisette must have found it? and my carelessness is to blame for all this confusion? *(to Christoph)* I have also done you wrong. Forgive me. I am truly ashamed to have been so rash.

LISETTE *(aside):* Jesus! Now it makes sense to me! Oh, I'm sure he wasn't too rash at all.

TRAVELER: Come we'll—

Scene 21

The Baron. The Traveler. Lisette. Christoph.

BARON *(quickly joins them):* Lisette, give the gentleman back his box this very instant! Everything is out in the open. He has confessed everything. And you weren't ashamed to take presents from someone like that? Well? Where is the box?

TRAVELER: So it really is true?

LISETTE: The gentleman's had it back again for ages. I thought that if you could accept someone's services, I could certainly accept that someone's presents! I knew as little about him as you!

CHRISTOPH: So, I guess my present has gone to blazes? Easy come, easy go!

BARON: But, dearest friend, how shall I show you my gratitude? For the second time you pull me out of equally great danger. I owe you my life. Without you, I would never have discovered my imminent misfortune. The warden, the man I considered to be the most honest on all my estates, was his godless accomplice. Ask yourself whether I could ever have foreseen this? If you had journeyed from me today—

TRAVELER: It's true—then the help which I thought I had rendered you yesterday would have been very incomplete. I consider myself most fortunate, that Heaven has selected me for this unexpected discovery, and now I rejoice as much as I previously trembled with the fear of making a mistake.

BARON: I admire the love you have for your fellow man as well as your magnanimity. Oh, I only hope that what Lisette reported to me is true!

Scene 22

The Lady and the others.

LISETTE: Well, why shouldn't it be true?

BARON: Come, my daughter, come! Join your plea to mine: beseech my savior to take your hand in marriage, and with your hand, my fortune. What can I give him in my gratitude that is more precious than you, whom I love just as much as him? Do not be at all surprised that I could make you such an offer. Your servant has revealed to us who you are. Allow me the inestimable pleasure of my gratitude. My fortune is equal to my station, and the latter equal to yours. Here you are safe from your enemies and will be among friends who will adore you. But suddenly you seem despondent? What am I to think?

LADY: Are you perhaps worried because of me? I assure you I will obey Papa with pleasure!

TRAVELER: Your generosity astonishes me. From the magnitude of the reward you offer me, I only now realize the smallness of my good deed. But what shall I answer you? My servant did not speak the truth and I—

BARON: Would to God that you really weren't who you said you were. Would to God your station were lower than mine. Then my reward would be a little more precious, and you would perhaps be less disinclined to grant my request.

TRAVELER *(aside):* Why do I not just reveal myself? Sir, your magnanimity fills my whole soul, but blame fate, not me, that your offer is in vain. I am—

BARON: Already married perhaps?

TRAVELER: No—

BARON: Well? What?

TRAVELER: I am a Jew.

BARON: A Jew? cruel fate!

CHRISTOPH: A Jew?

LISETTE: A Jew?

LADY: Oh, what difference does that make?

LISETTE: Sh! milady, sh! I'll explain later what difference it makes.

BARON: So are there cases then where Heaven itself keeps us from being grateful?

TRAVELER: You have made it unnecessary by the very fact that you want to be grateful.

BARON: Then I will at least do as much as fate allows me to do. Take my whole fortune. I would rather be poor and grateful than rich and ungrateful.

TRAVELER: This offer too is in vain in my case, as the God of my fathers has given me more than I need. For my whole reward I ask nothing but that in the future you judge my people a little less harshly and less categorically. I did not hide from you because I am ashamed of my religion. No! but I saw what you had a liking for me and a loathing for my nation. And anyone's friendship, whoever he may be, has always been invaluable to me.

BARON: I am ashamed of my conduct.

CHRISTOPH: And I'm just beginning to recover from my astonishment. What? You are a Jew and had the audacity to take an honest Christian into your service? You should have been serving me! That would have been right according to the Bible. Holy Christ! You insulted all of Christendom in me. That's why I couldn't figure out why he refused to eat any pork on the journey and was up to all kinds of other tomfoolery.—Don't think for one moment that I'll attend you any longer! And I'll bring charges against you into the bargain.

TRAVELER: I can't expect you to think any better than the rest of the common Christian horde. I will not remind you of the miserable conditions I wrenched you from in Hamburg. Nor will I force you to stay with me any longer. But because I am more or less satisfied with your services, and, moreover, because, just a while ago I harbored an unjustified suspicion against you, you shall keep as a reward that which caused my suspicion. (*Gives him the box.*) You can have your reward too. So, go wherever you want to!

CHRISTOPH: No, by Christ! There must be Jews who aren't Jews at all.

You are an honest man. Done! I'll stay with you! A Christian would have given me a kick in the ribs and no box!

BARON: All I see of you delights me. Come, let's see that the culprits are put into safe custody. Oh, how worthy of respect would all Jews be if they were all like you!

TRAVELER: And how delightful the Christians, if they all had your character!

(The Baron, the Lady and the Traveler off.)

Last Scene

Lisette, Christoph.

LISETTE: So, my friend, did you lie to me before?

CHRISTOPH: Yes, and for two reasons. Firstly, because I didn't know the truth and secondly, because for a box that one has to give back anyway, one can't really speak much of the truth.

LISETTE: And if it comes to that, are you really a Jew too, no matter how much you pretend?

CHRISTOPH: That question's too inquisitive for a young miss! Come on now!

(He puts his arm around her and they walk off together)

End of The Jews

Concerning the Comedy
THE JEWS

Amongst the acclaim which the two comedies in the fourth part of my writings have found, I count, and rightly so, the remarks of which one, *The Jews,* has been judged worthy. I ask in all urgency that it be not ascribed to any inability to tolerate criticism, if I now make ready to reply to them. That I do not overlook them in silence is, rather, a sign that they were not repugnant to me, that I have pondered them, and that I wish for nothing more earnestly, that to learn the legitimate opinions of the art critics, which I will thereupon, should they unhappily fail to convince me, acknowledge with thanks.

These remarks were made in the seventieth issue of the Göttingen *Journal of Scholarly Matters* of this year, and assented to in the Jena scholarly journals. I must, of necessity, reproduce them here, if I do not wish to confuse those of my readers who have not laid eyes on them. "The purpose of this comedy," as my opponent so kindly says, "is a matter of most serious moral philosophy, namely, to show the foolishness and unjustness of the hatred and contempt with which we usually treat the Jews. Therefore, one cannot read this comedy without that tale of an honest Jew in Mr. Gellert's *The Swedish Countess*— which was written with the same purpose—necessarily coming to mind.* On reading both of them, however, one's enjoyment, as we experienced only too well, is constantly interrupted by something we would like to make known, either to raise some misgivings about it, or for the future improvement of fictions of this kind. In all these plays the unknown traveler is so completely good, so noble, so concerned that he may perchance have wronged his neighbor and insulted him with his suspicion, that while it is not impossible, it is certainly all too improbable that, amongst a people of these principles, this life-style and this education, which cannot but repay its evil treatment by the Christians with all too much enmity, or, at least, indifference, towards Christians, such a noble spirit could evolve, as it were, on its own. This improbability disturbs our enjoyment all the more, the more we wish that such a noble and beautiful image could be true and could really exist. But even mediocre virtue and probity are to be found so rarely among this people that the few examples thereof do not diminish the hatred against them as much as one would wish. According to the principles of moral philosophy, which at least the greater part of them have accepted, even a general probity is scarcely possible, especially as almost the entire people must live by trade, which gives more opportunity for and temptation to deceit than other ways of life."

It can easily be seen that these objections come down to two points. Firstly, that an upright and noble Jew, in and of himself, is something improbable; secondly, that the use of such a Jew in my comedy is improbable. It is apparent that the second does not follow from the first; and it is equally apparent that I would really only be able to safeguard myself with respect to the latter if I were to prefer the love of mankind to my honor, and preferred to lose on the latter point rather than on the former. Nevertheless, however, I must first speak my mind on the latter.

Did I use an upstanding, noble Jew in my comedy against all

*Christian Fürchtegott Gellert's novel, *The Life of the Swedish Countess of G.* was published in two volumes in 1747–48. In the second part Count G., telling of his experiences as a Russian captive, extols the virtue and humanity of a Jew and a young girl.

probability?—I have still to analyze this according to the particular concepts of my opponent. He attributes the improbability of such a Jew to the contempt and oppression under which these people labor and to the necessity in which they find themselves of living exclusively from trade. Be that as it may; must one not necessarily conclude that the improbability would disappear as soon as these circumstances ceased to occasion it? When will they cease to do this, however? Doubtlessly after thay have been destroyed by other circumstances, that is, when a Jew is in a position not to feel the contempt and the oppression of the Christians so keenly, and does not see himself compelled to sustain a miserable life through the benefits of some small despicable trade. What more could be required for this than wealth? But yes, the appropriate application of this wealth is also required. Now let us see whether I did not introduce both into the character of my Jew? He is rich; he says himself that the God of his fathers has given him more than he needs; I portray him on a journey; indeed, I even exempt him from that ignorance in which one could assume him to be; he reads, and is not without his books even on his journey. So tell me, is it thus still really true, that my Jew would have had to have evolved on his own? If one were to insist, however, that wealth, better experience, and an enlightened intellect could only have no effect on a Jew, then I would have to say that this is exactly the prejudice that I have tried to weaken through my comedy; a prejudice that can only flow from pride or hate, and that not only makes Jews brutish people, but, in fact, puts them far beneath humanity. Now if this prejudice is insuperable in my fellow Christians, then I dare not flatter myself that my play will ever be seen with pleasure. Do I want to convince them that each and every Jew is upstanding and generous, or even to accept the majority as that? I say it bluntly, even if my character were a Christian, his character would be very rare, and if only rarity determines improbability, very improbable too.—

I have now slowly come to the first point. Is a Jew, as I have drawn him, in and of himself improbable: and why is he thus? One will refer to the above-named causes. But, cannot these in fact disappear just as easily in ordinary life as they do in my play? Certainly, in order to believe this, one must be better acquainted with Jews other than that abominable trash that roams around at fairs. But I prefer to let another talk here, whom this circumstance must touch more deeply; one from this nation itself. I know him too well to deny him here the testimony of a man who is as intelligent as he is learned and honest. He wrote the following letter on the occasion of the Göttingen objections to a friend among his people who is his complete equal in good qualities. I foresee that people will find it hard to believe, and may consider this letter rather to be a fiction of mine, but I offer to convince incontrovertibly those, to whom it is of great import, of the authenticity of the same. Here it is.*

"*Dear Sir*,

"I sent you herewith the seventieth issue of the Göttingen *Scholarly Journal*. Read the article about Berlin. The learned journalists reviewed the fourth part of Lessing's writings, which we have so often read with pleasure. What do you think they criticize in the comedy, *The Jews?* The protagonist, who, as they put it, is much too noble and much too generous. The pleasure, so they say, which we experience in the beauty of such a character, is disrupted by its improbability, and that, finally, nothing remains in our hearts but the mere desire for his existence. These thoughts made me blush with shame. I am not capable of expressing everything they caused me to feel. What a humiliation for our oppressed nation! What exaggerated contempt! That ordinary Christian people have from time immemorial regarded us as the dregs of nature, as open sores on human society. But from learned people I had always expected a juster judgment; from them I had assumed that unreserved fairness, for lack of which, we are generally criticized. How greatly mistaken I was, to have credited each Christian author with as much honesty as he demands of others.

"In truth! How can someone who still possesses a sense of decency, have the temerity to deny a whole nation the probability of being able to produce one single honest man? From a nation, from which, as the author of *The Jews* puts it, all prophets and the greatest kings arose? Does his cruel verdict have any foundation? What a disgrace for the human race! No foundation? What a disgrace for him!

"Is it not enough that we must feel the bitterest hatred of the Christians in so many cruel ways; are these injustices against us to be justified by calumnies?

"We continue to be oppressed; in the midst of free and happy citizens we must live under continual restrictions, indeed we are, moreover, exposed to the mockery and contempt of all the world; only virtue, the sole comfort of oppressed souls, the sole refuge of the abandoned, let them not try to deny us completely.

"And yet if they do deny us this, what do the learned reviewers gain thereby? Their criticism nevertheless remains irresponsible. In fact, the

*The letter was written by Moses Mendelssohn (1729–86) to Dr. Aaron Emmerich Gumpertz who introduced Lessing and Mendelssohn to each other.

character of the traveling Jew (I am ashamed when I consider him from this aspect) should be what is wonderful, what is unexpected in the comedy. Should the character of an arrogant citizen who lets himself be turned into a Turkish prince, not be as improbable as a Jew who is magnanimous?* Let someone who knows nothing of the contempt for the Jewish nation attend a performance of this play; he will surely yawn for long periods during the whole play, although for us, it has very many beautiful parts. The beginning will lead him to observe sadly, how far national hatred can be pushed, and at the end he will have to laugh. These good people, he will think to himself, have finally made the great discovery that Jews are people too. So humanely does a spirit think, that is cleansed of prejudices.

"Not that I wish by this observation to devalue the Lessing play; not at all! It is known that the poet in general, and when he is working for the stage in particular, must conform solely to that opinion prevalent among the people. Accordingly, however, the unexpected character of the Jew must have a very moving effect on the audience. And in this much the whole Jewish nation is greatly obliged to him, that he takes pains to convince the world of a truth which is necessarily of great importance to it.

"Must not this review, this cruel damning of souls have come from the pen of a theologian? These people think they greatly aid the Christian religion when they proclaim all the people who are not Christians assassins and highwaymen. I am far from thinking so insultingly of the Christian religion; that would doubtless be the strongest proof against its verity, if, in order to establish it, one had to cast all humanity from one's sight.

"What of importance can we advance against our harsh judges who all too frequently seal their judgments with blood. Do not all their reproaches boil down to the insatiable avarice which they, perhaps through their own fault, exult to find among the common Jewish masses? Let us concede this to them; will it then therefore cease to be probable that a Jew should have saved the life of a Christian who had fallen into the hands of thieves? Or should he have done it, must he then necessarily let that noble pleasure, which comes from having fulfilled his duty in such an important matter, be spoiled with base rewards? Certainly not! Not when he has been placed in such circumstances as the Jew in the play.

"But how can it be unbelievable that among a whole people of such

---

*A reference to Molière's *Le bourgeois gentilhomme*.

principles and education, such a noble and sublime spirit should evolve, so to speak, on its own? What an insult! then is all our morality forfeit? then does no instinct for virtue stir within in us any longer? then Nature neglected us cruelly when it distributed that noblest gift to people, the natural love of goodness. How far above such cruelty you are, benevolent Father.

"Whoever knows you better, dearest friend, and knows how to appreciate your talents, can lack for no example of how easily happy spirits, without model or education, soar aloft, perfect their invaluable talents, better mind and heart, and can rise to the ranks of the greatest men. I point out to all that you, noble friend, would have taken on the role of the Jew in the play if, on your scholarly journey, you had been placed in his circumstances. Indeed I would humiliate our nation if I wished to continue to cite individual examples of noble spirits. Only yours I could not overlook, because it is so dazzling, and because I all too often admire it.

"In any case, certain human virtues are more common among Jews than most Christians. Consider the violent aversion they have for murder. It will not be possible to cite one example where a Jew (here I omit professional thieves) is supposed to have killed someone. How easy it is, however, for many an otherwise honest Christian to rob his neighbor of his life over a mere insult. They say that there is baseness among the Jews. Very well! if baseness spares human blood, then baseness is a virtue.

"How sympathetic they are to all people, how charitable to the poor of both nations. And how harsh does the conduct of most Christians towards their poor deserve to be called. It is true, they carry these two virtues almost too far. Their sympathy is all too sensitive and almost hinders justice, and their charity is almost wastefulness. But if only all those who indulged in excess indulged in good excesses.

"I could still add much about their industry, about their admirable moderation, the sanctity in their marriages. But their social virtues are already enough to refute the Göttingen *Journal;* and I pity him who could read such a general condemnation without shuddering. I am, etc."

* * *

I also have the answer to this letter in front of me. But I have second thoughts about printing it here. It is written with too much passion, and the retorts against the Christians are a little too energetic. You can certainly believe me, however, that both correspondents, even without wealth, have been able to achieve virtue and erudition, and I am convinced that they would have more successors among their own people if the Christians would only allow them to hold their heads up a little higher.—

The remaining part of the Göttingen objections, wherein I am encouraged to write another, similar comedy, is far too flattering to me for me to be able to repeat it without vanity. It is certain that according to the plan offered there, a very engaging play could be made. Of course I must point out that then the Jews would be viewed only as an oppressed people, and not as Jews, and the goals that I had in finishing my play, would, for the most part, cease to exist.

Translated by Ingrid Walsøe-Engel

NATHAN THE WISE

A Dramatic Poem in Five Acts
Written in 1778/79

MOTTO:

Enter, for here too there are gods!

Apud Gellium

CHARACTERS

SULTAN SALADIN
SITTAH, *his sister*
NATHAN, *a rich Jew in Jerusalem*
RACHEL, [RECHA, *in Lessing's original*] *his adopted daughter*
DAYA, *a Christian, but in the house of the Jew, as companion to his*
daughter
A YOUNG TEMPLAR
A DERVISH
THE PATRIARCH OF JERUSALEM
A LAY BROTHER
AN EMIR and several MAMELUKES of Saladin

The scene is Jerusalem.

Act I

Scene 1

*Vestibule in Nathan's house.—Nathan returning from a journey.
Daya comes to meet him.*

DAYA: It's he, it's Nathan!—Endless thanks to God,
  That you at last return to us again.
NATHAN: Yes, Daya; thanks to God! But why "at last"?
  Had I intended sooner to return?
  And had I power to do so? Babylon
  Is from Jerusalem two hundred leagues
  By such a road as I perforce must follow,
  With side trips taken to both right and left;
  Collecting debts, you know, is certainly
  No business that proceeds apace, for which
  One needs but turn his hand.
DAYA: O Nathan, Nathan,
  How wretched, wretched meanwhile you might well
  Have come to be at home! Your house . . .
NATHAN: Took fire.
  So much I have already learned.—God grant
  That there's no evil I have yet to learn!
DAYA: And might have burned completely to the ground.
NATHAN: Then, Daya, we'd have built a new one here,
  A more convenient one.
DAYA: That's true enough!—
  But Rachel by a mere hair's breadth escaped
  From burning with it.
NATHAN: Burned? My Rachel? she?—
  I was not told of *that*.—Why then! I'd have
  No further need of houses.—Rachel burned
  But for a hair's breadth!—Ah! No doubt she is!
  Is burned in very truth!—Come, out with it!
  Speak out now!—Slay me, torture me no more.—
  I know she's burned to death.
DAYA: No, if she were,
  Would *my* lips be the ones to tell you so?

NATHAN: Why then affright me so?—O Rachel, Rachel!
    My Rachel!
DAYA: Yours? You call this Rachel yours?
NATHAN: If ever I must needs again forgo
    To call this child my child!
DAYA: And do you call
    All you possess with equal right your own?
NATHAN: Naught with a greater right! For see, all else
    That I possess, good fortune linked with nature
    Bestowed on me. This property alone
    I owe to virtue.
DAYA: O, how dear you make
    Me pay for all your noble goodness, Nathan!
    If goodness, exercised with such intent,
    Can still be "goodness" called.
NATHAN: With such intent?
    You mean . . .?
DAYA: My conscience . . .
NATHAN: Listen, Daya, let
    Me tell you first of all . . .
DAYA: I say, my conscience . . .
NATHAN: What handsome stuff I bought in Babylon.
    So rich, and yet so tasteful! I have brought
    No finer cloth, not even for my child.
DAYA: Quite useless! For my conscience, I must say,
    Will let itself no longer be benumbed.
NATHAN: And how the rings, the pendants for your ears,
    How brooch and necklace will appeal to you,
    Which I selected for you in Damascus:
    That I would like to see.
DAYA: That's just like you!
    If you can only give, and give, and give!
NATHAN: Take just as gladly as I give—and hush!
DAYA: And hush!—Who questions, Nathan, but that you
    Are honesty, greatheartedness itself?
    And yet . . .
NATHAN: And yet a Jew.—Not so,
    That's what you'd say?
DAYA: What I would like to say,
    You know quite well.

NATHAN: Then hush!
DAYA: I hold my tongue.
  Whatever wrong 'fore God results from this,
  And I cannot prevent, and cannot change,—
  Can *not*—be on your head!
NATHAN: Be on my head!—
  But now where is she? where in hiding?—Daya,
  If you're deceiving me!—Say, does she know
  That I have come?
DAYA: Why, this I ask of *you*.
  The fright still quivers through her every nerve,
  And fire is painted by her phantasy
  In every scene it paints. In sleep awakes,
  In waking sleeps her mind: hence now she's less
  Than beast, now more than angel.
NATHAN: Poor, poor child!
  What are we human beings!
DAYA: Long she lay
  This morning with her eyelids closed, and was
  As dead. Then starting up, she cried, "Hark, hark!
  I hear the camels of my father nearing!
  Hark, there's his gentle voice itself!"—But then
  Her eye grew dim again, and as her head
  Was left without the propping of her arm,
  It dropped upon the pillow.—I went through
  The gate, and saw you coming, really coming!
  What wonder! all her soul in every hour
  Was constantly with you—and him.—
NATHAN: With him?
  What "him" is that?
DAYA: With him who saved her life
  From fire.
NATHAN: Who was it? who?—And where is he?
  Who saved my Rachel for me, tell me, who?
DAYA: A youthful Templar, whom, some days before,
  They brought here to Jerusalem as captive
  And Sultan Saladin had pardoned.
NATHAN: What?
  A Templar, whom the Sultan Saladin
  Allowed to live? And by a lesser wonder
  Could Rachel not be rescued? God!

DAYA: Just so.
  Had he not bravely risked his life for her,
  His new-won life, her own would be no more.
NATHAN: Where is he, Daya, this heroic man?—
  Where is he? Come and lead me to his feet.
  Of course you gave as earnest what I left
  Of treasure in your hands? and gave him all?
  And promised more? far more?
DAYA: How could we, Nathan?
NATHAN: Not, not?
DAYA: He came, and no one knows from whence.
  He went, and no one knows where to.—Devoid
  Of previous knowledge, only by his ear
  Directed, spreading out his cloak in front,
  He boldly pressed through flame and smoke toward
  The voice that cried for help. We were assured
  That he was lost, when out of smoke and flame
  Sudden he faced us there, on sturdy arm
  Uplifting her. But cold and all unmoved
  By our exulting thanks, he sets his booty
  Upon the ground, darts off into the folk—
  And fades from sight!
NATHAN: But not, I hope, for ever.
DAYA: Thereafter for some days we still would see him
  Beneath the palm trees strolling back and forth,
  Which stand about the grave of Him who rose.
  I neared him with delight, expressed our thanks,
  Besought, enjoined, conjured—but once again
  To come before the gentle creature who
  Could find no peace or rest, until she had
  Wept out her thanks before his feet.
NATHAN: And he?
DAYA: In vain! He had no ear for our request;
  And poured such bitter scorn on me besides . . .
NATHAN: Until repelled by that . . .
DAYA: Quite the reverse!
  I went to meet him every day anew,
  And every day I bore his mockery.
  What did I not endure! What more had I
  Not suffered gladly!—But this long time now
  He comes no more to seek the lofty palms
  Which shade our Saviour's grave who rose again;

And no one knows what has become of him.—
You are amazed? You muse?

NATHAN: I'm thinking now
What impress this must make upon a soul
Like Rachel's. Think, to see oneself so scorned
By him whom one is so impelled to prize
Uncommonly; to be so thrust aside
And yet so much attracted;—on my word,
There must be long dispute twixt head and heart,
If hate of men or sadness shall prevail.
Oft it is neither; and our phantasy,
Which mingles in the strife, turns us to dreamers,
In whom the head plays heart, and then again
The heart must play the head.—A poor exchange!—
The latter, if I know my Rachel well,
Is Rachel's case: she dreams.

DAYA: And yet so gently,
So amiably!

NATHAN: That's dreaming all the same!

DAYA: Especially one—crotchet, if you will,
Is dear to her. She thinks her Templar knight
No earthly man nor born of human kind:
One of the angels, to whose watch and ward
Her little heart, from childhood on, was glad
To think her trusted, from the sheltering cloud
In which he cloaks himself, in fire as well,
To hover near her, all at once as Templar
Appeared to her.—Please do not smile!—Who knows?
Or smile and let her keep this one belief,
Which Jew and Christian share with Moslem too;—
A sweet delusion, if it be no more!

NATHAN: Sweet to me too!—Go, worthy Daya, go;
See what she's doing; I would speak with her.—
Then I will go to seek that wild, capricious
Protecting angel. If as yet he wills
To dwell among us here below; if still
He practices such graceless chivalry;
Then I will surely find him, and I'll bring
Him here.

DAYA: You're undertaking much.

NATHAN: If sweet
Delusion then makes way for sweeter truth:—

Believe me, Daya: to us human folk
A man is always dearer than an angel,—
Then you'll not censure me, I hope, not me,
To find your angel dreamer fully cured?
DAYA: You are so good, and yet so bad withal!
I'll go.—But hark, but look!—See, there she comes.

Scene 2

Enter Rachel.

RACHEL: Then it is really, wholly you, my father?
I thought you had but sent your voice ahead.
Where do you bide? What mountains, deserts, streams
Divide us yet? You're wall to wall with me,
And do not haste your Rachel to embrace?
Poor Rachel, who was burned while you were gone!—
Almost was burned! Almost. No, do not shudder.
It is a hideous death, to burn. O, O!
NATHAN: My child! My dear, dear child!
RACHEL: You had to cross
Euphrates, Tigris, Jordan; and—who knows
How many streams there were?—How often I
Trembled for you, before the fire had come
So near to me! For since the fire did come
So near to me, to die in water seems
Like rescue, sweet refreshment.—But you are
Not drowned at all; and I, I too am not
Burned up. How we will now rejoice, and praise,
Praise God! For He, He bore you and your boat
On his *invisible* angels' wings across
The treacherous rivers. Likewise it was He
Who showed my angel that he *visibly*
On his white wing should bear me through the fire—
NATHAN *(aside):* White wing! Ah yes, the white and forespread cloak
The Templar wore.
RACHEL: That he all visibly
Should bear me through the fire, which by his wing
Was blown aside.—So I have seen an angel,
My angel, face-to-face.
NATHAN: Quite meet for Rachel;
And she would see in him nought fairer, sure,
Than he in her.

RACHEL *(smiling)*: Whom do you flatter, father?
  The angel, or yourself?
NATHAN: And were it only
  A man—such as they daily are produced
  By Nature—who this service did for you:
  He must to you be angel. Must and would.
RACHEL: Not *such* an angel; no! a genuine one;
  For surely he was genuine!—Have you
  Yourself not taught me that it's possible
  That there are angels, and that God can do
  Such miracles for those who love Him well?
  I love Him.
NATHAN: And He loves you too; and does
  For you and others miracles every hour;
  Indeed, has done them from eternity
  For all of you.
RACHEL: I like to hear that.
NATHAN: What?
  Since it would sound quite natural, unexciting,
  If just a real and living Templar knight
  Had saved your life; would that be any less
  A miracle?—The greatest wonder is
  That to us all the true and genuine wonders
  Can come to be so commonplace, and should.
  Without this universal miracle,
  A thinking man might not have used the word
  For that which only children should so call,
  Who, gaping, only see the most uncommon,
  The latest happening.
DAYA: Come, Nathan, would you
  By suchlike subtleties completely shatter
  Her brain, already sadly overwrought?
NATHAN: Leave me in peace!—Were it for Rachel then
  Not miracle enough, that by a *man*
  Her life was saved, who first by no small wonder
  Must be preserved himself? Yes, no small wonder!
  For who has ever heard that Saladin
  Had spared a Templar's life? or that
  A Templar had desired he should be spared
  By him? or hoped it? offered for his freedom
  More than the leather belt which bore his sword;
  At most his dagger?

RACHEL: This I find conclusive.—
  He was no Templar, father; only seemed it.
  If captured Templars never, never come
  Save to sure death here in Jerusalem;
  If none so freely in this city walks
  About: how could at night of his free will
  A Templar save me?
NATHAN: See now, how ingenious!
  Now, Daya, you speak up. For it was you
  Who told me he was sent as captive here.
  No doubt you know still more.
DAYA: Well, yes. Indeed,
  That's what they say;—and yet they also say
  That Saladin this Templar spared because
  Of likeness to a brother he had loved
  Especially. But as it's twenty years
  Since death removed that brother,—he was called,
  I don't know how;—he lived, I don't know where:—
  The matter sounds so hardly—credible,
  That I suppose there's simply nothing to it.
NATHAN: Well, Daya! Tell me why that should be so
  Incredible. I hope not—such things happen—
  Because a thing still more incredible
  You'd like to think?—And why should Saladin,
  Who dearly loves his kinfolk, one and all,
  Not have possessed in younger years a brother
  Whom he loved specially?—Do faces not
  Resemble one another?—Is an old
  Impression lost?—Does a like cause no more
  Have like effects?—Since when?—What then is here
  Incredible?—But that, wise Daya, you
  Would think no miracle, and only yours
  Requi . . . deserve, I mean to say, belief.
DAYA: You mock.
NATHAN: Because you're mocking me.—But still,
  My Rachel, your deliverance even so
  Remains a wonder, wrought alone by Him
  Who stern resolves, the most ambitious plans
  Of kings—His sport if not His mockery—
  Delights to guide by feeble threads.
RACHEL: My father!

My father, if I'm wrong, you know it's not
By choice.
NATHAN: Contrariwise, you like to learn.—
   Look here! a forehead, arched this way or that;
   The profile of a nose, outlined like this
   And not like that; eyebrows which serpentine
   On sharp or blunted bone, or so, or so;
   A line, a curve, an angle, wrinkle, mole,
   A nothing, on a random countenance
   From Europe:—and you're saved from fire, in Asia!—
   Is that no wonder, wonder-avid folk?
   Why must you call an angel down from Heaven?
DAYA: What harm is there—if I may speak a word—
   In spite of all, if one should still prefer
   An angel to a man as rescuer?
   Does one not feel thereby so much the nearer
   To that mysterious First Cause of his rescue?
NATHAN: Nothing but pride! mere pride! The iron pot
   Wants to be drawn with silver tongs from out
   The fire, to think itself a pot of silver.—Bah!—
   And what's the harm, you ask me, what's the harm?
   No, what's the good, I'll ask you in return—
   For your "To feel oneself the nearer God"
   Is either nonsense or its blasphemy.—
   But there is harm; yes, truly, harm indeed.—
   Come, hark to me!—I'm sure, to him who saved
   Your life—and be it angel or a man—
   You both would give, and you, my Rachel, most,
   An ample service in return?—Not so?—
   Well, to an angel, what's the chance that you
   Can do him service, ample service, too?
   Thank him you can; can sigh and pray; can melt
   In ecstasy; and on his festal day
   Can fast, give alms.—All futile.—For I think
   In such a case you and your neighbor man
   Will always gain far more than he. He grows
   Not fat from all your fasting; grows not rich
   With your almsgiving; gets no greater glory
   From all your rapture, nor a greater power
   From all your trust. Not so? But if a man!
DAYA: It's true we'd have more opportunity,

Were he a man, to make him some return.
God knows how ready we were so to do!
But then, you see, he wanted, needed nothing;
Was in and with himself so self-contained
As only angels have the power to be.

RACHEL: And when at last he disappeared . . .

NATHAN: He did?—
How disappeared?—He showed himself no more
Beneath the palms?—Or did you really try
To see him further?

DAYA: No, indeed we didn't.

NATHAN: No, Daya, no? Now see what harm it does!—
You cruel dreamers!—Now what if this angel—
Has fallen sick? . . .

RACHEL: Sick!

DAYA: Sick! He won't do that!

RACHEL: What awesome chill assails me! Daya, feel!
My forehead, always warm, is turned to ice.

NATHAN: He is a Frank, not used to such a climate;
Is young; to tasks demanded by his order,
To hunger, waking, little used.

RACHEL: Sick, sick!

DAYA: It's possible, that's all that Nathan means.

NATHAN: Now there he lies, has neither friend nor coin
To pay for friendliness.

RACHEL: O dear, my father!

NATHAN: Lies without tending, comfort, or advice,
A prey to pain and death!

RACHEL: Where, where?

NATHAN: And he,
Who for a girl he'd never known nor seen—
Enough that she was human—plunged in fire . . .

DAYA: O spare her, Nathan!

NATHAN: Who the girl he'd saved
Would not approach or see again, to save
Her thanking him . . .

DAYA: O spare her, Nathan!

NATHAN: Nor
Desired to see her more—unless it were
That he a second time should save her life,—
Being a human soul . . .

DAYA: O stop, look here!
NATHAN: In dying now he lacks for comfort, all—
  Except awareness of his deed.
DAYA: Stop, stop!
  You're killing her!
NATHAN: And you have murdered him!—
  You could have killed him so.—Come, Rachel, Rachel!
  It's medicine, not poison, that I give.
  He lives!—Recover!—nor is sick, I think;
  Not even sick!
RACHEL: For sure?—not dead? not sick?
NATHAN: For sure, not dead!—For God rewards good deeds,
  Done here, among us.—Go!—But see how far
  It's easier to swoon in pious dreams
  Than do good actions? see how sluggish men
  Are fond of dreaming piously, because—
  Although at times of their intent not quite
  Aware—they'd shun the need of doing good?
RACHEL: O father, never leave me any more
  Alone!—But don't you think he might have gone
  Upon a journey?
NATHAN: Silly geese!—Of course.—
  I see out there a Mussulman who's eyeing
  With curious gaze my camels and their load.
  I wonder if you know him.
DAYA: Yes! your dervish.
NATHAN: Who?
DAYA: It's your dervish, and your chess companion.
NATHAN: Al-Hafi! That Al-Hafi?
DAYA: Treasurer
  Of Saladin.
NATHAN: Al-Hafi? Are you dreaming?
  It's he! It's really he!—He's coming here.
  Get in with you, be quick! (*Daya and Rachel leave.*)
  What shall I hear?

                    Scene 3

Enter Al-Hafi richly dressed.

DERVISH: Open your eyes, as wide as ever you can!
NATHAN: Is it you? Or is it not?—In such attire,
  A dervish! . . .

DERVISH: Well, why not? Can nought be made
  Out of a dervish, absolutely nothing?
NATHAN: Oh yes, enough!—But I had always thought
  A dervish—if a real one—would allow
  Nought to be made of him.
DERVISH: Now by the prophet!
  That I'm no real one, that may well be true.
  Yet if one must—
NATHAN: Must! Dervish!—Dervish must?
  No man needs must, and must a dervish, then?
  What must he?
DERVISH: What one warmly begs of him
  And he admits is good: that must a dervish.
NATHAN: Now, by our God, you speak the truth.—Let me
  Embrace you, man.—I hope you're still my friend?
DERVISH: And you don't ask what I have now become?
NATHAN: Despite what you've become!
DERVISH: Why, could I not
  Have come to be a fellow in the State
  Whose friendship you'd not want?
NATHAN: No, if your heart
  Is dervish still, I'll risk it. For your office
  Of State is but a robe.
DERVISH: Which yet must have
  Its honor.—Guess!—What do you think I'd be
  If you were king?
NATHAN: A dervish; and that's all.
  But on the side, I fancy, also—cook.
DERVISH: Of course! And thus my trade unlearn?—A cook!
  Not waiter too?—Confess that Saladin
  Knows me much better.—I'm his treasurer
  At present.
NATHAN: You?—for him?
DERVISH: Please understand:
  The smaller treasure—for his father wields
  The great one still—the treasure for his house.
NATHAN: His house is large.
DERVISH: And larger than you think;
  For every beggar man is of his house.
NATHAN: Yet Saladin so hates the beggar folk—

DERVISH: That he's resolved to wipe all beggars out
 Both root and branch—though he himself thereby
 Become a beggar.
NATHAN: Right!—That's what I mean.
DERVISH: He is one, too, as good as any! For
 His treasure is by sunset every day
 Much emptier than empty. Be the flood
 At morning never so high, by noon long since
 It's ebbed away—
NATHAN: Since channels have in part
 Absorbed it which to fill up or to block
 Is equally impossible.
DERVISH: You've hit it!
NATHAN: I know that game.
DERVISH: I grant it's not so good
 When princes play the vulture amid corpses.
 But if they're corpses 'mid the vultures, then
 It's ten times worse.
NATHAN: Not so, my dervish, no!
DERVISH: It's easy, friend, for you to talk.—See here:
 What will you give if I resign my post
 For you?
NATHAN: What does your post bring in?
DERVISH: To me?
 Not much. But you would make a splendid profit.
 For when the fund's at ebb—as frequently—
 You'll open up your sluices: make advances,
 And take in interest to your heart's desire.
NATHAN: And interest on interest?
DERVISH: Of course!
NATHAN: Till capital turns into interest.
DERVISH: That doesn't tempt you? Then you'll bid farewell
 To this our friendship, now. For I confess
 I counted much on you.
NATHAN: No, really? What
 Had you in mind?
DERVISH: I hoped that with your help
 My office I'd conduct in honor; that
 I'd always have full credit at your hands.—
 You shake your head?
NATHAN: Let's try to get this clear!

For one must make distinctions.—You? Why not?
Al-Hafi is as dervish always welcome
To all I have and can.—As treasurer
Of Saladin, Al-Hafi is a man
Who—whom—
DERVISH: I guessed it was so! You are ever
  As good as shrewd, as shrewd as you are wise!—
  But patience! What in Hafi you distinguish,
  Shall soon be quite distinct again.—See here
  This robe of honor, given by Saladin.
  Before it fades and turns to rags, such as
  Were fitter far to clothe a dervish, in
  Jerusalem you'll see it on a nail,
  And I'll be by the Ganges,* walking, barefoot
  And lightly clad, the hot sand with my teachers.
NATHAN: That sounds like you.
DERVISH: And playing chess with them.
NATHAN: Your greatest joy!
DERVISH: Imagine what seduced me!—
  That I myself no longer need go begging?
  That I might play the rich man among beggars?
  That I'd have power to turn the richest beggar
  Into a wretched Croesus† in a trice?
NATHAN: I fancy not.
DERVISH: A thing much more absurd!
  For once I felt myself sincerely flattered;
  By Saladin's good-hearted error flattered—
NATHAN: Namely?
DERVISH: He said that only a beggar knows
  How beggars feel; that none but a beggar could
  Have learned the proper way to give to beggars.
  Said he, "Your predecessor was too cold,
  Too rude for me. He gave ungraciously;
  Inquired so savagely of the receiver
  Before he gave; he thought it not enough
  To know the human need, no, he must learn
  The cause of it as well, so that the gift
  He'd stingily apportion to that cause.
  Al-Hafi won't do that! Nor Saladin

---

*The sacred river of northern India.
†The last king of Lydia (560–546 B.C.), whose great wealth has become proverbial.

In him appear so stingy-generous!
Al-Hafi is not like to clogged-up pipes,
Which take up crystal-clear and quiet water
And spray it out so cloudy and impure.
Al-Hafi thinks, Al-Hafi feels like me!"—
So sweetly sang the fowler's pipe, until
The simpleton was in the net,—I, fool!
Fool of an arrant fool!

NATHAN: Come, dervish, softly,
Speak softly!

DERVISH: Stuff!—It were not folly, then,
A hundred thousand people to oppress,
Exhaust and plunder, torture, throttle; and
To single persons play philanthropist?
It were not foppery, God's ample grace,
Which without choice on good and bad alike,
On mead and desert, now in rain, now sunshine,
Is spread abroad, to try to ape, and yet
To lock the everlasting fullness of His hand?
It were not foppery. . . .

NATHAN: Enough, enough!

DERVISH: No, let at least my own unhappy folly
Be mentioned too!—It were not foppery
To seek the goodly phases of this nonsense
And take, just for the sake of those good phases,
Your share in all that foppery? Not, not?

NATHAN: Al-Hafi, hurry with all speed to get
You back into your desert. For I fear
That being among men you might forget
To be a man.

DERVISH: You're right, I fear that too.
Farewell! *(Exit Al-Hafi.)*

NATHAN: So hasty? Wait, Al-Hafi, wait!
Your desert won't escape you, will it? Wait!
I wish he'd hear me! Hey, Al-Hafi, here!—
He's gone; and I'd have gladly asked of him
Some news about our Templar. Probably
He knows of him.

Scene 4

Enter Daya in haste.

DAYA: O Nathan, Nathan!
NATHAN: Well?
What now?
DAYA: He shows himself again! He shows
Himself again!
NATHAN: Who, Daya, who?
DAYA: He, he!
NATHAN: He? he?—When doesn't *he* appear? I see,
Your "he" is the only one.—That should not be!
And were he angel, that would not be right.
DAYA: Again he's strolling up and down beneath
The palms; and plucking dates from time to time.
NATHAN: And eats them?—As a Templar?
DAYA: Why torment
Me so?—Her greedy eye divined him there
Behind the interlacing palms; and now
It follows him. She begs you then—conjures
You rather—go to him without delay.
O haste! She'll signal to you from the window,
Which way he turns, this way or farther off.
O haste!
NATHAN: Dressed as I got down from my camel?—
Would that be proper?—Haste to him yourself,
Report my safe return. This gentleman,
You'll see, was loath to enter my abode
While I was gone; will not refuse to come
If I invite as father. Go and say
I beg him cordially . . .
DAYA: In vain! To you
He will not come.—In brief: he shuns all Jews.
NATHAN: Then go at least to hold him where he is;
At least that you may follow with your eyes
The course he takes.—Go, I will soon be there.
                    (Nathan hurries inside, Daya outside.)

Scene 5

An open space with palms, under which the Templar is walking up and down. A friar follows him at some distance and to one side, always as if about to address him.

TEMPLAR: He follows not to pass the time.—And look,
  See how he eyes my hands—My worthy brother . . .
  Or I might call you father, too, no doubt?
FRIAR: No, brother; just lay brother; at your service.
TEMPLAR: Ah, goodly brother, had I anything!
  God knows that I have nothing—
FRIAR: All the same
  Right hearty thanks! God grant a thousandfold
  What you would like to give. For it's the will
  And not the gift that makes the giver.—And
  I was not sent to follow you for alms.
TEMPLAR: Yet you were sent?
FRIAR: Yes, from the monastery.
TEMPLAR: Where I but now a pilgrim meal had hoped
  To find?
FRIAR: The benches were all filled, but yet
  You should return with me.
TEMPLAR: What for? It's true
  I've long dispensed with meat; but then, what odds?
  The dates are ripe, you know.
FRIAR: Sir, but beware
  Of too much of that fruit: that is not good,
  It clogs the spleen, makes mealancholy blood.
TEMPLAR: And what if sadness suits me?—Though, I think,
  Not just to give this warning you were sent?
FRIAR: O no!—My mission was to sound you out;
  To feel your pulse a bit.
TEMPLAR: And this you tell
  Yourself, like that?
FRIAR: Why not?
TEMPLAR *(aside)*:   A waggish brother!
  (aloud) Say, has the cloister more like you?
FRIAR: Don't know.
  I must obey, dear sir.
TEMPLAR: And you obey
  Without much questioning?

FRIAR: Would it else be
  Obedience, dear sir?
TEMPLAR *(aside):*   Upon my soul,
  Simplicity is always right. *(aloud)* No doubt
  You may reveal to me who is so eager
  To know me better?—Not yourself, I'll swear.
FRIAR: Would such a wish become or profit me?
TEMPLAR: Whom does it then become and profit, whom,
  To be so curious?
FRIAR: The Patriarch,
  I must believe.—For it was he who sent me.
TEMPLAR: The Patriarch! Knows he no better, then,
  Red cross on mantle white?
FRIAR: I know it well!
TEMPLAR: Well, brother, well?—I am a Templar knight;
  And captive—Further: taken at Tebnín,[*]
  The fort we thought to scale ere truce's end
  To march forthwith on Sidon;[†]—if I add:
  As one of twenty taken and alone
  By Saladin left living: then he knows,
  Your Patriarch, all that he needs to know;—
  More than he needs.
FRIAR: But hardly more, I think,
  Than he knows now.—He'd also like to know
  Wherefore my lord by Saladin was spared;
  Just he alone.
TEMPLAR: Do I know that?—Already
  My neck was bared, I knelt upon my cloak,
  The blow awaiting: keenly Saladin
  Observes my face, leaps toward me, makes a sign.
  They lift me up; I am unbound; I seek
  To thank him; see his eyes in tears: but mute
  Is he, am I; he goes, I stay.—And how
  All that's connected, let the Patriarch
  Himself unriddle.
FRIAR: From it he concludes
  That God for great and greater things must have
  Preserved you.
TEMPLAR: Yes, for mighty things indeed!

---

[*]A fortress north of Ptolemais, about fifteen miles from Tyre.
[†]A town on the Mediterranean.

To save a Jewess from the fire; to guide
To Sinai* curious pilgrims; and the like.
FRIAR: That's to be seen! But so far not so bad.
Perhaps the Patriarch himself meanwhile
Has more important business for my lord.
TEMPLAR: You think so, brother?—Has he given you hints
Already?
FRIAR: Yes, indeed!—All I should do
Is first sound out my lord, to see if he
Might be the man.
TEMPLAR: Why, well; go on and sound!
(aside) I wonder how he'll do this sounding.—*(aloud)* Well?
FRIAR: The quickest course will be to say right out
Just what the Patriarch wants.
TEMPLAR: Good!
FRIAR: He would ask
My lord to bear a letter.
TEMPLAR: Me? But I'm
No messenger.—And that should be a task
More glorious far than saving Jewish maidens
From death by fire?
FRIAR: It must be so!—For—says
The Patriarch—upon this letter hangs
For all of Christendom a mighty weight.
To have delivered it in safety—says
The Patriarch—will one day bring the bearer
A special crown in Heaven as reward.
And of this crown—so says the Patriarch—
No man is worthier than my lord.
TEMPLAR: Than I?
FRIAR: For to deserve this crown in Heaven—says
The Patriarch   there's scarce another man
More skillful than my lord.
TEMPLAR: Than I?
FRIAR: He says
You're free; can look about you everywhere;
You know how cities can be stormed and how
Defended; can—so says the Patriarch—
Best estimates the strength and weakness of

*Mt. Sinai, supposed to be the biblical Mt. Horeb; as it is far from Jerusalem, the
Templar would have been gone a long time.

The wall most lately built by Saladin,
The inner, second wall, most vividly
Describe it—says the Patriarch—to all
The host of God.

TEMPLAR: Good brother, if I but
Could know the detailed content of the note.

FRIAR: Ah that—I do not know so very well.
However, it is written to King Philip.*—
The Patriarch . . . I've often wondered how
A saint who lives in heaven otherwise
Can condescend to be so well informed
On worldly things. That must seem bitter to him.

TEMPLAR: Well then? The Patriarch?

FRIAR: Knows through and through,
Reliably, just how and in what strength,
From what direction Saladin, in case
The war breaks out again, will open up
His own campaign.

TEMPLAR: He knows that?

FRIAR: Yes, and wants
To let King Philip know it: so that he
Might estimate the danger, if it be
So great that at all costs the armistice,
Which your great Order nobly violated,
He should restore with Saladin.

TEMPLAR: Ah ha!
Ah what a Patriarch!—This bold, good man
Would make of me no common agent, but—
A spy.—Good brother, tell your Patriarch,
So far as you could sound me out, that this
Was not the task for me.—Say that I must
Regard myself as captive still; and that
The Templars' only calling is to use
The sword to smite, and not to act the spy.

FRIAR: I thought as much!—Nor am I much inclined
To chide my lord for it.—Though, to be sure,
The best is yet to come.—The Patriarch
Has wormed it out, the name and the location
Of that stronghold on Lebanon,† wherein

---

*Philip Augustus II of France (1165–1223), coleader of the Third Crusade with Richard I of England.
†A mountain range close to the Mediterranean.

Are kept the monstrous sums of gold with which
The Sultan's cautious father pays the troops
And other costs of war. From time to time
On hidden paths the Sultan to this fort
Betakes himself, but scantily attended.
You follow?

TEMPLAR: Never, never!

FRIAR: What would be
More simple than to seize the Sultan's person?
To make an end of him?—You shudder?—O,
A pair of pious Maronites* have offered
To dare the deed, if there's a doughty man
To lead them on.

TEMPLAR: And so your Patriarch
Has chosen me to be that doughty man?

FRIAR: He thinks King Philip out of Ptolemais†
Might send his men to lend a hand.

TEMPLAR: To me?
Me, brother, me? Have you not heard just now
What gratitude I owe to Saladin?

FRIAR: I have indeed.

TEMPLAR: And yet?

FRIAR: O well—so says
The Patriarch—that's very fine; but God,
Your Order . . .

TEMPLAR: Alter nought! Require of me
No knavish trick!

FRIAR: Of course not!—Only—says
The Patriarch—what seems a knavish trick
To human eyes may not seem so to God.

TEMPLAR: Then I should owe to Saladin my life
And take his from him?

FRIAR: Faugh!—and yet—so says
The Patriarch—still Saladin remains
A foe of Christendom, hence may not claim
The right to be your friend.

TEMPLAR: How friend? To whom
I merely would not play the thankless villain?

FRIAR: Quite true!—And yet—so says the Patriarch—

---

*A Syrian Christian sect founded in the seventh century; their central seat is still Mt. Lebanon.

†Ptolemais, another name for (Saint-Jean-d') Acre, a strong fortress on the Bay of Acre.

We are absolved of thanks, 'fore God and men,
If for *our* sake the service was not done.
And since it's rumored—says the Patriarch—
The Sultan had not spared your life unless
In your expression, in your very being,
Some semblance of his brother struck his eye . . .
TEMPLAR: The Patriarch knows this too, and all the same . . .?
Ah, were that definite! Ah, Saladin!
What? Nature should have shaped one single trait
In me that had your brother's form: to which
There were no correspondence in my soul?
This correspondence I could then suppress
To please a Patriarch?—No, Nature, no!
Thou'rt not so false! God does not contradict
Himself so in His works!—Go, brother, now.
Do not stir up the gall in me!—Go! go!
FRIAR: I go; and go more cheerful than I came.
My lord should pardon me. We cloister folk
Are under rule, we must obey the heads.

Scene 6

Daya, who has been observing the Templar for some time from a distance, now approaches him.

DAYA *(aside)*: The friar, it seems, left him in no good mood.
But I must risk my errand.
TEMPLAR: Excellent!—
How true the ancient saw, that monk and woman
Are as the devil's claws, alike and paired.
Today he passes me from one to the other.
DAYA: What do I see?—You, noble knight?—Thank God
A thousand times!—O speak, where have you been
In all this time?—I hope you've not been sick?
TEMPLAR: No.
DAYA: Quite, quite well?
TEMPLAR: Yes.
DAYA: We were so concerned
On your account.
TEMPLAR: You were?
DAYA: No doubt you were
Away?

TEMPLAR: You've guessed it.

DAYA: Just returned today?

TEMPLAR: No, yesterday.

DAYA: And Rachel's father too
Has just returned. So may she now have hope?

TEMPLAR: Of what?

DAYA: Of what so oft she begged of you.
Her father will invite you now himself
Most urgently. He comes from Babylon;
With twenty fully laden camels, with
Whatever of precious spices, jewels, stuffs,
That India, Persia, Syria, even China,
Esteem of highest worth.

TEMPLAR: I purchase nothing.

DAYA: His people honor him as though a prince.
But that they speak of Nathan as the Wise
And not the Rich, I've often thought that strange.

TEMPLAR: Perhaps they think that wise and rich are one.

DAYA: But most of all they should have called him good.
For you cannot conceive how good he is.
When he was told what Rachel owes to you:
What had he, in that moment, failed to do
And give to you!

TEMPLAR: Well!

DAYA: Try it, come and see!

TEMPLAR: See what? How quick a moment's time is fled?

DAYA: Had I, if he were not so good, myself
Put up with him so long? Do you suppose
I do not feel my worth as Christian woman?
It was not sung to me as cradle-song
That one day I'd accompany my husband
To Palestine for only this one end:
To rear a Jewish maiden. For my husband
In Emperor Frederick's* army was a noble
Esquire—

TEMPLAR: By birth a Swiss, who had the grace,
And honor too, within the selfsame stream
To drown with his Imperial Majesty.—
Woman! How often have I heard all this?
Will you then never cease thus to pursue me?

DAYA: Pursue you! gracious God!

*Friedrich Barbarossa (1123–1190), one of the leaders of the Third Crusade.

TEMPLAR: Yes, yes, pursue me.
   Once and for all, I won't see you again.
   Nor hear you! Will not endless have recalled
   A deed to which I gave no thought; and which,
   When I reflect, makes of myself a riddle.
   It's true, I'd not regret it. But look here:
   If such a case recurs, then you're to blame
   If I should act less quickly; should first off
   Inquire a bit—and then let burn what burns.
DAYA: Now God forbid!
TEMPLAR: Henceforth I beg at least
   You'll know me not. This I request. And keep
   The father off. For Jew is Jew. And I'm
   A Swabian* blunt. The image of the girl
   Has long since left my spirit; if indeed
   It once was there.
DAYA: But yours has not left *her*.
TEMPLAR: What good can that do? Tell me that.
DAYA: Who knows?
   For people are not always what they seem.
TEMPLAR: But rarely are they better. *(Starts off.)*
DAYA: Wait a bit!
   Why hasten?
TEMPLAR: Woman, do not make these palms to me
   Repellent, since I love to walk beneath them.
DAYA: Then go, you German bear! then go!—*(aside)*
      And yet
   I must not risk to lose the creature's trail.
                       (She follows him at a distance.)

Act II

Scene 1

The Sultan's palace. Saladin and Sittah are at chess.†

SITTAH: Where are you, Saladin? And how you play!

---

*Popular tradition in Germany makes fun of the Swabians (Schwaben), calling them honest but blunt and slow-witted.
†Saladin is known to have been passionately fond of chess.

SALADIN: Not well? I thought.

SITTAH: Quite well for me, perhaps.
Take back that move.

SALADIN: What for?

SITTAH: That leaves your knight
Uncovered.

SALADIN: True. Try that! I take it with
My pawn.

SALADIN: That's true again.—Then check!

SITTAH: What good
Is that? I shield my king, like this: and you
Are as you were.

SALADIN: This is a queeze, I see,
From which I can't escape without some loss.
Oh well! Then take the knight.

SITTAH: I'd rather not.
I'll pass him by.

SALADIN: You give me nothing, find
Your plan of greater value than my knight.

SITTAH: May be.

SALADIN: But reckon not without your host.
For, look! This move you hardly could foresee?

SITTAH: Not I indeed. Could I foresee that you
Would be so weary of your queen?

SALADIN: My queen!

SITTAH: It's plain to see: today I win my thousand
Dinars,* and not a farthing more.

SALADIN: How so?

SITTAH: You ask?—Because you're simply bent on losing.
Let's set aside the fact that such a game
Is not the most enjoyable to play:
Did I not always win the most with you
When I was loser? Did you ever fail
To pay the stake twofold, to comfort me
For losing it?

SALADIN: Well, well! So I suppose,
You lost on purpose when you lost, my sister?

SITTAH: At least this may be said: your open hand
Prevents me from improving on my game.

SALADIN: But we forget our playing. Make an end!

---

*Dinar (from Latin *denarius*) was a gold coin, first minted in the seventh century.

SITTAH: You will it so? Well, check! and double check!

SALADIN: Ah ha, that second check I did not see,
    Which at the same time overthrows my queen.

SITTAH: Could that have been averted? Let me see.

SALADIN: No; no; just take the queen. I never was
    Too lucky with that piece.

SITTAH: The playing-piece
    Alone?

SALADIN: Away with it!—That does no harm.
    For now again my cover is complete.

SITTAH: My brother has instructed me too well *(She leaves the
    queen.)*
    How courteously one should behave with queens.

SALADIN: Take it or not! For now I have no queen.

SITTAH: Why should I take it? Check! and check!

SALADIN: Keep on.

SITTAH: And Check!—and check!—and check!

SALADIN: And mate!

SITTAH: Not quite;
    You move the knight between; or what you will.
    All one!

SALADIN: Quite right!—For you have won; and now
    Al-Hafi pays.—Bid him be summoned! quick!—
    You were not so mistaken, Sittah; I
    Was absentminded, lost track of the game.
    And then: who'll always give us neutral* pieces
    Which nought recall and nothing designate?
    And was it with the Imam† I was playing?—
    Oh pshaw! A loss demands excuse. Not just
    The shapeless pieces, Sittah, can account
    For my defeat: your calm and rapid glance,
    Your skill . . .

SITTAH: Even so your only purpose is
    To blunt the sting of loss. Enough, you were
    Distracted; more than I.

SALADIN: Than you? What should
    Distract *your* mind?

---

*Lessing thought Mohammedans were forbidden to use chessmen which represented men or animals.
†Imam is the priest who conducts the service in a mosque; he would be sure to insist on the use of plain chessmen.

SITTAH: Not your distraction, truly!—
  When shall we play so zealously again?!
SALADIN: Why, then we'll play so much the lustier!—
  Ah! since the war begins again?—Well, let it!—Come on!—It was
    not I who drew the sword;
  I'd have renewed the armistice; and gladly
  In this way I had given a proper husband
  To Sittah. Richard's* brother he must be:
  He is the one.
SITTAH: If you can only praise
  Your Richard!
SALADIN: If your brother Melek† then
  Were given Richard's sister for his wife:
  Ha, what a house we'd have! Of all the first,
  Best houses in the world, the very best!—
  You see I am not slow to praise myself.
  I think that I deserve the friends I have.—
  What men would have been born to them, what men!
SITTAH: Did I not smile at once at your fine dream?
  You do not know the Christians, will not know them.
  Their pride is to be Christians, and not men.
  For even that which from their Founder's day
  With human nature spices superstition
  They don't love for its human worth: because
  Their Jesus taught it, by him it was done.—
  O well for them, that he was a good man!
  And well for them, that they can take his virtue
  On faith!—But what of virtue?—It's not that
  Shall overspread the world, but just his name;
  That name shall swallow all the names of men,
  Put them to shame. The name, the name alone,
  Is all they care for.
SALADIN: Otherwise you'd wonder
  Why they should ask that you and Melek both
  Should bear the name of Christians, ere you might
  Have Christians as your wedded lovers?
SITTAH: Yes!

---

*Richard I of England, called "Cocur de Lion" (1157–99), set out for the third Crusade in 1191. He and Saladin had great admiration for each other. History knows nothing of a plan to marry his brother to Sittah.
†Richard proposed in 1191 that Saladin's brother Melek should marry his widowed sister Joan, queen of Sicily.

Why is it only Christians who may claim
The love that God bestows on man and woman?
SALADIN: O, they believe such childishnesses that
It's not too hard to think this one among them.—
And yet you're wrong.—The Templars are to blame,
And not the Christians; are to blame as Templars,
And not as Christians. For through them alone
Our project came to nought. The town of Acre,
Which Richard's sister was to bring as dowry
To brother Melek, they will not give up.
To keep the knight's advantage out of danger,
They act the monk, the silly monk. In hope
Of playing us a clever trick, they would
Not wait until the armistice should end.—
Fine doings! Keep right on, good sirs, keep on!—
I'm quite content!—Were all else as it should be!
SITTAH: What else disturbs you? What else could there be
To rob you of composure?
SALADIN: What so long
Has robbed me of composure, now and ever.—
I was at Lebanon to visit father.
I fear he will succumb to care . . .
SITTAH: O dear!
SALADIN: He can't hold out, is pinched on every hand;
There's lack now here, now there—
SITTAH: What pinches, lacks?
SALADIN: What else but what I hardly deign to name?
Which, when I have it, seems superfluous,
And, when I lack it, indispensable.—
Where is Al-Hafi now? Has no one gone
To look for him?—Accursed, wretched money!—
(*Enter Al-Hafi*) Al-Hafi, welcome.

Scene 2

AL-HAFI: Sultan, I presume
The moneys due from Egypt have arrived.
I hope there's much.
SALADIN: Have you some news?
AL-HAFI: What, I?
I thought I should receive some here.

SALADIN: You'll pay
  Sittah a thousand dinars. *(abstractedly walking up and down)*
AL-HAFI: Pay! not get!
  O fine! For something that is less than nothing.—
  To Sittah?—her again? For a lost game?—
  Again a loss at chess?—The board still stands!
SITTAH: You don't grudge me my luck?
AL-HAFI *(eyeing the board)*: What, grudge you—if—
  You know the rest.
SITTAH *(making a sigh)*: Pst! Hafi! pst!
AL-HAFI *(still eyeing the board)*:   Don't grudge
  It to yourself.
SITTAH: Al-Hafi, pst!
AL-HAFI *(to Sittah)*:   The whites
  Were yours? You're checking?
SITTAH *(aside)*:   Good, he has not heard.
AL-HAFI: Now it's his turn to play?
SITTAH *(advancing)*:   You are to tell me
  That I can get my money.
AL-HAFI *(still intent on the game)*: Yes; you shall
  Receive it now as always.
SITTAH: Are you mad?
AL-HAFI: The game is not yet up. Look, Saladin,
  You have not lost.
SALADIN *(scarcely listening)*: O yes I have! Just pay!
AL-HAFI: Just pay and pay! Your queen is standing there.
SALADIN *(as before)*: No matter; she's not in the game.
SITTAH: Be quick
  And say that I can have the money fetched.
AL-HAFI *(still immersed in the game)*:
  Of course, the same as always.—All the same;
  And even if the queen is gone; you are
  Not mate on that account.
SALADIN *(steps up and overturns the board)*: I am; and want
  It so.
AL-HAFI: Oh ho!—Game like to winnings! And
  Paid just as won.
SALADIN *(to Sittah)*: What does he say? What's this?
SITTAH *(motioning from time to time to Hafi)*:
  You know his way. He likes to balk; he likes
  To be requested; feels a little envy.—

SALADIN: But not of you? Not of my sister, h'm?
    What is this, Hafi? Envy? you?
AL-HAFI: May be!
    May be!—I'd like to have her brain myself;
    Would like to be as good as she.
SITTAH: Meanwhile
    He's always paid me promptly up to now.
    And he will pay today. Just let him be!—
    So go, Al-Hafi, go! Be sure I'll have
    The money fetched.
AL-HAFI: No, no; I'll play no more
    This masquerade. For he must soon or late
    Be told the truth.
SALADIN: Who must? and what?
SITTAH: Al-Hafi!
    Is this your promise? Thus you keep your word?
AL-HAFI: How could I think that it would go so far?
SALADIN: Shall I learn nothing, then?
SITTAH: I beg, Al-Hafi,
    Be modest.
SALADIN: This is strange! What could my Sittah
    So solemnly, so warmly of a stranger,
    Yes, of a dervish, rather than of me,
    Her brother, ask in secrecy? It's time
    I should command, Al-Hafi.—Dervish, speak!
SITTAH: My brother, do not let a trifling thing
    Come closer to your thought than it is worth.
    You know that several times, in chess, I've won
    The selfsame sum from you. And since I need
    No money now; and since in Hafi's fund
    The money's not too plentiful; why then
    These items were not cashed. But have no fear!
    You shall not have them, brother, nor Al-Hafi,
    Nor yet the treasury.
AL-HAFI: If that were all!
SITTAH: More of the same.—That too I have let stand
    Which you had formerly to me allotted; that
    I have not touched for several months.
AL-HAFI: And still
    Not all!
SALADIN: Not yet?—Then speak!

AL-HAFI: Since we from Egypt
  Expected money, she . . .
SITTAH: Why listen to him?
AL-HAFI: Not only has had nothing . . .
SALADIN: Noble girl!
  But has advanced her own as well. Not so?
AL-HAFI: Maintained your court; all your expenditure
  Herself has paid.
SALADIN: Ha, there I see my sister! *(embracing her)*
SITTAH: Who had enriched me so, save you, my brother,
  That I could do this thing?
AL-HAFI: I think he will
  Make her as beggar-poor as he's become.
SALADIN: I poor? her brother poor? When had I more?
  When less in hand?—*One* dress, *one* sword, *one* horse—
  And then *one* God! What need have I of more?
  And when can I lack that? And yet, Al-Hafi,
  I still might chide you.
SITTAH: Brother, do not chide!
  Had I such power to lighten Father's cares!
SALADIN: Oh, Oh! You swiftly beat my joyousness
  To earth again!—To me, for me, there lacks
  No thing, nor can.—But he is lacking all,
  And thus we lack it too.—What shall I do?—
  From Egypt we may long get nothing yet.
  God knows the cause; for all is quiet there.—
  I'll gladly scrimp, retrench, and save, if only
  I am alone affected, and no other
  Need suffer want.—But what does that avail?
  One horse, one dress, one sword I have to have.
  Nor is there any haggling with my God.
  For as it is he is content with little:
  This heart of mine.—Upon the overflow,
  Al-Hafi, of your funds I'd firmly reckoned.
AL-HAFI: The overflow?—Confess: would you have failed
  To have me spitted, throttled at the least,
  Had you found overflow with me? Emmbezzlement,
  That I could risk.
SALADIN: Well, now, what's to be done?—
  Could you, to start with, draw on no one else
  But Sittah?

SITTAH: Would I have relinquished, Brother,
  This prior right? To Hafi? Even now
  I claim it still. For I am not as yet
  Quite high and dry.

SALADIN: Not high and dry as yet!
  That tops it all!—Go, Hafi, lay your plans!
  Take money whence you can! and as you can!
  Go, borrow, promise.—Only borrow not
  Of those I have enriched. For borrowing
  Of those might mean that I demand return.
  Go to the stingiest; they'll lend to me
  Most readily. For they are sure to know
  How fast their money doubles in my hands.

AL-HAFI: I know no one like that.

SITTAH: I just recall
  A rumor that your friend has now returned.

AL-HAFI *(startled):* My friend? Who should that be?

SITTAH: I mean the Jew
  You praise so highly.

AL-HAFI: Praise a Jew? and highly?

SITTAH: A Jew to whom—I still recall quite well
  The words you used of him—his God had given,
  Of all the goods of earth, in fullest measure,
  The greatest and the least.

AL-HAFI: What, said I so?—
  What did I mean by that?

SITTAH: The smallest: wealth.
  The greatest: wisdom.

AL-HAFI: This about a Jew?
  About a Jew you say I used these words?

SITTAH: You did not speak to me so of your Nathan?

AL-HAFI: Ah ha! of him! Of Nathan!—I admit
  I had forgotten him.—What, really? He
  Is home again at last? Well, well! Why then,
  He's likely not so badly off.—Quite right:
  The people used to call him wise. And rich.

SITTAH: The rich they call him more than ever now.
  The town is ringing with reports of all
  The treasures and the jewels he has brought.

AL-HAFI: Well, if he's rich again, without a doubt
  He's wise again as well.

SITTAH: What say you, Hafi,
  Suppose you went to him?
AL-HAFI: You mean to say:
  To borrow of him?—Ah, if you but knew him!
  He, lend?—Why, never to lend is just his wisdom.
SITTAH: You drew me once a very different picture.
AL-HAFI: Why, he might lend you goods, perhaps.
  But money?
  Not money, ever.—True, he's such a Jew,
  As you'll not often find. He has good sense;
  Good manners, too; can play chess well. And yet
  Stands out from other Jews no less in evil
  Than in the good.—You must not count on him.—
  He does give to the poor; perhaps as well
  As Saladin. If not as much: at least
  As willingly. Yet quite without pretense.
  And Moslem and Parsee,* and Jew and Christian,
  He treats alike.
SITTAH: And such a man . . .
SALADIN: How comes it,
  That of this man I never heard?
SITTAH: And he
  Would lend not to the Sultan, not to him,
  Who only needs for others, not himself?
AL-HAFI: Now there again you see the Jew in him;
  The common Jew!—Believe me!—For he is
  So envious, so jealous about giving,
  That every "God reward you" in the world
  He'd like to claim himself. And that is why
  He lends to none, that he may always have
  Something to give. Since generosity
  Is ordered in his law, not courteousness:
  His generous giving makes of him the most
  Discourteous fellow in the world. I grant
  Of late I've slightly fallen out with him;
  But think not that I'd fail to do him justice.
  He's good in all things, only not in that;
  Not that indeed. I'll hasten off at once
  And knock at other doors . . . For I recall

---

*An adherent of the ancient Persian religion called Zoroastrian.

A certain Moor, who's rich and stingy too.
I go; I go. *(He hurries out.)*
SITTAH: Why hurry, Hafi!
SALADIN: Let him!

Scene 3

Sittah. Saladin.

SITTAH: He hastes as though evading me!—Now what
  Is this? Has he been actually deceived—
  Or—would he just mislead us?
SALADIN: Can I tell?
  I scarcely know of whom you spoke; and of
  Your Jew, your Nathan, never heard till now.
SITTAH: Why, can it be that such a man remained
  Concealed from you, of whom the people say
  He's found the graves of Solomon and David
  And by a secret, mighty word has power
  To break their seals? And thence from time to time
  He brings to light the immeasurable wealth
  Which could proclaim no lesser source?
SALADIN: If truly
  This man derives his wealth from graves, be sure
  It's not from Solomon's nor David's, where
  Poor fools lie buried!
SITTAH: Yes, or miscreants!
  And of his wealth the source is richer far,
  More copious, than graves all full of gold.
SALADIN: For he's a trader; so I hear.
SITTAH: In truth,
  His beasts of burden travel all the roads,
  Traverse all deserts; and in all the ports
  At anchor lie his vessels. Formerly
  Al-Hafi told me this; and with delight
  He added, with what great nobility
  His friend bestowed what he did not disdain
  With zeal and shrewdness daily to acquire;
  Added, how free his mind of prejudice;
  His heart how open unto every virtue,
  With every beauty perfectly attuned.
SALADIN: Yet now Al-Hafi spoke so dubiously,

So coldly of him.
SITTAH: No, not cold; embarrassed.
As if he thought it dangerous to praise him,
And yet he would not chide him undeserved.—
Or is it really true that even the best
Among a people never quite escapes
That people's traits? that Hafi should have cause
In this regard to deprecate his friend?—
Well, be that as it may!—Suppose the Jew
Be more or less the Jew: if he be rich,
Enough for us!
SALADIN: I hope you would not take
His property by force?
SITTAH: What does that mean,
By force? With fire and sword? No, no, what need
With weaklings any force but their own weakness?—
Come with me to my harem for a while,
To hear a singing girl that I've just bought.
Meanwhile perhaps I'll ripen a design
I have for trying on this Nathan.—Come!

Scene 4

In front of Nathan's house, adjacent to the palms. Rachel and Nathan come out of the house. Daya joins them.

RACHEL: You've tarried very long, dear father; now
He'll hardly be here any more.
NATHAN: Oh well;
If here beneath the palms no longer, then
Some other place.—Be not disturbed.—But look!
Is that not Daya coming toward us?
RACHEL: Surely
She will have lost him.
NATHAN: Or as surely not.
RACHEL: Else she'd come faster.
NATHAN: She's not seen us yet . . .
RACHEL: She sees us now.
NATHAN: Is walking twice as fast.
But do be calm, be calm!
RACHEL: Would you prefer
A daughter that was calm in such a case?

Untroubled as to him whose benefaction
Had meant her life? Her life—to her so dear
Because she owes it first of all to you.
NATHAN: I would not have you other than you are:
    Not if I knew that in your soul were stirring
    A wholly different thing.
RACHEL: What, father, what?
NATHAN: You ask me that? So timid still? Whatever
    Goes on in you is innocence and nature.
    So let it cause you no concern. To me
    It causes none. But promise me, my child:
    That when your heart one day declares itself
    More audibly, you will conceal from me
    None of its wishes.
RACHEL: Just the very thought
    I might prefer concealment makes me tremble.
NATHAN: No more of this! For that, once and for all,
    Is settled now.—And here is Daya.—Well?
DAYA: He still is strolling here beneath the palms;
    And must at once appear around that wall.—
    See, there he comes.
RACHEL: Ah, seems irresolute:
    Where to? keep on? go down? turn right? turn left?
DAYA: No, no; he'll make the circuit of the cloister
    Again, I'm sure; then he must pass this spot.
    Agreed?
RACHEL: That's right!—And have you talked with him
    Already? How's his mood today?
DAYA: As ever.
NATHAN: See to it then that he does not perceive
    You here. Step back more. Better go inside.
RACHEL: Just one more look!—That hedge, that steals him from me!
DAYA: Come, come! Your father's right. You run the risk
    That if he sees you he will turn around.
RACHEL: The wretched hedge!
NATHAN: And if he should emerge
    Quite suddenly from it, he needs must see you.
    So get you gone!
DAYA: Come, come! I know a window,
    From which we can observe them.
RACHEL: What? you do? *(They go in.)*

Scene 5

Nathan. Templar.

NATHAN: I almost shrink from this strange man. Recoil
  Almost before his rugged virtue. How
  Can one be so embarrassed by a man?
  Look! there he comes! By Heaven! There's a youth
  Might be a man! I like it well, that glance,
  So good, defiant! and that sturdy stride!
  Only the shell is bitter, and the core
  Is sweet and good.—Where have I seen the like?—
  Your pardon, noble Frank* . . .
TEMPLAR: What?
NATHAN: Pray permit . . .
TEMPLAR: Permit what, Jew?
NATHAN: That I should be so bold
  As to address you.
TEMPLAR: Can I stop you? Yet
  Be brief.
NATHAN: Delay, and hasten not so fast,
  Nor so comtemptuously, to shun a man
  Whom you have put forever in your debt.
TEMPLAR: How so?—I almost guess. Not so? You are . . .
NATHAN: My name is Nathan; I'm the maiden's father,
  Whom your great heart delivered from the flames;
  I come . . .
TEMPLAR: Why, if to thank me:—stop! I have
  Endured already for this trifling thing
  Too many thanks.—And you especially
  Owe me no thanks at all. For did I know
  This girl to be your daughter? We are charged,
  As Templars, to rush forward to the aid
  Of anyone we see in some distress.
  Besides, my life was burdensome to me
  At just that moment. Very willingly
  I seized the chance to throw it in the breach
  To save another—were it nothing but
  A Jewish maiden's life.
NATHAN: Great! Great and monstrous!—

---

*A term used in the Levant to designate any European.

And yet I catch your drift. A modest greatness
Would hide behind the monstrous, merely to
Escape from admiration.—But if it
Thus scorns the gift of open admiration,
What sort of gift would it less quickly scorn?—
Sir Knight, were you no stranger here, nor yet
A prisoner, less boldly I would ask.
So speak, command: wherewith can you be served?
TEMPLAR: By you? With nought.
NATHAN: I am a wealthy man.
TEMPLAR: I never thought the richer Jew the better.
NATHAN: Is that a reason why you should not use
    The better thing he owns: his wealth?
TEMPLAR: All right
    I'll not refuse, for my poor mantle's sake.
    So soon as it is wholly worn and torn,
    And will not suffer either stitch or patch,
    I'll come to you and borrow for a new one,
    Or cloth or cash.—Put off that darkling look!
    And yet you're safe; as yet it's not worn out.
    You see: it's still in fairly decent shape.
    Just that one tip there has a filthy spot,
    For it is singed; that happened when I bore
    Your daughter through the fire.
NATHAN *(seizing the tip and eyeing it):* I find it strange
    That such an ugly spot, soiled by the fire,
    Bears better witness than a man's own lips.
    I'd like to kiss it now—that spot!—Forgive!—
    That was not meant.
TEMPLAR: What?
NATHAN: Why, a tear fell on it.
TEMPLAR: No harm! It has had other drops. *(aside)* But soon
    This Jew will put me in confusion.
NATHAN: Would
    You be so kind as send once to my daughter
    Your mantle?
TAMPLAR: What to do?
NATHAN: That she as well
    May press her lips upon this spot. For she,
    I think, must hope in vain to clasp your knees.
TEMPLAR: But, Jew—your name is Nathan?—Really, Nathan—

You choose your words most—well—most pointedly—
I am perplexed.—You speak the truth—I had . . .
NATHAN: Guise and disguise you, as you will. And still
  I'll find you out.—You were too good, too honest,
  To be more courtly.—There the maiden, all
  Emotion; here her female agent, all
  Submissiveness; the father far away—
  You were concerned for her good name; you fled
  Temptation; fled, in order not to conquer.
  For that I thank you too—
TEMPLAR: I must confess,
  You know just how the Templars ought to think.
NATHAN: Templars alone? and merely *ought*? and merely,
  Because the Order's rules command it so?
  I know how good men think; I know as well
  That all lands bear good men.
TEMPLAR: But different,
  You grant?
NATHAN: Oh yes: in color, dress, and shape.
TEMPLAR: And more or less in one land than the other.
NATHAN: This difference is not large. For everywhere
  The great man needs much room; and several,
  Too closely planted, break each other's limbs.
  The middling sort, like you and me, are found
  In numbers everywhere you care to look.
  Only, the one must not carp at the other.
  Only, the club must put up with the stick;
  Only, a hillock must not make pretense
  That it alone rose out of mother earth.
TEMPLAR: Well said indeed!—But do you know the folk
  That was the first to carp at other tribes?
  Was first to call itself the chosen people?
  Suppose that I did not exactly hate,
  But for its pride was forced to scorn that folk:
  The pride it then passed on to Christians, Moslem,
  Which says their god alone is the true god!
  You're startled at this from a Christian Templar?
  But when and where has pious frenzy, claiming
  The better god, intent on forcing him
  Upon the world at large, revealed itself
  In blacker form than here, and now? O he

Whose eyes drop not their present scales. . . . And yet
Be blind who will!—Forget what I have said;
And leave me! *(Starts to go.)*
NATHAN: Ha! You know not how much closer
I now shall cling to you.—O come, we must,
We must be friends!—Disdain my folk, as much
As ever you will. For neither one has chosen
His folk. Are we our folk? What is a folk?
Are Jew and Christian sooner Jew and Christian
Than man? How good, if I have found in you
One more who is content to bear the name
Of man!
TEMPLAR: By Heaven, yes! you have indeed!
You have in truth!—Your hand—I am ashamed,
To have misjudged you for a moment's time.
NATHAN: And I am proud of it. It's only baseness
That rarely is misjudged.
TEMPLAR: And what is rare
We hardly can forget.—Yes, Nathan, yes:
We must, we must become good friends.
NATHAN: We are
So now.—How happy will my Rachel be!—
And what a cheerful prospect opens out
Before my eyes!—Ah, wait until you know her!
TEMPLAR: I burn with eagerness.—Who rushes there
Out of your house? I think it is her Daya?
NATHAN: Quite right. So anxiously?
TEMPLAR: Our Rachel has
Not met with harm, I hope?

Scene 6

DAYA *(enter Daya in haste):* Oh Nathan, Nathan!
NATHAN: Well?
DAYA: Pardon, noble knight, that I'm compelled
To interrupt.
NATHAN: What is it, then?
TEMPLAR: What is it?
DAYA: The Sultan sends for you. The Sultan would
Have speech with you; O God!
NATHAN: The Sultan? me?

No doubt he's curious to see himself
The novelties I've brought. Send word and say
As yet I have unpacked but little, nothing.
DAYA: No, no; he would see nothing; would consult you,
Yourself, he said, as soon as ever you can.
NATHAN: Say I shall come.—Go back then quickly, go!
DAYA: O take this not amiss, most honored knight.—
O dear, we're so distressed, we cannot think
What he can want.
NATHAN: That will be shown. Go, go!
(Exit Daya.)

Scene 7

TEMPLAR: You do not know him yet?—I mean, in person?
NATHAN: Whom, Saladin? Not yet. Though I have not
Avoided him, I have not sought to know him.
For common talk spoke far too well of him
That I'd not rather trust it than to see.
But now—assuming that it's true—if he
By sparing of your life . . .
TEMPLAR: Indeed, so much
Is really true. The present life I live
He gave to me.
NATHAN: And by that gift to me
A double, triple life. This fact has changed
All things between us; has around me cast
A rope that binds me henceforth to his service.
I scarce, yes, scarce, can now await what he
Will first require of me. I am prepared
For everything; prepared as well to say
That I am so because of you alone.
TEMPLAR: As yet I could not give him thanks myself,
However often I might cross his path.
The impress that I made upon him came
As rapidly as then it disappeared.
Who knows if he remembers my existence.
And yet he must, for once at least, recall
My person, make disposal of my fate.
It's not enough that by his nod and will
I'm still alive: from him I have to learn

Whose will shall tell me how I am to live.

NATHAN: Quite right; so much the less will I delay.—
A word may fall that offers me excuse
To speak of you.—Forgive me, pray—I haste.—
But when may we receive you in my house?

TEMPLAR: When you permit.

NATHAN: No, when you will.

TEMPLAR: Today.

NATHAN: Your name?—I have to ask.

TEMPLAR: My name has been—
Is Curt von Stauffen.—Curt.

NATHAN: Von Stauffen?—Stauffen?

Templar: Why does that strike you so?

NATHAN: Von Stauffen?—Surely
Of that race there were more . . .

TEMPLAR: O yes, out here
A number now are rotting in the ground.
My uncle too—my father, I should say—
Why does your eye transfix me more and more?

NATHAN: It's nothing. I can't see enough of you.

TEMPLAR: Then I shall leave you first. The searcher's eye
Not seldom finds more than he wished to find.
I fear it, Nathan. Let the course of time,
Not curious prying, make us better known. *(Exit.)*

NATHAN *(looking after him in astonishment):*
"Not seldom has the searcher's eye found more
Than he desired."—As if he'd read my soul!—
Upon my word: that might befall me too.—
It's Wolf in growth and gait: his voice as well.
Precisely so he used to toss his head;
Just so the sword lay on his arm; his brows
Wolf used to stroke with leveled hand, as if
To hide the deep-set fire within his eyes.—
How such deep-graven images at times
Can sleep in us, until a word or tone
Arouses them.—Von Stauffen!—Yes, that's right;
Filnek and Stauffen; soon I will know more.
Our Daya—Well, come hither to me, Daya.
(Enter Daya.)

Scene 8

NATHAN: I'll wager, both your hearts are overweighed
  With need to learn far other news than what
  The Sultan wants.
DAYA: You don't take that amiss?
  You'd just begun to speak familiarly
  And kindly with him, when the Sultan's message
  Withdrew us from the window.
NATHAN: Tell her, then,
  She may expect him any moment now.
DAYA: For sure? for sure?
NATHAN: I hope I can rely
  Upon you, Daya? Be upon your guard,
  I beg of you; and you shall not regret it.
  Your conscience, too, shall find its recompense.
  I beg you only, do not spoil my plan.
  I beg you only, tell your tale and question
  Discreetly, with reserve . . .
DAYA: To think that you
  Remember that!—I go; and you go too.
  For look! I really think that from the Sultan
  Another comes, Al-Hafi, yes, your dervish. *(Exit.)*

Scene 9

AL-HAFI *(enters):* Well, well, I was about to call on you.
NATHAN: Why all the haste? What does he want of me?
AL-HAFI: Who?
NATHAN: Saladin.—I come, I come.
AL-HAFI: To whom?
  To Saladin?
NATHAN: Does he not send you?
AL-HAFI: Me?
  No. Has he sent already?
NATHAN: Yes, of course.
AL-HAFI: Then that's correct.
NATHAN: Why, what's correct?
AL-HAFI: Oh, that . . .
  I'm not to blame; God knows I'm not to blame.—
  How much I said of you, what lies I told
  To stave it off!

NATHAN: To stave what off?

AL-HAFI: Why, that
You've now become his treasurer. You have
My pity. But I will not see it done.
I go this moment; you've already heard
Whither I go; and know the way.—And if
You've messages to send along the way,
Then speak, I'm at your service. Yet it may
Not go beyond what nakedness can carry.
I go, so speak.

NATHAN: Al-Hafi, do remember
That not a word of this I know. So tell me
What you are babbling.

AL-HAFI: Surely you will take
Your purses with you?

NATHAN: Purses?

AL-HAFI: Yes, the cash
That you are to advance to Saladin.

NATHAN: And that is all it is?

AL-HAFI: I should stand by
And see him bleed you dry from top to toe?
Watch wastefulness from those once bursting barns
Of generosity just take and take,
Till even the mice in them cannot but starve?
Are you so simple as to think that one
Who needs your cash will take your counsel too?—
Oh, he, and counsel! When has Saladin
Accepted such?—Imagine, Nathan, what
Just now I suffered at his hands,

NATHAN: Well, what?

AL-HAFI: I come to him, just after he has played
Chess with his sister. Sittah's game's not bad;
There stood the game, which Saladin believed
Was lost, had given up, still on the board.
I take a look at it, and see at once
The game was far from lost.

NATHAN: Well, what a find
For you!

AL-HAFI: His king could be protected with a pawn
Upon her check.—Could I but demonstrate
The thing to you!

NATHAN: Oh, I can well believe it.
AL-HAFI: For thus the rook had open file, and she
　Was done for.—This I'd like to show to him
　And called him.—Think!
NATHAN: He shares not your opinion?
AL-HAFI: He doesn't even listen, in contempt
　He overturns the board.
NATHAN: Can such things be?
AL-HAFI: And says, he simply *wants* it to be mate;
　He wants it! Is that playing?
NATHAN: Hardly, no;
　That's playing with the game.
AL-HAFI: And yet the stake
　Was more than empty shells.
NATHAN: Oh, money, bosh!
　That was the least. But not to let you speak!
　Upon a point of such importance, not
　To listen to you! and your eagle glance
　Not to admire! that calls for vengeance; h'm?
AL-HAFI: Nonsense! I only tell you this, that you
　Can see yourself the kind of mind he has.
　In short, I cannot bear it any longer.
　I have to run around to filthy Moors
　And ask and beg that one will lend him money.
　And I, who for myself have never begged,
　Must borrow now for others. Borrowing
　Is much the same as begging: just as lending,
　At usury, is much the same as stealing.
　Among my Ghebers,
　[Parsees] on the Ganges, there
　I don't need either, and I need not be
　The tool of either. On the Ganges, now,
　There only men are found. Here, you alone
　Are worthy of our life upon the Ganges.—
　You'll go along?—Just leave him in the lurch
　With all this stuff he sets such store upon.
　He'll take it from you anyway in time.
　Join me, and forthwith all the worry's done.
　I'll get a gown for you. Come, come!
NATHAN: I think
　That's something to fall back on. But, Al-Hafi,
　I'll think it over. Wait . . .

AL-HAFI: You'll think it over?
This cannot be thought over.
NATHAN: Wait until
I come back from the Sultan; wait until
I take my leave . . .
AL-HAFI: To think things over, means
To seek for reasons to refuse. And who
Cannot resolve upon a moment's notice
To live his own life, he forever lives
A slave to others.—As you will!—Farewell!
Do as you like.—My way lies there; yours here.
NATHAN: Al-Hafi! First you have to verify
Your balance?
AL-HAFI: Rubbish! All the residue
In my account is not worth adding up;
What's owing me, you'll guarantee—or Sittah.
Farewell! *(Exit.)*
NATHAN *(looking after him):* I will—So noble, wild, and good—
What name for him?—I think, when all is said,
The genuine beggar is the genuine king!
(Exit at the other side.)

Act III

Scene 1

Nathan's house.

RACHEL: How, Daya, did my father choose his words?
"I might expect him any moment now?"
That sounds—agreed?—as if he would appear
At once—How many moments have gone by!—
Ah well: who thinks of moments that are past?—
I'll only live in each one as it comes.
That moment must arrive which brings him too.
DAYA: O, out upon that message from the Sultan!
Except for that I'm sure that Nathan would
Have brought him straight to us.
RACHEL: And when it has
Arrived, that moment; and in consequence

The warmest, deepest wish of mine has been
Fulfilled: what then?—what then?
DAYA: What then? Why then
I hope *my* dearest wish may likewise find
Fulfillment.
RACHEL: What within my breast will then
Replace it? It's forgotten how to swell
Without a wish of wishes to command it.—
Will there be nothing? I'm afraid! . . .
DAYA: My wish
Will take the place of that fulfilled one; mine.
My wish to see, in Europe, you in hands
More worthy of you.
RACHEL: Wrong.—What makes this wish
Your very own, prevents that it should ever
Be mine. What calls you is your fatherland:
Should mine not hold me? Should an image only
Of your beloved kin, which in your soul
Is not yet faded, have more weight with me
Than those I see, whom I can clasp and hear,
My people?
DAYA: You may struggle as you will!
The ways of heaven are the ways of heaven.
And were it your deliverer himself
Through whom his God, for whom he fights, should lead
Your person to that distant folk for whom
You once were born!
RACHEL: What are you saying, Daya,
What foolishness! Strange notions you do have!
"His God! for whom he fights!" Who can own God?
What God is that whom any man can own?
Who lets himself be fought for?—And how can
One know he's born *for* any spot on earth,
If not for that *on* which his birth took place?—
What if my father heard you!—How has he
Deserved that you should dream my happiness
As far away from him as possible?
And that the seeds of reason, which he sowed
So purely in my soul, you should now mix
With weeds or flowers from your native land?—
Beloved Daya, once for all, he will

Not see your pretty flowers on my soil.—
And I must tell you, that I feel my soil,
However fair they make it look, depleted,
Exhausted by your blossoms; feel myself
Amid their fragrance, faintly sour-sweet,
So giddy, so benumbed!—No doubt your brain
Is used to it. And so I do not chide
The stronger nerves which can endure it. But
It suits me not at all; and then your angel,
How close he came to making me a fool!—
I'm still ashamed, before my father, of
That farce!

DAYA: What farce!—As if pure reason dwelt
Nowhere but here!! Farce, farce! O, dared I speak!

RACHEL: Do you not dare? When was I not all ears,
As often as you chose to pass the hours
By telling of the heroes of your faith?
Have I not always heard with admiration
Their deeds, and wept at all their sufferings?
It's true, their faith has never seemed to me
Their most heroic trait. So much the more
Consoling was their doctrine, that submission
To God is wholly independent of
Our notions about God.—My father, Daya,
Has told us that so often; you yourself
Have often thought him right: why undermine
What you and he together have erected?—
My Daya, this is not the kind of talk
With which we best might meet our friend. For me
It's helpful. For to me it is important
Beyond all words to know if he . . . Hark, Daya!
What is that at our door? If it were *he!*

Scene 2

VOICE *(outside):* Please walk in here! *(Enter Templar.)*
RACHEL *(starts, composes herself, tries to fall at the Templar's feet):*
                              It's he!—My savior, ah!
TEMPLAR: This to prevent I have delayed: and yet—
RACHEL: If I would clasp the feet of this proud man,
It's but to thank our God and not the man.

He wants no thanks, as little as the bucket
Which showed such zeal in putting out the fire,
Which let itself be filled and emptied, quite
Indifferent: just so the man. He too
Was simply thrust into the fire, and so
By chance, I fell into his arms, and stayed
By chance, as might a spark upon his cloak;
Until I don't know what had cast us both
Out of the flames again.—What cause is there
For thanks?—Mere wine in Europe has impelled
To greater deeds by far.—And Templar knights
Are duty bound to act so; must indeed,
Like dogs of somewhat better training, fetch
From fire as well as water.

TEMPLAR *(observing her with astonishment and disquiet):* Daya,
    Daya!
If I had spells of bitterness and grief,
And took them out on you, why let her know
Each word of folly that escaped my tongue?
That was revenge beyond a proper measure!
I only hope henceforth you'll plead my cause
More kindly with her.

DAYA: I should hardly think
The tiny stabs which you have dealt her heart
Have harmed you there.

RACHEL: You say you suffered grief?
And were more stingy with that grief than with
Your life itself?

TEMPLAR: My good and gracious child!—
How is my spirit rent twixt eye and ear!—
Not *this* girl was it, no, not she indeed,
Whom from the fire I fetched.—Who could know her,
And not do as I did? Who then had waited
For me to come?—Still—fear—distorted looks—
(Pause, as he loses himself in contemplation of her.)

RACHEL: But as for me, I find you still the same.—
    (Pause continued; until she resumes talking, in order to break in
    upon his gazing.)
Well, Templar, tell us, do, where have you been
So long?—Almost I might inquire as well:
Where are you now?

TEMPLAR: I am—where I perhaps
  Ought not to be.—

RACHEL: Where you have been?—And where
  You think perhaps you ought not to have been?
  That is not good.

TEMPLAR: At—at—what is the name?
  At Sinai.

RACHEL: You have been at Sinai?—Good!
  Then I may surely learn reliably
  It it is true . . .

TEMPLAR: What? what? If it is true
  That there the spot is to be seen, where Moses
  Stood before God, when . . .

RACHEL: That is not the point.
  He stood 'fore God wherever he stood. Of that
  I know as much as I require.—No, what
  I'd like to learn from you is this: they say
  It's far less toilsome to ascend that mount
  Than to descend it.—Every time I climbed
  A mountain, it was just the opposite.—
  Well, Templar?—What?—You turn away from me?
  Look not at me?

TEMPLAR: Because I want to hear you.

RACHEL: Because you would not let me see that you
  Smile at my simpleness; yes, that you smile
  To find I have no weightier thing to ask
  About this holiest of all holy hills?
  Is that it?

TEMPLAR: Then into your eyes I must
  Gaze once again.—And now you cast them down?
  Repress your smile? just when I'd like to read
  In doubtful looks what I so plainly hear,
  What you so audibly confess—you're mute?—
  Ah, Rachel, Rachel! Justly did he say,
  "Wait till you know her!"

RACHEL: Who?—Of whom?—Who said it?

TEMPLAR: "Wait till you know her!" so your father said,
  To me, of you.

DAYA: Did I not say it too?
  Not I as well?

TEMPLAR: But speak, where is he now?

Where is your father? Is he with the Sultan?
RACHEL: Beyond a doubt.
TEMPLAR: Still there?—Forgetful me!
　No, no, he'd not stay there so long.—I think
　He's waiting for me by the cloister there;
　Quite certainly; I think we so agreed.
　Allow me! I will go to fetch him . . .
DAYA: That
　Is mine to do. Stay, Templar, stay. I'll bring
　Him here without delay.
TEMPLAR: Not so, not so!
　It is myself he wants to meet; not you.
　Besides, how easily he might . . . who knows? . . .
　With Saladin, you see, he might . . . you know
　The Sultan not! . . . he might have got into
　Embarrassment.—Believe me: there is danger
　Unless I go.
RACHEL: How so? what sort of danger?
TEMPLAR: Danger for me, for you, for him: unless
I swiftly, swiftly go. *(Exit.)*

Scene 3

RACHEL: What is this, Daya?
　So quickly?—What befell him? What new notion
　Impels him?
DAYA: Never mind. I think it is
　A not unhopeful sign.
RACHEL: A sign? Of what?
DAYA: That something stirs within him. Now it boils,
　Must not boil over. Let him be. Now its
　Your turn.
RACHEL: My turn for what? Like him, you grow
　Incomprehensible.
DAYA: Quite soon you can
　Repay him all the unrest that he made
　You suffer. But be not too hard on him,
　Too greedy for revenge.
RACHEL: What you are saying,
　I hope you know yourself.
DAYA: Well then, are you

Again so tranquil now?

RACHEL: Yes. Yes, I am . . .

DAYA: At least confess you're glad of his disquiet;
And that to this you owe the mood of peace
You now enjoy.

RACHEL: Of that I am aware!
For what at most I might confess to you
Is that I am myself amazed to find
How on a raging tempest in my heart
A calm like this could straightway thus ensue.
The sight of him, his speech, his actions have . . .

DAYA: Brought surfeit to you?

RACHEL: Surfeit's not the word;
No—far from that.—

DAYA: Assuaged the pangs of hunger.

RACHEL: Well, you might call it so.

DAYA: Not I, indeed.

RACHEL: He'll be for ever dear to me, yes, dearer
Than my own life; what though my pulse no more
Is altered by his very name; my heart
No longer, when I think of him, will throb
More strongly, faster.—Why this prattle? Come,
Come, Daya, once more join me at the window
Which looks toward the palms.

DAYA: And so I think
They are not quite assuaged, your hunger's pangs.

RACHEL: And now again I shall be seeing palms:
Not only him beneath the palms.

DAYA: This coldness
No doubt begins another fever spell.

RACHEL: How so? I am not cold. In truth, I see
With no less pleasure what I see with calm.

Scene 4

Saladin, Sittah. Audience chamber in the palace of Saladin.

SALADIN *(as he enters, speaks toward the door):* Bring the Jew here,
as soon as he arrives.
(to Sittah) He does not seem to hurry overmuch.

SITTAH: No doubt he was not right at hand; and not
So quickly found.

SALADIN: Ah, Sister, Sister!
SITTAH: My,
  You take this like a battle.
SALADIN: True, and one
  With arms I have not learned to wield. Shall I
  Dissemble; stir up apprehensions; set
  A trap or two; lure on to slippery ground?
  When did I so? Where could I learn the like?—
  And all this I must do, for what? For what?—
  To fish for money; money!—Yes, to scare
  Mere money from a Jew! And am I brought
  At last to stoop to such insipid wiles
  To gain the pettiest trifle of them all?
SITTAH: The smallest trifle, overly contemned,
  Will have its vengeance, brother.
SALADIN: All too true.—
  And now what if this Jew should prove to be
  The good and wise one, as the Dervish once
  Described the man to you?
SITTAH: Oh, in that case!
  No need for worry. For the snare is set
  To catch the stingy, fearsome Jew, the man
  Of wily ways, but not the good and wise.
  For such a Jew is ours without the snare.
  The joy of hearing how he'll find excuse;
  With what bold strength he'll either break the rope,
  Or else with sly precautions writhe his way
  Right past your nets; that you'll enjoy besides.
SALADIN: Well, that is true. Of course; I'm looking forward
  To that.
SITTAH: What else then can embarrass you?
  For if it's merely one of many; if
  He's merely Jew, as Jew: in sight of him
  You will not be ashamed so to appear
  As he thinks all men are? What's more, the man
  Who shows a better face is but to him
  A fool, a dupe.
SALADIN: And so I must do evil,
  Lest evil men think evil of my good?
SITTAH: Yes, brother, if you call it doing evil
  To use each thing according to its kind.

SALADIN: What could a woman's brain invent, it could
  Not also palliate!
SITTAH: What, palliate!
SALADIN: I only fear, this dainty, subtle thing
  Will crumble in my clumsy hand!—Such schemes
  Must be performed precisely as invented:
  With every skill and slyness.—Still, what odds!
  I dance as best I can; though to be sure
  I'd rather do it worse than better.
SITTAH: Come,
  Have confidence! For you I will go bail.
  If you but will.—How prone are men like you
  To make us think it was their sword alone,
  Their mighty sword had carried them so far.
  The lion is ashamed, it's true, when he
  Hunts with the fox:—of foxes, not of guile.
SALADIN: And that you women like to drag us men
  Down to your level!—Leave me, go!—I think
  I know my lesson.
SITTAH: What? I am to go?
SALADIN: You had not meant to stay?
SITTAH: Well, if not that . . .
  In sight of you—still, in this anteroom—
SALADIN: To listen there? Nor that, my sister, if
  I may insist.—Away! I hear the curtain;
  He comes!—Beware of lingering! I'll keep watch.
  (*As she withdraws, Nathan enters by another door; Saladin has
  seated himself.*)

Scene 5

SALADIN: Come nearer, Jew!—Still nearer!—Close to me!—
  And have no fear!
NATHAN: That's for your foe to feel!
SALADIN: You say you're Nathan?
NATHAN: Yes.
SALADIN: Wise Nathan?
NATHAN: No.
SALADIN: If you don't say it, yet the people do.
NATHAN: May be; the people!
SALADIN: Yet you don't suppose

That I am scornful of the people's voice?—
I long have had a wish to know the man
Whom they call wise.

NATHAN: And if it were in scorn
They called him so? If to the people "wise"
Were nothing more than "shrewd"? and shrewd were he
Who knew his interest well?

SALADIN: Of course you mean
His genuine interest?

NATHAN: Why then indeed
Most selfish were most shrewd. And shrewd and wise
Were one.

SALADIN: I hear you prove what you'd deny.—
Mankind's true interests, to the folk unknown,
Are known to you; at least you've tried to know them;
You've pondered them; and that alone produces
The wise man.

NATHAN: As each thinker thinks he is.

SALADIN: Enough of modesty! For when one longs
To hear dry season, constant modesty
Is sickening. *(He jumps up.)* Let's come to business, Jew.
But with sincerity!

NATHAN: Your Highness, I
Will surely serve you so that I shall seem
Well worth your custom.

SALADIN.   Serve me? what?

NATHAN: You shall
Obtain the best in all things; have it, too,
At lowest rates.

SALADIN: What do you mean? I hope
It's not your wares?—I'll let my sister haggle
And bargain with you. *(aside)* That's for listening ears!
(aloud) With you as merchant I have no concern.

NATHAN: Then doubtless you will wish to know what I
Have met or noted on my way about
The foe, who is indeed astir again? If I
May plainly speak . . .

SALADIN: That too is not the goal
I'm steering for with you. Of that I know
All that I need.—In short . . .

NATHAN: Command me, Sultan.

SALADIN: I seek instruction from you now in quite
  A different field.—Since you're accounted wise:
  Then tell me, pray—what faith, or moral law,
  Has most appeal for you?
NATHAN: Your Highness knows
  I am a Jew.
SALADIN: And I a Mussulman.
  The Christian stands between us.—Of these three
  Religions only one can be the true one.—
  A man like you does not remain where chance
  Of birth has cast him: if he so remains,
  It's out of insight, reasons, better choice.
  Well, then! such insight I would share with you.
  Let me the reasons know, which I have had
  No time to ponder out. Reveal to me
  The choice determined by these reasons plain—
  Of course in confidence—that I as well
  May make your choice my own.—This startles you?
  You weigh me with your eye?—It may well be
  No other sultan has had such caprice;
  Although I think it not unworthy quite
  Of any sultan.—Am I right?—Then speak!—
  Speak out!—Or would you have a moment's time
  To think it over? Good; I'll grant you that.—
  (aside) Has she been listening? I will go and see;
  I'll ask if she approves of me. *(aloud)* Reflect!
  Reflect, make haste! For I shall soon return.
  (He goes into the anteroom into which Sittah withdrew.)

Scene 6

NATHAN: H'm! h'm!—how strange!—I'm all confused.—What would
  The Sultan have of me?—I thought of money;
  And he wants—truth. Yes, truth! And wants it so—
  So bare and blank—as if the truth were coin!—
  And were it coin, which anciently was weighed!—
  That might be done! But coin from modern mints,
  Which but the stamp creates, which you but count
  Upon the counter—truth is not like that!
  As one puts money in his purse, just so
  One puts truth in his head? Which here is Jew?

Which, I or he?—But stay!—Suppose in truth
He did not ask for truth!—I must admit,
Suspicion that he used the truth as trap
Would be too small by far.—Too small?—What is
Too small for one so great?—That's right, that's right:
He rushed into the house incontinent!
One knocks, one listens, surely, when one comes
As friend.—I must tread warily!—But how?—
To be a Jew outright won't do at all.—
But not to be a Jew will do still less.
For if no Jew, he might well ask, then why
Not Mussulman?—That's it! And that can save me!
Not only children can be quieted
With fables.—See, he comes. Well, let him come!

Scene 7

SALADIN *(returning, aside):* There, now the coast is clear!—*(aloud)* I
   hope I come
Not prematurely?—You are at an end
With your deliberations.—Well then, speak!
No soul will hear us.
NATHAN: Let the whole world listen.
SALADIN: So sure is Nathan of his case? Now there
Is wisdom! Not to hide the truth! To stake
One's all upon it! Life and limb! One's goods
And blood!
NATHAN: Yes, when it's needful and of use.
SALADIN: Henceforth I may expect to hold by rights
One of my names, Reformer of the world
And of the law.
NATHAN: Indeed, a handsome title!
But, Sultan, ere I draw the final veil,
Allow me, please, to tell an ancient story.
SALADIN: Why not? I always was a friend of tales
Well told.
NATHAN: To tell them *well* is not, I fear,
My forte.
SALADIN: Proud modesty again?—Tell on!
NATHAN: In days of yore, there dwelt in eastern lands
A man who had a ring of priceless worth

Received from hands beloved. The stone it held,
An opal, shed a hundred colors fair,
And had the magic power that he who wore it,
Trusting its strength, was loved of God and men.
No wonder therefore that this eastern man
Would never cease to wear it; and took pains
To keep it in his household for all time.
He left the ring to that one of his sons
He loved the best; providing that in turn
That son bequeath to his most favorite son
The ring; and thus, regardless of his birth,
The dearest son, by virtue of the ring,
Should be the head, the prince of all his house.—
You follow, Sultan.

SALADIN: Perfectly. Continue!

NATHAN: At last this ring, passed on from son to son,
Descended to a father of three sons;
All three of whom were duly dutiful,
All three of whom in consequence he needs
Must love alike. But yet from time to time,
Now this, now that one, now the third—as each
Might be with him alone, the other two
Not sharing then his overflowing heart—
Seemed worthiest of the ring; and so to each
He promised it, in pious frailty.
This lasted while it might.—Then came the time
For dying, and the loving father finds
Himself embarrassed. It's a grief to him
To wound two of his sons, who have relied
Upon his word.—What's to be done?—He sends
In secret to a jeweler, of whom
He orders two more rings, in pattern like
His own, and bids him spare nor cost nor toil
To make them in all points identical.
The jeweler succeeds. And when he brings
The rings to him, the sire himself cannot
Distinguish them from the original.
In glee and joy he calls his sons to him,
Each by himself, confers on him his blessing—
His ring as well—and dies.—You hear me, Sultan?

SALADIN *(who, taken aback, has turned away):* I hear,

I hear you!—Finish now your fable
Without delay.—I'm waiting!
NATHAN: I am done.
For what ensues is wholly obvious.—
   Scarce is the father dead when all three sons
Appear, each with his ring, and each would be
The reigning prince. They seek the facts, they quarrel,
Accuse. In vain; the genuine ring was not
Demonstrable;—*(He pauses for a reply.)*
          almost as little as
Today the genuine faith.
SALADIN: You mean this as
The answer to my question? . . .
NATHAN: What I mean
Is merely an excuse, if I decline
Precisely to distinguish those three rings
Which with intent the father ordered made
That sharpest eyes might not distinguish them.
SALADIN: The rings!—Don't trifle with me!—I should think
That those religions which I named to you
Might be distinguished readily enough.
Down to their clothing; down to food and drink!
NATHAN: In all respects except their basic grounds.—
Are they not grounded all in history,
Or writ or handed down?—But history
Must be accepted wholly upon faith—
Not so?—Well then, whose faith are we least like
To doubt? Our people's, surely? Those whose blood
We share? the ones who from our childhood gave
Us proofs of love? who never duped us, but
When it was for our good to be deceived?—
How can I trust my fathers less than you
Trust yours? Or turn about.—Can I demand
That to your forebears you should give the lie
That mind be not gainsaid? Or turn about.
The same holds true of Christians. Am I right?—
SALADIN *(aside):* By Allah, yes! The man is right. I must
Be still.
NATHAN: Let's come back to our rings once more.
As we have said: the sons preferred complaint;
And each swore to the judge, he had received

The ring directly from his father's hand.—
As was the truth!—And long before had had
His father's promise, one day to enjoy
The privilege of the ring.—No less than truth!—
His father, each asserted, could not have
Been false to him; of such a loving father:
He must accuse his brothers—howsoever
Inclined in other things to think the best
Of them—of some false play; and he the traitors
Would promptly ferret out; would take revenge.
SALADIN: And then, the judge?—I am all ears to hear
   What you will have the judge decide. Speak on!
NATHAN: Thus said the judge: unless you swiftly bring
   Your father here to me, I'll bid you leave
   My judgment seat. Think you that I am here
   For solving riddles? Would you wait, perhaps,
   Until the genuine ring should rise and speak?—
   But stop! I hear the genuine ring enjoys
   The magic power to make its wearer loved,
   Beloved of God and men. That must decide!
   For spurious rings can surely not do that!—
   Whom then do two of you love most? Quick, speak!
   You're mute? The rings' effect is only backward,
   Not outward? Each one loves himself the most?
   O then you are, all three, deceived deceivers!
   Your rings are false, all three. The genuine ring
   No doubt got lost. To hide the grievous loss,
   To make it good, the father caused three rings
   To serve for one.
SALADIN: O splendid, splendid!
NATHAN: So,
   The judge went on, if you'll not have my counsel,
   Instead of verdict, go! My counsel is:
   Accept the matter wholly as it stands.
   If each one from his father has his ring,
   Then let each one believe his ring to be
   The true one.—Possibly the father wished
   To tolerate no longer in his house
   The tyranny of just one ring!—And know:
   That you, all three, he loved; and loved alike;
   Since two of you he'd not humiliate

To favor one.—Well then! Let each aspire
To emulate his father's unbeguiled,
Unprejudiced affection! Let each strive
To match the rest in bringing to the fore
The magic of the opal in his ring!
Assist that power with all humility,
With benefaction, hearty peacefulness,
And with profound submission to God's will!
And when the magic powers of the stones
Reveal themselves in children's children's children:
I bid you, in a thousand thousand years,
To stand again before this seat. For then
A wiser man than I will sit as judge
Upon this bench, and speak. Depart!—So said
The modest judge.
SALADIN: God! God!
NATHAN: Now, Saladin,
If you would claim to be that wiser man,
The promised one . . .
SALADIN *(rushing to him and seizing his hand, which he retains):*
                  I, dust? I, nothing? God!
NATHAN: What is the matter, Saladin?
SALADIN: Dear Nathan!—
The thousand thousand years your judge assigned
Are not yet up.—His judgment seat is not
For me.—Go!—Go!—But be my friend.
NATHAN: Nought else
Had Saladin to tell me?
SALADIN: Nought.
NATHAN: Nought?
SALADIN: Nothing.—
Why ask?
NATHAN: May I seek opportunity
To ask a favor?
SALADIN: And for that you need
An opportunity?—Speak out!
NATHAN: I have returned
From distant parts, where I collected debts.—
I've almost too much cash on hand.—The times
Are once more looking doubtful;—and I know
Not rightly where to find security.—

I wondered, then, if you perhaps—because
Prospective war needs money more and more—
Could use some.

SALADIN *(looking him fixedly in the eye)*: Nathan!—I'll not ask
    you if
  Al-Hafi has been with you;—nor explore
  If some suspicion urges you to make
  This voluntary offer . . .

NATHAN: A suspicion?

SALADIN: I'd be to blame.—Forgive me!—What's the use?
  I must confess to you—I was indeed
  Intending—

NATHAN: Surely not, the selfsame thing
  To ask of me?

SALADIN: Quite so.

NATHAN: Then both of us
  Are helped at once!—But that I cannot send
  All of my cash to you, ascribe that to
  The youthful Templar.—One well-known to you.—
  To him I first must pay a goodly sum.

SALADIN: A Templar? Surely you would not support
  My fiercest foes with means of yours?

NATHAN: I speak
  But of the one whose life you spared . . .

SALADIN: Ah! that
  Reminds me!—I had quite forgot the youth!—
  Where is he? Do you know him?

NATHAN: What? Then you
  Are not aware, how much of what you gave
  To him in mercy flowed through him to me?
  For, risking all his newly granted life,
  He saved my daughter from the fire.

SALADIN: He did?—
  Ha! So he looked, I thought. My brother would
  Have done the same, whom he so much resembles.—
  Is he still here? Then bring him to me!—For
  I've told my sister of her brother, whom
  She never knew, so many things that I
  Must have her see his living image too!—
  Go, fetch him!—Strange, how out of *one* good deed,
  Though but a child of passion, such a wealth

Of other goodly deeds is born. Go, fetch him!
NATHAN *(dropping Saladin's hand):* At once! And our agreement
    stays in force? *(Exit.)*
SALADIN: Too bad I did not let my sister listen!—
    To her!—How shall I tell her all of this?
    (Exit at the other side.)

Scene 8

*Under the palms in the vicinity of the monastery; the Templar is
waiting for Nathan.*

TEMPLAR *(struggling with himself, walks up and down; then he
    bursts out):*—The wearied victim pauses here.—What then!
I *will* not know just what goes on in me;
Nor yet anticipate what is to be.—
Enough to say, I fled in vain! in vain.—
Yet all I *could* was flee!—Now come what must!—
Too swift the blow for me to dodge its fall;
Although to shun it I so oft, so much,
Had used refusal.—Seeing her, whom I
So little craved to see—yes, seeing her
Meant the resolve to let her nevermore
Escape my sight—Resolve, how so? Resolve
Is purpose, action; and I merely suffered,
To see her and to feel myself enmeshed,
One texture with her being, was the same;
Remains the same.—To live apart from her
Is quite unthinkable; that would mean death—
And wheresoever after death we bide,
There too my death.—If that is love, why then—
The Templar loves indeed—the Christian loves
The Jewish maid indeed.—Well! What of that?—
In this the Land of Promise—hence to me
Of Promise likewise to eternity!—
I've rid myself of many a prejudice.—
What would my Order have? As Templar, I
Am dead; was from that moment dead to it,
Which made me prisoner to Saladin.
That head which he gave back, was it my own?—
No, it's a new one, ignorant of all
That was impressed on that one, bound it fast.—

And better, too, for my paternal heaven
More suitable. I feel that now. With it
I now begin to think as in these lands
My father must have thought; unless it's fables
They've told me of him.—Fables?—only quite
Believable; more credible, indeed,
They never seemed than now, when I but run
The risk of stumbling where he fell.—He fell?
I'd rather fall with men than stand with children—
His model guarantees me his applause.
Is there another whose applause I crave?
Nathan's, I wonder?—His encouragement,
Beyond applause, can hardly fail me less.—
Ha, what a Jew!—And one who likes to seem
Just Jew, no more!—He comes, and comes with haste;
Aglow with joy. But who comes otherwise
From Saladin?—Ho, Nathan!

Scene 9

NATHAN (*entering*):   Is it you?
TEMPLAR: You tarried very long with Saladin.
NATHAN: Oh, not so long. I was too much delayed
 In getting there.—Yes, truly, Curt; the man
 Matches his fame. His fame is but his shadow.—
 But first of all let me report to you . . .
TEMPLAR: What then?
NATHAN: He wants to see you; bids you come
 To him without delay. Escort me home,
 Where I have things to order for his service.
 Then we will go to him.
TEMPLAR: Your dwelling, Nathan,
 I'll enter not again, until . . .
NATHAN: Then you
 Have been there meanwhile? seen and spoken to her?—
 Well?—Tell me; how does Rachel please you?
TEMPLAR: Oh,
 Beyond all words!—And yet—I never will—
 Consent to see her more! Unless right here
 You promise me that I may see her face—
 For ever.

NATHAN: How should I interpret that?

TEMPLAR *(after a short pause, falling on his neck):* My father!

NATHAN: Well, young man!

TEMPLAR *(releasing him just as suddenly):* Not "son"?—I beg you!—

NATHAN: My dear young man!

TEMPLAR: Not "son"?—I beg you, Nathan!—
    Conjure you by the foremost bonds of nature!—
    Give not precedence to much later ties!—
    Suffice it just to be a man!—And thrust
    Me not from you!

NATHAN: My dear, dear friend! . . .

TEMPLAR: And "son"?
    Not "son"?—Not even then, if gratitude
    Had guided love to your dear daughter's heart?
    Not even then, if both but wait your nod
    To fuse and melt in one?—You say no word?

NATHAN: You have surprised me, Knight.

TEMPLAR: You are surprised?—
    Surprise you, Nathan, with your very thoughts?
    You'd not disown them, spoken by my lips?—
    And I surprise you?

NATHAN: Till I know for sure
    Which Stauffen was your father!

TEMPLAR: Nathan, not—
    At such a time, instead of feelings warm,
    You're curious?

NATHAN: For look you, I myself
    Once knew a Stauffen, and his name was Conrad.

TEMPLAR: And what if my own father bore that name?

NATHAN: Truly?

TEMPLAR: I bear my father's name: for Curt
    Is Conrad.

NATHAN: Well—my Conrad then was not
    Your father. For my Conrad was like you:
    A Templar; never married.

TEMPLAR: All the same!

NATHAN: What?

TAMPLAR: All the same he might quite well have been
    My father.

NATHAN: You are jesting.

TEMPLAR: And in truth

You're too pedantic!—For what were I now?
Granted, a by-blow or a bastard! Still
The stock is not to be despised at that.—
But give me leave to blink my pedigree,
I'll do as much by you. Not that I have
The slightest doubt of your descent. No, God
Forbid! You trace it, shoot by shoot, clear back
To Abraham. And backward from there on
I know it too; will take my oath on it.

NATHAN: You're growing bitter.—Do I merit that?—
Have I refused you?—No, I merely would
Not take you at your word this very moment.—
It's nothing more.

TEMPLAR: For sure?—And nothing more?
O, then forgive . . .

NATHAN: Come quickly, come!

TEMPLAR: Where to?
No!—With you to your house?—Not that, not that!—
There's fire there!—I'll await you here. Begone!—
If ever I see her more I'll see her then
Often enough. If not, then I have seen
Her far too much . . .

NATHAN: I'll hasten as I can. *(Exit.)*

Scene 10

TEMPLAR: More than enough!—The human brain can grasp
So boundlessly; yet on a sudden is
Sometimes so full! and of a trifle full!—
No use, no use; and let it be surcharged
With what it will.—Let me have patience now!
The soul will take the turgid stuff and blend
It soon in one, thus gaining space, and light
And order will return.—Say, is this love
The first I've known?—Or was what I have known
As love not love?—Is love none other than
I'm feeling now? . . .

DAYA *(who has stolen in from the side)*: Sir Knight! Sir Knight!

TEMPLAR: Who calls?
Well, Daya, you?

DAYA: I've stolen past him. But

He still could see us, where you stand.—So come
Closer to me, behind this tree.
TEMPLAR: What now?
    Such secrecy? What is it?
                         Ah, indeed
DAYA:
    It is a secret that impels me to
    Your side; a double secret. One is known
    To me alone; the other known to you.—
    Suppose we trade; your secret tell to me,
    Then I will tell you mine.
TEMPLAR: With pleasure.—If
    You'll tell me first what you consider mine.
    But that no doubt your secret will make clear.—
    So you begin.
DAYA: Imagine!—No, sir Knight:
    First you; I'll follow.—Be assured that mine
    Is nothing worth to you, unless I've yours
    Before.—Make haste!—For if I question you:
    You have confided nothing. Then my secret
    Remains my own; and you are rid of yours.—
    Alas, poor knight!—To think you men believe
    You *could* have a secret from our sex!
TEMPLAR: Often a secret we don't know we have.
DAYA: May be. And so indeed I must be kind
    Enough to give yourself the information.—
    What did it mean that to your heels you took
    So suddenly? and left us in the lurch?—
    And why don't you return with Nathan now?—
    Did Rachel have such slight effect on you?
    Or else, so much?—It *was* so much!—Teach me
    To know the fluttering of the captured bird,
    Stuck to the lime!—In short: confess at once
    You love her, love her close to madness; and
    I'll tell you something . . .
TEMPLAR: Madness? Truly; you
    Are quite a judge of that.
DAYA: Well, just admit
    The love at least; I'll let the madness go.
TEMPLAR: Because it's obvious?—A Templar knight
    Should love a Jewess! . . .

DAYA: Granted, that appears
  To make but little sense.—And yet at times
  There's more sense in a thing than we suspect;
  Would it be so amazing, if the Savior
  Should draw us to him by such ways as shrewdness
  Would not be like to choose?
TEMPLAR.   Such solemn tone?—
  (aside) But if I think of Providence instead
  Of Christ, is she not right?—*(aloud)* I grant, you make
  Me curious as I'm seldom wont to be.
DAYA: This is the land of wonders!
TEMPLAR *(aside):*   Well!—let's say
  Of wondrous things. Can it be otherwise?
  The whole world comes together here.—*(aloud)* Dear Daya,
  Assume as granted what you'd have me say:
  That I do love her; that I fail to see
  How I shall live without her; that indeed . . .
DAYA: Truly, sir Knight?—Then swear to make her yours;
  To save her; yes, to save her here on earth,
  Eternally in heaven.
TEMPLAR.   How?—How can I?—
  How can I swear what's not within my power?
DAYA: It is within your power. And with a word.
  A single word, I'll put it in your power.
TEMPLAR: That even her father would have no objection?
DAYA: Her father! stuff! He'll *have* to give consent.
TEMPLAR. Will *have* to, Daya?—Up to now he's not
  In robber's hands.—There's nothing that he *must* do.
DAYA: Well then, he must agree; and willingly.
TEMPLAR: Must, willingly!—But if I tell you, Daya,
  I've tried myself to touch this chord in him?
DAYA: And he did not respond in harmony?
TEMPLAR: No, in *disharmony,* which—wounded me.
DAYA: What say you?—What? You showed him but a shadow
  Of a desire for Rachel, and he failed
  To leap for joy?—he frostily withdrew,
  Made difficulties?
TEMPLAR: Just about.
DAYA: Then I
  Will hesitate no longer—*(pause)*
TEMPLAR.   Yet I see

You hesitate?

DAYA: He is so good a man!—
I owe him much myself.—To think that he
Should stop his ears!—God knows, with bleeding heart
I put such pressure on him

TEMPLAR: Daya, please
Free me at once from this uncertainty.
But if you are yourself unsure, if what
You have in mind should good or bad be called,
Shameful or laudable—then hold your peace!
I will forget you've something to conceal.

DAYA: That spurs instead of checking. Well; then learn;
Rachel is not a Jewess; is—a Christian.

TEMPLAR *(coldly):* Congratulations! Was the birthing hard?
Don't mind the labor pains!—Go on
With zeal to people heaven; now that you
Can add no more to earth.

DAYA: What, knight? Deserves
My news such scorn? That Rachel is a Christian:
That gladdens you, a Christian and a Templar,
Who love her well, no more?

TEMPLAR: Tremendously,
Since she's a Christian of your special brand.

DAYA: So that's your thought? Let it be so!—But no!
I'd like to see the one who should convert her!
Her fortune is, long since to be what she
Has lost the power to become.

TEMPLAR.   Explain
Or—go!

DAYA: She is a Christian; born of Christians;
And is baptized . . .

TEMPLAR *(hastily):* And Nathan?

DAYA: Not her father!

TEMPLAR: He's not her father?—Know you what you say?

DAYA: The truth, which often cost me bitter tears.—
No, he is not her father . . .

TEMPLAR: As his daughter
He reared her only? Reared this Christian child
As Jewess for himself?

DAYA: Quite so.

TEMPLAR: Not knowing

How she was born?—She never learned from him
That she was born a Christian, not a Jewess?
DAYA: No, never!
TEMPLAR: Did not merely rear the *child*
  In this delusion? Left the girl as well
  Thus uninformed:
DAYA: Too true!
TEMPLAR: Thus acted—Nathan?
  This wise, good Nathan should have been so free
  To falsify the voice of nature thus?—
  Thus to misguide the impulse of a heart
  Which, left alone, would take quite other ways?—
  You have indeed confided to me, Daya,
  A thing of weight—which may have consequences—
  Perplexes me—puts me in present doubt
  What I should do.—So give me time!—And go!
  He'll pass this place again. He might surprise us.
  So go!
DAYA: O, that would kill me!
TEMPLAR: I am quite
  Unfit to see him now. If you should meet him,
  Just tell him that again we'll come together
  At Saladin's.
DAYA: But let him not suspect
  A thing.—This should but give to the affair
  A final shove; should free you of all doubts
  Regarding Rachel!—If you take her then
  To Europe, surely, me you will not leave
  Behind?
TEMPLAR: That's to be seen. But go now, go. (*Both go out, Daya first.*)

Act IV

Scene 1

The cloisters of the monastery.

FRIAR: Yes, yes! no doubt the Patriarch is right!
  Although so far I've not had much success
  With what he's bid me do.—Why put on me

Just tasks like those?—I hate this subtlety;
I hate persuasion; hate to stick my nose
In everything; and hate to have my hands
In everything.—Did I forsake the world,
Myself alone, to get myself entangled
With worldly things? For others all the more?

TEMPLAR *(hurrying up to him):* Good brother! There you are. I long
    have sought you.

FRIAR: Me, sir?

TEMPLAR: Have you forgotten me so soon?

FRIAR: Oh no! I only thought that in my life
    Never again I'd get to see your face.
    Such was my prayer to God.—The dear God knows
    How bitter to me was the mission which
    I was obliged to lay before you; knows
    If I desired to find an open ear
    In you; and knows how greatly I rejoiced,
    With all my heart, that you so bluntly brushed
    Away from you, without much thought, all that
    Which does not grace a knight.—Yet you return;
    The seed has taken root.

TEMPLAR: You know, it seems,
    Why I have come? I scarcely know myself.

FRIAR: You've thought it through, and found, the Patriarch
    Is not so very wrong; that gold and honor
    His project might secure to you; and that
    A foe's a foe, and were he seven times
    Our angel. This you've weighed with flesh and blood,
    And come and will agree to serve.—Oh dear!

TEMPLAR: My good and pious man! be comforted
    It's not for that I come, . . . and would consult
    The Patriarch. As yet upon that point
    I think as then I thought; not for the world
    Would forfeit now the good opinion which
    An honest, dear, and pious man like you
    Once held of me.—I merely come to ask
    The Patriarch's advice upon a thing . . .

FRIAR: You ask the Patriarch? A knight a—*priest? (looking around
    fearfully)*

TEMPLAR: The thing is rather priestly.

FRIAR: All the same,

The priest won't ask the knight, and were the thing
All knightliness.
TEMPLAR: Because he has the right
  To make mistakes; which I am not included
  To envy him.—Of course, if I had but
  To act here for myself; of course, if I
  Had but to answer to myself; what need
  Had I of Patriarchs? But certain things
  I'd rather settle by another's will
  And badly, than quite well by mine alone.—
  Besides, as now I see, religion is
  Party as well; and one may think he is
  Unpartisan, yet find that willy-nilly
  He waves his party's flag. Since that is so,
  It's doubtless right.
FRIAR: On that I'll make no comment,
  Not sure I understand my lord.
TEMPLAR: And yet!—
  (aside) Let's see, what do I really want? Decree,
  Or counsel?—Simple-hearted, or refined?—
  (aloud) I thank you, Brother, for the friendly hint.—
  Why Patriarch?—Be you my Patriarch!
  For in the Patriarch it's more the Christian
  Whom I would ask, than the other way around.
  The case is this . . .
FRIAR: No further, sir, no further!
  What use?—You do misjudge me.—He who knows
  Too many things has many cares; and I
  Have vowed myself to *one* alone.—Oh, good!
  Hark! look! There comes, to my relief, himself.
  Remain right here. He has caught sight of you.

Scene 2

The Patriarch approaches through one of the choisters in full priestly regalia.

TEMPLAR: I wish that I could shun him.—Not my taste—
  A red-faced, fat, and all too friendly prelate!
  And what display!
FRIAR: You ought to see him dressed
  To go to court. But now he's only been
  Sick visiting.

TEMPLAR: How Saladin will pale
Before him!
PATRIARCH *(Approaching, motions to the Friar):*
Here!—No doubt that is the Templar.
What does he want?
FRIAR: Don't know.
PATRIARCH *(approaching him, as the Friar and retinue withdraw):*
Well, Knight!—Delighted
To see this fine young man!—Well, still so young!
With God's aid, something can be made of you.
TEMPLAR: But scarcely more, Your Worship, than you see.
And rather less, I think.
PATRIARCH. At least I hope
That such a pious knight for years may bloom
And flourish for the benefit and honor
Of Christendom and God's beloved cause!
Nor can this fail to be, if bravery
Of youth be guided by the mellowed counsel
Of age.—How else might I to you be helpful?
TEMPLAR: With that which youth like mine oft sadly lacks:
Advice.
PATRIARCH: Right willingly!—Yet the advice
Must be obeyed.
TEMPLAR: Not blindly?
PATRIARCH: Who says that?
No one, of course, must fail to use the reason
Which God has given him—where it belongs.—
But is that everywhere?—O no!—For instance:
If God should deign through his own angel's lips—
That is to say, a servant of His word—
To let us know a means whereby the weal
Of Christendom, the health of holy Church,
In any quite especial way can be
Advanced or strengthened: who may then presume
With reason to explore the will of Him
Who has created reason, and to test
The everlasting law of heaven's glory
By petty rules of vain and earthly honor?—
Enough of this.—What is it then, sir Knight,
On which for now you would have our advice?

TEMPLAR: Supposing, reverend Father, that a Jew
  Possessed an only child—call it a girl—
  Whom with the greatest care in all things good
  He had brought up, and loved more than his soul,
  And who most piously returned his love.
  And now we were informed, the child was not
  The Jew's own daughter: he had picked it up
  In childhood, bought or stolen—what you will;
  The girl was known to be a Christian child,
  Baptized; the Jew had merely reared her as a Jewess;
  And caused her to remain as Jewess and
  His daughter:—tell me, Father, in such case
  What should one do?

PATRIARCH: I shudder!—First, however,
  My lord should state if such a case is fact
  Or mere hypothesis. That is to say:
  If he has but imagined this, or if
  It has occurred, and so continues.

TEMPLAR: I
  Believed that was all one, if I but wished
  Your Worship's judgment.

PATRIARCH.   *One?* I pray you, mark
  How our proud human intellect can err
  In churchly things.—By no means! If the case
  Presented is but pastime of the mind:
  Would it be worth the toil to think it through
  In earnest? Then I'd urge my lord to try
  The theater, where such things *pro et contra*
  Could be discussed with general applause.—
  But if you do not play some trick on me
  With a theatric prank; and if the case
  Is fact; and should it even have transpired
  Within this diocese Jerusalem,
  Our well-beloved city:—then, indeed—

TEMPLAR: What then, pray?

PATRIARCH: First of all, upon the Jew
  The punishment must be inflicted, which
  Imperial and papal law decree
  For such a villanous and vicious crime.

TEMPLAR: It must?

PATRIARCH: And the aforesaid laws impose

Upon the Jew who to apostasy
Seduce a Christian soul—the funeral pyre,
The stake—

TEMPLAR: They do?

PATRIARCH: And how much more the Jew
Who forcibly a helpless Christian child
Withdraws from his baptism bond? For is
Not all that's done to children done by force?—
That is:—excepting what the church to them
May do.

TEMPLAR: But if the child, had not the Jew
Had pity on it, had perhaps succumbed
To misery?

PATRIARCH: All one! The Jew must burn.
For better if it died in misery
Than that for its damnation everlasting
It thus were saved.—Besides, why should the Jew
Forestall the Lord? Whom God would save, He can
Preserve without him.

TEMPLAR: Or despite the Jew
Make blessed, I should think.

PATRIARCH: All one! The Jew
Must burn.

TEMPLAR: I find that hard! The more that he,
So people say, has reared the girl not in
His faith, but rather in no faith at all,
And taught this child not more or less of God
Than reason would require.

PATRIARCH: All one! The Jew
Must burn. . . . Yes, for this cause alone deserves
To burn threefold!—What? let a child grow up
With no belief at all?—The solemn duty
Of faith to leave unmentioned to a child?
O, that is vile!—And I'm surprised, sir Knight,
That you . . .

TEMPLAR: The rest, Your Worship, if God will,
When I confess. *(Starts off.)*

PATRIARCH: What? fail a full account
To render me?—This criminal, this Jew,
Not name to me?—not fetch him here to me?—
But I know what to do! I'll go at once

To Saladin!—By the capitulation
His oath confirmed he *must* protect our rights;
In all the laws protect us, all the dogmas,
Which we account a part of our most holy
Religion! We have the original,
Thank God! We have his hand and seal. Yes, *we!*—
And easily I'll make him see what danger
Lies for the state itself in lack of faith.
All civic bonds dissolved and rent asunder,
When men need not believe.—Away! away
With such a crime! . . .

TEMPLAR: Too bad I can't enjoy
This splendid sermon with more leisure time!
For Saladin has sent for me.

PATRIARCH: He has?
Well then—Of course—Why then—

TEMPLAR: I will prepare
The Sultan, if Your Worship so desire.

PATRIARCH: Oh, oh!—I know that you have found much favor
With Saladin!—I beg you will report
But good of me to him.—It's only zeal
For God that does impel me. If I err
In overdoing, it's for Him.—I pray
You'll bear that fact in mind!—And then, sir Knight,
The matter of the Jew you have brought up
Was just a problem?—that's to say, was just—

TEMPLAR: A problem. *(Exit.)*

PATRIARCH *(to himself)*: Which however I must seek
To ferret out. That might be just the task
For Brother Bonafides. *(aloud):* Here, my son!
(He talks to the Friar while going off.)

The money provided by Nathan is being brought to the palace, and Saladin worries about how to spend it equitably. Sittah finds a small portrait of Assad, their lost brother, and Saladin affirms again that he can see his brother's face in the features of the Knight Templar. The Knight appears before him, Saladin addresses him as a "new Assad," and the young man assures him of his loyalty. He also confesses that he has fallen in love with Rachel and does not hide his disappointment in Nathan's vague hesitations. He also concedes that he has seen the Patriarch before coming to the Palace. Saladin promises to protect

Rachel, and Sittah wants to make her acquaintance quickly.
[Scene 3–5]

Scene 6

The open vestibule in Nathan's house, looking toward the palms; as in
Act I, Scene 1.—A part of the wares and jewels lie unpacked.

DAYA.   O, all is splendid!
 All choice! O, all—as only you can give it.
 Where, where is made this silver stuff with sprigs
 Of gold? What does it cost?—That's what I call
 A bridal dress! No queen could ask for better.
NATHAN: A bridal dress? Why only that?
DAYA: Oh well!
 Of course you did not think of that when you
 Were buying it.—But truly, Nathan, this
 And this alone is it! As if you'd picked
 It out as wedding dress. The background white,
 Denoting innocence; the golden streams
 Which everywhere meander through the ground,
 Denoting wealth. You see? Enrapturing!
NATHAN: Why all this show of wit? Whose bridal dress
 You symbolize so learnedly?—Are you
 Betrothed?
DAYA: I?
NATHAN: Who, then?
DAYA: I—good God!
NATHAN: Then who?
 Whose wedding dress are you describing here?—
 These things belong to you, and no one else.
DAYA: To me? And meant for me?—And not for Rachel?
NATHAN: What I have brought for Rachel, that is packed
 In quite another bale. Quick! take it hence!
 Pick up your stuff and go!
DAYA: You tempter, you!
 No, no, and even if it were the jewels
 Of all the world! I touch them not, unless
 You swear to me to take advantage of
 This opportunity, the like of which
 Heaven won't send you twice.
NATHAN: Advantage? what?—

And opportunity? for what?

DAYA: O act
Not so obtuse!—In brief: the Templar loves
Our Rachel: give her to him! Then your sin,
Which I no longer can conceal, will have
An end; the girl will thus return to Christians;
Once more be what she is; and is once more
What she became; and you, with all the good
For which we cannot give you thanks enough,
Will not have merely heaped up coals of fire
Upon your head.

NATHAN: Ah ha, the same old harp?—
Just strung with one new string, which, I'm afraid,
Cannot be turned nor made to hold.

DAYA: How so?

NATHAN: The Templar would be fine with me. I'd give
Him Rachel sooner than to any other.
But yet . . . Have patience.

DAYA: Patience? Is that not
Your ancient harp?

NATHAN: A few more days of patience! . . .
Look, look!—Who comes this way? A brother friar?
Go, ask him what he wants.

DAYA: What should he want?
(She goes to question him.)

NATHAN: Then give!—before he asks—*(aside)* If I but knew
How I could first accost the Templar, yet
Not tell the reason for my curious quest!
For if I tell him, and what I suspect
Is groundless: then in vain I've placed at stake
My interest as a father.—*(to Daya)* Well, what now?

DAYA: He wants to speak with you.

NATHAN: Then let him come;
And go the while.

Scene 7

Nathan and the Lay Brother.

NATHAN *(aside):* How gladly I'd remain
As Rachel's father!—Can't I *be* so still,

Though I should lose the name?—Indeed, with her
I'll keep the name as well, if once she knows
How much I crave it. *(to Daya)*—Go! *(Exit Daya.) (to the Friar)*
   how can I serve
Your need, good brother?
FRIAR: I've but little need.—
I'm happy, Nathan, still to see you well.
NATHAN: You know me, then?
FRIAR: Why, sir, who knows you not?
You have impressed your name on many a hand.
The impress is on mine, these many years.
NATHAN *(reaching for his purse):*
Come, Brother, I'll refresh the print.
FRIAR: No, thanks!
I'd steal it from the needy; I'll take nothing.—
But if you will permit me, I'll refresh
My name with you. For I've the right to boast
Of laying something in *your* hand, and not
Contemptible.
NATHAN: Forgive!—I am ashamed—
Remind me!—take as penance sevenfold
The value of it from me now.
FRIAR: But first
Be told how I myself this very day
Was minded of the pledge entrusted you.
NATHAN: A pledge entrusted me?
FRIAR: Not long ago ·
I sat as hermit, near to Jericho,
On Quarantana.* Arab robbers came,
Broke down my chapel and my cell, and dragged
Me off with them. But I escaped, with luck,
And journeyed hither to the Patriarch,
To beg of him another spot, where I
In solitude might serve my God unto
My blessed end.
NATHAN: I stand on coals, good brother.
Be brief. The pledge! The pledge entrusted me!

*A desert land between Jericho and Jerusalem, where Christ is said to have spent the
forty days (hence the name) of his temptation; a high, rugged mountain still bears the
same name.

FRIAR: One moment, Nathan.—Well, the Patriarch
 Assured me of a hermitage on Tabor,*
 So soon as one was free; but meantime bade
 Me stay as friar in the choister here.
 There I am serving, Nathan; wish myself
 A hundred times a day on Tabor. For
 The Patriarch employs me for such things
 As fill me with great loathing. For example:
NATHAN: Make haste, I beg you!
FRIAR: Well, it's coming now!
 Today somebody whispered in his ear:
 That hereabouts there lives a Jew who has
 A Christian child brought up as his own daughter.
NATHAN *(startled):* What's this?
FRIAR: Just hear me to the end.—The while
 He orders me to trace this Jew at once,
 If possible, and he is most enraged
 At such offense, which seems to him to be
 The very sin against the Holy Ghost;—
 That is, the sin, which of all sins we count
 The greatest sin, but that we, God be praised,
 Don't rightly know in what that sin consists;—
 At once my conscience wakes; and it occurs
 To me that I myself, in times gone by,
 Might well have given opportunity
 For this unpardonable sin.—I ask you,
 Did not a horseman, eighteen years ago,
 Bring you a baby girl, a few weeks old?
NATHAN: How so?—Well, yes—that's true—
FRIAR: Come, look at me
 Right sharply!—For that horseman, that was I.
NATHAN: Was you?
FRIAR.   The lord, from whom I brought it, was,
 If I am right—a Lord von Filnek—Wolf
 Von Filnek.
NATHAN: Right!
FRIAR: Because its mother had
 But lately died; and since the father was
 Dispatched—I think to Gaza†—suddenly,

---

*Mount Tabor, six miles southeast of Nazareth.
†A fortified seaport which Saladin attacked and took in 1170.

To where the infant could not follow him:
He sent it you. And as I think I found you
In Darun?*
NATHAN: Right again!
FRIAR: I would not wonder,
  If memory deceived me. I have had
  So many goodly masters; and this one
  I served but all too briefly. Very soon
  He fell at Ascalon;† I think he was
  A gallant gentleman.
NATHAN: He was! he was!
  To whom I owe so much, so much of thanks!
  Who more than once had saved me from the sword!
FRIAR: How fine! So much the gladder were you then
  To take his little daughter.
NATHAN: That you can
  Imagine well.
FRIAR: Well, then, where is it now?
  I surely hope the daughter has not died?—
  O better let it not have died!—And if
  Nobody knows of the affair: then all
  Is well.
NATHAN: Is well?
FRIAR: Have trust in me. For see,
  I think this way: if on the Good, which I
  Believe I'm doing, something very bad
  Too closely borders: then I'll rather not
  Perform the Good; because the Bad we know
  Reliable enough, but we are far
  From knowing what is good.—How natural,
  That if that Christian baby should be reared
  Most properly, you'd bring it up as yours.—
  And this you should have done in love and faith,
  And must get such reward? I can't see that.
  Admittedly, it had been shrewder if
  You'd had the Christian by another hand
  Brought up as Christian: in that case you'd not
  Have loved the daughter of your friend. And children

---

*Built not long before by a king of Jerusalem on a height near Gaza.
†Also named Ashkelon, a fortified seaport captured by Baldwin III in 1153, retaken by Saladin in 1187 and demolished in 1191.

Have need of love—and were it but the love
Of savage beasts—much more than Christian teaching.
For Christianity there's always time.
If but the girl before your eyes has grown
In health and soulfulness, in Heaven's eyes
She still is what she was. Is it not true
That Christendom is built on Jewish faith?
I've oft been angered, moved to bitter tears,
When Christians could so utterly forget
That our Lord Jesus was a Jew himself.

NATHAN: Good brother, you must be my advocate,
If hatred and hypocrisy should rise
Against me—for an act—Ah, for an act!
You only should be told of it!—But take
It with you to the grave! Mere vanity
Has never tempted me as yet to tell it
To any other. You alone I'll tell it.
To simple piety alone I'll tell it.
Since that alone can understand the deeds
God-fearing man can force himself to do.

FRIAR: I see you moved, your eyes are filled with tears?

NATHAN: At Darun you had found me with the child.
But you will hardly know that just before
In Gath* the Christians slaughtered all the Jews
With wives and children; know not, that among
These Jews my wife with seven hopeful sons
Was domiciled within my brother's house,
Sent to him for safekeeping, where they all
Were burned to death.

FRIAR: O righteous God!

NATHAN: And when
You came, three days and nights I had been lying
In dust and ashes, weeping unto God.—
Weeping? Far more: with God had argued, stormed,
Enraged, and cursed myself and all the world;
And sworn against the Christian world a hate
Irreconcilable—

FRIAR: I well believe it!

NATHAN: But bit by bit my reason found return.

---

*One of the five royal cities of Philistia, northwest of Jerusalem.

With gentle voice it spoke: "And yet God is!
That too was God's decree! Up then, and come!
Now practice what you long have understood;
And what is scarcely harder to perform
Than just to comprehend, if you but will.
Arise!"—I stood and cried to God: I will!
If Thou wilt, then I will!—Then you dismounted
And handed me the child, wrapped in your cloak.—
What you then said to me; or I to you:
I have forgotten. Only this I know:
I took the child, I bore it to my couch,
I kissed it, threw myself upon my knees,
And sobbed: O God! for seven *one* at least!
FRIAR: O Nathan, Nathan! You're a Christian soul!
    By God, a better Christian never lived!
NATHAN: And well for us! For what makes me for you
    A Christian, makes yourself for me a Jew!—
    But let's no longer melt each other's hearts.
    Here deeds are needed. And though sevenfold love
    Soon bound me to this single waif and girl;
    Though in the thought I perish, that anew
    I am to lose my seven sons in her:
    If Providence demands her at my hands
    Again—I shall obey!
FRIAR: See there!—So much
    I had myself been ready to advise you!
    And now your guardian angel has already
    So counseled you!
NATHAN: But still, the first chance claimant
    Must not abduct her!
FRIAR: Surely not!
NATHAN: Or one
    Who had not greater rights to her than I;
    At least he must have prior ones—
FRIAR: Of course!
NATHAN: Which blood and nature grant him.
FRIAR: Just my thought!
NATHAN: So quickly name the man who's kin to her
    As brother, uncle, cousin, or the like:
    I will not then withhold her, who was born
    And reared to be of any faith and house

The ornament.—I hope that of your lord
And of his race you know much more than I.
FRIAR: Alas, good Nathan, hardly that.—You have
    Already heard that all too brief a time
    I was with him.
NATHAN: Do you not know at least
    The mother's family?—Was she a Stauffen?
FRIAR: Quite possible!—I think so.
NATHAN: Was her brother
    Not named Conrad von Stauffen—and a Templar?
FRIAR: Unless I err. But stop! It comes to me
    That I possess from my lamented lord
    A little book. I drew it from his breast
    At Ascalon, when we interred him.
NATHAN: Well?
FRIAR: It's full of prayers. We call it breviary.—
    A Christian, so I thought, might have a use
    For that.—Not I, indeed.—I cannot read—
NATHAN: No matter.—To the point!
FRIAR: Well, in this book
    At front and back, as I've been told, and in
    My lord's own hand, are fully written down
    His relatives and hers.
NATHAN: O welcome news!
    Go! run! fetch me the book! I shall be glad
    To pay its weight in gold; a thousand thanks
    Besides! Haste! run!
FRIAR: Right gladly! But it is
    In Arabic, the writing of my lord. *(Exit.)*
NATHAN: All one! Just bring it!—God, if I could keep
    The maiden still, and purchase me besides
    A son-in-law like that!—I doubt it!—Well,
    Let be what may!—But who can it have been
    That let the Patriarch get wind of this?
    That I must not forget to ask.—What if
    It even came from Daya?

Scene 8

DAYA *(in haste, embarrassed):* Nathan, fancy!
NATHAN: Well, what?

DAYA: Poor child, she was in consternation!
There sends . . .
NATHAN: The Patriarch?
DAYA: The Sultan's sister,
The Princess Sittah . . .
NATHAN: Not the Patriarch?
DAYA: No, Sittah!—Don't you hear?—The Princess Sittah
Sends hither, has our Rachel fetched.
NATHAN: Has whom?
Our Rachel fetched?—And Sittah has her fetched?—
Well; if it's Sittah has her fetched, and not
The Patriarch . . .
DAYA: Why should you think of him?
NATHAN: You've not heard anything from him of late?
In truth? Nor whispered aught to him?
DAYA: I, him?
NATHAN: Where are the messengers?
DAYA: Outside.
NATHAN: I will
In caution's name accost them. Come!—If but
There's nothing of the Patriarch in this. *(Exit.)*
DAYA: And I have quite a different fear. Let's see!
The sole reputed daughter of a Jew
So rich were for a Mussulman not quite
Unmeet?—Then, flash! the Templar's out of luck.
He is: unless I risk the second step;
And to herself reveal just who she is!—
Take heart! Let me employ the earliest moment,
When I'm with her alone, for that.—Perhaps
I'll use the very one when I escort her.
A prior hint, while we are on our way,
Can do no harm, at least. Yes, yes! That's it!
It's now or never! On, and ever on! *(Follows Nathan.)*

Act V

Saladin's financial problems are over since Egypt has sent its seven-year tribute, and Saladin dispatches a trusted lieutenant to transport the greater part of the gold to his father in the mountains of Lebanon, where the treasures will be safe. [Scene 1–2]

Scene 3

The palms before Nathan's house; the Templar walking up and down.

TEMPLAR: And once for all, his house I will not enter.—
   He surely will appear again!—How soon,
   How gladly they were wont to notice me!—
   I should not wonder if he'd yet forbid
   My frequent strolling here before his house.—
   H'm!—I must say I'm very vexed.—And what
   Embittered me so much against him?—For
   He said, as yet he would refuse me nothing.
   And Saladin has taken on the task
   To win him over.—What? can it be true
   The Christian in me sends down deeper roots
   Than does the Jew in him?—Who knows himself?—
   Why else should I begrudge the little prey
   He took such pains to capture for himself
   Within the Christians' game preserve?—Of course:
   No paltry spoils, a creature such as that!
   A creature? Whose?—No creature of the slave
   Who floated to the desert shore of life
   The shapeless block, and disappeared. Much more
   The artist's, who in that abandoned block
   Thought out the form divine which he portrayed.—
   Ah! Rachel's sire in truth remains—despite
   The Christian who begot her—now and ever
   The Jew.—If I envision her as but
   A Christian girl, bereft of all the traits
   That only such a Jew could give to her:—
   Speak, heart—what would she have to win your praise?
   Naught! little! Even her smiling, were it nothing
   But gentle, lovely twitching of her muscles;
   Were that which makes her smile not worthy of
   The charm in which it's clothed upon her lips:—
   No, no; not even her smile! Far fairer smiles
   I've seen misspent on folly, frippery,
   On scoffing, flatterers, and paramours.—
   Did they enchant me then? Did they bring out
   In me the wish to flutter out my life
   Beneath their sunshine?—Not that I recall.
   And yet I'm out of sorts with him who gave,

And him alone, the higher worth she has?
How so? and why?—Do I deserve the gibe
With which the Sultan bade me go?—It's bad
Enough that Saladin could think it true!
How small he must have thought me then! and how
Contemptible!—And all that for a girl?—
Curt, Curt! this will not do. Change course! Suppose,
To cap all, Daya had but prattled something
Which could not well be proven.—See, at last
He comes, engrossed in conversation, from
His house!—Ah ha! with whom?—With him? My friar?—
Well! then he surely knows the whole! no doubt
Has been discovered to the Patriarch!—
What mischief have I in my folly done!—
See how one spark of passion can consume
So much intelligence!—Resolve at once
What now is to be done! I'll step aside
And wait; perhaps the Friar will depart.

Scene 4

NATHAN *(as they approach)*: Again, good brother, many thanks!
FRIAR:⠀⠀⠀⠀⠀⠀⠀And you
⠀As many!
NATHAN:⠀⠀I? from you? For what? For my
⠀Insistence in compelling you to take
⠀What you don't need?—If your insistence had
⠀Succumbed to mine; if you were not resolved
⠀To be more rich than I.
FRIAR:⠀⠀⠀⠀⠀⠀⠀⠀⠀The book does not
⠀Belong to me in any case; belongs
⠀Much rather to your daughter; so to speak,
⠀It is her sole paternal heritage.—
⠀Oh well, she now has you.—May God but grant
⠀That you may never need repent that you
⠀Have done so much for her!
NATHAN:⠀⠀⠀⠀⠀⠀⠀⠀Can I repent?
⠀I never can. No fear of that!
FRIAR:⠀⠀⠀⠀⠀⠀⠀⠀⠀Well, well!
⠀These Patriarchs and Templars . . .
NATHAN:⠀⠀⠀⠀⠀⠀⠀⠀Have no power

To do me so much harm that anything
Could cause me to regret: that least of all!—
And are you then so very certain that
A Templar's egging on your Patriarch?
FRIAR: It scarce can be another. Such a knight
Had just had talk with him; and what I heard
Resembled this.
NATHAN: And yet there is but one
Here in Jerusalem. And I know him;
He is my friend; a noble, frank young man!
FRIAR: Quite right; that's he!—But what one is, and what
One must be in this world, that is not always
The same.
NATHAN: Too true.—Let anyone who will,
Proceed to do his best or worst! For with
Your book, good brother, I'll defy them all;
And with it I'll go straight to Saladin.
FRIAR: Good luck! So then for now I'll leave you here.
NATHAN: And haven't even seen her?—Come again,
Come soon, and often.—On this day, I hope,
The Patriarch learns nothing yet!—But stay!
Tell him the truth if you desire.
FRIAR: Not I.
    Farewell! *(Exit.)*
NATHAN: And don't forget us, Brother!—God!
O that right here beneath the open sky
I could fall on my knees! See how the knot
Which often caused me fear unties itself!—
O God! how light I feel, that now no more
There's anything to hide in all the world!
That I can walk so freely before men,
As in Thy sight, O Thou who needest not
To judge a man according to his deeds,
The which indeed so seldom are his deeds!

Scene 5

Templar approaches Nathan from the side.

TEMPLAR: Ho, Nathan, wait; take me along!
NATHAN: Who calls?—
It's you, sir Knight? Where were you, when I thought

To meet you at the Sultan's?

TEMPLAR: We but missed
Each other. Do not take offense!

NATHAN: Not I;
But Saladin . . .

TEMPLAR: You had just gone . . .

NATHAN: And so
You saw him after all? Then all is well.

TEMPLAR: But he would have us come to him together.

NATHAN: So much the better. Come along. My course
Was to him anyway.—

TEMPLAR: May I inquire
Who left you there just now?

NATHAN: Why, don't you know him?

TEMPLAR: Was it that good old soul, the Friar, whom
The Patriarch sends out to be a ferret?

NATHAN: May be! It's true he's with the Patriarch.

TEMPLAR: Not bad, that trick: to send the simple out
Before rascality.

NATHAN: If stupid, yes;—
But not if pious.

TEMPLAR: Which no Patriarch
Believes in.

NATHAN: This is one I'll vouch for. He
Will never help his Patriarch in what
Is wicked.

TEMPLAR: Such at least is his pretense.—
But has he said nothing to you of me?

NATHAN: Of you? No, not by name.—Indeed, he scarce
Can know your name.

TEMPLAR: That's true.

NATHAN: But of a Templar
He did say something . . .

TEMPLAR: What?

NATHAN: But you he could
Not possibly have meant!

TEMPLAR: Who knows? Let's hear it.

NATHAN: That to his Patriarch one had accused me . . .

TEMPLAR: Accused you?—That is, by his leave—a lie.—
O hear me, Nathan!—I am not a man
Who's able to deny the truth. And what

I did, I did! But neither am I one
Who'd make defense of everything he did
As if well done. Why should I be ashamed
Of error? Have I not the best resolve
To better it? And don't I know, perhaps,
How far a man can get with such resolve?—
O hear me, Nathan!—Yes, I am the Templar
The Friar had in mind, who's said to have
Accused you.—Oh, you know what made me vexed,
What caused my blood to boil in every vein!—
I, imbecile!—I came, in soul and body
Prepared to throw myself into your arms.
How you received me—cold—lukewarm—the which
Is even worse than cold; how formally
You were at pains to seek evasions; how
With questions quite irrelevant you seemed
To which to give me answer: even now
I scarce may think of this, if I would keep
Composure.—Hear me, Nathan!—Being in
This fermentation, Daya stole to me
And flung her secret in my face, which seemed
To me to hold the explanation of
Your dubious behavior.

NATHAN: How?

TEMPLAR: O let
Me finish!—I imagined that this child
Which you had shrewdly wrested from the Christians
You would be loath to yield to them again.
To make it short, I thought it would be good
To put the dagger at your throat.

NATHAN: Hm, good?
Where is the good in that?

TEMPLAR: O hear me, Nathan!—
It's true; I did a wrong!—And I presume
You are not guilty.—And that silly Daya
Knew not what she was saying—hates you, too—
And only wants to get you into trouble.—
May be, may be!—I'm just a stupid puppy,
Who tries to play both ends against the middle;
Does now too much, and now by far too little.—
That too may be. Forgive me, Nathan.

NATHAN: If
  You come at me like that—
TEMPLAR: In short, I sought
  The Patriarch!—but mentioned not your name.
  That's falsehood, I repeat! I merely placed
  The case before him in a general way,
  Asked his opinion.—Well, that too might well
  Have stayed undone: of course!—Did I not know
  The Patriarch as scoundrel? Could I not
  Have questioned you at once?—Was I obliged
  Thus to subject your daughter to the risk
  Of losing such a father?—Well, what odds?
  The prelate's villainy, which always stays
  Consistent, brought me by the straightest path
  Back to myself again.—For hear me, Nathan;
  Just hear me out!—Suppose he knew your name:
  What then, what then?—He cannot take the girl
  From you unless she's no one's but your own.
  And from *your* house he could but drag her to
  The convent.—So—give her to me! Just give
  The girl to me; and let him come. I think
  He'll hardly dare to take my wife from me.—
  Give her to me; and quickly!—Say she be
  Your child, or not; be Christian, Jewess, neither!
  All one, all one! I will not question you
  About it, never, not in all my life.
  No, be that as it may!
NATHAN: You think I find
  It very needful to conceal the truth?
TEMPLAR: Well, be that as it may!
NATHAN: I've not denied
  To you or those who'd have a right to know—
  That she's a Christian, only foster daughter
  To me.—But why I've not to her revealed it?—
  I think that only calls for *her* forgiveness.
TEMPLAR: Which you'll not need of her.—Do her the favor
  That she may always see you as your child!
  And spare her this disclosure! —For as yet
  You only have control of her. But give
  Her life to me! I beg you, Nathan: do!
  It's I alone who for a second time
  Can rescue her—and will.

NATHAN: Yes—could have, could have!
  No longer now. It is too late for that.
TEMPLAR: How so? too late!
NATHAN: Thanks to the Patriarch . . .
TEMPLAR: The Patriarch? And thanks to him? What for?
  You mean *he* should have merited our thanks?
  For what, for what?
NATHAN: That now we know to whom
  She is related; know into whose hands
  She can be safely laid.
TEMPLAR: Let him give thanks
  For that who will have greater cause!
NATHAN: From them
  You too must now receive her; not from mine.
TEMPLAR: Poor Rachel! Think of all you must endure,
  Poor Rachel! What for other orphans were
  A blessing turns to your misfortune.—Nathan!—
  Where are they now, these kinsfolk?
NATHAN: Where they are?
TEMPLAR: And *who* are they?
NATHAN: A brother specially
  Has come to light, to whom you'll have to sue
  For her.
TEMPLAR: A brother? What is he, this brother?
  A soldier? Or a churchman?—Let us hear
  What I may look for.
NATHAN: Neither one, I think,—
  Or both at once. I know him not so well.
TEMPLAR: What else?
NATHAN: A goodly man! In whom, I hope,
  Our Rachel will not be so badly off.
TEMPLAR: A Christian, though!—At times I cannot tell
  What I should think of you:—take no offense,
  Good Nathan!—Must she not the Christian play,
  Midst Christians? Not at last become what she
  Has now played long enough! Will not the weeds
  At last choke down the wheat you finely sowed?
  And that leaves you so calm? In spite of that,
  I hear you say yourself that with her brother
  She won't be badly off?

NATHAN: I think and hope it!—
And if with him there should be something lacking,
Has she not you and me beside her?
TEMPLAR: O!
With him what should be lacking? Will he not
Provide his sister well with food and clothing,
With finery and sweetmeats plentiful?
What needs a sister more?—Oh yes, a man
Besides!—Oh well, him too in course of time
Will brother soon provide; he's easily found!
The Christianer the better!—Nathan, Nathan!
Think of the angel you had formed, whom now
Others will ruin!
NATHAN: Have no fear! She will
Continue to prove worthy of our love.
TEMPLAR: Don't say that! Do not say it of *my* love!
For that will not be cheated, not of jot
Or tittle! nor of any name!—But stop!—
Does she suspect already what awaits her?
NATHAN: Perhaps; although I wouldn't know from whom.
TEMPLAR: That too's all one; she shall in either case—
She must find out what fate has now in store
At first from me. My notion, not to see
Or speak to her again, till I should have
The right to call her mine, is void. I haste . . .
NATHAN: Where to?
TEMPLAR: To her! To find out if her soul,
Though maidenly, has manhood in its veins
Enough to make the sole resolve which would
Be worthy her!
NATHAN: Which one?
TEMPLAR: This: not to pay
Much heed henceforth to you and to her brother—
NATHAN: And?
TEMPLAR: Follow me, regardless; even though
At last she should be married to a Moslem.
NATHAN: Remain! You will not find her. She's with Sittah,
The Sultan's sister.
TEMPLAR: What? Since when? and why?
NATHAN: And if you'd like to find the brother too
There with them: come along.

TEMPLAR: The brother? which?
   Sittah's or Rachel's?
NATHAN: Both, perhaps. Come, come!
   (Nathan leads him off.)

Sittah welcomes Rachel, and the young woman tells her about Daya's assertion that she is not Nathan's natural daughter. Rachel, confused, cannot believe that she originally comes from a Christian family. [Scene 6]

Scene 7

SALADIN *(entering):* What's all this? Sittah?
SITTAH: She's beside herself!
SALADIN: Who is it?
SITTAH: Why, you know . . .
SALADIN: Our Nathan's daughter?
   What ails her?
SITTAH: To your senses, child!—The Sultan . . .
RACHEL *(dragging herself on her knees to Saladin's feet, her head
   lowered to the floor):* I'll not get up! not sooner!—do not care
   Sooner to see the Sultan's face!—admire
   The glory of eternal justice shining
   With goodness in his eyes, upon his brow . . . .
SALADIN: Get up . . . get up!
RACHEL: Until he promise me . . .
SALADIN: Come! I will promise . . . Be it what it will!
RACHEL: Not more nor less than leave to me my father;
   And me to him!—I still don't know who else
   Desires to be my father; or who can.
   Nor would I know. Is blood then all that makes
   The father? blood alone?
SALADIN *(lifting her up):* I see, I see!—
   Who was so cruel as to put such thoughts
   Into your head? For is the fact established?
   And proven?
RACHEL: Must be! For my Daya claims
   To have it from my wet-nurse.
SALADIN: From your wet nurse!
RACHEL: In dying she had felt herself obliged
   To tell it her.

SALADIN: Just dying?—And not driveling
  Already?—What if true!—Yes, blood alone
  Is far from all that makes a father! scarce
  Can make the father of a beast! at most
  Confers the first right to acquire that name!—
  Don't let yourself be frightened!—And you know
  What I suggest? So soon as fathers twain
  Are fighting for you:—quit them both: and take
  A third one!—Take me then to be your father!
SITTAH: Do that, do that!
SALADIN: I'll be to you a good,
  A right good father!—Stop! I have a thought
  Much better yet.—What need have you of fathers,
  I'd like to know? Suppose they die? Let's look
  Betimes for someone who would like to live
  While keeping step with us! Know you of none? . . .
SITTAH: Don't make her blush!
SALADIN: That's just what I had planned.
  For blushing beautifies the ugly ones:
  And should it not make lovely ones more lovely?—
  I've bade your father, Nathan, and another—
  One other hither. Can you guess him?—Hither!
  You'll grant me your permission, Sittah?
SITTAH: Brother!
SALADIN: At sight of him you must blush very much,
  Dear girl!
RACHEL: At sight of whom? I, blush?
SALADIN: Dissembler!
  Then blanch instead!—Do what you will and can!—
  (A slave-girl enters and approaches Sittah.)
  Could they be here already?
SITTAH *(to the slave):*   Show them in.—
  It's they, my brother! *(Enter Nathan and Templar.)*

Scene 8

SALADIN: Ah, my good, dear friends!—
  First I must tell you, Nathan, that your gold
  You can have fetched again, so soon as you
  Desire it!
NATHAN: Sultan! . . .

SALADIN: Now I'm at your service
  In turn . . .
NATHAN: Ah, Sultan!
SALADIN: Now the caravan
  Is here. And once again I'm richer than
  I've been this long time.—Tell me what you need
  To undertake some major project! For
  You too, you too, you men of business, can
  Not have too much of cash!
NATHAN: And why speak first
  Of such a trifle?—There I see an eye
  In tears, which I am far more willed to dry. *(Goes to Rachel.)*
  You've wept? What ails you?—aren't you still my daughter?
RACHEL: My father! . . .
NATHAN: Yes, we understand each other.
  Enough!—Be cheerful! Be composed! If but
  Your heart is still your own! If but no loss
  Can menace still your heart!—Your father is
  Not lost to you!
RACHEL: No other, no!
TEMPLAR: No other?—
  Then I've deceived myself. What one fears not
  To lose, one has not thought to own, and never
  Desired.—All's well, all's well!—That alters, Nathan,
  That alters all!—We came, O Saladin,
  At your command. But now it seems I had
  Misled you: so concern yourself no more.
SALADIN: Again so rash, young man!—Shall everything
  Conform to you? and all men guess your thoughts?
TEMPLAR: Well, don't you hear, and see it, Sultan?
SALADIN: Truly,
  It's bad enough that you were not more sure
  Of your own case.
TEMPLAR: I am so now.
SALADIN: Whoever
  Presumes like that on any benefaction
  Would take it back. What you have rescued, is
  Not yours to own. Else were the robber, whom
  His greed lures into flames, a hero quite
  As good as you! *(going to Rachel, to lead her to the Templar)*
    Come, darling maiden, come!

Don't judge him too severely. For if he
Were otherwise; were not so warm and proud;
He never would have made attempt to save you.
Weigh one against the other.—Come! And shame him!
Do what he ought to do! Confess to him
Your love! Make offer of yourself to him!
And if he scorns you; if he should forget,
How in this act you do far more for him
Than he for you . . . What did he do for you?
Just smoked himself a bit!—is that so much?—
Then he has nothing of my brother Assad!
He only wears his mask, bears not his heart.
Come, dear . . .

SITTAH: Now go, dear, go! It's still not much
For all your gratitude; it's nothing yet.

NATHAN: Halt, Saladin! Halt, Sittah!

SALADIN: What, you too?

NATHAN: One other has a voice here . . .

SALADIN: Who denies it?—
Indubitably, Nathan, there's a vote
That's due a foster father such as you!
The first one, if you will.—You see I know
All sides of the affair.

NATHAN: No, no, not all!—
I speak not of myself. There is another;
A very different one, whom, Saladin,
I beg you first to hear.

SALADIN: Who?

NATHAN: It's her brother!

SALADIN: What, Rachel's brother?

NATHAN: Yes!

RACHEL: My brother? Then
I have a brother?

TEMPLAR (*starting up from his sullen, silent inattention*):
          Where? where is this brother?
Not yet at hand? I was to meet him here.

NATHAN: Be patient!

TEMPLAR (*in utmost bitterness*): He's palmed off a father on her:
How should he fail to find a brother too?

NATHAN: Forgive him, do!—
I do so gladly.—Who can say what we

In his position, at his age, would think!
(going to him in a friendly manner)
Of course, sir Knight!—Distrust leads to suspicion!—
If only you your *true* name had revealed
To me at once . . .

TEMPLAR: What?

NATHAN: You are not a Stauffen!

TEMPLAR: Who am I then?

NATHAN: Your name's not Curt von Stauffen!

TEMPLAR: Then what's my name?

NATHAN: It's Leu von Filnek.

TEMPLAR: What?

NATHAN: You start?

TEMPLAR: I should! Who says so?

NATHAN: I; who can
Tell you much more. Yet charge you with no lie.

TEMPLAR: You don't?

NATHAN: For it may be, that other name
Is yours by right as well.

TEMPLAR: It is indeed!
(aside) God put that on his tongue!

NATHAN: Yes, for your mother—
She was a Stauffen. And her brother, whom
Your parents asked in Germany to rear
Their child, when they, to flee that rugged climate,
Returned here to this land:—his name was Curt
Von Stauffen; possibly as his own child
Adopted you!—How long is it since you
Came hither with him? Is he still alive?

TEMPLAR: What shall I answer?—Nathan! To be sure!
You're right. But he is dead. I only came
With final reinforcements of our Order.—
But tell me—what has all this tale to do
With Rachel's brother?

NATHAN: Now, your father . . .

TEMPLAR: What
You knew him too? Him too?

NATHAN: He was my friend.

TEMPLAR: He was your friend? How wonderful! . . .

NATHAN: He called
Him Wolf von Filnek; but he was no German . . .

TEMPLAR: You know that too?

NATHAN: Was only married to
   A German; only briefly went with her
   To Germany . . .

TEMPLAR: Enough! I beg you, stop!—
   But Rachel's brother? Rachel's brother . . .

NATHAN: That
   Is you!

TEMPLAR: I? I her brother?

RACHEL: He my brother?

SITTAH: Brother and sister!

SALADIN: Really! Is it true?

RACHEL *(going toward him):*   Ah! my brother!

TEMPLAR *(stepping backward):* Her brother!

RACHEL *(stops and turns to Nathan):*   It cannot be! His heart
   Knows nothing of it!—We're impostors! God!

SALADIN *(to the Templar):* Impostors?—what? You think that? You
   can think it?
   Impostor, you! For everything's a lie
   In you: your face and voice and walk! You're nothing!
   What, not acknowledge such a sister? Go!

TEMPLAR *(approaching him humbly):* Do not you too misread my
   wonderment!
   Misjudge not in a moment, in the like
   Of which I think you never saw your Assad,
   Both him and me! *(swiftly to Nathan)*
                    You take and give me, Nathan!
   And both in full!—But no, you give me more
   Than you are taking! Infinitely more!
   (throwing his arms about Rachel)
   Oh, you my sister, darling sister!

NATHAN: Blanda
   Von Filnek!

TEMPLAR: Blanda, Blanda!—And not Rachel?
   No more your Rachel!—Heavens! You disown
   Your daughter, give her back her Christian name?
   Disown her for my sake!—O Nathan, Nathan!
   Why should she suffer? she!

NATHAN: No thought of that!—
   O children mine, dear children!—For should not
   My daughter's brother be my child as well—

Soon as he will? *(As he surrenders to their embraces, Saladin joins his sister in uneasy astonishment.)*

SALADIN: What say you to this, Sister?

SITTAH: I'm greatly moved . . .

SALADIN: And I—I'm shivering,
  Almost afraid of yet a greater shock!
  Prepare yourself for that as best you can.

SITTAH: What?

SALADIN: Nathan, just a word with you! one word!—
  *(As Nathan goes to him, Sittah joins the others to express her
    sympathy; Nathan and Saladin speak more softly.)*
  Hark to me, Nathan! Said you not just now
  That—

NATHAN: What?

SALADIN: Her father had from Germany
  Not come; was not a German born?
  What was he, then? Whence else could he have come?

NATHAN: That's something he would not reveal to me.
  And from his lips I know no word of it.

SALADIN: But he was not a Frank? no Westerner?

NATHAN: O, that he made no effort to conceal.—
  He spoke by preference Persian . . .

SALADIN: Persian? Persian?
  What need I more?—It's he! Was he!

NATHAN: What, who?

SALADIN: My brother! not a doubt! My Assad! not
  A doubt!

NATHAN: Well, if you hit on that yourself:—
  Take the assurance in this volume here.
                        (Hands him the breviary.)

SALADIN *(opening it eagerly)*: His writing! Ah! That too I'd know
    again!

NATHAN: As yet they do not know. It lies with you
  Alone, how much of it they shall be told!

SALADIN *(paging in the book)*: I not to recognize my brother's
    children?
  My niece and nephew—as I would my own?
  Not recognize them? I? And let you have them? *(aloud)*
  It's they. It's they, my Sittah! See, it's they!
  And both are my . . . that is, your brother's children!
                        (He rushes to embrace them.)

SITTAH *(following him):* What do I hear?—Could not be otherwise!
SALADIN *(to the Templar):* And now, you spitfire, now you'll have to
    love me!
  (to Rachel) And now I am what I proposed to be!
  Whether you will or no!
SITTAH: I too, I too!
SALADIN *(back to the Templar):* My son; my Assad!
  Yes, my Assad's son!
TEMPLAR: I of your blood!—So then those dreams of mine,
  With which they rocked me in my childhood, were—
  More than just dreams! *(falling at his feet)*
SALADIN *(raising him):* Just see that scoundrel here!
  He knew some of the truth, and yet he could
  Consent to make me murder him! You wait!
      (Amid silent embraces on all sides the curtain falls.)

Translated by Bayard Quincy Morgan

ERNST AND FALK CONVERSATIONS FOR THE FREEMASONS

Written in 1778/80

First Conversation

ERNST: Of what are you thinking, friend?

FALK: Of nothing.

ERNST: But you're so silent.

FALK: That's exactly the reason. Who thinks when he is enjoying something? And I am enjoying this refreshing morning.

ERNST: You're right. And you would have only needed to turn my question back upon me.

FALK: If something were to enter my mind, I would speak about it. There's nothing better than thinking aloud with a friend.

ERNST: Indeed.

FALK: If you have enjoyed this fine morning enough, or if something has occurred to you, well then, go ahead and say something. I can't think of anything.

ERNST: Very well! I do recollect that I have been wanting to ask you about something for some time.

FALK: Well then, ask away.

ERNST: Is it true, friend, that you are a Freemason?

FALK: That's the question of someone who is not one.

ERNST: Of course! But answer me more straightforwardly. Are you a Freemason?

FALK: I believe myself to be one.

ERNST: That's the answer of someone not quite sure of his position.

FALK: Far from it! I'm rather quite sure of my position.

ERNST: Then of course you certainly well know, if and when, where, and by whom you were admitted.

FALK: Indeed I do. But that wouldn't reveal very much.

ERNST: No?

FALK: Who is it that doesn't admit, and who doesn't get admitted?

ERNST: Explain yourself.

FALK: I believe myself to be a Freemason; not so much because I was admitted by older Masons into a legally constituted lodge, but rather because I realize and see what Freemasonry is, and why, when, and where it existed and why and by what means it is fostered or hindered.

ERNST: And you nevertheless express yourself so irresolutely? "I believe myself to be one"!

FALK: An expression to which I have simply grown accustomed. Not, of course, as if I lacked conviction, but rather because I don't care to put myself directly in anybody's way.

ERNST: You're answering me as if I were a stranger.

FALK: Stranger or friend!

ERNST: You've been admitted, you know everything . . .

FALK: Lots of others have also been admitted and think they know everything.

ERNST: Could you have been admitted without knowing what you know?

FALK: Unfortunately.

ERNST: How so?

FALK: Because many of those who do the admitting don't even know it themselves, while the few who know, are not allowed to express it.

ERNST: So then could you know, what you know, without being admitted?

FALK: Why not? Freemasonry is not some arbitrary thing, not something superfluous, but rather it's a necessity, founded in the essence of man and civil society. As a result a person ought to be just as able to arrive at it through his own reflection as be led to it through instruction.

ERNST: Freemasonry is not arbitrary, you say? Doesn't it have words, signs, and customs, every one of which could be different and therefore arbitrary?

FALK: It does. But these words, signs, and customs, none of these is Freemasonry.

ERNST: Freemasonry is not something superfluous? Well then, what did people do when Freemasonry did not yet exist?

FALK: Freemasonry has always existed.

ERNST: All right, what is it then, this necessary, indispensable Freemasonry?

FALK: As I just gave you to understand, something that even those who know are not able to say.

ERNST: An absurdity then.

FALK: Don't be too hasty.

ERNST: Anything I can conceive of, I can express in so many words.

FALK: Not always, and at least many times not always in such a way that others acquire from these words the exact same concept which I thereby possess.

ERNST: If not exactly the very same, at least an approximate one.

FALK: An approximate concept would be useless or even dangerous here. Useless if it contained not enough, and dangerous if it contained the slightest excess.

ERNST: That's strange! If even the Freemasons who know the secret of their order are not able to convey it in so many words, how do they spread their order nevertheless?

FALK: Through deeds. They let good men and youths, whom they consider worthy of close company, surmise, guess, or observe their deeds, insofar as they can be observed. The latter find them to their taste and perform similar deeds.

ERNST: Deeds? Deeds of Freemasons? I know of none except for their speeches and songs, which for the most part are more attractively printed than thought out and expressed.

FALK: That's something they have in common with quite a few speeches and songs.

ERNST: Or am I to take for their deeds, the things they praise themselves for in these speeches and songs?

FALK: As long as they don't merely praise themselves for them.

ERNST: Besides, what is it that they praise themselves for? Nothing but things that we expect from every good individual or upright citizen. They are so full of friendship, so altruistic, so obedient, so patriotic.

FALK: Well? Is that nothing?

ERNST: Nothing!—to single one's self out from other people. Who should not be that way?

FALK: Should!

ERNST: Who doesn't have motive and opportunity enough even outside of Freemasonry to be like that?

FALK: But within it and through it, one motive more.

ERNST: Don't give me anything about accumulated motives. It's much better to impart all possible intentional powers to one single motivating desire. The number of such motivational forces is like the number of gears in a machine. The greater the number of gears, the more changeable.

FALK: I can't contradict you there.

ERNST: And what sort of one motive more? One that minimizes or renders all others suspect! And purports to be the strongest and the best!

FALK: My friend, be reasonable. Hyperbole. Confusion born of all those shallow songs and speechifying. Experimentation. The work of zealot disciples.

ERNST: Which is to say, Brother Speaker is a windbag.

FALK: Which is only to say, what Brother Speaker praises about the Freemasons, is precisely not their deeds. For at the very least Brother Speaker is not just an empty windbag, and deeds do speak for themselves.

ERNST: Ah, now I see what you're aiming at. How could these deeds not be obvious to me from the outset, these deeds which speak for themselves. I'd almost like to say cry out for themselves. It's not enough that the Freemasons support one another, support one another in the most energetic way; after all, that would only be a quality necessary in any sort of group. What is it they don't do for the entire population of every state whose citizens they are?

FALK: For example? Just so that I can see whether or not you are on the right track.

ERNST: For example the Freemasons in Stockholm! Didn't they just erect a large orphanage?

FALK: Let's hope the Freemasons in Stockholm have shown themselves active on other occasions as well.

ERNST: What other occasions?

FALK: Any other ones, I mean.

ERNST: And the Freemasons in Dresden! The ones who are keeping poor young girls busy working. Having them make lace or do knitting—just so the orphanage might not get too large.

FALK: Ernst! You know quite well what I mean, when I remind you of your name.

ERNST: All right then, no more sarcastic remarks! How about the Freemasons in Braunschweig? The ones who have poor talented boys instructed in drawing.

FALK: Why not?

ERNST: And the Freemasons in Berlin! Supporting Basedow's Philanthropic Educational Institute.*

FALK: What's that, you say? The Freemasons? Supporting the educational institute? Whoever told something like that?

ERNST: It was all over the newspaper.

FALK: The newspaper! I'd have to see the receipt written in Basedow's very own hand. And I'd have to be sure that the receipt was not to Freemasons in Berlin but to *those* Freemasons.

ERNST: What's that? Then you don't approve of Basedow's institute?

FALK: Not approve? Who can approve of it more?

ERNST: Well then, surely you don't begrudge him such support?

---

*An institute for the education of the young opened in Dessau in 1774 by Johann Bernhard Basedow.

FALK: Begrudge him? Who doesn't wish him well more than I?

ERNST: Now wait a minute! You're confusing me completely.

FALK: I do believe I am. And I'm wrong to do so. After all, *those* Freemasons can do a thing which they don't do *as* Masons.

ERNST: And is that supposed to hold for all their other good deeds as well?

FALK: That might be. It might be that all the good deeds you have just mentioned to me, to use a scholastic expression for the sake of brevity, are only their good deeds *ad extra*.

ERNST: What do you mean by that?

FALK: Only their deeds to catch the eye of the populace as a whole, those deeds that they perform merely because they are intended to catch the eye of the populace.

ERNST: To gain respect and toleration?

FALK: That could well be.

ERNST: But what about their real deeds? You've nothing to say?

FALK: Suppose I have already given you an answer? Their true deeds are their secret.

ERNST: Ho, ho! Therefore not explainable in words either?

FALK: Probably not. I can and will tell you only this much, the true deeds of the Freemasons are so great, so farseeing, that whole centuries may well pass before it will be possible to say, this is what they have done! Nevertheless, they have done all that is good that still exists in the world—note that: in the *world*. And they continue to contribute to all good that will still come to be in this world—note that: in this *world*.

ERNST: Oh go on! You're pulling my leg.

FALK: Really, I'm not. But look there! There goes a butterfly I've got to have. It's the one from the spurge caterpillar. In haste, I'll add only this: the true deeds of the Freemasons have as their goal, rendering what in general are customarily termed good deeds, superfluous.

ERNST: And yet they are nevertheless good deeds as well?

FALK: There can be none better. Just think about it for a minute. I'll be right back.

ERNST: Good deeds which have as their goal making good deeds superfluous? That's a riddle. And I'm not going to waste my time thinking about a riddle. I'd rather lie down here for a while under this tree and watch the ants.

Second Conversation

ERNST: Well? Where have you been? And no butterfly yet either?

FALK: It lured me on from bush to bush, as far as the brook. And then suddenly it was on the other side.

ERNST: Ah, yes indeed. There are those who lure you on like that.

FALK: Have you thought about it?

ERNST: About what? That riddle of yours? I won't catch that pretty butterfly either! That's also why it's not going to give me any more trouble. Talking about Freemasonry with you once is plenty. Never again. It's perfectly clear to me, you're just like all the rest of them.

FALK: Like all the rest of them? The rest of them don't say that sort of thing.

ERNST: They don't? Well then, it certainly looks as if there are heretics among the Freemasons. And as if you are one of them. But all heretics still always have something in common with true believers. And that's what I was talking about.

FALK: What was it you were talking about?

ERNST: True believers or heretical Freemasons—they all play with words and let themselves be asked questions and give answers without answering.

FALK: Do you think so? Well then, let's talk about something else. Because there was a time when you tore me out of a comfortable state of silent admiration.

ERNST: There's nothing easier than to put you back into that state. Just sit down right here next to me and take a look.

FALK: At what then?

ERNST: The goings-on in and around this anthill here. What activity, and yet what orderliness! Everyone is carrying or dragging or pushing something, and not a one gets in the other's way. Just look there. They're even helping one another.

FALK: Ants live in society like the bees.

ERNST: And yet in an even more amazing society than bees. Because they don't have anybody among them who keeps them together and governs them.

FALK: Order must therefore be capable of existing without government.

ERNST: If every individual knows how to govern himself, why not?

FALK: Do you think it will ever come to that among humankind?

ERNST: Hardly likely.

FALK: Too bad!

ERNST: I'll say!

FALK: Get up and let's be going. Otherwise they'll crawl all over you, those ants of yours, and I've just had something occur to me that I do have to ask you just now. I haven't got the faintest idea about your attitude toward it at all.

ERNST: About what?

FALK: About civil society among humankind in general. What do you think of it?

ERNST: It's a very good thing.

FALK: No doubt about it. But do you consider it an end or a means?

ERNST: I don't understand you.

FALK: Do you believe that men were created for the state? Or states for men?

ERNST: Some seem to maintain the former. The latter seems, however, to be more likely.

FALK: I think so too. States unite men so that through and in such a union every individual can all the more perfectly and more securely enjoy his measure of happiness. The sum of the individual happiness of all members is the happiness of the state. Beyond this, there is none whatsoever. Every other happiness of the state, by which however few individual members suffer or *are compelled* to suffer, is a cover-up for tyranny. Nothing else!

ERNST: I wouldn't care to say that so loudly.

FALK: Why not?

ERNST: A truth which everyone judges according to his own situation can easily be misused.

FALK: Do you know, friend, you are already halfway a Freemason?

ERNST: Me?

FALK: You. Because you already recognize truths which are better left unsaid.

ERNST: But which *could be* said.

FALK: The wise man *cannot* say, what is better left unsaid.

ERNST: All right then. Just as you will. But let's not start over about the Freemasons again. I certainly don't want to hear any more about them.

FALK: Pardon me! But at least you see my readiness to tell you more about them.

ERNST: You're joking. All right then! Man's life in civil society. The governmental forms of all states are nothing more than means for the achievement of human happiness. What comes next?

FALK: Nothing more than means. And means of man's invention. Although at the same time I also won't deny that nature so arranged things that mankind would soon have had to arrive at such an invention.

ERNST: This has probably led to some considering modern society to be the ultimate end of nature. Because everything, our passions as well as our needs, all have led to such an end. Consequentially, it must seem to be the ultimate goal towards which nature proceeds. That's what they concluded. As if nature had not also needed to produce the means in a purposeful way! As if nature had had as its end the happiness of some abstract idea—such as the state, the fatherland and so on—rather than the happiness of every really existing individual.

FALK: Very good! You're meeting me halfway on the right path. For now tell me this, if the governmental forms of states are a means— means of human invention—are they alone to be exempt from the destiny of human means?

ERNST: What do you call the destiny of human means?

FALK: That which is inevitably associated with human means, and which differentiates them from infallible divine means.

ERNST: What is that?

FALK: That they are not infallible. That they frequently not only fail to correspond to their intent, but that instead even bring about exactly the opposite.

ERNST: An example! If you can think of one.

FALK: Well, maritime commerce and ships are a means to reach distant lands, and they are also the reason why many persons never reach them.

ERNST: Particularly those who suffer shipwreck and drown. Now I think I comprehend what you're driving at. But certainly the reasons are clear why so many individual persons don't gain anything in the way of happiness through the forms of state government. There are all kinds of governments. State governments have many kinds of forms. Therefore one is better than the others. Many a one is quite lacking, obviously in conflict with its goals. And the best has per- haps yet to be created.

FALK: Let's not even take that into account! Imagine that the best form of government which could be conceived of has already been created. Imagine that all the people in the entire world have already accepted this best form of government. Don't you think that even then, pre- cisely as a result of this best form of government, that things will have to take place which are extremely injurious to human happiness, and of which man in his natural state would have simply had no idea whatsoever?

ERNST: I believe that if things of that sort were to come about as a result of the best form of government, then it wouldn't be the best form of government.

FALK: And that a better one would be possible? Well then, I'll accept this better one as the *best* and ask the very same thing.

ERNST: It looks to me as if from the start you are doing a bit of quibbling on the basis of our assumption that every means of human invention, which you declare one and all forms of state government to be, can't be anything except faulty.

FALK: Not just that.

ERNST: And it would be difficult for you to name one of those injurious things.

FALK: Which necessarily would have to proceed from the best form of government? Oh, I'll give you ten for one.

ERNST: Just one for a start.

FALK: Let's assume then, that the best form of government has been created. Let's assume that all persons in the world live under it. Would therefore all persons in the world constitute just one state?

ERNST: Not very likely. Such a gigantic state would not be capable of being governed. It would therefore have to subdivide into several small states which would all be governed by the same laws.

FALK: That is, the people would still then be Germans and Frenchmen, Dutchmen and Spaniards, Russians and Swedes, or whatever else they might be called.

ERNST: Absolutely!

FALK: Well then, we've got *one* there already. Because it's true, isn't it, that each of these smaller states would have its own interests? And every individual citizen of them would have the interests of his own state?

ERNST: How could it be otherwise?

FALK: These differing interests would frequently collide with one another, just as they do now, and two members of two different states would be just as unable to encounter one another in an impartial state of mind as right now a German encounters a Frenchman, or a Frenchman an Englishman.

ERNST: Very probably!

FALK: That is, whenever at the present a German encounters a Frenchman, or a Frenchman an Englishman or vice versa, it is no longer *just one person* encountering *just another person*, who on the basis of their similar natures are reciprocally drawn to one another, but rather *one sort of person* encounters *another sort of person*, both of whom are aware of their differing inclinations, which makes them cool, reserved, and distrustful toward one another, long before they have the slightest bit to do with each other as individuals.

ERNST: That is unfortunately true.

FALK: Well then, it is therefore also true that the means which unites men to assure them of their happiness precisely through this union, separates them at the very same time.

ERNST: If you understand it that way.

FALK: Go one step further. Many of the smaller states would have a completely different climate, consequently totally different needs and gratifications, as a consequence of that totally different customs and morals, as a consequence of that a totally different morality, consequently totally different religions. Don't you agree?

ERNST: That's quite a step!

FALK: Men would then still be Jews and Christians and Turks and the like.

ERNST: I don't bring myself to say no.

FALK: If they were to do that, they would also, whatever they might want to be called, behave towards one another in exactly the same way as our Christians and Jews and Turks have behaved all along. Not merely *just as persons* towards *just other persons*, but as *one sort of persons* towards *another sort of persons* who argue for a certain spiritual preference and establish rights on the basis thereof, which would never occur to man in his natural state.

ERNST: That's a very sad state of affairs, but unfortunately nevertheless also very probable.

FALK: Just probable?

ERNST: Because you see, under any circumstances, I would have thought, just as you've postulated, that if all states had the same form of government, that they all probably could have the same religion too. In fact, I really don't understand how having the same form of government without having the same religion could even be possible.

FALK: Neither do I. Actually, I just assumed that position in order to cut off your way out. The one is assuredly just as impossible as the other. One state—several states. Several states—several forms of state government. Several forms of state government—several religions.

ERNST: Yes indeed. So it would seem.

FALK: So it is. Now let me show you the second misfortune which—

totally contrary to its intention—civil society causes. It cannot unite men without dividing them; not divine them, without establishing rifts between them, without putting walls among them.

ERNST: And how terrible these rifts are! How impossible these walls so often are to cross!

FALK: Now let me still add the third. As if it were not enough that society divides and separates mankind in various peoples and religions, this division—if in a few large parts, of which each were of itself a whole—would still always be better than no whole at all. No indeed, civil society continues its division on into every one of these parts as well, so to speak right on into infinity.

ERNST: How so?

FALK: Or do you really think that a state could be conceived of without differences of class? Be it good or bad, closer or less close to perfection, it is impossible that all its members can have the same relationship to one another. Even though they all participate in the legislative process, yet they cannot have an equal share, at least not an equally direct share. As a result there will be more and less prominent members. And if at the beginning all possessions of the state are equally distributed among them, nevertheless this equality of distribution cannot go on even for two generations. Somebody will know how to use his property better than somebody else. In the same manner, somebody will have to distribute his less wisely employed property among several more descendants than the other. As a result, there will be richer and poorer members.

ERNST: That's obviously true.

FALK: Well then, just consider, how much evil there probably exists in the world which does not have its origin in this difference of classes.

ERNST: If only I could contradict you somehow! But what basis would I have to contradict you anyway? Well then, it's true, mankind can be united only by division, and only kept unified through unceasing division. It's simply the way things are. And it simply can't be any other way.

FALK: Just what I've been saying!

ERNST: Well then, what are you driving at with all of this? Trying to sour me on civil society? To make me wish the idea of uniting in states had never occurred to mankind?

FALK: Do you really misunderstand to such an extent? If civil society had only that one good thing about it, that within it alone human reason can be cultivated, I would bless it still, even if it had far greater failings.

ERNST: As the saying goes, whoever wants to enjoy the fire has to put up with the smoke.

FALK: Exactly! But just because smoke can't be avoided when there's fire, does that mean that the chimney ought not to have been invented? And the fellow who invented the chimney, did doing that make him an enemy of fire? Do you see, that's what I've been driving at.

ERNST: At what? I don't understand you.

FALK: The metaphor was actually quite fitting. If men cannot be united in states in any other way than through these divisions, does that therefore make them a good thing—these divisions, I mean?

ERNST: Probably not.

FALK: Do they therefore become sacred—these divisions?

ERNST: In what way sacred?

FALK: That it might be forbidden to lay hands on them?

ERNST: With the intent . . . ?

FALK: With the intent of preventing them from tearing apart more than necessity demands. With the intent of rendering their consequences as harmless as possible.

ERNST: How could that be forbidden?

FALK: But it can also not be bidden either, bidden by means of civil laws. Because civil laws never extend beyond the borders of their state. And this would in fact lie beyond the borders of each and every state. As a result it could only be an *Opus supererogatum** and one would only wish that the wisest and best persons of every individual state would voluntarily submit themselves to this *Opus supererogatum*.

ERNST: That could only be wished for, but wished for very much indeed.

FALK: I would think so! It's very much to be wished for that there might be in every state men who were above the prejudices of the populace and who would know exactly where patriotism ceases to be a virtue.

ERNST: Very much to be wished for.

FALK: Very much to be wished that there might be in every state men who would not succumb to the prejudices of the religions to which they had been born; who did not believe that everything they recognize as good and true must of necessity be good and true.

ERNST: Very much to be wished for.

FALK: Very much to be wished that in every state there might be men

---

**Opus supererogatum:* a concept of scholasticism—"good works" going beyond ordinary expectations.

not blinded by social eminence and not repelled by social insignificance, in whose company the individual of high estate is happy to reach out to those below, and a person of low estate is quickly raised up.

ERNST: Very much to be wished.

FALK: And if it were to be fulfilled, such a wish?

ERNST: Fulfilled? Well, I suppose of course there is such a man, here or there, at one time or another.

FALK: Not just here and there, not just at one time or another.

ERNST: At certain times, and in certain countries, even a few of them.

FALK: What if right now there were men of that sort everywhere? And that there will be their like at all times?

ERNST: Would to God!

FALK: And that these men don't live scattered about impotently. Not always in some invisible church.

ERNST: That's a beautiful dream!

FALK: To be brief about it—and what if these men were the Freemasons?

ERNST: What's that you say?

FALK: What if it were the Freemasons, who were to make it *just one* of their endeavors to draw those divisions, whereby men become so alien to one another, as close together as possible?

ERNST: The Freemasons?

FALK: I say, *just one* of their endeavors.

ERNST: The Freemasons?

FALK: Oh forgive me. I had forgotten again that you didn't wish to hear any more about the Freemasons. They're just waving to us to come to breakfast. Come along!

ERNST: Hold it! Wait a minute! The Freemasons, you say?

FALK: Our conversation led me to them again against my will. Do forgive me! Come on! Over there, in a larger group we'll soon find a more appropriate topic for discussion. Come along!

Third Conversation

ERNST: You've been avoiding me all day in the crowd of people here. But I'm following you right into your bedroom.

FALK: Do you have something so important to tell me? I'm tired of mere conversation for today.

ERNST: You're making fun of my curiosity.

FALK: Your curiosity?

ERNST: Which you were able to arouse so masterfully this morning.

FALK: What was it were we talking about this morning?

ERNST: About the Freemasons.

FALK: Well then? In the intoxication of that Pyrmont mineral water we were drinking, I didn't reveal the mystery to you, did I?

ERNST: Which, as you say, can't be revealed anyhow.

FALK: Ah, of course. That reassures me once more.

ERNST: But you did tell me something about the Freemasons I didn't expect, something that caught my attention, made me think.

FALK: And what might that have been?

ERNST: O don't torture me like this! You remember it for sure.

FALK: Ah yes. It's gradually coming back to me. And that was what so preoccupied you the whole day long among your gentleman and lady friends?

ERNST: That was it! And I won't be able to fall asleep if you don't at least answer one more question for me.

FALK: It all depends on the question.

ERNST: Well then, how can you prove to me, at least make it seem probable for me, that the Freemasons really have such great and worthy intentions?

FALK: Did I say anything to you about their intentions? I don't recollect doing so. Rather, since you were unable to get any sort of idea of the true deeds of the Freemasons, I merely sought to call your attention to a point, where a great deal can still take place of the sort of thing our cleverest political minds can't even dream of. Perhaps the Freemasons are working around that. Perhaps just around that! Merely to disabuse you of your prejudice that all those places still in need of repair have been found and occupied, or that all the undone tasks have already been distributed among the necessary hands.

ERNST: Twist about now however you want. It suffices that from your descriptions I now envision the Freemasons as people who have voluntarily taken it upon themselves to labor against the unavoidable evils of the state.

FALK: That idea can at least not cause any shame for the Freemasons. Stay with it! Just be sure you grasp it in the right way! Don't go mixing things into it which don't belong. The unavoidable evils of the state! Not of just any state. Not those unavoidable evils which, once it has been assumed, necessarily precede from an assumed form of civil government. The Freemasons never involve themselves in that sort of thing. At least not as Freemasons. The amelioration and cure of things like that they leave to the individual citizen, who may occupy himself with it according to his judgment, his courage, and at his own peril. It's evils of a totally different sort, a much higher sort, which are the object of their endeavors.

ERNST: I understood that quite well. It is not those evils which make for a dissatisfied citizen, but evils without which even the happiest citizen cannot be.

FALK: Right! Against those—how did you put it?—laboring against those?

ERNST: Exactly!

FALK: That phrase does overdo it a bit. Laboring against them! Abolishing them completely? That can't be. For the state itself would have to be destroyed along with them. They mustn't even be suddenly made apparent to those who as yet have no perception of their existence. At best, creating an awareness in the individual from afar, fostering the way it sprouts, transplanting the seedlings, cultivating and thinning it, that can be called laboring against them in a case like this. Do you now understand why I say, although the Freemasons have always been at work, nevertheless centuries can pass without it ever being possible to say, this is what they have done?

ERNST: And I comprehend the second part of the riddle too—good deeds which render good deeds unnecessary.

FALK: Exactly! Now go and study those evils and learn to identify every one of them and balance all of their effects against one another; and let me assure you that this study will reveal things to you which on gloomy days will seem like utterly depressing, incontrovertible objections to Providence and virtue. This insight, this illumination, will make you calm and happy—without *being called* a Freemason.

ERNST: You put so much emphasis on this *being called.*

FALK: Because one can be something without being called it.

ERNST: That's good! I understand. But to come back to my question, which I merely have to clothe a bit differently: since now I really do know them, these evils against which the Freemasons proceed . . .

FALK: You know them?

ERNST: Didn't you just name them for me?

FALK: I named a few of them for you as a sample. Merely a few of those which are obvious even to the most shortsighted eye, a few of the most indisputable, the widest-ranging ones. But how many more aren't there still, which although not so obvious, not so indisputable, not so wide-ranging, are yet any less certain, any less necessary!

ERNST: Well then let me limit my question merely to those examples which you yourself have named for me. How can you prove to me from these examples that the Freemasons are really concentrating their intentions upon them? You're silent? You're thinking about it?

FALK: In truth, not about what I could give as an answer to this question! But I don't know what might be its cause, why you even ask me that question?

ERNST: But you will answer my question if I explain its cause to you?

FALK: That I promise you.

ERNST: I know and fear the sharpness of your mind.

FALK: The sharpness of my mind?

ERNST: I fear you're passing off your speculations to me as fact.

FALK: Much obliged!

ERNST: Does that insult you?

FALK: On the contrary, I really must thank you for calling something sharpness of mind, which you could well have called something entirely different.

ERNST: Not at all. But I do know how easily someone who is sharp of mind deceives himself, how easily he applies or imputes plans or intentions to others, which never ever occurred to them.

FALK: But where do we get the conclusions we draw regarding people's plans and intentions? From their individual actions, wouldn't you say?

ERNST: Where else? And this brings me back to my question. From what individual and indisputable activities of the Freemasons, can we deduce that it is also merely *secondarily,* their intent, through and in themselves, to again unite those divisive forces named by you, which the state and states in general necessitate among individuals?

FALK: And, moreover, not to the disadvantage of the state or states in general.

ERNST: All the better. They perhaps need not be activities from which we can derive something like that. If they are just certain characteristics, particular details, which are directed toward it or emerge from it. Something of that sort must have served as the starting point of your speculations, assuming your system were only a hypothesis.

FALK: Your distrust keeps on showing itself. But I hope it will disappear when I make a basic principle of the Freemasons clear to you.

ERNST: And what might that be?

FALK: Something of which they have never made a mystery, and according to which they have always acted before the eyes of the entire world.

ERNST: Which is?

FALK: Which is: to accept into their order every worthy man of fitting disposition, regardless of fatherland, regardless of religion, regardless of social standing.

ERNST: Really!

FALK: Of course this basic principle seems rather to presume men of the sort who are already beyond these divisive factors, than having the intent of creating them. But of course the niter must already be in the air before it adheres to the walls as saltpeter.

ERNST: Oh yes indeed!

FALK: And why should the Freemasons not have been allowed to make use here of a commonplace ruse? Carrying out a part of one's secret intentions quite openly to mislead the suspicion which always presumes something entirely different than what it sees.

ERNST: Why not?

FALK: Why shouldn't the artist who can *make* silver deal in old silver fragments, so that people will all the less suspect that he can make it?

ERNST: Why not?

FALK: Ernst! Don't you hear me? You're answering as if in a dream, it seems.

ERNST: No, my friend. But I have enough. Enough for this night. Tomorrow, at first light, I am returning to the city.

FALK: Already? And why so soon?

ERNST: You know me so well and ask that? How much longer does your water cure last?

FALK: I just started it day before yesterday.

ERNST: Well then, I'll see you again before you have finished it. Farewell! Good night!

FALK: Good night! Farewell!

Postscript

The spark ignited the fire. Ernst departed and became a Freemason. What he found there at the outset is the material of a fourth and fifth conversation, with which—the path divides.

Fourth Conversation

FALK: Ernst! Welcome! Back again at last! I'm long since finished with my water cure.

ERNST: And feel the better for it? Glad to hear it.

FALK: What's that? Never has a "glad to hear it" been expressed with more irritation.

ERNST: And I am irritated too, and it wouldn't take much for me to be angry at you as well.

FALK: At me?

ERNST: You've lured me into taking a foolish step. Look here. Give me your hand. What do you say now?* Shrugging your shoulders? That's all I need.

FALK: Lured you?

ERNST: It can well be, without intending to do so.

FALK: Yet nevertheless I am to blame.

ERNST: The man of God speaks to the people of a land where milk and honey flow and the people are not to yearn for it? And not to grumble about the man of God when, instead of leading them to the promised land, he leads them into a barren desert?

FALK: Now, now! The damage can't be as great as all that! Furthermore, I see that you have already been at work *at the graves of our forefathers.*

ERNST: But they were not surrounded with *flames,* but rather with smoke.†

FALK: Well then, wait until the smoke passes and the flame will light and warm you.

ERNST: The smoke will suffocate me before the flame casts any light for me, and I can clearly see that others who can better endure the smoke will be the ones warmed by it.

FALK: I do hope you're not speaking of people who gladly put up with acrid smoke, as long as it's the smoke from someone else's fine and juicy kitchen?

ERNST: I see you do know that sort.

FALK: I've heard of them.

ERNST: All the more then, whatever could induce you to lead me out onto this ice? And then to dazzle me with things whose groundlessness you knew only too well?

FALK: Your irritation is making you far too unjust. Am I supposed to have talked with you about the Freemasons, without having made it clear in more than just one way how useless it is for every honorable man to become a Freemason? How useless? Why, as a matter of fact, how harmful.

ERNST: That may well be.

---

*Ernst has offered his friend the secret handshake of Freemasonry.
†"Graves of our forefathers," "flames": accessories of Masonic rituals, usually accorded only to "Masters."

FALK: I suppose I didn't tell you that one could fulfill the highest obligations of Masonry without being called a Freemason?

ERNST: On the contrary, I recall that very point. But you know quite well, when that imagination of mine spreads out its wings, and begins to beat them—can I hold it down? I reproach you with nothing except that you offered it such a lure.

FALK: Which you have also very quickly become weary of reaching. And why did you not tell me a word about your intention?

ERNST: Would you have advised me against it?

FALK: Certainly! Who would want to convince an impetuous child to take up the walker again, just because he still falls now and then? I am not making you any compliment there; you were already too far along to start all over again from that point. At the same time there was no making an exception of you. Everyone must tread that path.

ERNST: I would not regret having trodden it if I could but promise myself more from the path still ahead. But one empty promise after another, and not a thing but empty promises!

FALK: If it really is empty promises you've been getting! What sort of things are they promising you?

ERNST: You know perfectly well, all about the Scottish Rite, the Scottish knights.*

FALK: Ah yes, quite right. But what is the Scottish knight supposed to be a promise of?

ERNST: Who knows that!

FALK: And your fellows, the other novices of the order, don't they know anything either?

ERNST: Oh them! They know so much! They expect so much! One of them wants to make gold, another is looking to conjure up spirits, and the third wants to reorganize the [Knights Templars].† You're smiling? That's all you're doing? Just smiling?

FALK: What else am I to do?

ERNST: Show some irritation against such dunderheads!

FALK: If there were not *one thing* which reconciles me to them again.

ERNST: And what would that be?

FALK: That I recognize in all of these fanciful dreams a striving towards truth that from all of these paths of error the direction of the true path can be ascertained.

*Scottish Rite: a branch of Freemasonry.
†Originally * * * in first editions. Johann Georg Hamann, the philosopher and literary contemporary of Lessing, who after the author's death republished *Ernst und Falk* in the *Königsberger Zeitung* in May 1781, interpreted these to mean the Order of Knights Templars.

ERNST: Even from the gold-making business?*

FALK: Even from the gold making. Whether gold can really be made or cannot be made doesn't make the slightest difference to me. But I am very absolutely certain that rational persons would only wish to be able to make it with Freemasonry in mind. Furthermore, the very first person who comes along into whose hands the philosopher's stone falls will in that very same instant become a Freemason. And it really is an astonishing thing, that is proven by all the accounts regarding real or alleged alchemy, that the world is constantly in a dither about.

ERNST: And the conjurors of spirits?

FALK: More or less the same can be said of them. It is impossible that the spirits can pay heed to the voice of any other person except a Freemason.

ERNST: How seriously you are able to say such things!

FALK: By all that's holy, no more seriously than they are.

ERNST: Would that were so! But finally, those rejuvenated [Knights Templars], if God's willing?

FALK: Those most completely!

ERNST: You see! You don't know what to say about the likes of them. After all [Knights Templars] really did exist at one time. But gold makers or conjurors of spirits perhaps never existed. And obviously it is easier to tell how the Freemasons relate to such imaginary beings than to real ones.

FALK: It's true indeed, here I can express myself only in an paradox. Either or . . .

ERNST: That's fine too. If one at least knows that one of two propositions is true. Well then! Either those "would be [Knights Templars] . . ."

FALK: Ernst! Before you finish saying one more mocking remark! On my word! These—these very individuals are either on the right path for sure, or so far from it that not even a shred of hope is left for them ever to find it.

ERNST: I've got to listen to the likes of that as well. For to ask you for a more precise explanation . . .

FALK: Why not? Private matters have been made into the great mystery long enough.

ERNST: What do you mean by that?

---

*Gold making: tricksters and mountebanks such as Cagliostro maintained in the eighteenth century that they had penetrated the secrets of the Freemasons and were able to make gold as a result.

FALK: The mystery of Freemasonry, as I've already told you, is that very thing which the Freemason *cannot* let pass his lips, even if it were possible he *wanted* to do so. But private matters are things which can no doubt be expressed and which people have concealed, at certain times only, and in certain lands, in part because of envy, suppressed in part because of fear, or in part avoided saying out of prudence.

ERNST: For example?

FALK: For example! Something like this relationship between [Knights Templars] and Freemasons. It can well be that at one time it was necessary and expedient not to reveal it. But now—now on the contrary, it can be exceedingly harmful if a mystery is made of this relationship any longer. Rather it ought to be loudly proclaimed and merely the proper point ascertained in which the [Knights Templars] were the Freemasons of their time.

ERNST: May I know it, this point?

FALK: Read the history of the [Knights Templars] with care! You must guess it. And you will guess it for certain, and it was precisely that reason why you ought not to have become a Freemason.

ERNST: O, that I am not sitting among my books at this moment! And if I guess it, will you acknowledge to me that I have guessed it?

FALK: You will discover at the same time that you don't need such an acknowledgment. But to return to my paradox! It is this very point alone from which the decision can be derived—If all Freemasons who are now full of the [Knights Templars], perceive and feel this point, well be unto them! Well be to the world! A blessing on all they seek to do! A blessing on all they leave undone! If, however, they do not perceive or feel it, this point, if a mere consonance has seduced them, if *the Freemason who works in the* [Temple], has led them to the [Templars], if they have merely fallen in love with the [Templars] on the ———, if they are only really looking to distribute lucrative— ———, or juicy sinecures among themselves and their friends—well then, may heaven above send us a goodly portion of compassion, so that we can control our laughter.*

ERNST: Just look at that! It seems that you can still get impassioned and bitter.

FALK: Unfortunately! I thank you for that remark of yours, and am once more as cold as ice.

---

*An obscure passage that Hamann interpreted to read, "If *the Freemason who works in the Temple* has led them to the Templars; if they have merely fallen in love with the red cross on the white cloaks, if they are only really looking to distribute the order's lucrative estates, juicy sinecures . . ."

ERNST: And what in your opinion of these two cases is probably that of these gentlemen?

FALK: I fear it is the latter. Would that I were deceiving myself! For if it were the former, how could they have such a peculiar scheme?—to reconstitute the [Knights Templars]? That great point in which the [Knights Templars] were Freemasons no longer exists. At least, Europe is long since beyond it and needs no further extraordinary assistance in the matter. What in the world is it they are after? Do they too wish to become a sponge full of water which the powerful someday squeeze dry?* But who am I asking this question of? Against whom is it directed? Did you tell me—were you able to tell me that any others except the neophytes of the order were dragging themselves down with caprices of this sort, such as alchemy, spirit conjuring, [the Knights Templars]? Any others besides children, or people who have no reservation in misusing children? But children become men! Just let them alone! It suffices, as I have already said, that already in the toy I see that weapon which someday these men will bear with a sure and certain hand.

ERNST: When you get right down to it, my friend, it is not these childish things which make me indignant. Without even suspecting that something of a serious nature could be behind them, I simply looked right past them. Barrels, thought I, thrown out to distract the young whales.† But what gnaws at me is that everywhere I see nothing, hear nothing but these childish things. That not a soul wishes even to hear of those things which you led me to expect. I may hum this tune as often as I want, to whomsoever I please, no one cares to join in, always and everywhere, nothing but the deepest silence.

FALK: You mean to say . . .

ERNST: That equality which you declared to me to be the basic principle of the order, that equality which filled my entire soul with such an unexpected hope of at last being able to breathe it in the company of men, who understand how to think beyond any sort of social differences, without transgressing against one individual to the disadvantage of another.

FALK: Well then?

---

*Sponge: at the insistence of Philip IV of France, the Pope disbanded the Knights Templars. All their extensive properties then fell to the crown in France, Spain, and England.
†Barrels: an old seaman's custom.

ERNST: Does it still exist? If ever it did exist! Just let some enlightened Jew come along and present himself! "Oh yes," they say. "A Jew? Of course, a Freemason has to be at the very least a Christian." *Except that it doesn't make the slightest difference, what kind of Christian.* Without discrimination in regard to religion really means: without discrimination in regard to the three religions publicly tolerated in the Holy Roman Empire.* Do you agree as well?

FALK: I can't really say I do.

ERNST: Just let some honest shoemaker, who has leisure enough to have a few good ideas while at his last, even if he were a Jacob Böhme or a Hans Sachs.† Just let him come along and present himself! "Oh yes," they say, "a shoemaker. Why of course, a shoemaker." Just let some loyal, highly experienced, well-tested servant come along and present himself. "Yes indeed," they say, "of course, that sort of people don't themselves get to choose the color of their coat—and after all amongst ourselves we are such a select society."

FALK: And just how select a society are they really?

ERNST: Dear me! Why naturally there's not a thing I could find any other fault with there, except that it is *just* select society of which the whole world is so weary. Princes, counts, Herr von this or Herr von that, officers, councillors of every stripe, merchants, artists—all of the sort who prattle on enthusiastically amongst themselves in the lodge, without, you can be sure, taking any cognizance of class difference—but the fact of the matter is, they all really belong only to *one* class, and that unfortunately is . . .

FALK: It was, I daresay, not like that in my day. But then, perhaps! I don't know. I can only guess. I've been too long a time without any sort of connection with lodges of whatever sort they might be.‡ Not to be permitted to enter a *lodge just right now,* for the time being, and to be *excluded from Freemasonry,* are nevertheless still two very different things.

ERNST: How so?

FALK: Because a lodge is related to Freemasonry as the church is to faith. From the visible well-being of a church one can draw no conclusions, none at all, about the faith of its members. Indeed,

---

*Three religions: the Lutheran, Protestant Reformed (Calvinist), and Roman Catholic.
†Jacob Böhme, Hans Sachs: two famous shoemakers of German cultural history. Böhme (1575–1624), a baroque mystic, author of *Aurora, oder das Morgenrot* (The dawn). Sachs (1494–1576), a famous Nuremberg poet and playwright of the Reformation era.
‡After several unsuccessful attempts, Lessing joined a Masonic lodge in Hamburg in 1771. He did not, however, participate in meetings either there, or later in the last years of his life in Braunschweig and Wolfenbüttel.

there is a certain external well-being of the latter of which it would be a miracle if it were capable of existing along with true faith. Moreover, they never got along well with one another. Instead, one of them has always destroyed the other, as history itself teaches us. And so too, I fear, I fear . . .

ERNST: What?

FALK: To put it briefly! I simply cannot get the way I hear lodges are being run today into my head. Having a treasury, acquiring capital, investing this capital, seeking to place it for the best return, wanting to acquire property, looking for privileges from kings and princes, using the esteem and power of the latter for the suppression of other brothers of a different rite than the one which they so enthusiastically desire to make into the primary thing—if that goes on for some length of time! How glad I will be to have prophesied falsely!

ERNST: Good grief! What's to happen then? That's not the way the state is run nowadays. And besides, even among the persons who make or enforce its laws there are already too many Freemasons—

FALK: Fine! If therefore they also have nothing to fear from the state, what kind of influence do you think such a form of government is likely to have upon them? Will they not obviously arrive once more at exactly the point they wanted to tear themselves away from? Will they not cease to be what they desire to be? I'm not sure if you completely understand me—

ERNST: Just go on talking!

FALK: Of course!—yes, it is true—nothing lasts forever—Perhaps this is supposed to be the very way that Providence has chosen to put an end to the present scheme of Freemasonry—

ERNST: Scheme of Freemasonry? What do you mean by scheme?

FALK: Well! Scheme, exterior, visible appearance.

ERNST: I still don't know—

FALK: You surely do not believe that Freemasonry has always played at Freemasonry?

ERNST: Now what is that supposed to mean? Freemasonry has not always played at Freemasonry?

FALK: In other words, do you really think that that which Freemasonry is, has always been called Freemasonry? But look there. Past noon already! There come my guests already! You are, of course, going to stay?

ERNST: I did not want to, but now I'll probably have to. It looks like a double enrichment awaits me.

FALK: But at table, please, not a word.

Fifth Conversation

ERNST: At last they're gone. Oh those jabberers! And did you notice, by the way, or did you not want to notice, that the one with a wart on his chin—whatever his name is—is a Freemason? He banged on his glass about it often enough.

FALK: Indeed I heard him quite well. I even noticed in his comments, something which probably did not catch your attention, he is one of those who do their fighting for America over here in Europe.*

ERNST: That's probably not the worst thing about him.

FALK: And he's got the bizarre idea that the Congress is a lodge and that with weapons in hand, the Freemasons are finally founding their empire over there.

ERNST: Are there actually *dreamers* like that?

FALK: There must actually be.

ERNST: And how did you get that little worm out of him?

FALK: From a trait which you will also one day get to know somewhat better.

ERNST: Good God, if only I had known that I was deceiving myself *so terribly* in these Freemasons!

FALK: Don't worry. A Freemason calmly awaits the rising of the sun and lets the candles burn as long as they want or can. Putting candles out and when they are out, finally recognizing that the stumps have got to be lit again or maybe even new ones set up, that's nothing for a Freemason.

ERNST: That's what I think too. Anything that costs blood is certainly not worth blood.†

FALK: Splendid!—now ask what you will. I've got to answer.

ERNST: That means there will be no end to my questions.

FALK: Only you can't find a starting point.

ERNST: Did I understand you correctly, or did I misunderstand you when we were interrupted? Did you contradict yourself or did you not? Because, as a matter of fact, when you told me that time *Freemasonry had always existed,* I understood it to mean that not only its essence, but its present mode of being also derives from time immemorial.

FALK: If it were only the same thing for both of them! In its essence, Freemasonry is just as old as civil society. Both could not do other-

---

*Referring to the contemporaneous American War for Independence, i.e., far from the scene of battle.

†An expression of Benjamin Franklin.

wise except to orginate together. Why, it may even be that civil society is just an offshoot of Freemasonry. After all, even at its burning point the flame is also an offshoot of the sun.

ERNST: Something like that shimmers before my mind's eye as well.

FALK: Be they mother and daughter or sister and sister, the fate of both has always been interwoven. In whatever condition civil society found itself, Freemasonry everywhere has also found itself and vice versa. It has always been the surest characteristic of a healthy and strong form of state government, that it allowed Freemasonry to flower alongside it, just as it is now the infallible indication of a weak, timid state, if it will not openly tolerate what it nevertheless must tolerate covertly, whether it wishes to or not.

ERNST: By which is meant, Freemasonry!

FALK: Surely! For it is based not in *external unions,* which ever so easily degenerate into civil organizations, but instead in the mutual feelings of like-thinking minds.

ERNST: And who takes it upon himself to oversee the latter?

FALK: All along, of course, it has been necessary for Freemasonry at every time and place to adapt or shape itself according to civil society, for the latter was always the stronger. As varied as civic society has been, Freemasonry has not been able to refrain from assuming just as many varied forms; except that every new form had its new name, as is only natural. How could you ever think that the term *Freemasonry* might be older than that prevailing manner of political thought according to which it has been precisely evaluated?

ERNST: And what is this prevailing manner of thought?

FALK: That I'll leave to your own study and research. It's enough for me to tell you that the term *Freemason,* used to indicate a member of our secret brotherhood, was never heard before the beginning of this century. You can be reliably certain that before this time it never appeared in any printed book and I'd like to see the fellow, who thinks he can show it to me in just one older handwritten document.

ERNST: You mean the German term.

FALK: By no means! I mean the original English term *Free-Mason,* as well as every other translation derived from it, in whatever language you choose.

ERNST: That can't be! Just think about it for a moment. Not in one single printed book before the beginning of the present century? Not a single one?

FALK: Not a one.

ERNST: Nevertheless, I myself . . .

FALK: You did? Has some of that dust that people are still haven't stopped around gotten into your eyes too?

ERNST: But certainly the passage in . . .

FALK: In *Londinopolis?** Am I right?—Dust!

ERNST: And the Acts of Parliament under Henry VI?†

FALK: Dust!

ERNST: And the privileges which Charles XI, king of Sweden granted the Lodge of Gothenburg?‡

FALK: Dust!

ERNST: And Locke?

FALK: What sort of lock?

ERNST: The philosopher. His letter to the duke of Pembroke, his notes about an interrogation written by Henry VI in his own hand?§

FALK: That must be a brand-new discovery. That's one I don't know. But Henry VI again? Dust and nothing more than dust!

ERNST: It can't be!

FALK: Do you know a more genteel term for distorted words, or forged documents?

ERNST: And they could be able to get away with that for so long in the eyes of the world without being punished?

FALK: Why not? There are far too few intelligent folk to be able to contradict every single inanity as soon as it appears. It's sufficient that no statute of limitations takes effect in such cases. Of course, it would certainly be better if people didn't undertake any sort of inanity whatsoever before the eyes of the public. Because precisely the most disgraceful of them, so disgraceful, that is, for the very reason that no one takes the trouble to oppose them, can in the course of time attain the appearance of very solemn and sacred things. Then a thousand years later everybody says, "Would anyone have been capable of just going off and writing something like that if it had not been true? Nobody contradicted those trustworthy gentlemen back in those days, and you want to contradict them now?"

ERNST: Oh history! history! What art thou! [. . .]

Londinopolis, by James Howell, London, 1657. He speaks only about the professional organization of Masons.

†Henry VI (1442–71): Parliamentary documents of the era also mention only illegal meetings and organizations of Masons, i.e., handworkers.

‡Charles XI (1660–97): the so-called privileges proved to be counterfeits of the eighteenth century, by means of which the Swedish Masonic lodges sought to protect themselves by claiming long-standing legitimacy.

§Both the letter attributed to Locke and the royal proceedings proved to be falsifications.

Postlude

A sixth conversation which took place between these friends cannot be reconstructed in this way. But the essential matter thereof is intended to be critical comments on the fifth conversation, which are at present still being withheld.

Translated by William L. Zwiebel

SELECTIONS FROM LESSING'S PHILOSOPHICAL/ THEOLOGICAL WRITINGS

On the Proof of the Spirit
and the Power (1777)
The Testament of John (1777)
The Education of the Human Race
(1780)
The Religion of Christ (1780)

On the Proof of the Spirit and the Power

> . . .because of the prodigious miracles which
> may be proved to have happened by this
> argument among many others, that traces of
> them still remain among those who live
> according to the will of the Logos.

Origen, *Contra Celsum*, I.2

To Herr Director Schumann at Hannover, Brunswick, 1777

Sir, who could be more eager to read your new work than I? I hunger for conviction so much that like Erisichthon* I swallow everything that has even the appearance of nourishment. If you do the same with this pamphlet, we are the men for one another. I am, with the regard that one inquirer after truth never ceases to bear for another,

Yours etc.—

Fulfilled prophecies, which I myself experience, are one thing; fulfilled prophecies, of which I know only from history that others say they have experienced them, are another.

Miracles, which I see with my own eyes, and which I have the opportunity to verify for myself, are one thing; miracles, of which I know only from history that others say they have seen them and verified them, are another.

That surely, is beyond controversy? Surely there is no objection to be made against that?

If I had lived at the time of Christ, then of course the prophecies fulfilled in his person would have made me pay great attention to him. If I had actually seen him do miracles; if I had had no cause to doubt that these were true miracles; then in a worker of miracles who had

---

*Because Erisichthon (in Ovid's *Metamorphoses*) fells a sacred oak in Ceres' grove, Ceres punishes him. Erisichthon is stricken with an insatiable hunger which eventually drives him to eat himself.

been marked out so long before, I would have gained so much confidence that I would willingly have submitted my intellect to his, and I would have believed him in all things in which equally indisputable experiences did not tell against him.

Or: if I even now experienced that prophecies referring to Christ or the Christian religion, of whose priority in time I have long been certain, were fulfilled in a manner admitting no dispute; if even now miracles were done by believing Christians which I had to recognize as true miracles: what could prevent me from accepting this proof of the spirit and of power, as the apostle calls it?

In the last instance Origen was quite right in saying that in this proof of the spirit and of power the Christian religion was able to provide a proof of its own more divine than all Greek dialectic. For in his time there was still "the power to do miraculous things which still continued" among those who lived after Christ's precept; and if he had undoubted examples of this, then if he was not to deny his own senses he had of necessity to recognize that proof of the spirit and of power.

But I am no longer in Origen's position; I live in the eighteenth century, in which miracles no longer happen. If I even now hesitate to believe anything on the proof of the spirit and of power, which I can believe on other arguments more appropriate to my age: what is the problem?

The problem is that this proof of the spirit and of power no longer has any spirit or power, but has sunk to the level of human testimonies of spirit and power.

The problem is that reports of fulfilled prophecies are not fulfilled prophecies; that reports of miracles are not miracles. These, the prophecies fulfilled before my eyes, the miracles that occur before my eyes, are immediate in their effect. But those—the reports of fulfilled prophecies and miracles, have to work through a medium which takes away all their force.

To quote Origen and to cite his words that "the proof of power is so called because of the astonishing miracles which have happened to confirm the teaching of Christ" is of little use if one keeps from one's readers what Origen says immediately thereafter. For the readers will also turn up Origen and find with surprise that he argues for the truth of the miracles which happened with the foundation of Christianity εκ πολλων μεν αλλων,* thus, from the narrative of the evangelists; chiefly

---

*"εκ πολλων μεν αλλων": for many other reasons.

and particularly, however, he argues their truth on the basis of miracles which were still happening.

If then this proof of the proof has now entirely lapsed; if then all historical certainty is much too weak to replace this apparent proof of the proof which has lapsed: how is it to be expected of me that the same inconceivable truths which sixteen to eighteen hundred years ago people believed on the strongest inducement, should be believed by me to be equally valid on an infinitely lesser inducement?

Or is it invariably the case, that what I read in reputable historians is just as certain for me as what I myself experience?

I do not know that anyone has ever asserted this. What is asserted is only that the reports which we have of these prophecies and miracles are as reliable as historical truths ever can be. And then it is added that historical truths cannot be demonstrated: nevertheless we must believe them as firmly as truths that have been demonstrated.

To this I answer: *first*, who will deny (not I) that the reports of these miracles and prophecies are as reliable as historical truths ever can be? But if they are only as reliable as this, why are they treated as if they were infinitely more reliable?

And in what way? In this way, that something quite different and much greater is founded upon them than it is legitimate to found upon truths historically proved.

If no historical truth can be demonstrated, then nothing can be demonstrated by means of historical truths.

That is: *accidental truths of history can never become the proof of necessary truths of reason.*

I do not for one moment deny that in Christ prophecies were fulfilled; I do not for one moment deny that Christ performed miracles. But since the truth of these miracles has completely ceased to be demonstrable by miracles still happening at the present time, since they are no more than reports of miracles (however incontroverted and incontrovertible they may be), I deny that they can and should bind me in the least to a faith in the other teachings of Christ. These other teachings I accept on other grounds.

Then *secondly*: what does it mean to accept an historical proposition as true? to believe an historical truth? Does it mean anything other than this: to accept this proposition, this truth as valid? to accept that there is no objection to be brought against it? to accept that one historical proposition is built on one thing, another on another that from one historical truth another follows? to reserve to oneself the right to estimate other historical things accordingly? Does it mean anything other than this? Anything more? Examine carefully.

We all believe that an Alexander* lived who in a short time conquered almost all Asia. But who, on the basis of this belief, would risk anything of great, permanent worth, the loss of which would be irreparable? Who, in consequence of this belief, would forswear forever all knowledge that conflicted with this belief? Certainly not I. Now I have no objection to raise against Alexander and his victory: but it might still be possible that the story was founded on a mere poem of Chœrilus† just as the ten-year siege of Troy depends on no better authority than Homer's poetry.

If on historical grounds I have no objection to the statement that Christ raised to life a dead man; must I therefore accept it as true that God has a Son who is of the same essence as himself? What is the connection between my inability to raise any significant objection to the evidence of the former and my obligation to believe something against which my reason rebels?

If on historical grounds I have no objection to the statement that this Christ himself rose from the dead, must I therefore accept it as true that this risen Christ was the Son of God?

That the Christ, against whose resurrection I can raise no important historical objection, therefore declared himself to be the Son of God; that his disciples therefore believed him to be such; this I gladly believe from my heart. For these truths, as truths of one and the same class, follow quite naturally on one another.

But to jump with that historical truth to a quite different class of truths, and to demand of me that I should form all my metaphysical and moral ideas accordingly; to expect me to alter all my fundamental ideas of the nature of the Godhead because I cannot set any credible testimony against the resurrection of Christ: if that is not a μεταβασις εις αλλο γενος,‡ then I do not know what Aristotle meant by this phrase.

It is said: "The Christ of whom on historical grounds you must allow that he raised the dead, that he himself rose from the dead, said himself that God had a Son of the same essence as himself and that he is this Son." This would be quite excellent! if only it were not the case that it is not more than historically certain that Christ said this.

---

*Alexander the Great (356–323 B.C.).
†Chœrilus: Lessing often refers to Choerilus, a poet who accompanied Alexander. Lessing considered him a poor poet.
‡"μεταβασις εις αλλο γενος": a change in genres.

If you press me still further and say: "Oh yes! this is more than historically certain. For it is asserted by inspired historians who cannot make a mistake."

But, unfortunately, that also is only historically certain, that these historians were inspired and could not err.

That, then, is the ugly, broad ditch which I cannot get across, however often and however earnestly I have tried to make the leap. If anyone can help me over it, let him do it, I beg him, I adjure him. He will deserve a divine reward from me.

And so I repeat what I have said above in the same words. I do not for one moment deny that in Christ prophecies were fulfilled. I do not for one moment deny that Christ did miracles. But since the truth of these miracles has completely ceased to be demonstrable by miracles still happening now, since they are no more than reports of miracles (even though they be narratives which have not been, and cannot be, impugned), I deny that they can and should bind me to the very least faith in the other teachings of Christ.

What then does bind me? Nothing but these teachings themselves. Eighteen hundred years ago they were so new, so alien, so foreign to the entire mass of truths recognized in that age, that nothing less than miracles and fulfilled prophecies were required if the multitude were to attend to them at all.

But to make the multitude attentive to something means to put common sense on to the right track.

And so it came about, so it now is. And what it hunted out to the left and right of this track are the fruits of those miracles and fulfilled prophecies.

These fruits I may see before me ripe and ripened, and may I not be satisfied with that? The old pious legend that the hand which scatters the seed must wash in snails' blood seven times for each throw, I do not doubt, but merely ignore it. What does it matter to me whether the legend is false or true? The fruits are excellent.

Suppose that a very useful mathematical truth had been reached by the discoverer through an obvious fallacy. (Even if such an instance does not exist, yet it could exist.) Should I deny this truth? Should I refuse to use this truth? Would I be on that account an ungrateful reviler of the discoverer, if I were unwilling to prove from his insight in other respects, indeed did not consider it capable of proof, that the fallacy through which he stumbled upon the truth *could* not be a fallacy?

I conclude, and my wish is: may all who are divided by the Gospel of

John be reunited by the Testament of John. Admittedly it is apocryphal, this testament. But it is not on that account any the less divine.

The Testament of John

. . . who lay at the Lord's breast and drew the rivulets of his teachings from the purest source.

Jerome*

HE: You were very quick with this pamphlet [*On the Proof of the Spirit and of Power*]; but the pamphlet shows it.

I: Really?

HE: You usually write more clearly.

I: The greatest clarity I have always regarded as the greatest beauty.

HE: But I see you let yourself be carried away. You begin to think that you can just make allusions to things which are not understood by one in a hundred readers; which perhaps you yourself learnt about only yesterday or the day before . . .

I: For example?

HE: Don't be too learned.

I: For example?

HE: Your obscure remark at the end. Your Testament of John. I have searched in vain through the pages of my Grabius and Fabricius† for it.

I: Must everything be a book, then?

HE: Is this Testament of John not a book? What is it, then?

I: The last will of John, the last remarkable words of the dying John which he repeated over and over again. Cannot they also be called a Testament?

HE: Certainly they can. But I am now less curious about it. Neverthe-

---

*See John 13:23ff.

†Johann Ernst Grabe (1666–1711), *Spicilegium SS. Patrum ut et Hoereticorum seculi post Christum natum, I, II, et III* (Further selections on the church fathers and heretics of the first, second, and third centuries) (Oxford, 1698 or 1714); Johann Albert Fabricius (1668–1738), *Codex Apocryphus Novi Testamenti* (Apocrypha of the New Testament), 3 vols. [Hamburg 1703–19].

less, what are these words? I am not very well read in the Abdias,* or wherever else they may occur.

I: They are to be found in a less-suspect writer. Jerome preserved them for us in his *Commentary on Paul's Epistle to the Galatians.* Turn them up there. I hardly think that you will like them.

HE: Who knows? Just quote them to me.

I: Out of my head? Giving the circumstances which I can now remember or which seem to be probable?

HE: Why not?

I: For John, the good John who wished never again to be separated from his Church which he had gathered together at Ephesus, this single congregation was a sufficiently large stage for his teaching of wonders and his wonderful teaching. John was an old man, so old that . . .

HE: That the pious and simple folk thought he would never die.

I: Yet they saw him day by day approaching nearer to death.

HE: Superstition sometimes trusts the senses too much, sometimes too little. Even when John was already dead, superstition still held on to the belief that John *could* not die, that he slept and was not dead.

I: How close superstition often gets to the truth.

HE: But tell me more of the story. I cannot listen to you speaking in favor of superstition.

I: With a speed as hesitant as a friend wrenching himself from the arm of a friend to hasten to the embrace of his lady, gradually and visibly John's pure soul was separated from his equally pure but decayed body. Soon his disciples could not even carry him to church. And yet John would not neglect any assembly; he would allow no assembly to disperse without his address to the community which would rather have been deprived of its daily bread than of this address.

HE: Which often may not have been very carefully prepared.

I: Do you prefer what has been carefully prepared?

HE: It all depends.

I: Is it quite certain that John's address was never that. For it always came straight from his heart. It was always simple and short; and every day became simpler and shorter, until finally he reduced it to the words . . .

HE: To what?

---

*Abdias, bishop of Babylon, was the alleged author of an apocryphal history of the apostles in ten books; for the Latin text cf. Fabricius; English summary in M. R. James, *The Apocryphal New Testament*, 462ff.

I: "Little children, love one another."

HE: Short and good.

I: Do you really think so? But one so quickly becomes tired of the good and even of the best, if it begins to be an everyday thing. At the first assembly at which John could say no more than "Little children, love one another," these words had a wonderful effect. So it was also in the second, third, and fourth assemblies; for the people said, the weak old man cannot say anything more. But when the old man now and then had good and cheerful days again, and still said nothing more, and still had nothing further for the daily assembly than "Little children, love one another"; when they saw that it was not that the old man was only able to say these few words but that he deliberately chose not to say more: then "Little children, love one another" became insipid, flat, and meaningless. Brethren and disciples could hardly listen any more without feeling sick of it, and finally had the audacity to ask the good old man: "But, Master, why do you always say the same thing?"

HE: And John?

I: John replied: "Because it is the Lord's command; because this alone, this alone, if it is done, is enough, is sufficient and adequate."

HE: So that is your Testament of John?

I: Yes.

HE: It is well that you have called it apocryphal.

I: In contrast to the canonical Gospel of John. But still I think it divine.

HE: In the same sort of way that you would perhaps call a pretty girl divine.

I: I have never called a pretty girl divine, and am not in the habit of misusing this word. What I here call divine Jerome calls *dignam Ioanne sententiam.* *

HE: Ah, Jerome!

I: Augustine relates† that a certain Platonist said that the beginning of John's Gospel, "In the beginning was the Word," etc., deserves to be inscribed in letters of gold in all churches in the most prominent places.

HE: Of course. The Platonist was quite right. Oh, the Platonists! Quite certainly Plato himself could not have written anything more sublime than these opening words of John's Gospel.

I: That may be. At the same time I, who do not make much of the

---

*"Dignam Ioanne . . .": a statement worthy of John.

†Compare *City of God,* X, 29, 2.

sublime writing of a philosopher, think that it would be far more appropriate if what was inscribed in letters of gold in all our churches in the most prominent places was the Testament of John.

HE: Hm!

I: "Little children, love one another."

HE: Yes, yes.

I: It was by this Testament of John that formerly one who was of the salt of the earth used to swear. Now he swears by the Gospel of John, and it is said that since this change the salt has become a little stale.

HE: Another riddle?

I: He that has ears to hear let him hear.

HE: Yes, yes, now I see your point.

I: What do you see?

HE: That is how some people always draw their head out of the noose: It is enough if they keep to Christian love; it does not matter what becomes of the Christian religion.

I: Do you count me as one of these people?

HE: Whether I would be right in doing so, you must ask yourself.

I: Then may I say a word for these people?

HE: If you want to do so.

I: But perhaps I do not understand you either. Is then Christian love not the Christian religion?

HE: Yes and no.

I: In what way no?

HE: For the dogmas of the Christian religion are one thing, practical Christianity, which it affirms to be founded upon these dogmas, is another.

I: And in what way yes?

HE: Inasmuch as only that is true Christian love which is founded upon the Christian dogmas.

I: But which of the two is the more difficult? To accept and confess the Christian dogmas, or to practice Christian love?

HE: It would not help you even if I admitted that the latter is by far the more difficult.

I: How then should it help me?

HE: It is all the more ridiculous that those people I mentioned make the road to hell so burdensome for themselves.

I: In what way?

HE: Why should they take on themselves the yoke of Christian love when it is not made either easy or meritorious for them by the dogmas?

I: Yes of course. This is a risk that we have to run. I only ask: Is it wise of certain other people, on account of this risk which these people run with their unchristian Christian love, to deny to them the name of Christians?

HE: *Cui non competit definitio, non competit definitum.** Have I invented that?

I: But suppose, nevertheless, we could interpret the definition a little more widely. We might follow the saying of a certain good man: "He who is not against us is for us." You know this good man?

HE: Very well. He is the same who in another place says: "He who is not with me is against me."

I: Yes indeed. Of course. That reduces me to silence. Oh, you alone are a true Christian. And as well read in the Scripture as the devil.

* * *

JEROME, *in Epist, ad Galatas,* c. 6.

The blessed Evangelist John, having lived to a ripe old age in Epheus, could scarcely be brought to church any more, and then only supported on the arms of his disciples. He could no longer speak at length, and yet at each gathering he reiterated, "Children, love one another." Finally the disciples and brothers who were with him grew tired of always hearing the same thing and they said, "Master, why do you always repeat yourself?" John answered with dignity, "Because this is the commandment of our Lord, and if it alone is achieved, this will suffice."

---

* "*Cui non competit* . . .": The definition does not fit one who does not concur with the definition.

The Education of the Human Race

For the same reasons, this is all in a certain sense true, and in a certain sense false.

Augustine

Edited by Gotthold Ephraim Lessing

Editor's Preface

I have published the first half of this essay in my *Contributions*. Now I am in a position to give the remainder.

The author has set himself upon a high eminence from which he believes it possible to see beyond the limits of the allotted path of his present day's journey.

But he does not call away from his road any wanderer hastening home whose one desire is to reach his night's lodging. He does not ask that the view which enchants him should also enchant every other eye.

And so, I would suppose, he may be allowed to stand and wonder where he stands and wonders.

Would that from the immeasurable distance which a soft evening glow neither entirely conceals nor wholly reveals to his gaze, he could bring some guiding hint, for which I have often felt myself at a loss!

This is what is in my mind. Why are we not more willing to see in all positive religions simply the process by which alone human understanding in every place can develop and must still further develop, instead of either ridiculing or becoming angry with them? In the best world there is nothing that deserves this scorn, this indignation we show. Are the religions alone to deserve it? Is God to have part in everything except our mistakes?

The Education of the Human Race

1. What education is to the individual man, revelation is to the whole human race.

2. Education is revelation coming to the individual man; and revelation is education which has come, and is still coming, to the human race.

3. Whether it can be of any advantage to the science of instruction to consider education from this point of view I will not here inquire; but in theology it may unquestionably be of great advantage, and may remove many difficulties, if revelation be conceived of as an education of the human race.

4. Education gives man nothing which he could not also get from within himself; it gives him that which he could get from within himself, only quicker and more easily. In the same way too, revelation gives nothing to the human race which human reason could not arrive at on its own; only it has given, and still gives to it, the most important of these things sooner.

5. And just as in education, it is not a matter of indifference in what order the powers of a man are developed, as it cannot impart to a man everything at once; so also God had to maintain a certain order and a certain measure in his revelation.

6. Even though the first man was furnished at once with a conception of the One God; yet it was not possible that this conception, freely imparted and not won by experience, should subsist long in its clearness. As soon as human reason, left to itself, began to elaborate it, it broke up the one immeasurable into many measurables, and gave a distinguishing mark to every one of these parts.

7. Hence naturally arose polytheism and idolatry. And who can say for how many millions of years human reason would have been lost in these errors, even though at all places and times there were individual men who recognized them *as* errors, had it not pleased God to afford it a better direction by means of a new impulse?

8. But when he neither could, nor would, reveal himself any more to *each* individual man, he selected an individual people for his special education; and that the most rude and the most ferocious, in order to begin with it from the very beginning.

9. This was the Hebrew people, about whom we do not even know what kind of divine worship they had in Egypt. For so despised a race of slaves could not have been permitted to take part in the worship of the Egyptians; and the God of their fathers had become entirely unknown to them.

10. It is possible that the Egyptians had expressly prohibited the Hebrews from having a god or gods, and having destroyed their faith, had brought them to the belief that they had no god or gods whatsoever; that to have a god or gods was the prerogative only of the superior Egyptians; this perhaps in order to be able to tyrannize over

them with a greater show of fairness. Do Christians treat their slaves much differently even now?

11. To this rude people God caused himself to be announced at first simply as "the God of their fathers," in order to make them familiar and at home with the idea of a God belonging to them too.

12. Following this, through the miracles with which he led them out of Egypt and planted them in Canaan, he testified of himself to them as a God mightier than any other god.

13. And as he continued demonstrating himself to be the mightiest of all, which only one can be, he gradually accustomed them to the idea of the One.

14. But how far was this conception of the One below the true transcendental conception of the One, which reason, so late, teaches us only to conclude with certainty out of the conception of the infinite!

15. Although the best of the people were already more or less approaching the true conception of the One, the people as a whole could not for a long time elevate themselves to it. And this was the sole reason why they so often abandoned their one God, and expected to find the One, i.e., the mightiest, in some other god belonging to another people.

16. But of what kind of moral education was a people so raw, so incapable of abstract thoughts, and so entirely in their childhood, capable? Of none other but such as is adapted to the age of children, an education by rewards and punishments addressed to the senses.

17. Here too, then, education and revelation come together. As yet God could give to his people no other religion, no other law than one through obedience to which they might hope to be happy, or through disobedience to which they must fear to be unhappy. For as yet they envisaged nothing beyond this life. They knew of no immortality of the soul; they yearned after no life to come. But now to reveal these things, when their reason was so little prepared for them, what would it have been but the same fault in the divine rule as is committed by the vain schoolmaster who chooses to hurry his pupil too rapidly and boast of his progress, rather than thoroughly to ground him?

18. "But," it will be asked, "to what purpose was this education of so rude a people, a people with whom God had to begin so entirely from the beginning?" I reply: "In order that in the process of time he might all the better employ particular members of this nation as the teachers of all other peoples. He was bringing up in them the future teachers of the human race. These were Jews, these could only be Jews,

only men from a people which had been educated in this way."

19. Then further. When the child by dint of blows and caresses had grown and was now come to years of understanding, the Father sent it of a sudden into foreign lands: and here it recognized at once the good which in its Father's house it had possessed, and had not been conscious of.

20. While God guided his chosen people through all the degrees of a child's education, the other nations of the earth had gone on by the light of reason. The most part had remained far behind the chosen people. Only a few had got in front of them. And this, too, takes place with children, who are allowed to grow up on their own; many remain quite raw; some educate themselves to an astonishing degree.

21. But as these more fortunate few prove nothing against the use and necessity of education, so the few heathen nations, who hitherto seemed to be ahead of the chosen people even in the knowledge of God, prove nothing against a revelation. The child of education begins with slow but sure footsteps; it is late in overtaking many a more happily placed child of nature; but it *does* overtake it; and thenceforth can never be overtaken by it again.

22. Similarly—putting aside the doctrine of the unity of God, which in a way is found, and in a way is not found, in the books of the Old Testament—the fact that the doctrine of immortality at least is not to be found in it, but is wholly foreign to it, and all the related doctrine of reward and punishment in a future life, proves just as little against the divine origin of these books. For let us suppose that these doctrines were not only wanting there, but even that they were not even true; let us suppose that for mankind all was over in this life; would the being of God be for this reason less demonstrated? Would God on this account be less at liberty, would it less become him, to take immediate charge of the temporal fortunes of any people out of this perishable race? The miracles which he performed for the Jews, the prophecies which he caused to be recorded through them, were surely not for the few mortal Jews, in whose time they happened and were recorded: his intentions there concerned the whole Jewish people, the entire human race, who, perhaps, are destined to remain for ever here on earth, even though every individual Jew and every individual man dies and is gone for ever.

23. Once more, the absence of those doctrines in the writings of the Old Testament proves nothing against their divinity. Moses was sent from God even though the sanction of his law extended only to this life. For why should it extend further? He was surely sent only to the Israelitish people, to the Israelitish people *of that time,* and his com-

mission was perfectly adapted to the knowledge, capacities, inclinations of the *then existing* Israelitish people, as well as to the destiny of the people that was to come. And this is sufficient.

24. So far ought Warburton* to have gone, and no further. But that learned man overdrew his bow. Not content that the absence of these doctrines did not *discredit* the divine mission of Moses, it must even be a *proof* to him of the divinity of the mission. If he had only sought this proof in the suitability of such a law for such a people!

But he took refuge in the hypothesis of a miraculous system continued in an unbroken line from Moses to Christ, according to which God had made every individual Jew just as happy or unhappy as his obedience or disobedience to the law deserved. The miraculous system, he said, had compensated for the lack of those doctrines [of eternal rewards and punishments] without which no state can subsist; and precisely this compensation proved what that lack at first sight appeared to deny.

25. How well it was that Warburton could by no argument prove or even make likely this continuous miracle, in which he placed the essence of the Israelitish theocracy! For could he have done so, then indeed, but not until then, he would have made the difficulty really insuperable, for me at least. For the truth which the divinity of Moses' mission was to restore, would, in fact, have been actually made doubtful by it: a truth which God, it is true, did not at that time want to reveal; but which, on the other hand, he certainly did not wish to make harder of attainment.

26. I will illustrate by something that is a counterpart to the process of revelation. A primer for children may fairly pass over in silence this or that important piece of the science or art which it expounds, when the teacher considers that it is not yet suitable for the capabilities of the children for whom he was writing. But it must contain absolutely nothing which bars the way to the knowledge which is held back, or which misleads the children away from it. Rather, all the approaches towards it must be carefully left open; and to lead them away from even one of these approaches, or to cause them to enter it later than they need, would alone be enough to change the mere imperfection of the primer into an actual fault.

27. In the same way, in the writings of the Old Testament, those primers for the Israelitish people, rough, unpracticed in thought as they

---

*The English theologian William Warburton (1698–1779) defended Christianity against deism.

are, the doctrines of the immortality of the soul, and future recompense, might be fairly left out: but they were bound to contain nothing which could even have delayed the progress of the people for whom they were written, in their way to this great truth. And what, to say the least, could have delayed them more than the promise of such a miraculous recompense in this life—promised by him who makes no promise that he does not keep?

28. For even if the strongest proof of the immortality of the soul and of a life to come were not to be alleged from the inequality of the distribution of the material rewards in this life, in which so little account appears to be taken of virtue and vice; yet it is at least certain that without this difficulty—to be resolved in the life to come—human reason would still be far from any better and firmer proofs, and perhaps even would never have reached them. For what was to impel it to seek for these better proofs? Mere curiosity?

29. An Israelite here and there, no doubt, might have extended to every individual member, of the entire state those promises and threatenings which applied to it as a whole, and been firmly persuaded that whosoever is pious must also be happy, and that whoever was unhappy must be bearing the penalty of his wrongdoing, which penalty would at once change itself into blessing, as soon as he abandoned his sin. One like this appears to have written Job, for the plan of it is entirely in this spirit.

30. But it was impossible that daily experience should confirm this conviction, or else it would have been all over, for ever, with the people who had this experience, so far as all recognition and reception were concerned of the truth as yet unfamiliar to them. For if the pious man were absolutely happy, and it was also a necessary part of his happiness that his satisfaction should be broken by no uneasy thoughts of death, and that he should die old and "full of days":* how could he yearn for another life? and how could he reflect upon a thing for which he did not yearn? But if the pious did not reflect on it, who then should reflect? The transgressor? he who felt the punishment of his misdeeds, and if he cursed this life must have so gladly renounced that other existence?

31. It was of much less consequence that an Israelite here and there should directly and expressly have denied the immortality of the soul and future recompense, on the grounds that the law had no reference to it. The denial of an individual, had it even been a Solomon,† did not

*Cf. Genesis 25:8 and 35:29.
†Ecclesiastes 3:19–21.

arrest the progress of the common reason, and was in itself, even, a proof that the nation had now taken a great step nearer to the truth. For individuals only deny what the many are thinking over; and to think over an idea about which before no one troubled himself in the least, is halfway to knowledge.

32. Let us also acknowledge that it is a heroic obedience to obey the laws of God simply because they are God's laws, and not because he has promised to reward those who obey them now and hereafter; to obey them even though there be an entire despair of future recompense, and uncertainty respecting a temporal one.

33. Must not a people educated in this heroic obedience towards God be destined, must they not be capable beyond all others of executing divine purposes of quite a special character? Let the soldier, who pays blind obedience to his leader, also become convinced of his leader's wisdom, and then say what that leader may not venture to do with his aid.

34. As yet the Jewish people had worshipped in their Jehovah rather the mightiest than the wisest of all gods; as yet they had rather feared him as a jealous God than loved him: this, too, is a proof that the conceptions which they had of their eternal One God were not exactly the right conceptions which we should have of God. However, now the time has come for these conceptions of theirs to be expanded, ennobled, rectified, to accomplish which God availed himself of a perfectly natural means, a better and more correct measure, by which they got the opportunity of appreciating him.

35. Instead of, as hitherto, appreciating him in contrast with the miserable idols of the small neighboring peoples, with whom they lived in constant rivalry, they began, in captivity under the wise Persian*, to measure him against the "Being of all Beings" such as a more disciplined reason recognized and worshipped.

36. Revelation had guided their reason, and now, all at once, reason gave clearness to their revelation.

37. This was the first reciprocal influence which these two (reason and revelation) exercised on one another; and so far is such a mutual influence from being unbecoming to the author of them both, that without it either of them would have been useless.

38. The child, sent into foreign lands, saw other children who knew more, who lived more becomingly, and asked itself, in confusion, "Why do I not know that too? Why do I not live so too? Ought I not to

---

*The Persian refers to Cyrus the Younger (424?–401 B.C.).

have learned and acquired all this in my Father's house?" Thereupon it again sought out its primer, which had long been thrown into a corner, in order to push the blame on to the primer. But behold, it discovers that the blame does not rest upon books, but the blame is solely its own, for not having long ago known this very thing, and lived in this very way.

39. Since the Jews, by this time, through the medium of the pure Persian doctrine, recognized in their Jehovah not simply the greatest of all national deities, but God; and since they could the more readily find him and show him to others in their sacred writings, inasmuch as he was really in them; and since they manifested as great an aversion for sensuous representations, or at all events were shown in these Scriptures as possessing an aversion as great as the Persians had always felt; it is not surprising that they found favour in the eyes of Cyrus with a divine worship which he recognized as being, no doubt, far below pure Sabeism,* but yet far above the rude idolatries which in its stead had taken possession of the land of the Jews.

40. Thus enlightened respecting the treasures which they had possessed without knowing it, they returned, and became quite another people, whose first care it was to give permanence to this enlightenment amongst themselves. Soon apostasy and idolatry among them was out of the question. For it is possible to be faithless to a national deity, but never to God, after he has once been recognized.

41. The theologians have tried to explain this complete change in the Jewish people in different ways; and one, who has well demonstrated the insufficiency of these explanations, wanted finally to give, as the true reason—"the visible fulfilment of the prophecies which had been spoken and written respecting the Babylonian captivity and the restoration from it." But even this reason can only be true in so far as it presupposes the exalted ideas of God as they now are. The Jews must now, for the first time, have recognized that to do miracles and to predict the future belonged only to God, both of which powers they had formerly ascribed also to false idols; this precisely is the reason why miracles and prophecies had hitherto made so weak and fleeting an impression upon them.

42. Doubtless the Jews became better acquainted with the doctrine of immortality among the Chaldeans and Persians. They became more familiar with it, too, in the schools of the Greek philosophers in Egypt.

43. However, as this doctrine did not correspond with their Scriptures in the same way that the doctrines of God's unity and attributes

*Sabeism refers to worship of the stars, a practice in Saba.

had done—since the former were entirely overlooked by that sensual people, while the latter would be sought for: and since too, for the former, previous exercising was necessary, and as yet there had been only *hints* and *allusions,* the faith in the immortality of the soul could naturally never be the faith of the entire people. It was and continued to be only the creed of a certain section of them.

44. An example of what I mean by "previous exercising" in the doctrines of immortality, is the divine threat of punishing the misdeeds of the father upon his children unto the third and fourth generation. This accustomed the fathers to live in thought with their remotest posterity, and to feel in advance the misfortunes which they had brought upon these innocents.

45. What I mean by an "allusion" is something which might merely excite curiosity, or call forth a question. As, for instance, the common figure of speech which describes death by "he was gathered to his fathers."

46. By a "hint" I mean something which contains some sort of germ, from which the truth which up to now has been held back, may be developed. Of this character was the inference of Christ from God's title as "the God of Abraham, Isaac, and Jacob."* This hint appears to me to be undoubtedly capable of development into a strong proof.

47. In such exercises, allusions, hints, consists the *positive* perfection of a primer; just as the above-mentioned quality of not putting difficulties or hindrances in the way to the truths that have been withheld, constitutes its *negative* perfection.

48. Add to all this the clothing and the style.

(1) The clothing of abstract truths which could scarcely be passed over, in allegories and instructive single circumstances, which were narrated as actual occurrences. Of this character are creation in the image of growing day; the origin of evil in the story of the forbidden tree; the source of the variety of languages in the story of the tower of Babel, etc.

49. (2) The style—sometimes plain and simple, sometimes poetical, throughout full of tautologies, but of such as call for a sharp wit, since they sometimes appear to be saying something else, and yet say the same thing; sometimes seem to say the same thing over again, and yet to mean or to be capable of meaning, basically, something else:—

50. And there you have all the good qualities of a primer both for children and for a childlike people.

*Matthew 22:32.

51. But every primer is only for a certain age. To delay the child, that has outgrown it, longer at it than intended, is harmful. For to be able to do this in a way which is at all profitable, you must insert into it more than there is really in it, and extract from it more than it can contain. You must look for and make too much of allusions and hints; squeeze allegories too closely; interpret examples too circumstantially; press too much upon words. This gives the child a petty, crooked, hairsplitting understanding: it makes him full of mysteries, superstitious, full of contempt for all that is comprehensible and easy.

52. The very way in which the rabbis handled *their* sacred books! The very character which they thereby imparted to the spirit of their people!

53. A better instructor must come and tear the exhausted primer from the child's hands—Christ came!

54. That portion of the human race which God had wished to embrace in one plan of education, was ripe for the second great step. He had, however, only wished to embrace in such a plan that part of the human race which by language, habits, government, and other natural and political relationships, was already united in itself.

55. That is, this portion of the human race had come so far in the exercise of its reason, as to need, and to be able to make use of, nobler and worthier motives for moral action than temporal rewards and punishments, which had hitherto been its guides. The child has become a youth. Sweetmeats and toys have given place to an awakening desire to be as free, as honored, and as happy as its elder brother.

56. For a long time, already, the best individuals of that portion of the human race had been accustomed to let themselves be ruled by the shadow of such nobler motives. The Greek and Roman did everything to live on after this life, even if it were only in the memories of their fellow citizens.

57. It was time that another *true* life to be expected after this one should gain an influence over the youth's actions.

58. And so Christ was the first *reliable, practical* teacher of the immortality of the soul.

59. The first *reliable* teacher. Reliable, by reason of the prophecies which were fulfilled in him; reliable by reason of the miracles which he achieved; reliable by reason of his own revival after a death by which he had put the seal to his teaching. Whether we can still *prove* this revival, these miracles, I put aside, as I leave on one side *who* the person of Christ was. All *that* may have been at that time of great importance for

the first acceptance of his teaching, but it is now no longer of the same importance for the recognition of the *truth* of his teaching.

60. The first *practical* teacher. For it is one thing to conjecture, to wish, and to believe in the immortality of the soul, as a philosophic speculation: quite another thing to direct one's inner and outer actions in accordance with it.

61. And this at least Christ was the first to teach. For although, before him, the belief had already been introduced among many nations, that bad actions have yet to be punished in the life to come; yet they were only such actions as were injurious to civil society, and which had, therefore, already had their punishment in civil society too. To preach an inward purity of heart in reference to another life, was reserved for him alone.

62. His disciples have faithfully propagated this teaching: and even if they had had no other merit than that of having effected a more general publication among other nations of a truth which Christ had appeared to have destined for the Jews alone, yet if only on that account, they would have to be reckoned among the benefactors and fosterers of the human race.

63. If, however, they mixed up this one great truth together with other doctrines whose truth was less enlightening, whose usefulness was less considerable, how could it be otherwise? Let us not blame them for this, but rather seriously examine whether these very commingled doctrines have not become a new directing impulse for human reason.

64. At least, it is already clear from our experience that the New Testament Scriptures, in which these doctrines after some time were found preserved, have afforded, and still afford, the second, better primer for the race of man.

65. For seventeen hundred years past they have occupied human reason more than all other books, and enlightened it more, were it even only through the light which human reason itself put into them.

66. It would have been impossible for any other book to become so generally known among such different nations: and indisputably, the fact that modes of thought so completely diverse from each other have turned their attention to this same book, has assisted human reason on its way more than if every nation had had its *own* primer specially for itself.

67. It was also most necessary that each people should for a time consider this book as the *non plus ultra* of their knowledge. For the

youth must believe his primer to be the first of all books, so that his impatience to be finished with it may not hurry him on to things for which he has not yet laid the foundations.

68. And that is also of the greatest importance now. You who are cleverer than the rest, who wait fretting and impatient on the last page of the primer, take care! Take care that you do not let your weaker classmates notice what you are beginning to scent, or even see!

69. Until these weaker fellows of yours have caught up with you, it is better that you should return once more to this primer, and examine whether that which you take only for variations of method, for superfluous verbiage in the teaching, is not perhaps something more.

70. You have seen in the childhood of the human race, in the doctrine of the unity of God, that God makes immediate revelations of mere truths of reason, or has permitted and caused pure truths of reason to be taught, for a time, as truths of immediate revelation, in order to promulgate them the more rapidly, and ground them the more firmly.

71. You learn in the childhood of the human race the same thing, in the doctrine of the immortality of the soul. It is *preached* in the second, better primer as revelation, not *taught* as a result of human reason.

72. As we by this time can dispense with the Old Testament for the doctrine of the unity of God, and as we are gradually beginning also to be less dependent on the New Testament for the doctrine of the immortality of the soul: might there not be mirrored in this book also other truths of the same kind, which we are to gaze at in awe as revelations, just until reason learns to deduce them from its other demonstrated truths, and to connect them with them?

73. For instance, the doctrine of the Trinity. How if this doctrine should in the end, after countless waverings to one side or the other, merely bring human reason on the path to recognizing that God cannot possibly be One in the sense in which finite things are one, that even his unity must be a transcendental unity which does not exclude a sort of plurality? Must not God at least have the most perfect conception of himself, i.e., a conception which contains everything which is in him? But would everything be contained in it which is in him, if it contained merely a conception, merely the possibility even of his necessary reality, as well as of his other qualities? This possibility exhausts the being of his other qualities. Does it exhaust that of his necessary reality? I think not. Consequently either God can have no perfect conception of himself at all, or this perfect conception is just as necessarily real (i.e., actually existent) as he himself is. Admittedly the

image of myself in the mirror is nothing but an empty representation of me, because it only has that of me which is reflected by rays of light falling on its surface. If, however, this image contained everything, everything without exception, which is contained in me, would it then still be a mere empty representation, or not rather a true double of myself? When I believe that I recognize in God a similar reduplication, I perhaps do not so much err, as that my language in insufficient for my ideas: and so much at least remains for ever incontrovertible, that those who want to make the idea acceptable to the popular intelligence could scarcely have expressed themselves in a more apt and comprehensible form than by giving the name of a Son whom God begets from eternity.

74. And the doctrine of original sin. How if finally everything were to convince us that man, standing on the first and lowest step of his humanity, is by no means so much master of his actions that he is *able* to obey moral laws?

75. And the doctrine of the Son's satisfaction. How if everything finally compelled us to assume that God, in spite of that original incapacity of man, chose rather to give him moral laws, and forgive him all transgressions in consideration of his Son, i.e., in consideration of the living embodiment of all his own perfections, compared with which, and in which, all imperfections of the individual disappear, than *not* to give him those laws, and thus to exclude him from all moral bliss, which cannot be conceived of without moral laws?

76. Let it not be objected that speculations of this nature upon the mysteries of religion are forbidden. The word *mystery* signified, in the first age of Christianity, something quite different from what it means now: and the development of revealed truths into truths of reason, is absolutely necessary, if the human race is to be assisted by them. When they were revealed they were certainly not truths of reason, but they were revealed in order to become such. They were like the "facit" said to his boys by the mathematics master; he goes on ahead of them in order to indicate to some extent the lines they should follow in their sums. If the scholars were to be satisfied with the "facit," they would never learn to do sums, and would frustrate the intention with which their good master gave them a guiding clue in their work.

77. And why should not we too, by means of a religion whose historical truth, if you will, looks dubious, be led in a similar way to closer and better conceptions of the divine Being, of our own nature, of our relation to God, which human reason would never have reached on its own?

78. It is not true that speculations upon these things have ever done

harm or been injurious to civil society. Reproach is due, not to these speculations, but to the folly and tyranny which tried to keep them in bondage; a folly and tyranny which would not allow men to develop their own thoughts.

79. On the contrary, though they may in individual instances be found wanting, speculations of this sort are unquestionably the most fitting exercises of the human reason that exist, just as long as the human heart, as such, is capable to the highest degree of loving virtue for its eternal blessed consequences.

80. For this selfishness of the human heart, which wishes to exercise its understanding only on that which concerns our bodily needs, succeeds in blunting rather than in sharpening it. It is absolutely necessary for it to be exercised on spiritual objects, if it is to attain its perfect illumination, and bring out that purity of heart which makes us capable of loving virtue for its own sake alone.

81. Or is the human species never to arrive at this highest step of illumination and purity?—Never?

82. Never?—Let me not think this blasphemy, All Merciful! Education has its goal, in the race, no less than in the individual. That which is educated is educated for a purpose.

83. The flattering prospects which are opened to the youth, the honor and well-being which are held out to him, what are they more than means of educating him to become a man, who, when these prospects of honor and well-being have vanished, shall be able to do his *duty?*

84. This is the aim of *human* education, and does the divine education not extend as far? Is nature not to succeed with the whole, as art succeeded with the individual? Blasphemy! Blasphemy!

85. No! It will come! it will assuredly come! the time of the perfecting, when man, the more convinced his understanding feels about an ever better future, will nevertheless not need to borrow motives for his actions from this future; for he will do right because it *is* right, not because arbitrary rewards are set upon it, which formerly were intended simply to fix and strengthen his unsteady gaze in recognizing the inner, better, rewards of well-doing.

86. It will assuredly come! the time of a new eternal gospel, which is promised us in the primers of the New Covenant itself!*

87. Perhaps even some enthusiasts of the thirteenth and fourteenth

*Revelation 14: 6.

centuries had caught a glimmer of this new eternal gospel, and only erred in that they predicted its arrival as so near to their own time.

88. Perhaps their "Three Ages of the World" were not so empty a speculation after all, and assuredly they had no bad intentions when they taught that the new covenant must become as antiquated as the old has become. There remained with them the same economy of the same God. Ever, to put my own expression into their mouths, ever the selfsame plan of the education of the human race.

89. Only they were premature. They believed that they could make their contemporaries, who had scarcely outgrown their childhood, without enlightenment, without preparation, at one stroke men worthy of their *third age*.

90. And it was just this which made them enthusiasts. The enthusiast often casts true glances into the future, but for this future he cannot wait. He wants this future to come quickly, and to be made to come quickly through him. A thing over which nature takes thousands of years is to come to maturity just at the moment of his experience. For what part has he in it, if that which he recognizes as the best does not become the best in his lifetime? Does he come again? Does he expect to come again? It is strange that this enthusiasm is not more the fashion, if it were only among enthusiasts.

91. Go thine inscrutable way, Eternal Province! Only let me not despair of thee because of this inscrutableness. Let me not despair of thee, even if thy steps appear to me to be going backward. It is not true that the shortest line is always straight.

92. Thou hast on thine eternal way so much that thou must concern thyself with, so much to attend to! And what if it were as good as proved that the great, slow wheel, which brings mankind nearer to its perfection, is only set in motion by smaller, faster wheels, each of which contributes its own individual part to the whole?

93. It is so! Must every individual man—one sooner, another later— have traveled along the very same path by which the race reaches its perfection? Have traveled along it in one and the same life? Can he have been, in one and the selfsame life, a sensual Jew and a spiritual Christian? Can he in the selfsame life have overtaken both?

94. Surely not that! But why should not every individual man have been present more than once in this world?

95. Is this hypothesis so laughable merely because it is the oldest? Because human understanding, before the sophistries of the Schools had dissipated and weakened it, lighted upon it at once?

96. Why may not even I have already performed all those steps towards my perfection which merely temporal penalties and rewards can bring man to?

97. And, once more, why not all those steps, to perform which the prospects of eternal rewards so powerfully assist us?

98. Why should I not come back as often as I am capable of acquiring new knowledge, new skills? Do I bring away so much from one visit that it is perhaps not worth the trouble of coming again?

99. Is this a reason against it? Or, because I forget that I have been here already? Happy is it for me that I do forget. The recollection of my former condition would permit me to make only a bad use of the present. And that which I must forget *now*, is that necessarily forgotten for ever?

100. Or is it a reason against the hypothesis that so much time would have been lost to me? Lost?—And what then have I to lose?—Is not the whole of eternity mine?

The Religion of Christ

For the Father also seeketh those who thus worship him.

St. John

1. It is a question whether Christ was more than a mere man. That he was a real man if he was a man at all, and that he never ceased to be a man, is not in dispute.

2. It follows that the religion of Christ and the Christian religion are two quite different things.

3. The former, the religion of Christ, is that religion which as a man he himself recognized and practiced; which every man has in common with him; which every man must so much the more desire to have in common with him, the more exalted and admirable the character which he attributes to Christ as a mere man.

4. The latter, the Christian religion, is that religion which accepts it as true that he was more than a man, and makes Christ himself, as such, the object of its worship.

5. How these two religions, the religion of Christ and the Christian

religion, can exist in Christ in one and the same person, is inconceivable.

6. The doctrines and tenets of both could hardly be found in one and the same book. At least it is obvious that the former, that is the religion of Christ, is contained in the evangelists quite differently from the Christian religion.

7. The religion of Christ is therein contained in the clearest and most lucid language.

8. On the other hand, the Christian religion is so uncertain and ambiguous, that there is scarcely a single passage which, in all the history of the world, has been interpreted in the same way by two men.

Translated by Henry Chadwick

ACKNOWLEDGMENTS

Every reasonable effort has been made to locate the owners of rights to previously published translations printed here. We gratefully acknowledge permission to reprint the following material:

Excerpts from *Men in Dark Times,* copyright © 1955 by Hannah Arendt and renewed 1983 by Mary McCarthy West, reprinted by permission of Harcourt Brace Jovanovich, Inc.

Minna von Barnhelm. Translation by Kenneth J. Northcott. Reprinted by kind permission of The University of Chicago Press: Chicago and London, 1972. Copyright © 1972 The University of Chicago Press.

"On the Proof of the Spirit and of Power," "The Testament of John," "The Education of the Human Race," and "The Religion of Christ," reprinted from *Lessing's Theological Writings,* translated and edited by Henry Chadwick with the permission of the publishers, Stanford University Press. Copyright 1956 by A. and C. Black Ltd.

THE GERMAN LIBRARY
in 100 Volumes

Wolfram von Eschenbach
Parzival
Edited by André Lefevere

Gottfried von Strassburg
Tristan and Isolde
Edited and Revised by Francis G. Gentry
Foreword by C. Stephen Jacger

German Medieval Tales
Edited by Francis G. Gentry
Foreword by Thomas Berger

German Humanism and Reformation
Edited by Reinhard P. Becker
Foreword by Roland Bainton

Immanuel Kant
Philosophical Writings
Edited by Ernst Behler
Foreword by René Wellek

Friedrich Schiller
Plays: Intrigue and Love and Don Carlos
Edited by Walter Hinderer
Foreword by Gordon Craig

German Literary Fairy Tales
Edited by Frank G. Ryder and Robert M. Browning
Introduction by Gordon Birrell
Foreword by John Gardner

F. Grillparzer, J. H. Nestroy, F. Hebbel
Nineteenth Century German Plays
Edited by Egon Schwarz in collaboration with
Hannelore M. Spence

Heinrich Heine
Poetry and Prose
Edited by Jost Hermand and Robert C. Holub
Foreword by Alfred Kazin

Heinrich Heine
The Romantic School and other Essays
Edited by Jost Hermand and Robert C. Holub

Heinrich von Kleist and Jean Paul
German Romantic Novellas
Edited by Frank G. Ryder and Robert M. Browning
Foreword by John Simon

German Romantic Stories
Edited by Frank G. Ryder
Introduction by Gordon Birrell

German Poetry from 1750 to 1900
Edited by Robert M. Browning
Foreword by Michael Hamburger

Karl Marx, Friedrich Engels, August Bebel, and others
German Essays on Socialism in the Nineteenth Century
Edited by Frank Mecklenburg and Manfred Stassen

Gottfried Keller
Stories
Edited by Frank G. Ryder
Foreword by Max Frisch

Wilhelm Raabe
Novels
Edited by Volkmar Sander
Foreword by Joel Agee

Theodor Fontane
Short Novels and other Writings
Edited by Peter Demetz
Foreword by Peter Gay

Theodor Fontane
Delusions, Confusions and The Poggenpuhl Family
Edited by Peter Demetz
Foreword by J. P. Stern
Introduction by William L. Zwiebel

Wilhelm Busch and others
German Satirical Writings
Edited by Dieter P. Lotze and Volkmar Sander
Foreword by John Simon

Writings of German Composers
Edited by Jost Hermand and James Steakley

German Lieder
Edited by Philip Lieson Miller
Foreword by Hermann Hesse

Arthur Schnitzler
Plays and Stories
Edited by Egon Schwarz
Foreword by Stanley Elkin

Rainer Maria Rilke
Prose and Poetry
Edited by Egon Schwarz
Foreword by Howard Nemerov

Robert Musil
Selected Writings
Edited by Burton Pike
Foreword by Joel Agee

Essays on German Theater
Edited by Margaret Herzfeld-Sander
Foreword by Martin Esslin

German Novellas of Realism I and II
Edited by Jeffrey L. Sammons

Friedrich Dürrenmatt
Plays and Essays
Edited by Volkmar Sander
Foreword by Martin Esslin

German Radio Plays
Edited by Everett Frost and Margaret Herzfeld-Sander

Max Frisch
Novels, Plays, Essays
Edited by Rolf Kieser
Foreword by Peter Demetz

Gottfried Benn
Prose, Essays, Poems
Edited by Volkmar Sander
Foreword by E. B. Ashton
Introduction by Reinhard Paul Becker

German Essays on Art History
Edited by Gert Schiff

Hans Magnus Enzensberger
Critical Essays
Edited by Reinhold Grimm and Bruce Armstrong
Foreword by John Simon

All volumes available in hardcover and paperback editions at your bookstore or from the publisher. For more information on The German Library write to: The Continuum Publishing Company, 370 Lexington Avenue, New York, NY 10017.